Hermeneutics

Ancient and Modern

Hermeneutics
Ancient and Modern

GERALD L. BRUNS

Yale University Press   New Haven and London

Designed by Jill Breitbarth and set in Sabon type by Compset, Inc.,
Beverly, Massachusetts.
Printed in the United States of America by BookCrafters, Inc.,
Chelsea, Michigan.

Chapter 3 of the present work appeared in a slightly different version
in *Critical Inquiry* 10, no. 3 (March 1984), 462–80. © 1984 by the
University of Chicago.

Library of Congress Cataloging-in-Publication Data
Bruns, Gerald L.
Hermeneutics ancient and modern / Gerald L. Bruns.
p.   cm.
Includes index.
ISBN 0-300-05450-5 (alk. paper)
1. Hermeneutics—History.   I. Title.
BD241.B78   1992
121'.68—dc20   92-14839 CIP

A catalogue record for this book is available from the British Library.

The paper in this book meets the guidelines for permanence and
durability of the Committee on Production Guidelines for Book
Longevity of the Council on Library Resources.

10   9   8   7   6   5   4   3   2   1

For Lew and Lucien Bruns

But peace, peace,
            to all who wander
For whatever reason
            from their stony lands
Bringing all the heavy cargo
            of their legends
Humming in a cipher
            in their lucid, spinning minds!
—John Matthias, "To V. V.: On Our Translation
of the Kossovo Fragments"

Contents

Preface

In 1967 I read an essay by Hans Kimmerle called "Hermeneutical Theory or Ontological Hermeneutics," which was an attempt to defend Friedrich Schleiermacher's conception of hermeneutics as a systematic, procedural *approach* to the texts of our cultural past against Hans-Georg Gadamer's idea of hermeneutics as a discipline of reflection in which our own historicality is what is at issue.[1] Since that time, hermeneutics has been something I have been struggling to get clear about. At first it seemed that understanding the difference between analysis and reflection might give some substance and point to the profession I was then, to no one's satisfaction, trying to pursue; I mean, I thought hermeneutics might help me bring my professional and intellectual lives together. But it was many years before anything like this sort of reconciliation took place, and even so the arrangement has proved to be like one of those Jamesian relationships in which parties survive chiefly by speaking tacitly. For reasons that historians of recent criticism have made plain, hermeneutics is not obviously compatible with a university career in literary studies. In literary studies we learn mainly new ways to approach old texts, and Schleiermacher is never thought of. Yet even though we have multiplied our approaches over the years and have enlarged and refined our theory of the text, now for example taking the contextual weave of culture as the place of the text's action, the analytical outlook that Schleiermacher already took for granted has remained pretty much steadfast and foundational. Hermeneutics as a reflection on, among other things, this analytical steadfastness has aroused little interest among literary critics. Nor has hermeneutical reflection helped to advance itself by emphasizing that things of the past tend to be open-ended with respect to the present and future, this being what recent criticism worries most about. Whence we have redoubled our commitment to the obsolescence of things by thinking of ourselves as postmodern. Meanwhile hermeneutics plods along, as if it belonged to other sorts of history. My thought, which I don't think here, is that the history of criticism is only one of the histories of hermeneutics. I leave open for another time the question of whether ignorance of hermeneutics among literary critics is invincible or merely strategic. All I can say now is that my friends who read this book will not find a new angle on doing literary or cultural studies. But I don't mean by this to excuse them from reading it.

I began trying to write this book in the early 1970s, and since then I seem to have written bits and pieces of it several times over before ever really getting started. In fact most of what I have written toward this project has been discarded or survives in mercifully forgotten publications. In *Inventions: Writing, Textuality, and Understanding in Literary History* (1982), I tried to treat hermeneutics in terms of historical topics rather than strictly as a set of theoretical problems, and the present (journeyman's) effort follows this earlier model. There are two fugitive pieces from the late 1970s that I don't mind remembering for the usual sentimental reasons, even though they would have to be substantially rewritten to be consistent with what I have said in this book.[2]

One could, for reasons that the conclusion will make clear, take this book as a slowly unfolding gloss on the lines from John Matthias's poem that I have quoted as an epigraph.[3]

Between 1981 and 1989 I presented different versions of the first two chapters as lectures at various universities. I recall with great pleasure my conversations with Michael Davidson and Steven Cassedy during my visit to the University of California, San Diego, in 1982. I'm especially indebted to Eugene Garver and the faculty and students at St. John's University in Collegeville, Minnesota, where I presented chapter 1 in November 1986, and to the audience and participants at Florida State University, where in

February 1989 chapter 2 received some much-needed criticism, especially from Mary Lefkowitz and Jon Levenson. Chapter 3 first appeared in *Critical Inquiry*, 10, no. 3 (March 1984), 462–80, and was subsequently reprinted in *Canons*, ed. Robert von Hallberg (Chicago: University of Chicago Press, 1984), pp. 65–84. Much of the material in chapters 4 and 5 was originally developed for a seminar at Luther College, Decorah, Iowa, in February 1985. The questions and criticisms of the participants in the seminar have proved invaluable to my entire project. An earlier version of chapter 5 was originally presented at a conference on the Bible and Critical Theory at the University of Colorado in April 1986, and subsequently published in *The Book and the Text: The Bible and Critical Theory*, ed. Regina Schwartz (London: Basil Blackwell, 1989). Chapter 8, now slightly revised, appeared in *The Centennial Review*, no. 4, 33 (Fall 1989), 393–418, and was originally presented at Michigan State University in February 1989 as part of a series on "Wordsworth and the Modern World." Part of chapter 9 appeared in *Research in Phenomenology*, 18 (Fall 1989), 191–201, and was originally presented as a paper at an annual meeting of the Society for Phenomenology and Existential Philosophy at the University of Notre Dame in October 1988. Chapter 10 was presented in June 1988 at a workshop on the Institutions of Interpretation at The Institute for Advanced Studies, Hebrew University of Jerusalem, and was subsequently published in *New Literary History*, 22, no. 1 (Winter 1991), 1–21. Sections of chapter 11 were presented as a commentary on John Caputo's *Radical Hermeneutics* at the annual meeting of the Society for Phenomenology and Existential Philosophy at Northwestern University, October 1989. An earlier version of chapter 12 was presented at a conference on Paul Ricoeur at the University of Iowa, April 1990. I am grateful for permission to reprint this copyrighted material.

I've been the beneficiary of arguments, exchanges, and conversations with many people over the past twenty years, some of whom have read parts or all of this book with varying degrees of amusement, suspicion, and alarm. My thanks particularly to Ralph Berry, Daniel Boyarin, Joe Buttigieg, Jack Caputo, Steve Fredman, Eugene Garver, Clint Goodson, Jay Holstein, David Morris, David O'Connor, Richard Palmer, Marjorie Perloff, Herman Rapaport, Regina Schwartz, Gary Shapiro, David Stern, Steve Watson, Michael Vander Weele, and Joel Weinsheimer. Don Marshall has been a searching critic of these pages and a continuing inspiration to get things right. Geoffrey Hartman, as he well knows, is godfather to this book. I am grateful to David Burrell, C.S.C., for his criticisms and corrections of chapter 6 and for allowing me to see the manuscript of his translation (with Nazih

Daher) of al-Ghazālī's treatise on the ninety-nine names of God. Georgia Warnke's writings on hermeneutics and Fred Dallmayr's on nearly everything have been of enormous help to me. I also wish to thank the participants in my National Endowment for the Humanities seminar on the Early History of Interpretation, held at the University of Iowa during the summer of 1981, especially Roger Lundin and Brice Wachterhauser. I owe a great deal to Sanford Budick, Wolfgang Iser, and the participants in the workshop on the Institutions of Interpretation at the Center for Literary Studies, Hebrew University of Jerusalem. My students and colleagues in my courses on the history of interpretation, both at Iowa and at Notre Dame, put me onto things and corrected my mistakes on a regular basis, thus demonstrating that no one person, working alone, can ever get into the spirit of hermeneutics, much less make sense of it.

Part of this book was written during 1985–86 while I was a Guggenheim Fellow and also a fellow at the Institute for Advanced Studies at Hebrew University in Jerusalem. My thanks for their support.

Hermeneutics

Ancient and Modern

Introduction

WHAT IS HERMENEUTICS ABOUT?

> Men who wish to know about the world must learn about it in
> its particular details.
> —Heraclitus (D35, trans. Guy Davenport)

Let me try to situate my book by taking up, in some fairly familiar ways, the question of what sort of thing hermeneutics might be and what its point is. The simplest answer is that hermeneutics is a tradition of thinking or of philosophical reflection that tries to clarify the concept of *verstehen*, that is, understanding. What is it to make sense of anything, whether a poem, a legal text, a human action, a language, an alien culture, or oneself? The difficulty is that this is not an entirely coherent question; or rather, the question of understanding turns up in many different contexts and has application in many intellectual disciplines, some of which are hardly intelligible to one another. So there is a problem about how to frame the question.[1]

The possibility that understanding is not purely and simply one thing suggests that the best way to approach hermeneutics is through its history. But this history is itself multiple and highly conflicted and would have to be written in different ways. One way would be as a conceptual history of the sort that Richard Palmer laid out for us.[2] A useful version of such a history is Michael Ermarth's essay "The Transformation of Hermeneutics: Nineteenth-Century Ancients and Twentieth-Century Moderns," which argues that we ought not to think of earlier forms of hermeneutical reflection as being superseded by more recent efforts.[3] Earlier for Ermarth means Friedrich Schleiermacher's attempt to generalize the ancient motto of philology, namely, that understanding a text means understanding it first as well as and then even better than its author does, and it includes Wilhelm Dilthey's efforts to develop from Schleiermacher's ideas an epistemological justification of the *Geisteswissenschaften*. "How," Dilthey wanted to know, "can an individually structured consciousness reconstruct—and thereby know objectively—the distinct individuality of another."[4]

Like most conceptual histories that we are likely to write, this one is dominated by a Copernican Revolution, namely, Martin Heidegger's idea that understanding is not an activity of consciousness but a condition of belonging to a world. This so-called ontological turn produced a fundamental split between two hermeneutical theories. The first might be called transcendental, and its centerpiece is Edmund Husserl's idea that understanding is of ideal entities called meanings rather than of minds.[5] Understanding means reproducing an ideal state of the sort one finds in geometry, not someone else's state of consciousness. When we understand a geometrical expression, we understand not Euclid but what Euclid understood, or what anyone can understand who understands geometry, which consists of ideal objects like triangles and statements that are analytically true of triangles. Understanding is like translating, which presupposes an ideality of meaning or an ideal object that can be transported without loss across historical, cultural, and linguistic boundaries. Geometric expressions are absolutely translatable and identical in every language, culture, and historical period.[6] The words and propositions of natural language are perhaps not so ideal as geometrical terms and expressions, but they are close. They have a univocality and universality about them; they can be handed down from past to present without (on the whole) leaving anything essential behind. Otherwise they would not be intelligible. The univocal and universal is what is understandable ("A universal thought dispenses with communication," says Emmanuel Levinas), whereas what is singular is equivocal and refractory and may resist meaning altogether.[7] In fact, the terms and concepts of language are in constant need of clarification. Certain of them are no problem: a spade is a spade, a smile is just a smile, but justice is difficult to clarify conceptually, and Plato's *dikē* may not be identical with (or translatable as) John Rawls's "justice," which may simply mean that the concept of justice is therefore not fully intelligible, not coherent with itself but historically embedded and to that extent heterogeneous and opaque, lacking in the ideal intelligibility of the Pythagorean theorem. But at least we know what it would be for the concept of justice to be fully intelligible, even though, situated as we are, we always fall short in our efforts to determine it rigorously and without equivocation. Perhaps we need not always fall fatally short. One could, for example, write a reasonably coherent history of the concept of justice from Homer to Rawls. But doing such a thing might then bring home the problem of how to choose among rival conceptions of justice. And then one would have to wrestle with the Nietzschean problem, formulated memorably in Fragment 481 of *The Will to Power*, that there is no way to adjudicate among rival versions of anything, because everything is internal to interpretation.[8]

Opposed to transcendental hermeneutics, at least at first glance, is Heidegger's analysis of understanding as a mode of practical involvement or concern with others and with a world.[9] Understanding is of forms of life, and also internal to them. It entails being able to speak the language spoken by those around you and taking as natural or intelligible (not needing explanation) the ways of acting, thinking, and feeling that are local and current. Heidegger's favorite example is knowing what a hammer is for. Knowing this presupposes the sharing of a world made up of (among other possibilities) garages and hardware stores, of houses being built and tacks in the carpet.[10] At this level the way to understand understanding would not be through conceptual clarification and the construction of theories; rather, one can hardly *not* understand it, because it discloses itself most powerfully in its disruption or when it withholds itself, as when we find ourselves in a strange land or suffer alienation or exclusion. That is, the reality of understanding seems to show itself most clearly in moments of epistemological crisis or in the breakdown of everyday practice. Franz Kafka's "Metamorphosis" gives us a sort of comic nightmare version of what this might be like, but one could just as well consult one's own experience, where merely growing up entails the loss of a world. Understanding is a condition of being at home, whereas meaninglessness is isolation, randomness, the absence of contexts (think of how Gregor Samsa resists efforts to remove the furniture from his room: somehow his identity is internal to these objects). The upshot is that understanding is always situated, always answerable to what is at hand, in place, already going on. It always presupposes some sort of initiation or integration into an already-understood world.[11] Obviously, this doesn't rule out Husserl's idea, but it does mean that to arrive at what is universal and univocal one has to try to reflect oneself out of one's situation, and the question of how far one can do this is controversial. What are the limits of reduction? Can one understand the world by repressing one's involvement with it?

This is the question that worries Ermarth in his essay, but of course not just Ermarth, since it suggests that understanding is excessive with respect to the propositional attitude in which we make statements about things; or, in other words, excessive with respect to judgments of true or false; or one might say excessive with respect to philosophy.[12] In fact, Heidegger himself is very clear (and, to some, excessive) on this point when he says that assertion requires that we disengage ourselves from the object of our assertion— that is, put ourselves, so to speak, in a position of just staring at it.[13] This is what objectivity comes down to, whereas understanding and interpretation are themselves events of intimacy or of internal connection with people and things. Heidegger takes this in the strongest sense possible when he says that interpretation is always grounded in what we have or see or know in advance. It is simply the clarification of what is already understood and not a special act (like translation) that produces understanding where it is missing. This does not mean that one always understands everything; rather, it means that understanding always proceeds from the inside and that interpretation is essentially an explication not of objects but of situations in which we are involved or have to do with what is at hand. In a well-known statement, Heidegger says that "an interpretation is never a presuppositionless apprehending of something presented to us. If, when one is engaged in a particular kind of interpretation, in the sense of exact textual interpretation, one likes to appeal [beruft] to what 'stands there,' [but] then one finds that what 'stands there' in the first instance is nothing other than the obvious undiscussed assumption [Vormeinung] of the person who does the interpreting" (Being and Time, pp. 192–93). The hermeneutical circle in this event is never purely philological, that is, it is not simply an exegetical movement between the parts and the whole of a text that is present before us as an object. Instead, it is an ontological movement between the text and our situation as interpreters of it.

What sort of movement is this, and what is at stake in it? It would not be too much to say that this is the regulating question not only of hermeneutics after Heidegger (for example, in Hans-Georg Gadamer's *Truth and Method*) but in much of post-World-War-II thinking (for example, in controversies about rationality in Anglo-American analytical philosophy). Let me illustrate this with a brief look at Peter Winch's famous essay "Understanding a Primitive Society."[14] This essay draws on the later writings of Ludwig Wittgenstein, whose work can also be seen as forcing us to explore the breach between the transcendental and the everyday. Take this question:

What would happen if you gave an account of a move in chess that would be unintelligible to chess players? Peter Winch applies a question of roughly this Wittgensteinian type to the problem that Western anthropologists face in giving accounts of alien cultures. The case in question is the Azande tribe, which is given to strange practices: they plant seeds and harvest the ensuing crops, but in addition they perform magical rites (of some sort), in the absence of which, or so they evidently believe, no crops will grow from the planted seeds. The anthropologist, in this case E. E. Evans-Pritchard, is in this position: he just knows better, that is, he can't help knowing that magical rites don't matter—under proper environmental conditions seeds will grow into crops no matter what, or anyhow without any mediation of magic and witchcraft.

Winch's point is that if the anthropologist says, appealing to his superior knowledge, that the believers in magical rites are, well, irrational, the anthropologist is wrong—and not just wrong but "crucially wrong." According to Evans-Pritchard, "'Scientific notions are those which accord with objective reality,' whereas the rites of the tribe under study do not" (p. 308). Against this Winch argues that the concept of reality cannot be external to a language in which it makes sense to use that concept. "Reality is not what gives language sense. What is real and what is unreal shows itself *in* the sense that language has" (p. 308). But there are multiple languages, and it won't do to import into one language a concept of reality that has application only in another; the same goes for the concept of rationality. As Winch put it in a book called *The Idea of Social Science and Its Relation to Philosophy*, "Criteria of logic are not a direct gift from God, but arise out of, and are only intelligible in the context of, ways of living or modes of social life. It follows that one cannot apply criteria of logic to modes of social life as such. For instance, science is one such mode and religion is another; and each has criteria of intelligibility peculiar to itself."[15]

This is a line of thinking to which Alasdair MacIntyre objected, arguing that it's all very well to say that criteria of logic are internal to forms of life, but this doesn't deprive us of the warrant to criticize Azande magic as being, among other things, bad science. "It seems to me," MacIntyre said, "that one could only hold the belief of the Azande rational *in the absence of* any practice of science and technology in which criteria of effectiveness and kindred notions had been built up. But to say this is to recognize the appropriateness of scientific criteria of judgment from our standpoint."[16] But appropriate to whom? Winch's reply is that it is not obvious either that Azande witchcraft is simply a primitive form of science or that we are further along in the history of rational criticism and inquiry than they are and so are in a position to judge the coherence of their beliefs. Azande witchcraft belongs to a different sort of history and a different category of practice, one which Winch tries to characterize in terms of the expression of "an attitude to contingencies, one . . . which involves recognition that one's life is subject to contingencies, rather than an attempt to control these" (p. 321). As if magical rites were in some sense reflective and philosophical rather than scientific and instrumental. At all events, they are not translatable into the terms in which MacIntyre would judge them.

Then follows what seems to me to be the crucial paragraph in Winch's essay:

> [What is it] for us to see the *point* of the rules and conventions followed in an alien form of life? MacIntyre speaks as though our own rules and conventions are somehow a paradigm of what it is for rules and conventions to have a point, so that the only problem that arises is in accounting for the point of the rules and conventions in some other society. But in fact, of course, the problem is the same in relation to our own society as it is in relation to any other; no more than anyone else's are *our* rules and conventions immune from the danger of being or becoming pointless. So an account of this matter cannot be given simply in terms of any set of rules and conventions at all: our own or anyone else's; it requires us to consider the relation of a set of rules and conventions to something else. In my discussion of Zande magical rites just now what I tried to relate the magical rites to was a sense of the significance of human life. This notion is, I think, indispensable to any account of what is involved in understanding *and learning from* an alien culture (p. 321; my italics).

This paragraph shifts the ground of the argument between MacIntyre and Winch as radically as Heidegger shifts the ground of hermeneutics from the transcendental to the ontological. For the point of trying to understand an alien form of life is no longer descriptive and evaluative; rather, it is now reflective and self-critical. Winch asks: "What is involved in understanding and learning from an alien culture?" MacIntyre had wanted to insist that because of the history of *our* rationality we cannot help seeing and criticizing the incoherence of Azande practices. Winch turns this argument back on MacIntyre: it is because of the history of *our* rationality that we cannot help seeing (if we know where to look) in Azande practices a criticism of our own rationality.[17] MacIntyre had imagined the Azande questioning their own criteria upon acquaintance with ours (and who can say this didn't take place?). But on Winch's account, rational criticism itself undergoes a critical reversal in its encounter with Azande magic.

"What we may learn by studying other cultures," Winch says, "are not merely possibilities of different ways of doing things, other techniques. More importantly we may learn different possibilities of making sense of human life, different ideas about the possible importance that the carrying out of certain activities may take on for a man, trying to contemplate the sense of his life as a whole." Winch complains (not altogether fairly) that MacIntyre can see in Azande magic only "a (misguided) technique for producing consumer goods. But a Zande's crops are not just potential objects of consumption: the life he lives, his relations with his fellows, his chances for acting decently or doing evil, may all spring from his relation to his crops. Magical rites constitute a form of expression in which these possibilities and dangers may be contemplated and reflected on—and perhaps also thereby transformed and deepened" (p. 321). Our inability to grasp the coherence of Azande witchcraft may derive not from the incoherence of these practices but from our own inability to make sense of things except in terms of "'efficiency of production'—production, that is, for consumption. This again is a symptom of what Marx called the 'alienation' characteristic of man in industrial society. . . . Our blindness to the point of primitive modes of life is a corollary of the pointlessness of much of our own life" (p. 321).

Winch's essay is sometimes taken simply as an argument for seeing alien cultures in their own terms and hence as a brief for cultural relativism, with each culture following its own peculiar norms of rationality. But his reconceptualization of understanding in terms of *learning from* as against description and evaluation according to universal criteria comes out instead as an argument *against* relativism in favor of an idea that is very close to what MacIntyre himself has recently been arguing (in defense of something like a cross-cultural theory of rationality), namely, that our encounter with alien traditions may, and indeed ought to, compel us to reflect critically on our own intellectual and cultural situation. What MacIntyre calls "the rationality of traditions" consists precisely in such critical self-reflection brought on by the conflict of interpretation among traditions.[18] And in a way that is slightly more congenial to Winch's position Charles Taylor has argued that our encounter with alien cultures ought to compel us to develop not a neutral language in which to describe the alien but rather "a language of perspicuous contrast" that "forces us to redescribe what we are doing. . . . We are always in danger of seeing our ways of acting and thinking as the only conceivable ones. That is exactly what ethnocentricity consists in. Understanding other societies ought to wrench us out of this; it ought to alter our self-understanding."[19]

In *Anthropology as Cultural Critique*, George Marcus and Michael M. J. Fischer have indicated that a critical turn of precisely this sort is now going on (or seems about to happen) in anthropology. They offer as a research program "two techniques of critique in anthropology," the epistemological and the cross-cultural. The one "arises from the very nature of traditional anthropological work: going out to the periphery of the Euro-centric world where conditions are *supposed* to be most alien and profoundly revising the way we normally think about things in order to come to grips with what in European terms are exotica. The challenge of serious cultural criticism is to bring the insights gained on the periphery back to the center to raise havoc with our settled ways of thinking and conceptualization."[20] The other matches "ethnography abroad with ethnography at home. The idea is to use the substantive facts about another culture as a probe into the specific facts about a subject of criticism at home" (p. 138). Marcus and Fischer seem generally disappointed in recent attempts at cultural criticism in anthropology as well as in other disciplines, including philosophy and literary criticism. Their objections are generally methodological, however, and do not detract from what one might call the hermeneutical point, which is that the present task of understanding in the human sciences is not to reflect itself out of the situation in which it occurs; that is, the task of understanding is not to objectify itself but to reflect on itself and its situation critically in the light of what it discovers in its objects of study.[21] Winch puts the point of such hermeneutical reflection plainly when he says that his "aim is not to engage in moralizing, but to suggest that the concept of *learning from* which is involved in the study of other cultures is closely linked with the concept of *wisdom*" (p. 322).[22]

Winch's essay entitled "Understanding a Primitive Society" does not belong to the conceptual history of hermeneutics, but it is deeply involved with the subject of hermeneutics, that is, with its *Sache*—what hermeneutics is *about*.[23] And the context of argument that developed out of Winch's essay, and which is still expanding in multiple directions, seems to me as good an example as any of what sort of thing hermeneutics is. It is not a method or system or theory or any sort of position to be defended or advanced but exactly a context of argument about understanding—a context whose boundaries are determined not by conceptual traditions, much less by school disciplines, but by the thing itself, that is, by the question of what it is that happens (what the practical consequences are) when we try to make sense of something. What sense this question will have for us, however, is determined by how we frame it, and there are multiple, intersecting, and conflicting frames. Hermeneutics, as I understand it, is this whole network of lines and angles on the question of *verstehen*. There is no getting outside of this network and giving a comprehensive view of it, which is one reason

why it is not easy to give a conceptually coherent account of what hermeneutics is. But although this book is not an attempt at a comprehensive view,
it does try to give some sense of the historical dimensions of what hermeneutics is about—dimensions that tend to get disregarded when we try to
situate hermeneutics simply within the history of German philosophical idealism, or even within modern and contemporary controversies about the
nature and limits of rationality or about what practical rationality might
finally come down to.

For me, as for many people of my generation and disciplinary background, the question of understanding first took coherent shape in an attempt to get clear about what Gadamer was after in *Truth and Method*.[24]
This has never been an easy book to read, and when it was first put into
my hands I could make only poor sense of it. Why did a book that claimed
to revive hermeneutics present itself in the first instance as a critique of
aesthetics and historicism? The answer is that such a critique is what finally
opens up hermeneutics as an open-ended region of thinking. If, for example,
we start out from the modern theory of subjectivity that comes down to us
from Descartes and Kant, and which aesthetics and historicism embody in
symmetrical ways, the question of understanding will not seem worth taking up, because it will always seem like a weak and confused form of the
problem of knowledge, which is all that it was, on Gadamer's reading, in
Dilthey's effort to ground the human sciences. This is unfair to Dilthey, but
at all events Gadamer was determined to start out from Heidegger's theory
of the historicized subject—and he was determined to avoid what would
seem to follow, namely, the Nietzschean dilemma that if understanding always moves within horizons where it is not possible to determine things as
such, once for all, or in a way that a change in perspective will not require
us to revise, then there can be no such thing as understanding; rather, everything is simply interpretable otherwise in every direction and without end.
Gadamer's idea is that Heidegger's hermeneutics of facticity or the everyday
shows a way out of the Nietzschean impasse of an endless conflict of interpretations precisely because it shifts the question of understanding from the
theoretical plane of seeing from a perspective to the practical plane of involvement and participation in an ongoing action. For Gadamer this is a
shift from *epistēmē* to *phronēsis*, as if the Kantian problem of knowledge
could be (as many in fact do think it can be) rewritten as an Aristotelian
problem of practical reason. So with respect to a discourse or a text, *verstehen* is less knowing what the text means in itself than it is knowing how we
stand with respect to it in the situation in which we find ourselves. For
Gadamer, the task of hermeneutics is to clarify situations of this sort—call

them "hermeneutical situations": situations, as I try to suggest in this book, that call for something more than the construction of meanings. Gadamer's idea that understanding only shows itself in action is meant to be taken seriously.

It is worth stressing that Gadamer does not so much answer Nietzsche as redescribe him in essentially Aristotelian terms. This might help to explain why Husserlians like E. D. Hirsch see in Gadamer little more than another version of modern relativism leading to skepticism, nihilism, and despair, while deconstructionists like John Caputo see in him the defender of a metaphysics of obsolescence.[25] In fact, borrowing from Alasdair MacIntyre, one could say that Gadamer clarifies our historical situation—clarifies, one might say, our modernity—namely, that we are caught, many of us, in an agonistic dialogue between Nietzsche and Aristotle, these two names representing the only two languages in which one could conceivably conduct a reasonably coherent life of reflection and inquiry.[26] The difference between Anglo-American analytic philosophy and Continental thinking might be seen as a difference between two responses to this dialogue. The analytic philosopher (like MacIntyre) thinks we should face up to the logic of our situation and choose either Nietzsche or Aristotle, whereas the Continental philosopher would say—and I think this would be Gadamer's counsel—that we should enter into the movement, the give and take, of this agonistic struggle, not to resolve it one way or another but rather to grasp its meaning and its point, that is, to understand it and ourselves as belonging to it, since, after all, we do belong to it and cannot stand outside of it to see who between the two has the better argument. One could say that hermeneutics is a mode of belonging to this argument, or of working through it, in a reflective way, always wanting to know where it leads, what will come of it— always wanting to know the consequences.

This certainly comes out in those sections of Gadamer's *Truth and Method* that seem to move back and forth between two seemingly incompatible positions: (1) that what a text, especially a classical text, has to say to us is inescapable, rather in the way a law or a destiny is inescapable, as if there could be no question or opportunity of misunderstanding it, and (2) that we understand a text differently if we understand it at all, because our understanding is determined at least in part by the objectivity or, better, inescapability of history, that is, by the concrete situations in which we find ourselves, in which case there is always going to be a conflict of interpretations among people situated differently.[27] For Gadamer, however, these two positions are not or need not be alternative states of affairs. The question between them is not whether the meaning of a text is determined by the author or by the reader (Gadamer doesn't really make use of anything like an analytic concept of meaning); rather, the two positions taken together describe the movement of understanding itself, where understanding does not stop with the determination of meanings but is an ongoing critical reflection in which we see ourselves and what matters to us in the light of the text, even as we see the text in the light of ourselves and our interests. It is a mistake, or at the very least fatally reductive, to see this movement as occurring along a plane between the mind and its objects. For what is understood in a text is never reducible, for example, to another's meaning, rather what one understands, in the light of another's meaning, is a subject matter (*Sache*). Because of who we are and how we are situated the text has a claim on us, and part of what we understand is the substance and force of this claim, and also how we are to respond to it. Part of what we understand might be the necessity of getting out from under this claim—a point that Jürgen Habermas stresses in his criticism of Gadamer, Gadamer's reply being, if I understand, that doing such a thing (disengaging from tradition, for example) is not a matter of applying the right method of emancipation, say, a "depth hermeneutics," rather it would require nothing short of a radical transformation of who we are, a conversion, one might say, to a new or at all events different mode of existence, a different form of life or different tradition.[28] It remains to be seen what this means. Certainly Augustine, to take an obvious example, got out from under the claims of Roman tradition not by way of an emancipatory hermeneutics but by entering into an alternative history, although it is arguable how far behind he left the one when he gave himself over to the other. As Donald Davidson put it in another context, "speaking a language is not a trait [anyone] can lose while retaining the power of thought."[29] At the same time, however, it is far from obvious that historicality and tradition add up to a theory of confinement that requires us always to reconcile ourselves to our antecedents and to coerce the future into agreement with the past. Certainly, in spite of declarations in Gadamer's name, I have never found where in his writings he promotes such theory. Rather, if we exist historically we are always in a state of *in-between*, like the anthropologist who can neither study strange worlds without experiencing their powers of transformation nor abide in familiar regions without seeing, as if from the outside, the arbitrariness of their exclusions and constraints. It is always a state in which something is called for in the way of decision and action.

Hence the idea that hermeneutics is a kind of phenomenology of the between. Its task is not, for example, to produce such events as translations of meaning, conversion experiences, cultural critiques, or new interpretations of Shakespeare; instead, it is to study these things (among endless others) for the light that they shed on its object, that is, the *Sache* of its thinking, namely, the question of understanding. What is it for any of these things—the persistence of geometry across cultures, Augustine's (or Gregor Samsa's) spiritual crisis, mental bondage and the experience of scales falling from one's eyes, the divestitures of tragedy, the study of alien cultures or of the marginal or popular reaches of one's own—what is it for any of these things to happen? And what are their consequences? This is, in effect, what hermeneutics wants to know. Gadamer put it this way: "Given the inter-mediate position in which hermeneutics operates, it follows that its work is not to develop a procedure of understanding, but to clarify the conditions in which understanding takes place" (*Truth and Method*, p. 295). Gadamer may, of course, be thinking (Kant-like) of logical conditions of possibility. But for me this work of clarification cannot be purely theoretical, or at all events theory must always be historically mediated, because understanding is a region of unpredictable events and untheorizable practices that can never be conceptually reduced. One must study these events and these prac-tices in all of their bewildering heterogeneity.

One might say the same of hermeneutics—that it cannot be contained within the limits of a theory, not even within the sort of conceptual history that locates it as a branch of German philosophical idealism. My purpose in this book at any rate has been to stretch the limits of this conceptual history so as to include accounts of hermeneutical reflection and practice that belong to the histories of interpretation, or at least to a certain version of these histories, one made up of certain classic hermeneutical scenes and culturally distinctive interpretive practices. What can hermeneutics learn from these histories about what matters to it? Or, indeed, what can it learn about itself, since as I try to show, it belongs to these unruly, many-sided interpretive traditions? What can we learn from the situations in which Soc-rates or Thucydides or Philo of Alexandria found themselves? What can we learn from the ancient rabbis or the Sufi mystics? And what from Luther or Wordsworth?

Of course, many of my colleagues (particularly those in literary criticism) will be impatient with these questions, taking them to be of interest mainly to antiquarians and nostalgia artists. From the standpoint of literary criti-cism hermeneutics belongs to a history that is over and done with, a history of commentary that presupposes along its way a message-bearing or postal-service theory of discourse; whereas literary criticism, an intrepid and pow-erfully supersessionist discipline, thinks of itself as having got beyond her-meneutics. By elevating itself from history to metahistory, criticism has brought the history of commentary to an end. Its task is no longer to decipher discourses in their singularity but to lay bare the deep structures, the modes of production, the networks, strategies, manipulations, and negotiations of discourse and culture as such. Michel Foucault's preface to *The Birth of the Clinic* gives a classic anatomy of the case:

> *Commentary* questions discourse as to what it says and intended to say; it tries to uncover that deeper meaning of speech that enables it to achieve an identity with itself, supposedly nearer to its essential truth; in other words, in stating what has been said, one has to re-state what has never been said. In this activity known as commentary which tries to transmit an old, unyielding discourse seemingly silent to itself, into another, more prolix discourse that is both more archaic and more contemporary—is concealed a strange attitude towards language: to comment is to admit by definition an excess of the signified over the signifier; a necessary, unformulated remainder of thought that language has left in the shade—a remainder that is the very essence of that thought, driven outside its secret—but to comment also presupposes that this unspoken element slumbers within speech (*parole*), and that, by a superabundance proper to the signifier, one may, in questioning it, give voice to a content that was not explicitly signified. By opening up the possibility of commentary, this double plethora dooms us to an endless task that nothing can limit: there is always a certain amount of signified remaining that must be allowed to speak, while the signifier is always offered to us in an abundance that questions us, in spite of ourselves, as to what it 'means' (*veut dire*). Signifier and signified thus assume a substantial autonomy that accords the treasure of a virtual signification to each of them separately; one may even exist without the other, and begin to speak of itself: commentary resides in that supposed space. But at the same time, it invents a complex link between them, a whole tangled web that concerns the poetic values of expression: the signifier is not supposed to 'translate' without concealing, without leaving the signified with an inexhaustible reserve; the signified is revealed only in the visible, heavy world of a signifier that is itself burdened with a meaning that it cannot control. Commentary rests on the postulate that speech (*parole*) is an act of 'translation,' that it has the dangerous privilege images have of showing while concealing, and that it can be substituted for itself indefinitely in the open series of discursive repetitions; in short, it rests on a psychologistic interpretation of language that shows the stigmata of its historical origin. This is

an exegesis, which listens, through the prohibitions, the symbols, the concrete images, through the whole apparatus of Revelation, to the Word of God, ever secret, ever beyond itself. For years we have been commenting on the language of our culture from the very point where for centuries we had awaited in vain for the decision of the Word.[30]

In place of commentary Foucault proposes "a structural analysis of discourses that would evade the fate of commentary by supposing no remainder, nothing in excess of what has been said, but only the fact of its historical appearance. The facts of discourse would then have to be treated not as autonomous nuclei of multiple significations, but as events and functional segments gradually coming together to form a system" (p. xvii).[31] It is this system that now requires study. As Louis Althusser expressed it in a comparable statement, we must break with the "religious myth of reading" that concerns itself with hidden *meanings,* for what is hidden is not a meaning but a structure: "the truth of history cannot be read in its manifest discourse, because the text of history is not a text in which a voice (the Logos) speaks, but the inaudible and illegible notation of the effects of a structure of structures."[32]

What Foucault says about commentary seems true enough. Commentary is always unsatisfiable with respect to whatever is placed before it. Something is always left unsaid and undone, and it is this unfinished portion that commentary listens for and works for in whatever it studies. And there is no doubt that hermeneutics is a name for the desire to know what it is that inspires commentary, or what provokes its desire for what remains undone. Why is it that, historically, or except among philosophers of a certain analytical stripe, no text is ever taken as being merely explicit?

And certainly, given its history—its heavy burden of German romantic idealism—the local inclination of hermeneutics might well be to study texts like Walter Benjamin's "The Task of the Translator," with its idea that in "all language and linguistic creations there remains in addition to what can be conveyed something that cannot be communicated," namely, language itself, or what Benjamin calls "that ultimate essence, pure language," which exists nowhere by itself but is internal to, even imprisoned by, the natural languages that we speak and write.[33] Benjamin states that "in this pure language—which no longer means or expresses anything but is, as expressionless and creative Word, that which is meant in all languages—all information, all sense, and all intention finally encounter a stratum in which they are destined to be extinguished" (p. 80). The task of the translator is not simply to duplicate the meaning of an alien text in one's own language but, rather, "to release in [one's] own language that pure language which is under the spell of another, to liberate the language imprisoned in a work in his re-creation of that work" (p. 80). The notion of a pure language, a language uncontaminated by mere speech, may be one of modernity's great unkillable ideas.

But it is also true that Foucault's writings, and the whole analytic of discourse and culture that his work has helped inspire, are entailed in what hermeneutics is about. From a hermeneutical standpoint Foucault emerges as one of the great allegorists in the history of interpretation, where an allegorist is someone who deals with alien discourses by recontextualizing them within his or her own conceptual scheme. Foucault gives us some idea of what his scheme looks like in "The Order of Discourse," in which he says that what is inexplicit about a text is not a meaning but the way the text is inscribed in a network of relations whose purpose is the production and control of discourse.[34] The lesson that hermeneutics takes from Foucault is that commentary itself has to be situated within this network, or more accurately that understanding has to be understood in terms of its agencies and effects as well as in terms of its self-conscious tasks. So when hermeneutics tries to clarify the conditions in which understanding takes place, it must always recognize that these conditions are social and political in ways it may not always be possible to analyze. In any event understanding is always appropriative, or perhaps it would be better to say that it is always caught up in a struggle with what it seeks to understand, for it is also the case that understanding, being situated, is always exposed to what it confronts and is not always certain to be dominant.

One passage in Foucault's "The Order of Discourse" stands out in this regard because it describes what one might call the originary hermeneutical scene:

> What civilization, in appearance, has shown more respect toward discourse than our own? Where has it been more and better honoured? Where have been depended more radically, apparently, upon its constraints and its universal character? But, it seems to me, a certain fear hides behind this apparent supremacy accorded, this apparent logophilia. It is as though these taboos, these barriers, thresholds and limits were deliberately disposed in order, at least partly, to master and control the great proliferation of discourse, in such a way as to relieve its richness of its most dangerous elements; to organise its disorder so as to skate round its most uncontrollable aspects. It is as though people had wanted to efface all trace of its irruption into the activity of our thought and language. There is undoubtedly in our society, and I would not be surprised to see it in others, though taking different forms and

modes, a profound logophobia, a sort of dumb fear of these events, of this mass of spoken things, of everything that could possibly be violent, discontinuous, querulous, disordered even and perilous in it, of the incessant, disorderly buzzing of discourse. (pp. 228–29)

Here, in a way, is Foucault's version of Benjamin's notion of a pure language imprisoned in its discursive effects, but what is interesting is Foucault's conception of discourse as a kind of transcendental anarchy that human culture must struggle to bring under control; that is, the purity of discourse consists in an unconstrained freedom rather than in an undistorted message or uncontaminated system of pure relations. This is an idea not to be lost sight of. Of course, we should not imagine that discourse for Foucault is ever external to the systems that produce and contain it—"the existence of systems of rarefaction does not imply that, over and beyond them lie great vistas of limitless discourse, continuous and silent, repressed and driven back by them, making it our task to abolish them and at last to restore it to speech. Whether talking in terms of speaking or thinking, we must not imagine some unsaid thing, or an unthought, floating about the world, interlacing with all its forms and events" (p. 229). Rather, the point has to do with the fragility of these systems of control, or with what one might call their historicality or temporal eccentricity, their variable rigor or looseness or porousness.[35] The fact is that discourse is always excessive with respect to its occasions, so that even in the case of Foucault's own analytical project there always remains more to be accounted for than the operations of deep structure.

Indeed, an important lesson to learn from Foucault is that deep-structure analysis itself always comes at a high cost: inevitably it has to sacrifice what is historically singular and unrepeatable in favor of what is regular and schematic.[36] So naturally one is always tempted (as I am in this book) to step back from metahistory into an old-fashioned historicism that studies the contingent bits and pieces of the surface, telling several stories at once, interrupting itself with its own ignorance, losing its way, muddling one part of its subject in the bargain of trying to understand another. There is really no overcoming one's fascination with particulars. The book that follows is an attempt to stretch the conceptual history of hermeneutics in order to produce a less narrow, more heterogeneous and complicated picture of its ancient and modern boundaries, but it will be apparent at once that this attempt is far from being either systematic or rigorously and exhaustively empirical—how could it be, given the vastness and intractability of its subject? If hermeneutics were as self-contained as geometry, or as coherent as a branch of philosophy, or even as tractable as one of the discursive or textual fields that an archaeologist might analyze, or (most unlikely of all) as methodologically self-conscious as a school or movement in literary criticism, one might have been able to confine it sufficiently to deal with it comprehensively and conclusively, thus finally getting beyond it, or in control of it, in some nontrivial way. But in fact hermeneutics is a loose and baggy monster, or anyhow a less than fully disciplined body of thinking whose inventory of topics spreads out over many different historical, cultural, and intellectual contexts. Hermeneutics is "anarchic," in Rainer Schürmann's sense of this word; it does not try to assault its *Sache* but rather tries to grant what is singular and unrepeatable an open field.[37]

At all events there is no way to understand hermeneutics except through a piecemeal study of the different topics in its vast inventory—for example, the interpretation of oracles, the silencing of the muses, the quarrel of philosophy and poetry, the logic of allegory, the extravagance of midrash, mystical hermeneutics, the rise of literalism and the individual interpreter, the relation of self-understanding and the understanding of other people, not to mention the topics that belong more strictly to philosophical hermeneutics itself, particularly as these relate to the problem of historicality or the finitude of understanding: appropriation, power, authority, tradition, the conflict of interpretations, experience, critique, practice, action, freedom, and so on. My purpose has been to engage these topics out of a historical as well as theoretical interest, or in terms of their emergence in various episodes within various histories of interpretation and hermeneutical reflection, and not just as concepts in need of theoretical clarification.

The Ancients

I

Truth and Power in the Discourse of Socrates

> We believe we are at home in the immediate circle of beings.
> That which is, is familiar, reliable, ordinary. Nevertheless, the
> clearing is pervaded by a constant concealment [*Verbergen*] in
> the double form of refusal and dissembling [*des Versagens und
> des Verstellens*]. At bottom, the ordinary is not ordinary; it is
> extraordinary, uncanny. The nature of truth, that is,
> unconcealedness [*der Unverborgenheit*], is dominated
> throughout by a denial [*von einer Verweigerung*]. Yet this
> denial is not a defect or a fault, as though truth were an
> unalloyed unconcealedness that has rid itself of everything
> concealed. If truth could accomplish this, it would no longer
> be itself. This denial, in the form of a double concealment,
> belongs to the nature of truth as unconcealedness. Truth, in its
> nature, is untruth.
> —Heidegger, "The Origin of the Work of Art"

It is in the spirit of these words by Heidegger that I want
to ask about the discourse of Socrates—how he talks, how he sounds, and
also what it is to understand him; and I mean all of this to be taken point-
edly as a hermeneutical question. What is it for anyone, including Socrates,
to understand Socrates? This is the question at issue in Plato's *Apology,*
where Socrates talks about himself and claims to tell the truth about himself, and it is at issue again in the *Symposium,* where a drunken Alcibiades
claims to speak the truth of Socrates (215a), as if anyone, not just Socrates,
could do such a thing.

It is by no means clear, however, what sense can be given to the phrase
"speak the truth." Heidegger makes us think back to the play of dissembling
and recognition in the *Odyssey,* and to Hesiod's muses, who are proud of
their ability to speak many *pseudea* as if they were true (*etumoisin omoia*),
although, or so they claim, they could speak *alēthea* if they wanted to
(*Theogony,* 25). Or think of the enigmas of Heraclitus, who says, "Nature
loves to hide [*phūsis krūptesthai philei*]" (D123).[1] According to Heidegger,

this saying should be translated in a way that doesn't update it with easy modernisms like "nature." *Phusis* is not obviously translatable at all. He suggests the following: "Self-revealing loves self-concealing," where "loves" means something like "is true to" in the sense of being faithful (at one with, without being the same as). Heidegger reads this saying against the background of his etymology of *alētheia*, which frequently is translated as "truth" but which Heidegger renders as "unconcealedness." *Alētheia* is rooted in the word for forgetfulness (*lēthē*, which for Heidegger means that *lēthē* belongs to truth, is internal to it; but *alētheia* also entails words for secrecy, hiddenness, or escaping notice (as in the famous motto of Epicurus, *lathē biosas:* "Live in hiding").

Heraclitus also says: "The lord whose oracle is in Delphi neither speaks nor conceals, but gives a sign [*sēmainei*]" (D93). In antiquity, speaking the truth frequently meant speaking darkly, where a dark saying is not so much secret speech as a saying of what cannot be put into words and which must be looked for elsewhere (as, for example, in one's life). An *ainigma* is not the same as an *akousma* (something heard), and it is not something decipherable like a *sumbolon* (password); it is a saying that sheds its light elsewhere than where we stand, perhaps on things we know nothing about or have forgotten.

We can draw some rough boundaries for this way of thinking by appealing to Parmenides and also to his dark counterpart, Gorgias. On the one hand, there is the saying of the goddess Dikē in Parmenides' song about *Being and Non-Being:* "What there is to be said and thought [*legein te noein*] must needs be: for it is there for being, but nothing is not. I bid you ponder that, for this is the first way of inquiry from which I hold you back, but then from that on which mortals wander, knowing nothing, two-headed: for helplessness guides the wandering thought in their breasts, and they are carried along, deaf and blind at once, dazed, indiscriminating hordes, who believe that to be and not to be are the same and not the same; and the path taken by them all is backward-turning" (Fr. 6). There is the way of the speakable and the way of the unspeakable, and then there is that other way in which people say what they please: the way of wandering and ambiguity in which we end up going in circles. What do we do, however, when we find ourselves along this way, as inevitably we will, being mortal as we are? The rule of Parmenides is the philosopher's counsel of silence, still in force today: what we cannot talk about we must pass over without speaking. (Paradoxically, however, the goddess, whom we might take to be an allegory of the just word, disregards her own counsel halfway through her speech: "Here I end my trustworthy discourse and thought concerning the truth [*en tō soi pauo piston logon ēde noēma amphis alētheiēs*]; henceforth learn the beliefs [*doxas* of mortal men, listening to the deceitful order of my words [*kosmon emōn epeon apatēlon*]" [D8]).

On the other hand, there are the sayings of Gorgias as we have them from Sextus Empiricus: "For in his book *Concerning the Non-Existent* or *Concerning Nature* [*peri tou mē ontos ē peri phuseos*] [Gorgias] tries to establish successively three main points—firstly, that nothing exists; secondly, that even if anything exists it is incomprehensible [*akatalepton*] to man; thirdly, that even if anything is incomprehensible, yet certainly it is inexpressible and incommunicable to one's fellow-creatures [*anexoiston kai anermēneuton tō pelas*]" (*Against the Logicians*, 1.65; Loeb trans.). This reads like a parody of Parmenides: *phūsis* not only likes to hide, it is *not;* but even if it were, there would be no putting it into words, at least not in a way that would make sense to others. Gorgias locates everything on that middle way that Dikē forbids us to follow. For Gorgias, however, the indeterminacy of things strengthens rather than weakens language, making it the most powerful thing there is. The rule of Gorgias would go roughly as follows: given a state of affairs in which you cannot tell the difference between the same and not the same, you must take things in your own hands and by means of discourse make the case for what is or is not, construing it as you will or in terms of your own interests, because there is nothing else for it: in a world in which everything withholds itself or dissembles, anything goes, or anyhow will go to those strong enough to make their version of the case prevail. Hence the theme of Gorgias' *Defense of Helen:* persuasion (*peitho*) is equivalent to abduction by force (*bia*). It is the seduction, or the conquest, of the will (or the world) by means of language (Fr. 11.12–13).

I want to situate the question of how Socrates is to be understood—including the question of his own self-understanding—within this opposition between Parmenides and Gorgias, or between the philosopher's counsel of silence and the rhetorician's counsel of speech, or between the discourse of truth and the discourse of power. This framework certainly suits the ambiguity of Socrates, whom I will eventually want to figure (following a suggestion from his speech in the *Symposium*) as Hermes, god of interpreters and philosopher of the shuttle, that is, the dialectician who goes back and forth endlessly between the One and the indeterminate Two. Of course, there are many versions of Socrates, authorized and unauthorized—remember the tradition which has it that at his trial Socrates chose to remain silent; or conversely, as Guido Calogero once argued, that the true forerunner of Socrates is Gorgias, since the *Apology* is so obviously modeled on the *Defense of Helen,* which turns on the Socratic principle that *nemo sua sponte peccat:* no one willingly does wrong (pp. 409–10).² And so perhaps the real question about Socrates has less to do with the truth of what he says than with its power. This is the question that Alcibiades raises in the *Symposium* when he speaks of the talk of Socrates as a satyric enchantment (215e) and also as a kind of snakebite (217e). The truth of Socrates, Alcibiades says, lies in his power over other people—a point that Socrates, who has the chance, does not dispute.

It is certainly true that Socrates belongs, as all of us do, to that middle way in which things go this way or that and have to be stabilized by con-structions (requiring to be authorized or enforced) of what is or is not the case. This is the realm over which the goddess Peitho (not Dikē) presides. It is a frankly political realm, but also, as the *Symposium* reminds us, an erotic realm as well. It is the place of hermeneutics. As Gorgias says, Peitho is the goddess of inducement, or the compulsion of pleasure; but she is also, as Alexander Mourelatos says in his close philological study of the word *peith-ein,* "the patron of civilized life and of democratic institutions. Peitho in this context is the spirit of agreement, bargain, contract, consensus, exchange, and negotiation in a free *polis.*"³ However, we still need to know what it is to speak the truth in such a place.

Plato's *Apology* will help us reflect on this question. What does Socrates say about Socrates? How does he talk, how does he sound, when he claims to speak the truth (which, incidentally, is something he almost never claims to do)? In the *Apology* he does not hold back. He begins:

> How you, men of Athens, have been affected by my accusers, I do not know; but I, for my part, almost forgot who I was [*egō d' oun kai autos hup autōn oligon emauton epelathomēn*], so persuasively [*pi-thanōs*] did they talk; and yet there is hardly a word of truth [*alēthes*] in what they have said. But I was most amazed by one of the many lies that they told—when they said that you must be on your guard not to be deceived by me [*mē hup emou exepatēthēte*], because I was a clever speaker [*hōs deinou ontos legein*]. For I thought it was the most shame-less part of their conduct that they are not ashamed because they will immediately be convicted by me of falsehood by the evidence of fact [*oti autika hup emou exelegchthēsontai ergo*], when I show myself to be not in the least a clever speaker who speaks the truth [*ton talēthe legonta*]. For if this is what they mean, I would agree that I am an orator [*rhetōr*]—not after their fashion. Now they, as I say, have said little or nothing true; but you shall hear from me nothing but the truth [*umeis d' emou akousesthe pasan tēn alētheain*]. Not, however, men of Athens, speeches finely tricked out with words and phrases, as theirs

are, nor carefully arranged, but you will hear things said at random with words that happen to occur to me [*alla akousesthe eikē legomena tois epituchousin onomasin*]. For I believe that what I say is just [*pisteuō gar dikaia einai a legō*]; and let none of you expect anything else. For surely it would not be fitting [*prepoi*] for one of my age to come before you like a youngster making up speeches. And, men of Athens, I urgently beg and beseech you, if you hear me making my defense with the same words which I have been accustomed to speak both in the market place at the bankers' tables, where many of you have heard me, and elsewhere, not to be surprised or to make a disturbance on this account. For the fact is that this is the first time I have come before the court [*dikasterion*], although I am seventy years old; I am therefore an utter foreigner [*xenos*] to the manner of speech [*lexeōs*] here. Hence, just as you would, of course, if I were really a foreigner, pardon me if I spoke in that dialect and that manner of speech [*tē phōnē te kai tō tropō elegon*] in which I had been brought up, so now I make this request of you, a fair one, as it seems to me, that you disregard the manner of my speech—for perhaps it might be worse and perhaps better—and observe and pay attention merely to this, whether what I say is just or not [*ei dikaia legō ē mē*]; for that is the virtue [*aretē*] of a judge, and an orator's virtue is to speak the truth [*de talēthē legein*]. (17a–18a; Loeb trans.)

If you want to know what it is to speak the truth in front of other people, and also what it sounds like for the truth to get spoken, here you begin to get an answer, because what Socrates calls attention to here is something like the *lexis* of truth telling, where *lexis* is concerned with how words look or sound (how they make their appearance). Whatever it is, speaking the truth is the opposite of speaking cleverly or skillfully, where the word for *clever* is, interestingly, *deinos,* which in its Homeric (and also Sophoclean) sense means "terrible" or "fearful" and implies awesome force or strange power. *Deinos* is Odyssean and Oedipean; in short, heroic. Think of Antenor's description of Odysseus' power of speech in the *Iliad:*

> Odysseus looked the fool at first,
> But when he let the great voice go from his chest, and the words
> came drifting down like the winter snows, then no other mortal
> man beside could stand up against Odysseus.
> (3.221–223; Lattimore trans.)

In its sophistic sense *deinos* had come to mean "clever," but the note of power had not by any means diminished—anyhow the point to notice is the opposition between power and truth in the way Socrates characterizes himself as a speaker. "One should speak the truth," Democritus said, "not speak at length [*alēthomutheein chreōn, ou polylogeein*]" (Fr. 225; Freeman trans.).

Truth does not come in the form of a prepared speech. It just "comes out," as if on its own (or under its own power), as if one could speak it not by design or intention but only as if possessed by it, which is frequently how Socrates figures himself when he speaks, namely, as one who does not speak on his own or in his own name, in his own voice or on his own authority. This is how he speaks, for example, in the *Phaedrus* (another text on truth telling): in his second speech on love he speaks the speech of Stesichorus (son of Euphemus, Man of Pious Speech). This speech, however, in which philosophy is figured as a kind of madness or divine possession, is not a memorized text; Socrates hasn't memorized the words, only the subject: the words don't matter, which is one reason why truth-telling is rhetorically weak. The truth is naturally unrhetorical in the sense of not being persuasive of itself: "Knowledge of truth," says Socrates, "does not give the art of persuasion" (260d; Loeb). Hence the artlessness of truth telling—"you will hear things said at random with the words that happen to occur to me": it is whatever pops into the speaker's head—provided that the speaker is in his right mind, or self-possessed: or (since the Greeks had no word for self—*de nobis ipsis silemus:* of ourselves we are silent) possessed by *sophrosune*, rightmindedness. Truth happens only to those who are not beside themselves (paranoid). (In a moment, however, we will have to reflect on the truth of drunken outbursts.)

Thus, in one respect the problem that Socrates faces in the *Apology* is simply the traditional one of why the truth persuades so few. The problem is not only Heraclitean (most men do not know what is happening to them) but Odyssean as well: few people recognize what they see and hear. Barefoot Socrates before the assembly is like a beggarly Odysseus before the suitors: even the hooting is the same. Socrates will sound barbarous, speaking as if he were in the marketplace, whereas the assembly is listening for a terrific rhetorical display—but disregard my lexis, Socrates says, "and pay attention merely to this, whether what I say is just or not [*ei dikaia legō ē mē*]."

However, here things begin to grow complicated. The speech of Socrates is unadorned—not "finely tricked out with words and phrases"—but we must understand that unadorned discourse is not the same as talking straight. Plain speech is not plain speaking. Truth telling has metaphors of its own, as when, in this case, Socrates turns the question of *alētheia* into a question of *dikē*. What is it for Socrates to speak (not just the truth but) justly? Speaking justly means being in one's right mind when speaking, but it means more: justice enlarges upon truth by introducing the question of propriety or fitness. What, after all, would it be fitting for Socrates to sound like or to say? This is what the question of Socratic lexis come to: it is not just that Socrates promises not to lie; it is that he will stay in character when he speaks. He may be out of place in the assembly—in every sense in violation of its decorum—but he will not allow himself to slip out of character (out of his right mind). Speaking justly means preserving a Socratic decorum, and this means speaking truthfully not only *about* Socrates but *as* Socrates (the Socrates of the agora). To speak the truth in this case is not merely not saying anything contrary to the facts (as we shall see, facts can be taken this way or that). Truth telling is, rather, a complex rhetorical and ethical undertaking in spite of its indifference to words.

In order to tell the truth, Socrates has to exhibit himself; that is, the Socrates of Socrates has to shine out or disclose itself—and it's hard to say exactly what this means. It isn't enough to say (as we would today without hesitation) that Socrates has an inwardness to express. In fact, he has less of an interiority than Odysseus does.[4] In place of a display of words Socrates must display a character—not an *ego*, however, but an *ethos* in the antique sense of ethical difference: the just man, for example, or the wise man, or perhaps the man not so wise, or the *eiron* (the man who never talks straight). But more than this, Socrates has a *phūsis* to show, namely, that which he almost forgot when he heard the charge against him delivered with such force (*deinos*) and persuasion (*peithō*). Speaking the truth means bringing this *phūsis* out into the open—but remember that *phūsis krūptesthai philei*. Perhaps this dark saying will help us gain some insight into what it is for Socrates to be ironic.

One approach would be to say that the task of Socrates in speaking before the assembly is to appear to be what he is, the word *appear* carrying the double meaning of semblance and emergence. Here the question of speaking the truth is not only one of agreement between appearance and reality but also one of the conditions in which reality makes its appearance within the human world that the assembly represents.

I can try to clarify this point by referring to the Homeric axiom that you are what you appear to be—and, more to the point, you are what is said about you. The heroic quest for fame is not vainglorious; it is a quest for the truth about oneself: it is a desire to be put into words, where one will at last be fully what one is. One emerges in one's actions and in the stories that such actions produce, and one cannot be counted as real—as really *there*—except as one emerges in this guise. It is not that one's reality—one's *phūsis*, if that is the word for it—is hidden or separate from action and story; it is that action and story are the way of coming into being for the hero. And as one comes into being, so one can go out again, as Odysseus learns to his sorrow. Remember that Odysseus is not himself for much of his time away from Ithaca—there is, for example, a terrific disparity between the naked nobody who washes up on the shores of Phaeacia and the Odysseus about whom Damodocos sings at the Phaeaician court. To speak technically, one might say that empirically the two are the same man but phenomenologically only one of them is the true Odysseus. The task of Odysseus in any case is to live up to his name, to restore himself to the norm of what is said about him; short of this he is just not himself and might as well be a beggar (someone without a story to tell, unless it is a story—like the story of Eumaeos [*Odyssey*, 15.390–492]—of how a hero was bereft of everything that made him what he was).

This is why it matters so much how Odysseus is clothed, how he looks, and how he can be made to resemble the man everyone has heard about. In this regard he has the frequent help of Athene:

And Athene, she who was born from Zeus, made him
Bigger to look at and stouter, and on his head
Made his hair flow in curls, like the hyacinth flower.
As when some man whom Hephaistos and Pallas Athene have taught
Art of all kinds, and he turns out graceful handiwork;
So she poured grace upon his head and shoulders.
(6.229–35; Cook trans.)

In other words, embellishment is required for the Odysseus of Odysseus (his *phūsis*) to shine out, make its appearance, or appear to be what it is—in short, for Odysseus to be in character. The point is, however, that this *phusis* of Odysseus—call it the truth of him—is not what we would call an ego identity that Odysseus simply carries around with him wherever he goes. Indeed, it is something that Telemachus can possess to the extent that he comes to resemble his father. The question of whether Telemachus is true to his father is one of identity as well as of fidelity. It's a wise child that knows its father (*Odyssey*, 1.216)—this is how one's self-knowledge (or one's self-emergence; *phusis*) begins to take shape. In a similar way, the main question is not whether the poet's song is true to Odysseus but whether Odysseus is true to the poet's song. In the Homeric scheme, poetry is truth, but it is possible for the human world to be false to it. In this, poetry resembles the law. Thus, understanding Odysseus—*being* Odysseus (being true to him)—means being true to what is said about him. If it is difficult to say in this case where saying ends and being begins, that is the way it is with sayings that require us to live up to them. The mystery of the logos is reflected in the task of being what is said about you.

This can be illustrated in a slightly different way by the Oedipus of Sophocles. Unlike Odysseus, Oedipus lives in a world of multiple and intersecting stories whose truth or falsity wait upon Oedipus himself. He is renowned as the man who emancipated Thebes by unriddling the *ainigma* of the Sphinx; and at the outset of *Oidipos Tyrannos* he is called upon to be himself again—"look to your name" (47), the supplicant says, "show you are the same man still" (53; Arnott trans.)—but *phusis* likes to hide: Oedipus is not himself; or, rather, he is also, without knowing it, or without understanding what he knows, the man who has done the unspeakable. He already knows this about himself—has heard about it anyhow—from an oracle's response to his question about who his father really is:

> Phoebus sent me away
> No wiser than I came, but something else
> He showed me, sad and strange and terrible:
> That I was doomed to mate with my own mother,
> Bring an abhorrent brood into the world;
> That I should kill the father who begat me.
> When I heard, I fled from Corinth, ever since
> Marking its whereabouts only by the stars,
> To find some place where I should never see
> This evil oracle's calamities fulfilled,
> And in my travels reached that very place
> Where, as you tell me, Laius met his death.
> (761–72)

The task of Oedipus—call it the task of self-understanding—is to recognize not himself exactly but the truth of what was said about him, which means understanding how the oracle's prophecy maps onto—fits and finally replaces—the story he is accustomed to tell about his life. In effect, Oedipus finds himself compelled to revise his autobiography to make it consistent with what he hears from others (a drunk in Corinth, Apollo, Tiresias, messengers, and herdsmen): the truth of what is said shines out in him, that is, shines out unmistakably in his life and action. Here the law or logos is not poetry but prophecy, but the upshot is the same: the meaning of what is said lies in the way it is binding upon Oedipus, or in the way he lives up to it.

In the case of Socrates we should imagine the following: the same rule applies (you are what is said about you), only now what is said is no longer *epos*, or prophecy, but talk: free-floating or fugitive *doxa*, things people hear and repeat (*akousmata*), sayings that circulate anonymously and that sometimes take the form of *diabolai* (slanderings) and *katēgorēmena* (accusations: literally, talk that brings one down). Remember how Socrates continues in the *Apology*: "For many accusers [*katēgoroi*] have risen up against me before you, who have been speaking for a long time . . . saying 'There is a certain Socrates, a wise man, a ponderer over the things in the air, and one who has investigated the things beneath the earth and who makes the weaker argument the stronger. . . .' And . . . all these are most difficult to cope with; for it is not even possible to call any of them up here and cross-question him, but I am compelled in making my defence to fight, as it were, absolutely with shadows and to cross-question when nobody answers" (18b–e).

One way to think about Socrates is to say that he is the first hero in Greek tradition whose adversary is the *pseudos*, that is, not just the lie but the impostor: the pseudo-Socrates. Both Odysseus and Oedipus confront only the truth about themselves—they come to terms with themselves in new ways as their lives unfold, even when this means coping with violent changes that produce unforeseen identities. Odysseus is the cunning sacker of cities (*Iliad*) but also the much-suffering Odysseus (*Odyssey*); Oedipus the unriddler of the Sphinx is also Oedipus the transgressor of the unspeakable. All that this means, however, is that their lives have produced or fulfilled many stories, and so they answer to many names. Socrates, by contrast, seems to have entered into a different order of things: he belongs to that middle way between being and nothing in which things exist not in themselves as self-identical entities but only in their versions, among which serious disagreements occur—and among which, therefore, one is required to choose.

Here is a short list of the versions of Socrates circulating in Athens: (1) the Socrates of the old accusation (which I have just quoted); (2) the Socrates of the new accusation, which essentially embellishes the old, saying that in addition to "investigating the things beneath the earth and in the heavens and making the weaker argument the stronger" Socrates is guilty of "teaching others these things" (19b–c); and (3) the sophistic Socrates (the Socrates who resembles Gorgias, Prodicus, Hippias, and other "wise men" to whom young Athenians resort): "and if you have heard that I undertake to teach people and that I make money by it, that is not true either" (19d–e).

It is important to understand that none of these versions is obviously false. This is what the goddess in the song of Parmenides warned us about: in the human world there is always a likeness (fading into indeterminacy) between what is and what is not the case. This is why for Plato what we would call correspondence theories of truth always fall short of the truth—think of what the *Seventh Letter* says about "the Weakness of the logos [*tōn logon asthenes*]" (343a). Truth is not correspondence but disclosure: "It is only when all these [*logoi*], names and definitions, visual and other sensations, are rubbed together and subjected to tests in which questions and answers are exchanged in good faith and without malice that finally, when human capacity is stretched to its limit, a spark of understanding and intelligence flashes out and illuminates the subject at issue" (344b; Hamilton trans.). In any case, each of the *diabolai* concerning Socrates contains the presumptive charge of *anosion,* which translates as impiety or unholiness, but which in this case means specifically *oude theous nomizein,* "not recognizing the gods of the city." And we know from the *Euthyphro* that Socrates is on entirely ambiguous terms with the gods: "Is not this, Euthyphro, the reason why I am being prosecuted, because when people tell such stories about the gods I find it hard to accept them?" (6a); and before his conversation with Euthyphro is out Socrates will have delivered a magnificent insult to the gods by figuring piety, by analogy, with the care and feeding of animals (13a–c) and then with commerce, or *emporikē* (14e). Of course, perhaps Socrates is not insulting the gods but only ridiculing the way we practice piety—who can tell?

The problem here is twofold. On the one hand, the question at issue has to do with power and authority in interpretation. How can one's version of one's self, one's self-understanding or self-construction, get counted as true—or even emerge—when the field is already commanded by versions that are more powerful in their probability? Anyone may speak the truth, but how can one make it plain that *that* is what one is actually doing? How, in this case, can the truth be made sufficient to the occasion so that Socrates will shine out unmistakably as being "such a man as I say I am" (30c)?

On the other hand, there is the question of what it would be for Socrates to do such a thing. If he does shine out as what he is, what will appear? The problem here is both rhetorical and not rhetorical. We know, for example, that Socrates cannot become rhetorical in the normal fashion of displaying a winning version of himself, and so he gives us abnormal rhetoric, which is, however, but one rhetoric the more: the rhetoric of truth telling is to appear to be without guile, cunning, design, or duplicity—in short, unrhetorical—but of course the extemporaneity of Socrates is no less cunning for being just what it is, else why should he call attention to it and to his whole manner of speaking? This, we want to say, is what the rhetoric of irony looks like. However, it would not be enough to say that Socratic irony is simply a figure of speech, a rhetorical *lexis* that we can learn to figure out one way or another; rather, irony is essential to Socratic *phūsis*. It is being rather than style; it is not something Socrates can put on or take off. The hermeneutical problem in this event would be that the truth of Socrates would lie in its resistance to interpretation in the plain sense of exegesis or the construction of meaning, that is, the construction of an intelligible and forceful version of the case. We should imagine that it is the *phūsis* of Socrates to baffle or bewilder such that his "shining-out," or *alētheia,* is bound to leave us as much in the dark as ever. And this indeed seems to be how it works. The point about Socrates is that we never know how to take him.

"So listen," he says. "And perhaps I shall seem to some of you to be joking [*paizein*]; be assured, however, I shall speak perfect truth to you" (20d). We know better than to say that truth telling means (necessarily) being serious, because this is just what Socrates never is: his being is his being playful, turning things upside down like a lord of misrule. "Tell me, Chaerephon," Callicles says in the *Gorgias,* "is Socrates in earnest [*spoudazei*] about this, or only joking [*paizei*]?" (481b). Socrates never allows us to believe our ears. He always speaks audaciously and against the grain of what is said, as in the *Gorgias,* when he turns a Homeric commonplace on its head by compelling Polus to agree that it is better to suffer injustice than to cause it. Or, again, in the *Republic,* his questions overturn every known definition of justice until an enraged Thrasymachus can take it no more and challenges Socrates to talk straight for once in his life: "If you really want to know what justice is, stop asking questions and then playing to the crowd by refuting anyone who answers you. You know perfectly well that it's easier to ask questions than to answer them. Give us an answer yourself, and tell us what you think justice is" (336c–d; Lee trans.).

For Thrasymachus, the "well-known irony of Socrates [*eiōuthua eirōneia Sōkratous*]" (337a) is not just his not saying what he means but his refusal to mean anything at all—his refusal to put anything but questions into words. Socratic irony in this sense is a kind of Parmenidean silence that takes the form of dissembling speech, that is, a discourse characterized by darkness or reserve—a holding back of the kind dramatically represented by the *daimon* of Socrates, which makes its appearance as a compulsive restraining force whenever Socrates is tempted to come forward (go public) in the way of speech and action (31d, 40b; *Phaedrus,* 242c): tempted, in other words, to turn himself from an *eirōn* into an *alazōn* like Odysseus or

Oedipus or (better) Protagoras and Alcibiades. Socratic irony is *Versagen,* or speech without saying.

However—and appropriately perhaps—this is a matter on which it is difficult to speak without getting tangled in contradictions. I have already mentioned that when Socrates does speak positively, that is, when he does say something about something—as in his second speech on love in the *Phaedrus* or in his (unreservedly dogmatic) account of love in the *Symposium*—he does so in the name of someone else (Stesichorus, Diotima). This is consistent with his characterization of himself in the *Theaetetus* as a kind of midwife: "But the greatest thing about my art is this, that it can test in every way whether the mind of the young man is bringing forth a mere image, an imposture [*eidolon kai pseudos*], or a real and genuine offspring. For I have this in common with midwives: I am sterile in point of wisdom, and the reproach which has often been brought against me, that I question others but make no reply myself about anything, is a true reproach; and the reason of it is this: the god compels me to act as midwife, but has never allowed me to bring forth" (150c–d; Loeb trans.). Socrates will even speak in the name of Homer and the poets and tell a tale "as the truth" even though it will appear to his interlocutor as an obvious fabrication (Gorgias, 523a: *on su men ēgēse muthon, hōs egō oimai, egō de logon. ōs alēthē gar onta soi lexō a mello legein*). Frequently—as in the *Gorgias,* the *Phaedrus,* and even the *Republic*—recourse to storytelling is a way of finessing the weakness of the logos, that is, the liability of our words to get away from us and to run around in circles like the statues of Daedalus (*Euthyphro,* 15b). Stories, being memorable, are a way of holding opinions without having to fix them in exact words or a text. But storytelling is also the sign of a defect in one's company that puts the true give-and-take out of the question. The whole point of the *Phaedrus* is that it is a long way from philology to dialectic; one can speak along this way only as truthfully as the occasion will bear (*Phaedrus,* 257a). Under these circumstances, the *muthos* may be the only way of avoiding a *macrologia,* or of eliminating unnecessary words: "To tell what it [the soul] really is would be a matter for utterly superhuman and long discourse, but it is within human power to describe it briefly in a figure; let us therefore speak in that way" (246a). On these occasions, as always, it is necessary to pay close attention to how Socrates sounds, and usually this means that one has to cope with Socratic joking: "You're making fun of our discourse, Socrates," Phaedrus says: *skōpteis ton logon emōn* (264e). The irony is that making fun of a *logos* does not necessarily mean that it is empty; in fact, Socrates will normally praise questionable talk and declare himself spellbound by it (*Protagoras,* 328d). The deeper irony may be this: it is not absolutely out of the question that the *pseudos* is a way (sometimes the only way) for something to show itself, if only deceptively.

In the essay "Plato's Unwritten Dialectic," Hans-Georg Gadamer says that "in his dialogues Plato fails to deal adequately with the problem of the pseudos. For pseudos does not lie in falsely speaking of one thing as another but only of speaking of it as something which it is not."⁵ Evidently we must imagine that there are false sayings that are just false (*diabolai* or *pseude katēgoremēna*), but also false sayings—deceptions—in which something begins to show itself. In the *Cratylus*—in the midst of lunatic punning and absurd etymologies—Socrates says that the *logos* is able to "signify everything [*to pan sēmainei*]," but at the same time it makes things hard to grasp because it is always moving them around and around, "and is duplicitous, both true and false [*kai esti diplous, alēthes te kai pseudes*]." The pun here on the god Pan is part of this runaround with words, which continues as follows:

SOCRATES.   Is not the truth that is in him [*Pan*] the smooth or sacred form which dwells above among the gods, whereas falsehood [*pseudos*] dwells among men below, and is rough like the goat of tragedy, for tales and falsehoods [*muthoi te kai ta pseude*] have generally to do with the tragic or goatish life, and tragedy is the place of them?

HERMOGENES.   Very true.

SOCRATES.   Then surely Pan, who is the declarer of all things [*pan*] and the perpetual mover [*aei polon*] of all things, is rightly called *aipolos* (goatherd), he being the two-formed son of Hermes, smooth in his upper part, and rough and goatlike in his lower regions. And, as son of Hermes, he is speech or the brother of speech, and that brother should be like brother is no marvel. But, as I was saying, my dear Hermogenes, let us get away from the gods. (408c–d; Jowett trans.)

A number of things need to be sorted out here. The figure of Pan is a short way of making a long point about the Platonic *logos,* namely, that it is never logocentric: the One is always tied to the indeterminate Two. Pan is "two-formed son of Hermes"—an epithet that applies not only to Socrates' interlocutor, Hermogenes, but also to Socrates himself, who is no less duplicitous than Pan. This is the point that Alcibiades tries to make in the *Symposium* when he compares Socrates to Marsyas, the satyr who bewitches mankind

with his words (215b–d), but it is a point already (covertly) made by Diotima in her characterization of Eros as a hermeneutical *daimonion* who
shuttles back and forth between the gods and men, that is, between *alētheia*
and *pseudos,* being and nothing, wisdom and ignorance—and who (of
course) looks just like Socrates: shoeless, ugly, impoverished, cunning in
pursuit of the beautiful and the good (Phaedrus, Agathon), a lover of wisdom and "a master of jugglery, witchcraft, and artful speech" (203d–e).

The *Republic* is a valuable text in this connection, because it is the one
case in which Socrates is not allowed to get away with his customary mimetic dodge of putting what is questionable into someone else's mouth.
Thrasymachus insists that Socrates speak *in propria persona,* and although
Socrates manages to disarm Thrasymachus in his usual manner—"you seem
to have fascinated Thrasymachus into a premature submission, like a snake
charmer" (385b)—Glaucon will not be put off: "What we want from you,"
Glaucon says, "is not only a demonstration that justice is superior to injustice, but a description of its essential effects, harmful or otherwise, which
each produces on its possessor" (367a–b). And Socrates complies, saying
not what *he* thinks justice is, however, nor even what he would like to say,
but only what must be said under the circumstances: if one were going to
construct a just city (not a friendly city, mind you, but a *just* city and nothing else), what would it look like? Socrates speaks under necessity, saying
what he is bound to say: we would call it logical argument: if A, then B
must follow: "whithersoever the wind of the argument blows, there lies our
course [*all hopē an ho logos hōsper pneuma pherē, tautē iteon*]" (394d).
Yet—and here is the crucial point—Socrates makes no claim for the truth
of what he says. Logic is no guarantor of truth (as Cicero, repeating an old
line, said of the Greeks: *contentionis cupiodores quam veritatis* [*De Ora-
tore,* 1.11.47–48]). In fact, at one point, when Socrates engages the hard
practical question of how the ruled can be made to accept their rulers, his
argument fills him with shame, because it appears that in order to get the
citizens of the *polis* to accept their several subordinate stations in the system
it will be necessary to tell them a powerfully persuasive story (*pseudomen-
ous peisai malista* [414c])—"a sort of Phoenician tale," Socrates calls it—
about the way the rulers are made of gold and are therefore fit to rule,
whereas the rest of us are variously composed of silver, bronze, and iron
(414b-15c). Even Glaucon is astonished at this: "It is not for nothing," he
says, "that you were so ashamed [*ēschunou*] about coming out with your
lie [*pseudos legein*]" (414e). Doesn't this, after all, make the *pseudos* foundational for a just *polis?*

Socrates, however, is careful to emphasize the speculative and nonserious nature of his account, which sometimes threatens to get serious anyhow, especially when the dignity of philosophy is at stake. One must take care, Socrates says, not to make philosophy look ridiculous, the more so in these times when no one any longer takes her for what she is:

—[But] here again I am making myself a little ridiculous.
—In what way?
—I forgot, I said, that we were jesting [epaizomēn], and I spoke with too great intensity. For, while speaking, I turned my eyes upon philosophy, and when I saw how she is undeservedly reviled, I was revolted, and, as if in anger, spoke too earnestly to those who are in fault.
—No, by Zeus, not too earnestly for me as a hearer.
—But too much so for me as a speaker, I said. (536b–c; Loeb trans.)

It would be well to recall here the advice that the old Parmenides gave to the young Socrates, who was always so irrepressible when it came to defining the beautiful, the good, and the just. "Believe me," Parmenides said, "there is something noble and inspired [kalē men oun kai theia] in your passion for argument [dialegomenou enthade], but you must make an effort and submit yourself, while you are still young, to a severer training in what the world calls idle talk [adoleschias] and condemns as useless. Otherwise the truth will escape you" (135c–d). For the truth is that the beautiful, the good, and the just cannot be put into words—not, at any rate, in isolation but only in respect to something other than themselves. What the young Socrates had to learn was reserve and the ability to speak of things in other terms than in the as such of conceptual determination.

The talk old Parmenides had in mind is Eleatic rather than Athenian. The Sixth Letter, for example, tells us that the serious and the playful are like brother and sister (323d); they belong together: the one or the other could not exist in isolation. Thus they are like Being and the Other (te on kai thateron), which, according to the Eleatic Stranger in Plato's Sophist, weave through all things and through one another, so that it becomes possible for us even to transgress the rule of Parmenides and to say that which is not (259a–b). The hard truth (which must seem like madness) is that this transgression is indispensable to philosophy, for if it were not possible to say that which is not, speech itself—and therefore philosophy—would be out of the question (260a). The pseudos is born—it exists, even though it is a shock to the logos to say such a thing—in the interweaving of Being and Nothing that makes discourse possible, but we are not to take alarm at this, the Stranger tells the young Theaetetus, for without this interweaving everything would remain isolated from everything else and nothing could be predicated of anything (259e), in both senses of this phrase. This would leave us in the nightmare world of the Sophist (254e) where it would never be possible to tell the difference—the otherness of the not-being (the "is-not")—between what is and is not the case.

One could not talk seriously this way unless one were willing to let one's *logos* go free without worrying how it might sound, because it is bound to sound very strange, especially to Athenian ears accustomed to the smooth exfoliation of the long speech. The discourse of the Eleatic Stranger, in which young Theaetetus is instructed in the nature of true and false speaking, is an example of *adoleschia,* which means both idle or empty talk and also the subtlety of dialectical conversation. There is nothing comforting to the ears in such talk; on the contrary, it is frequently painful, and when it goes on in public it always sounds silly. This is the point that Socrates makes in the *Theaetetus,* in which we hear the *adoleschia* of Socrates as he initiates the young Theaetetus into the intricacies of the question, What is knowledge? The conversation threatens to go on endlessly. No resolution of the question is in sight when the conversation is broken off because Socrates has to go to the portico of the King-Archon to hear the charge of Meletus and Anytus. Mercifully his *adoleschia* is punctuated by canny asides and mimetic interludes, as when Socrates impersonates Protagoras and allows the old sophist to defend himself against the Socratic *adoleschia:* "'Our estimable Socrates here frightened a little boy by asking if it was possible for one and the same person to remember and at the same time not to know one and the same thing, and when the child in his fright said "no," because he could not foresee what would result, Socrates made poor me a laughing-stock in his talk'" (166a). This is a merciful mimesis because the problem with dialectical conversation is that it takes time—too much time for it to go on in public. No wonder, Socrates says, "that those who have spent long time in the study of philosophy appear ridiculous when they enter the courts of law as speakers" (172c). In public one's *logos* is not free but is bound to the clock and to the restlessness of one's audience (172d–73b). Dialectical conversation is meant to go on privately among friends—and perhaps also silently, which is the mode of conversation that gives Socrates his definition of *dianoia,* or what is called thinking: it is "the talk which the soul has with itself" in order to arrive at an opinion, one way or another, about whatever comes up. Socrates emphasizes that it is "talk which has been held, not with someone else, nor aloud, but in silence with oneself" (190a). Perhaps it is related to the "word which is written with intelligence [*epistēmes graphetai*] in the soul of one who learns [*manthanontos psuchē*], which is able to defend itself and knows to whom it should speak and before whom to be silent" (*Phaedrus*, 276a). In this event one is at least required to appear ridiculous in no one's eyes but one's own, which is perhaps why it is the better part of irony to take everyone seriously except oneself.

For our purposes, however, the main point about *adoleschia*—whence we get our word *adolescence*—is that it belongs to the same semantic field as *paideia* (the teaching of children), *paidia* (child's play), and *paizein* (to be playful, to joke). But now we see that *paizein* is something like a philosophical way of speaking, or at least a way of speaking that is on the way to philosophy. In any event, here would be the proper context in which to situate the figure of Socrates as he addresses the assembly, saying: "And perhaps I shall seem to some of you to be joking [*paizein*]; be assured, however, I shall speak perfect truth to you" (20d).

Recall that Socrates was about to explain why it is that there is such talk about a certain Socrates, a wise man, and so on. Perhaps it is the case, he says, that he is wise in some sense, but this is not a claim that he makes on his own authority (for he knows that he is not wise); rather, he will, true to form, bring it out of another's mouth:

And, men of Athens, do not interrupt me with noise, even if I seem to you to be boasting; for the word which I speak is not mine, but the speaker to whom I shall refer it is a person of weight. For of my wisdom—if it is wisdom at all—and of its nature, I will offer you the god of Delphi as a witness. You know Chaerephon, I fancy. . . . And you know the kind of man [he] was, how impetuous in whatever he undertook. Well, once he went to Delphi and made so bold as to ask the oracle this question; and, gentlemen, don't make a disturbance at what I say; for he asked if there was anyone wiser than I. Now the Pythia replied that there was no one wiser. And about these things his brother here will bear you witness, for Chaerephon is dead.

But see why I say these things; for I am going to tell you whence the prejudice against me has arisen. For when I heard this, I thought to myself: "What in the world does the god mean, and what riddle is he propounding [*ti pote legei ho theos, kai ti pote ainittetai*]? For I am conscious that I am not wise either much or little. What then does he mean by declaring that I am the wisest? He certainly cannot be lying, for that is not possible for him." And for a long time I was at a loss as to what he meant; then with great reluctance I proceeded to investigate [*zētēsin*] him somewhat as follows (21b).

What Socrates describes here is what we would now call an epistemological crisis. This is a rupture in one's self-understanding that requires the rewriting of one's narrative or the story of one's life. What happened to Socrates, for example, is just what happened to Oedipus when he heard what the oracle said about *him;* and what follows now in the case of Socrates is what followed then. An attempt is made to find the oracle's saying empty, but the very making of the attempt turns into the action that proves the oracle's fulfillment, or that which makes it true—namely, the making of one's life. It is axiomatic, after all, that whatever you do to escape your fate will become the exact steps that lead you to it. Willy-nilly the mystery of the *logos* continues to lie in the task of living up to what is said about you. What this means, however, is that the truth of the *logos* may lie less in its logical self-identity and less still in its correspondence to a world of self-subsistent entities than in its fulfillment in the world of *ergon,* that is, in the world of deed and action.

The oracle's saying produces the life of Socrates just as it once produced the life of Oedipus; or perhaps we should say that it produced his *way* of life. Socrates questions the oracle's saying, not directly—"We may not question gods," as Electra says (556)—but indirectly by questioning himself and others. "I went to one of those who had a reputation for wisdom," he says, "thinking that there, if anywhere, I should prove the [saying] wrong"; but of course he proves just the opposite, making himself a hateful nuisance in the bargain by making people look like fools. Nevertheless, he says,

> I thought I must consider the god's business of the highest importance. So I had to go, investigating the meaning [*chrēsmon:* answer] of the oracle, to all those who were reputed to know anything. And by the Dog [*kai ēn ton kuna*], men of Athens—for I must speak the truth to you—this, I do declare, was my experience [*ē mēn egō epathon:* this is what happened to me]: those who had the most reputation seemed to me almost the most deficient, as I investigated *at the god's behest* [*kata ton theon;* emphasis mine], and others who were of less repute seemed to be superior in the matter of being sensible. So I must relate to you my wandering as I performed my Herculean labors, so to speak, in order that the oracle might prove irrefutable. (21e–22a)

There is much here that is very strange: Socrates swears "by the dog"; he compares his way of life to a heroic tale of wandering and Herculean labor; he began by seeking to prove the oracle wrong, but now, without making anything of it, he speaks of proving the oracle "irrefutable." But the greatest crux is Socrates' claim that he was just following orders in undertaking his famous *elenchos:* what is this "at the god's behest [*kata ton theon*]"? Socrates drops this in as if it were a throwaway line—"as I investigated at the god's behest"—but there isn't any divine command or any evidence that the god desired anything at all from Socrates. The oracle was simply given a question—"Is there anyone wiser . . . ?"—and his answer was (as always) brief: "no one," or words to that effect. So on what ground does Socrates speak of *kata ton theon?*

Socrates doesn't simply drop this in once but plays several variations on it:

1. at 23b: Therefore I am still even now going about and searching and investigating at the god's behest [*kata ton theon*] anyone . . . who I think is wise; and when he does not seem so to me, I give aid to the god [*to theo boēthōn:* help the god out] and show that he is not wise. And by reason of this occupation I have no leisure to attend to any of the affairs of the state worth mentioning, or of my own, but am in vast poverty on account of my service to the god [*dia tēn tou theou latreian*, where *latreia* means "labor," "service," "servitude"].
2. at 28e: the god gave me a station, as I believed and understood, with orders to spend my life in philosophy and in examining myself and others [*tou de theou tattontos, hōs egō ōēthēn te kai hupelabon, philosophounta me dein zēn kai exetazonta emauton kai tous allous*].
3. at 30a: For know that the god commands me to do this, and I believe that no greater good ever came to pass in the city than my service to the god [*ē tēn emēn tō theō hupēresian*, where *hupēresia* means "the service or duty of rowers," from *hupēretein*, "to serve on board ship," "to do hard labor," "to obey or act under instructions." Here the implication is that of abject servitude, as in the *Euthyphro*, 13d, where *hupēretikē* means something like bondage to a despot].
4. at 33c: But, as I believe, I have been commanded to do this by the god through oracles and dreams and in every way in which any man was ever commanded by divine power to do anything whatsoever.

From a purely analytical point of view, as generations of scholars have remarked, all of this is entirely cockeyed. A review of learned opinion is given by Reginald Hackforth in *The Composition of Plato's* Apology, to which Hackforth adds his own ideas that Socrates believed that he had been sent by the god to serve his people but that he had never explained why he believed this—at least did not do so at his trial—and that the whole business about the divine imperative is Plato's attempt to fill a gap in the historical record: "Plato thought, wrongly but not unnaturally, that there must have been some explanation [for why Socrates believed himself to be on a divine mission], and that it was a pity that Socrates had not given it, because it would have impressed the judges favourably: when he came to write his *Apology,* in which, as I have argued, his purpose was to influence contemporary opinion in favour of Socrates, he thought that it would subserve that purpose if he showed that Socrates, accused of impiety, might have defended his life-work as obedience, not merely to God, but to God speaking through the mouth of the Pythian priestess."[6]

From a hermeneutical standpoint, however, there is really nothing surprising in what Socrates claims. It is not that Socrates, in his account of his way of life and its foundations, has left something unexplained or out of account that Plato had clumsily to supply; it is that there is nothing requiring to be supplied—no missing facts or inferences. There is only the oracle's dark saying and the question of what sort of construction can be placed on it that will allow it to shed its light on how things are. What we get from Socrates is his construction, and there is nothing awfully wrong about it. What would have to be the case for the oracle's saying to make sense? This is essentially what Socrates sets out to determine. What has to be studied is not the text but the world, or one's life in it.

The point is that his construction is an appropriation and application of the oracle's saying to the situation in which he finds himself; it is not the recovery of an original intention or a hidden meaning. Oracles do not have original meanings, only belated ones. In any event you can't ask an oracle what he means. Oracles are like statues and texts and cannot be interrogated, except in the figural sense that others must speak or answer for them (*Phaedrus,* 275d–e). The meaning of the oracle's saying is hidden not in the mind of Apollo but (if anywhere) in time, and only time will tell whether the saying is full or empty, binding or idle, forceful or weak. The task of Socrates is to make time speak; the oracle has spoken and said all it is going to say.

We are dealing here with the hermeneutics of prophecy, whose conventions are strange to us, although they shouldn't be and wouldn't be if we studied the law (for example) hermeneutically as well as analytically. There is an analogy of law and prophecy, as the ancients knew, since both belong to the category of discourses that depend upon the future for their intelligibility. A legal text, after all, must always be situated before it can be understood, and this means situating it not only in the time of its composition but also in the time of those to whom it continues to apply; it cannot simply be analyzed as if it were a historical document or a logical proposition. The same is true of the oracular text. What we call the ambiguity of legal and prophetic texts—their resistance or irreducibility to logical and historical exegesis—is just their openness to the future. What they mean exactly remains to be seen: only time tells the truth. Thus the primary question that Socrates faces is not what was in Apollo's mind when he gave his answer but what he, Socrates, has to do—how he has to live—in order for the oracle's saying to come out either true or false. Laws and prophecies have to be situated in the lives of those who are called upon to interpret them. Socrates, in any case, must henceforward see himself in the light of what the oracle has said about him, true or false. His construction of the sense of the oracle is not the reconstruction of an original intention but his own self-construction: his understanding of the oracle is how he comes to understand himself in the light of what the oracle has said. In virtue of what the oracle has said, Socrates situates himself in his own life in a certain way.

Recall how this works: Socrates, bewildered by the oracle's answer, sets out to prove it wrong by interrogating those who are supposed to know what they are talking about, and this interrogation turns into a way of life, what Socrates calls "spending my life in philosophy": pursuing, via the *elenchos*, wisdom, which (like *phūsis*) loves to hide—hence the endless quest or questioning. But the point is that his way of life proves the oracle true. The way taken by Oedipus, which led him to the fatal crossroads (or his destiny), did no less. The oracle's saying was not historical or descriptive but prophetic—which means also, in a certain sense, ethical, since character is fate. What *this* means is that the oracle is the foundation of the Socratic way of life (philosophy), even as this way of life proves to be the foundation of the oracle, or that which supports it—shows the truth of it. Thus philosophy finds *its* destiny, which is to be foundational, giving the sense and truth of things. The oracle is unintelligible—empty (just talk)—except in the context which Socrates provides for it, the context which fulfills the oracle's saying.

One could say that the analytical gap here (what can the god mean?) is hermeneutically filled when Socrates takes the oracle's saying as binding on him in the way of action (what is to be done?), that is, binding as a law or a call—*kata ton theon:* a motion of the god, which is perhaps something like a hint or a wink that one can make sense of only by following it out to see where it leads (it could lead nowhere). "The lord whose oracle is at Delphi neither speaks nor conceals but gives a sign"—not a sign in the semiotician's sense but rather in the sense of hint or wink. The oracular text does not express a meaning but opens up a path. Socrates is, analytically, acting on his own authority or in his own name when with great reluctance he proceeds to investigate the saying (looking, however, not for what is behind the saying but what is in front of it in the world), but prophetically he acts in Apollo's, whose saying gives his life its direction or its meaning.

Another way to put this would be to speak of the dialogical relationship between Apollo and Socrates, where dialogue is to be understood less on the I-Thou model of intersubjectivity and mutual agreement (knowing others as we know ourselves, a meeting of minds) than on the model of conversation, where one speaker "picks up" on the saying of another and puts it into play, not to reproduce what was said but to bring out what was left unsaid by seeing where it leads. In the interpretation of law and prophecy (and perhaps of all human discourse) the main question is, Where does it take us? This is what goes on in understanding, where one is not engaged in divining other minds but in picking up on what is said and carrying on in perhaps a new or unforeseen direction. The hermeneutical metaphor of "taking" what is said one way or another implies that understanding is not just a state of mind but also a movement or undertaking: understanding only fulfills itself in action. As Gadamer says, it is more being than consciousness. Thus Socrates took the oracle's saying as a sign that he should do something rather than think something.

At 22d–e, at any rate, Socrates makes it plain that he is not simply the reader of a sacred text but, rather, has been appropriated by it and has appropriated it in his turn; he is made by it in the event of making it his own. He puts it into play and is set in motion by it; it speaks the truth of Socrates, who makes it speak, as one would the law, to the situation at hand. And so he says, "I asked myself in behalf of the oracle [*huper tou chresmou*] whether I should prefer to be as I am, neither wise in their wisdom [the politicians, poets, and artisans whom he has been questioning] nor foolish in their folly. . . . I replied then to myself and to the oracle that it was better for me to be as I am." It is in the context of this dialogue that Socrates is at last able to give an account of himself and (what amounts to the same thing) an account of the oracle's riddle: "It is likely," he says, "that the god is really wise, and by his oracle means [*legein:* says] this: 'Human wisdom is of little or no value.' And it appears that he does not really say this of Socrates, but merely uses my name, and makes me an example, as if he were to say, 'This one of you, O human beings, is wisest, who, like Socrates, recognizes that he is of no account in respect to wisdom'" (23a–b).

Socrates treats his interpretation with a shrug of the shoulders, but it has a number of virtues: (1) it takes the oracle at its word, and no more, because the oracle did not say anything about anyone being wise, but speaking negatively had implied only that no one was wiser than Socrates, who may amount to nothing or, in any case, has nothing to say; (2) it takes Socrates at his word, which is that he feels keenly that he has nothing to say, notwithstanding what is said about him; and (3) we are all taken into account, implicated in these words, for the self-understanding of Socrates is not his own affair or merely between him and his god but is a play in which all of us have been taken up; or, in other words, we all have a part in this conversation, as the assembly who listens to Socrates well knows. Understanding Socrates means acting (or refusing to act) in a certain way.

Here is where the speech of Alcibiades in the *Symposium* becomes important. "I shall speak the truth now," Alcibiades says, and "if I say anything that is false . . . take me up short and say that there I am lying; for I will not lie if I can help it" (214e–15a). What Alcibiades gives us is an account of what it is to be taken up in the discourse of Socrates and what happens when you try (as Alcibiades has) to get out of it, that is, to break free of Socrates, who is, Alcibiades says, as captivating or as spellbinding as the satyr Marsyas, who could ravish mankind with his flute. But Socrates is more powerful still: "so soon as we hear you, or your discourses in the mouth of another,—even though such a person . . . a poor speaker, and whether the hearer be a woman or a man or a youngster—we are all astounded and entranced" (215d). He would not speak of this, Alcibiades says, if he were not drunk—and remember that Oedipus first began to learn the truth about himself from a drunk. And, like Oedipus, the truth Socrates learns, or at all events hears, is dark and perhaps unspeakable in its way: there is something monstrous about him. He is a seducer of young men whom, however, he does not love, or for whom he has no feeling, because he is incapable of feeling: he can walk barefoot in the snow and stand stock still for a day and a night without discomfort; he can drink the night through without getting drunk, and he can spend the night in bed with the most beautiful man in Athens without getting an erection. The truth of Socrates is that he has killed what is human in himself, and he makes our own humanity seem hateful to us in turn, so that if we ever come under his spell we will never again be able to look upon ourselves without loathing: "what a wondrous power he wields" (216d).[7]

Wine, Alcibiades says, "is truthful" (217e). And the secret truth about Socrates is as follows:

> I share the plight of the man who was bitten by the snake: you know it is related of one in such a plight that he refused to describe his sensations to any but persons who had been bitten themselves, since they alone would understand him and stand up for him if he should give way to wild words and actions in his agony. Now I have been bitten by a more painful creature, in the most painful way that one can be bitten: in my heart, or my soul, or whatever one is to call it, I am stricken and stung by his philosophic discourses [*philosophia logon*],

which adhere more fiercely than any adder when once they lay hold of a young and not ungifted soul, and force it to do or say whatever it will; I have only to look around me, and there is a Phaedrus, an Agathon, an Eryximachus, a Pausanias, an Aristodemus, and an Aristophanes—I need not mention Socrates himself—and all the rest of them; every one of you has had his share of philosophic frenzy and transport [tēs philosophou te kai bakcheias], so all of you shall here. You shall stand up alike for what then was done and for what now is spoken. (218a–b)

It is possible to read this speech as the true indictment of Socrates—the indictment brought against him by his friends rather than by his enemies: that is, by those who experienced the terrible reserve of Socrates, his ability to close himself up or turn in upon himself in monumental self-possession. The other side of this, of course, is that Alcibiades does not just want to love Socrates; he wants to break him, to break his self-possession or to break in upon that reserve in order to possess Socrates—and his wondrous power—for himself alone. But one cannot possess Socrates this way; he cannot be grasped as an object. The epistemological lesson might be that Socrates is finally unknowable and unspeakable and that one can begin to understand him only by turning oneself into him—not so much by transforming oneself into his image and likeness, which Aristodemus does, but by living through his life, or his way of life: something we can do, perhaps, only at a tragic cost to ourselves.

Thucydides, Plato, and the Historicality of Truth   2

Here I end my trustworthy discourse.
—Parmenides

It must be acknowledged that hermeneutics belongs to the realm of opinion, or rhetoric, rather than to the realm of truth, or philosophy.[1] But it seems part of every hermeneutical desire to cross the threshold of rhetoric and to speak, well, philosophically. My purpose in this chapter is to consider one or two ancient examples of this desire. These examples are related to the question of tradition, that is, the question of how we stand with respect to all that comes down to us from the past. A main problem about tradition is that things do not seem exactly to come down to us in this way, as if past were a cornucopia or bountiful heaven. Foundational for Western experience is the idea that time is an insatiable consumer: instead of coming down to us from the past, things disappear into it, including the mechanisms of tradition itself: memories fade or grow heavy with dreams; manuscripts on winter nights are not always for reading. And so we are always in a position like that of Thucydides when he undertook to write his account of the Peloponnesian War. Like Socrates vis-à-vis the oracle, this is a classical hermeneutical scene, one on which Thucydides himself reflected in a famous passage. Let me start with something like a close reading of this passage:

(1.21.1) Still, from the evidence [*tekmērion*] that has been given, anyone would not err who should hold the view that the state of affairs in antiquity was pretty nearly as I have described [*diēlthon*: narrated] it, not giving greater credence to the accounts, on the one hand, which the poets have put into song, adorning and amplifying their theme, and, on the other, which the chroniclers [*logographoi*] have composed with a view rather of pleasing the ear than of telling the truth [*alēthesteron*], since their stories cannot be tested [*anexelegkta*] and most of them have from the lapse of time won their way into the region of the fabulous [*muthōdes*] so as to be incredible. (2) He should regard the facts [*eurēsthai*] as having been made out [*de ēgēsamenos*] with sufficient accuracy, on the basis of the clearest signs [*ek tōn epiphanestatōn semeiōn*], considering that they have to do with early times. (3) And so, even though men are always inclined, while they are engaged in war, to judge the present one the greatest, but when it is over to regard ancient events with greater wonder, yet this war will prove, for men who judge from actual facts [*ap autōn tōn ergōn skopousi*], to have been more important than any that went before.

(22.1) As to the speeches that were made by different men, either when they were about to begin the war or when they were already engaged therein, it has been difficult to record [*diamnēmoneusai*] with strict accuracy [*akribeian*] the words actually spoken, both for me as regards that which I myself heard, and for those who from various other sources have brought me reports. (2) Therefore the speeches are given in the language in which, as it seemed to me, the several speakers would express, on the subjects under consideration, the sentiments [*ta deonta*] most befitting the occasion, though at the same time I have adhered as closely as possible to the truth of what was said [*tēs xumpasēs gnōmēs tōn alēthōs lechthentōn, outōs eirētai*]. (3) But as to the facts of the occurrences of the war [*ta d' erga tōn prachthentōn en tō polemō*], I have thought it my duty to give them, not as ascertained from any chance informant, nor as seemed to me probable, but only after investigating [*epexelthōn*: reviewing] with the greatest possible accuracy [*dunaton akribeia*] each detail, in the case of both the events in which I myself participated and of those regarding which I got my information from others. (4) And the endeavour to discover [*eurisketo*] these facts was a laborious task, because those who were eyewitnesses of the several events did not give the same reports about the same things, but reports varying according to their championship of one side or the other, or according to their recollection. (5) And it may well be that the absence of the fabulous from my narrative will seem less pleasing to the ear; but whoever shall wish to have a clear view [*to saphes skopein*] both of the events that have happened and of those which will some day, in all human probability, happen again in the same or a similar way—for these to judge my history [narrative] profitable will be enough for me. (6) And, indeed, it has been composed, not as a prize-essay to be heard for the moment, but as a possession for all time.[2]

This text gives, among other things, the theory or, say, the rhetoric of history writing. There are, Thucydides says, three ways of giving an account of past events. First, there is the way the poets do it, that is, by an account put into song and by the enlargement or embellishment of received material. Poetry here is not *poiēsis* but just fabulous discourse, the sort of thing that has to be allegorized in order to bring it down to earth or under the control of reason. Second, there is the way logographers or local chroniclers do it, by an account made to resemble a beautiful speech and restricted to matters of local interest. And then there is the way Thucydides does it. What Thucydides promises is an account prevented from becoming poetic or logographic by the desire to tell the truth.

The question is: What does it mean to tell the truth? This may not be the same as asking, How do you know or go about knowing (for sure) that such and such is, or was, the case? What Thucydides seems to be proposing is not so much a research program or method of arriving at the truth as a way of giving an account that, in contrast to other ways of doing such a thing, can be *taken* as true by those who hear it. I mean that Thucydides represents himself as instituting the truth, not just finding and speaking it (not just reproducing it). He poses the question of truth not from the standpoint of the knowing subject but rhetorically from the standpoint of his audience—as he puts it, the one "who would not err [by holding] the view that the state of affairs in antiquity was pretty much as I have narrated it." What Thucydides has in mind here is the problem of persuading an audience that it is being told the truth. This is not just a logical problem of deciding between appearance and reality; rather, it is a hermeneutical problem of authority, or (more accurately) a problem of what will be allowed to stand as an authoritative or authorized version of past events. Before deciding between true or false, one has to determine what the truth looks like, what will pass for it, and by whose lights. This is what Thucydides wants to get clear about beforehand.

The rhetoric of truth telling, which comes down to us from the fifth century, is based on the idea that the truth isn't pretty and perhaps it is not very interesting: if it's beguiling or amazing or colorful, it isn't true. (Philosophy has always staked its reputation on the drabness of truth: think of what Kant says about *The Critique of Pure Reason*, that he deliberately wrote it without wit or charm because he was determined to command assent from his reader by the sheer force of his argument, not by the beauty of his expression.)[3] Thucydides already knows this rhetoric very well. But what is interesting is how the audience—or, rather, how the way Thucydides characterizes his audience—enters into this problem, for it appears that the authority possessed by a version of past events depends on the character of the audience for whom it is composed. Certainly this is what Thucydides is thinking of when he says that he has composed his account "not as a prize-essay to be heard for the moment, but as a possession of all time." Thucydides imagines for himself a special audience (one might well think of calling it a philosophical audience), as against the usual audience before whom songs are sung and long speeches are performed. (One might mention here that Herodotus evidently read portions of his history aloud to an assembly and composed his great work for just such an oratorical occasion.) Accordingly, Thucydides formulates the question of truth telling within the domain of the eye rather than of the ear; that is, his audience is not being asked to hear anything but is invited to see for itself and to regard what is said from a point raised up out of time (the standpoint of the gods). Poets put things into song and logographers desire to please the ear, but Thucydides promises his audience "a clear view [*to saphes skopein*] both of the events that have happened and of those which will some day, in all human probability, happen again in the same or a similar way." What Thucydides proposes, in other words, is a philosophical rather than poetic or oratorical account of past events—an account that is more of a monument than a performance, because it is meant to be preserved for all time. One speaks for the moment but one writes for the ages.

This may not be quite right. To call Thucydides' account, or his audience, philosophical is probably to import an Aristotelian category, which may not be quite applicable in this case. This way of thinking, however, does help to explain why Thucydides characterizes his audience as an individual rather than as a group (here we may think of the difference between the way Aristotle characterizes audiences in the *Poetics* and his characterization of it in the *Rhetoric*.) I had once thought to say that Thucydides imagines his audience as a reader rather than as a listener and that the distinction between eye and ear that Thucydides relies upon corresponds to a distinction between writing and speech, where writing becomes the medium of truth, or the medium in which such a thing as telling the truth becomes possible, as against the word spoken or sung, which is designed to fill the telling with interest, the better to captivate the audience. The spoken word is the medium of hearsay, whereas the written word is rooted in the eyewitness report (or what in antiquity was known as the autopsy). This view would be consistent with the thesis of Jack Goody and Ian Watt (among many others) that writing is an intrinsically philosophical medium, in contrast to speech or song, which belongs not to the realm of the imaginary exactly but to a realm where the imaginary can come into power because nothing is accessible to a second look or a second thought.[4] Writing fixes and distances what is said, exposes it to critical reflection; but speech lets words fly, and it's hard, when listening, not to get carried away (the later Heidegger exploits this thought in his notion of thinking as listening and letting go [*Gelassenheit*]). Here might be the place to mention Eric Havelock's impression that "behind the prose of Herodotus as he describes the epic contest between Greeks and Persians on the mainland one hears the epic hexameters as they are recited—meaning that he was remembering them—whereas in the Archeology of Thucydides we view a reader of a Homeric text who looks carefully for detail in order that he may correct it."[5] This attitude— that of giving a second look to a text with a view toward correction, is what makes history possible. As Havelock says, "The true parent of history was not any one 'writer' like Herodotus but the alphabet itself," because the alphabet makes possible the otherness or pastness of the past (p. 23). Writing, in other words, is the source of the alienation that produces the historical-critical attitude.

My own thought had once been that writing is the medium of history, whereas philosophy belongs to conversation or dialogue, and rhetoric belongs to oratory as poetry to song. But this thought holds only on paper. We must not forget that these categories of discourse belong to a later period and cannot simply be mapped onto what Thucydides thought he was writing. We don't really know what he thought he was writing—we can't even say that he thought of himself as writing in contrast to speaking (a distinction that seems peculiar to our own time). Let us merely say that Thucydides imagines his audience not as a reader rather than as a listener but simply as someone who is not part of a crowd—someone who is more like a member of a conversation than a member of an assembly: someone, in other words, who can interrupt or answer back. One remembers that Socrates will frequently complain against the long speech or spellbinding oration—the macrologia—which never allows anyone to stand outside of it and give a second thought to anything said along the way. What Thucydides proposes, however, is the sort of account that can be put to the test not empirically, of course, but dialectically, that is, by being subject to another's discourse—subject to correction or to a second authority. Thus Thucydides imagines a self-possessed and critical audience, one that will keep its presence of mind and not get caught up in the heat of the narrative. There are things that such an audience would not allow to pass and that Thucydides will not allow to pass either, not merely when he writes (sifting his evidence, as we say), but already beforehand when he listens to those who report to him of the war. Havelock has written some excellent things about the psychology of the poetic performance in Homeric antiquity, in which everyone who listens is swept up as a participant in the story being told. What we need to do is to join to this a description of the Thucydidean performance, which is not something in which to participate but something to stand outside of and to regard with an eye toward improvement or toward the truth.

The principle implicit here is logically simple and obviously familiar, but in the present context it is complicated in a number of interesting ways. The principle is that truth telling means speaking under (or as if under) interrogation, or under subjection to another's thoughts. Truth telling presupposes dialogue or a dialogical situation. To see how this principle works for Thucydides, however, you must remember that he never once makes an appeal to memory as foundational, as the source or authority of his account—unlike Herodotus, who writes explicitly as a stay against forgetfulness. On the first page of his account, in place of the usual invocation to a goddess of memory, Thucydides explains that he began writing at the *outset* of the war, when it became clear to him that this war would be greater in scope and consequence than any before, specifically, of course, greater than Trojan and Persian wars. The work of Thucydides is really a preemption of memory and a circumvention of that which memory authorizes, namely, tradition (or, as Havelock would say, *oral* tradition, or the process by which things normally get handed down from the past).[6] The tacit appeal of Thucydides to his (let us say) philosophical audience replaces the Homeric appeal to the daughters of memory as a way of underwriting the truth of what will follow. What will follow from Thucydides is an entirely new way for the facts to get handed down—not a new process of knowledge but a new process of tradition. The old tradition is characterized by embellishment and the rhetorical desire to repeat everything; the new tradition is characterized by interrogation and second thoughts and the determination to speak something called the truth. The lesson of poets and logographers or, at a higher level, of Homer and Herodotus is that there is just no getting at the facts once they begin to recede into the past. Thucydides means to beat the past to the facts—to get to the facts before they get assimilated by memory into tradition, that is, before they get turned into stories that "cannot be tested" and that, with the "lapse of time," win "their way into the region of the fabulous."

Beating time to facts means, of course, doing without a certain kind of narrative transcendence. Here we need to look closely at the special problem that Thucydides faces, which he formulates at 22.1 through 22.4. How can you tell the truth of history from the inside of it, that is, not just from the perspective of the beginning and the moment-by-moment unfolding of things—as against the normal perspective of the end and of the whole—but from the perspective of your own historicality or embeddedness in the event? How, in other words, can you tell the truth from a temporal instead of a divine or Rankean perspective? According to Arthur Danto, you can't, because you are, all of us are, "temporally provincial with respect to the future."[7] The historicality of the teller puts truth telling out of the question because of the enormity of what cannot be known. Danto's point is incontestable, but it covers up an interesting idea, which is that the divine perspective hardly requires any notion of truth at all, just as it hardly requires a notion of philosophy, as Socrates will observe in the *Phaedrus*. Owing to their plenitude, the gods have neither the love nor the need of wisdom. If you naturally can never get things wrong, it will never occur to you to try to get things right. In a similar way the issue of truth hardly arises in Homer—the lie, as we saw earlier, is the one adversary that Odysseus (in contrast to Socrates) doesn't really have to face. Or say that in Homer questions of how things stand are decided by force rather than by argument. War is a method of instituting facts. By contrast, the production of history by the alienation of writing produces a notion of truth in the same stroke. There can be no notion of truth except in virtue of the awareness of historicality, and vice versa: you can't have a notion of history without a corresponding notion of truth. History makes the subject of truth arise. But in exactly what form does it arise in the case of Thucydides?

Here we get to the hard part. When you relinquish memory and tradition you close up the great Homeric inventory of things to say, or that whence all discourse arises—and in the same breath you confront temporality itself, or that which slips away, taking with it exactly what you want to put into words. The problem is, rhetorically, a problem of invention, or of the historicality of the inventory. What do you say when there is no longer any having anything to say, what to say having slipped away in natural course of things? It is at this point, the closing of the Homeric inventory, that philosophy begins; I mean that this is the point at which the philosopher, from

Parmenides to Wittgenstein, learns the counsel of silence and the desire of speechless wonder. The Socratic inventory contains only questions followed by bewildered moments of not knowing what to say. The rhetorician, by contrast, is the one who plunges ahead in defiance of lying or making things up. What do you say when there is no longer any knowing what to say, and yet you make bold to say it, and (bolder still, boldest of all) you claim to speak the truth as well? It is this dramatic rhetorical threshold—the limits of invention or of discourse, or perhaps one should say the limits of history—in any case, it is this threshold of the unspeakable truth that Thucydides crosses.

Let me try to clarify this with two observations. The first is that Thucydides thinks of himself as engaged in a kind of writing and not in a kind of knowing. Herodotus used the word *historia* to describe his undertaking—and it is hard for us not to think of *historia* as an epistemological program, that is, as a certain kind of rigorous mental functioning that supports the queen of the human sciences: call it *inquiry* or, more rigorously still, *research*—naturally we think of it as something going on between the mind of Herodotus and the past of Greece, something that did not go on between Homer and what came down to him (by whatever means it came). Thucydides, however, refers to what he is doing as a *syngraphe* of "the war waged by the Peloponnesians against the Athenians" (1.1.1). The word *syngraphe* here means the "writing up" of an account or the "writing down" of the facts of the war—getting them all down in one place. Hence, some scholars refer to the "monograph" of Thucydides.

But writing down, documenting, what, exactly? My second observation has to do with what counts as a fact for Thucydides. This is a slippery matter, but it appears that what Thucydides takes to be a fact differs from our own conception in several important respects. For us, the word *fact* refers to the empirical authority that a piece of information acquires once it has been independently established as certain or objective (that is, not the product of any subjective outlook). Facts are, as we say, brute-data verifiable. A fact is information given not, of course, by an informant but by formal procedures underwritten by a theory of knowledge as the documentation of given states of affairs. So we speak of facts as things lying around waiting to be gathered up. Facts are collectors' items. It is not wrong to see this modern theory anticipated in the strong experiential and visualist bias of Thucydides' practice: he has written down, he says, only those events in which he himself participated or which were recounted to him not by "any chance informant" but in the reports of eyewitnesses. Hence the special and, one might say, historic point Thucydides makes about his accuracy or precision (*akribeia*) in determining what will go into his account (or count as fact), namely, that he took into account (and so, in a manner of speaking, was able to correct) the natural defects of human reporting. Thucydides has been praised by many generations of scholars for the way in which he guides himself by empirical norms in accounting for what happened. Here I should mention the comparison that Eric Voegelin makes between Thucydides' historiographical method and the Hippocratic method of investigating diseases, whereby the investigator proceeds not on the basis of philosophical hypotheses concerning the constitution of human nature but by means of accumulated observations of particular cases. Here, for example, is Thucydides on the plague: "I shall simply set down its nature, and the symptoms by which it perhaps may be recognized by the student, if it should ever break out again. This I can the better do, as I had the disease myself, and watched its operation in the case of others" (1.68).[8]

Still, the empirical is not just given for observation but is always mediated by the discursive, as at 21.2, where Thucydides says that his audience "should regard the facts as having been made out with sufficient accuracy, on the basis of the clearest signs, considering that they have to do with early times." The word for *fact* here is *ēuresthai,* literally, that which was found, from *eurisko,* to find, whereby we obtain the rhetorical concept of invention or the finding of things to say among all that has or can be said. Figuring facts this way, what we have in Thucydides is perhaps less a new method of historical knowledge than a new theory of rhetorical invention, that is, a conception of finding things to say about past events that preempts memory and removes the necessity (and also the authority) of tradition. Where do facts come from, after all? In the case at hand they derive chiefly from what Thucydides is told and how he construes it, whence he speaks of signs (*semeia*) coming down to him from the past and requiring to be made out in a certain way, as if he were engaged in a sort of reverse augury. I don't think *augury* is too strange a word to use here, but it is true that most scholars try to get Thucydides beyond interpretation by mapping onto his augury our scientific models of inductive reasoning and causal explanation.[9] This works well enough a good bit of the time, but some things fit inside this map more easily than others; in fact, quite a lot gets left out. For example, the word for fact that Thucydides normally uses is *ergon,* which is specifically a work or deed of war. That *ergon* should be translated as "fact" rather than as "work" is worth thinking about, but my point here is that since Homer the Greeks had traditionally distinguished between *ergon* and *epos* (or *ergon* and *logos*) as the basic components of war and history. In addition to the works or accomplishments of war, and inseparable from them, there is also *what was said,* often of a formal nature: or, in other words, history is already rhetorical in the nature of the case. A mute combat would have neither reason nor occasion to occur or would be as vacuous or artificial as speech without action. History not only belongs to the world of discourse, it *is* that world at every turn, because events are continuous in every direction with the discourse of those engaged in them. History is as much linguistical as it is factual. And of course no one has addressed the linguisticality of history quite so aggressively as Thucydides.[10]

Students of history will see directly where this leads, namely, to the illustrious problem of the Thucydidean speeches. Scholars have never wearied of the paradox that major portions of Thucydides' great work are just speeches that he could never have heard and that would have come to him as the most general reports at best—in short, speeches that are simply original compositions contributed to history by Thucydides himself. Forgery would be our word for it. Every school child will remember the funeral oration of Pericles, but there are between 50 and 150 of these speeches, depending on whether you count forms of indirect discourse. Downright scholarly dismay over the presence of these speeches is less serious now than it was years ago in the heyday of positivism, but the problem remains that for most scholars (I'm thinking here of Simon Hornblower's book on Thucydides as well as Virginia Hunter's work) the norms of history writing remain relentlessly empirical and analytical—history writing is nothing if not documentation all the way down—hence it is necessary to conclude that some parts of Thucydides' text may pass as history, but in the speeches Thucydides was doing something else (something subjective and artful or maybe just false).[11] As Danto has shown, this is the only position one can maintain on analytical grounds. The speeches just cannot count as documents on any definition; or say that they are documents that constitute what they document: there is nothing outside the text. This has driven some scholars to an Aristotelian compromise which says that we should figure the speeches not as fictions or "mere inventions," not as just false, but rather as hypotheses; they are philosophical rather than poetic or historical in their truth. That is, they are to be read as philosophical essays that are not so much part of the war as about it—political and psychological explanations of what was happening, disguised or represented as what was happening.[12] In any case, the *syngraphe* of Thucydides is more philosophical than history, but more historical than poetry.

This Aristotelian, form-critical method of accounting for the speeches makes good sense from several points of view, but it does seriously weaken the force of the claim that Thucydides nevertheless makes in their behalf,

namely, that the speeches are constitutive of the historical record, notwithstanding their own constitution as rhetorical inventions. The truth of history calls for these speeches and would remain incomplete without them.
The speeches are not the medium of anything but part of the substance: part
of the res itself and not about it.

Here we should consider closely, if we can, what Thucydides himself says:
"As to the speeches that were made by different men, either when they were
about to begin the war or when they were already engaged therein, it has
been difficult to record with strict accuracy the words actually spoken, both
for me as regards that which I myself heard, and for those who from various
other sources have brought me reports. Therefore the speeches are given in
the language in which, as it seemed to me, the several speakers would express, on the subjects under consideration, the sentiments [ta deonta] most
befitting the occasion, though at the same time I have adhered as closely as
possible to the truth of what was said [tēs xumpasēs gnōmēs tōn alēthōs
lechthentōn, outōs eirētai]."

This last line is a Thucydidean crux (on which one should consult an
essay by John Wilson, "What Does Thucydides Claim for His Speeches,"
which is about the difficulty, almost the impossibility, of making good English sense of the Greek: he suggests "keeping as closely as possible to the
main points of what was actually said," thus erasing or anyhow smudging
what looks like a truth claim).[13] Still, the upshot is clear: from a strictly
documentary standpoint we are no longer in the domain of history writing
but have crossed over into rhetoric, specifically the world of rhetorical impersonation where truth gives way to probable constructions. In other
words, if you are looking for the place where history and rhetoric divide,
here you have it. Thucydides' construction of the past is rhetorical rather
than documentary, and the threshold that divides the two is the analytic
limit of what is knowable (documentable). Nevertheless, the specific claim
of Thucydides is that in giving these speeches (forging these documents) he
has given us their truth; he has given the truth of what was said, even
though it was not possible to retain the exact words of anything spoken.

From a hermeneutical point of view, however, another account of what
Thucydides is up to may be worth trying out. Let me construct this account
with the help of two models.

First, it is plausible to think of Thucydides as being engaged in a translation from a language no longer accessible into one (the one he is writing)
that will make it possible for these speeches to be understood. I mean that
there is a division of letter and spirit implicit in Thucydides' claim of the
sort that elsewhere in the ancient world makes the translation of meaning

(including the radical translation of allegory) possible. But, of course, the translation that Thucydides attempts is not of one language to another but of the oral into the written or of memory into manuscript. We know from studies by Havelock on the alphabetization of Homer and by Birger Gerhardsson on the transmission of the oral Torah that this translation is not simply a transcription or documentation of what was said but involves a collaboration (perhaps one could say a dialogue) of the oral and the written, the exact nature of which we cannot be sure of, although we can be certain that it is not reflected in our current notions of how speech and writing are related.[14] (But, of course, we don't think of writing as simply the documentation of speech.) My point here, however, is that the position occupied by Thucydides is comparable to the antique scribe who is required to produce a text for what is said where none has ever existed, that is, in the absence of any textual tradition or where writings handed down in tandem with oral tradition are rudimentary, garbled, or incomplete in the manner of crib sheets, or *hypomnemata,* arguably the earliest form of writing. The hermeneutical task in these circumstances would not be to reproduce anything verbatim but rather to produce for the first time a total, coherent, finished, permanent, authoritative, canonical, or monumental version of what was said, notwithstanding the fact that what was said is not and never was in a form amenable to this task. The function of this monumental version is not simply to preserve but, prior to this, to institute—to settle and establish or lay down once for all—just what was said. On this model, at any rate, Thucydides is not only the historian of the Peloponnesian War but its lawgiver and scribe as well: his purpose is not to construct a picture of the war but to establish it in its twofold nature as a formal narrative of *erga* and *logoi.* So we could think of him as constructing a sort of institution, call it the cultural institution (the canon) of history.

Consider, therefore, Thucydides in relation to his reports of what was said by Archidamus or Themistocles, Pericles or Cleon or the Spartan generals: there is no use merely reproducing such reports, because the whole truth of what was said cannot be contained in any report of it but includes also the situation in which the speech occurred. The task of Thucydides is to produce a text that does not merely give the *gist* of what was said—a meaning such as a report can epitomize—but gives rather the *truth* of the relationship between the speech and the situation that called for it. History, as Geoffrey Hartman says in an essay on history writing, must be written in an "answerable style."[15] The emphasis that Thucydides places on the situation or occasion of discourse should not be dismissed. Thucydides is in the position of the scribe who is required to produce a text that he cannot be the author of, nor yet is he simply an amanuensis or someone taking dictation—in other words he is not a mimetic but a hermeneutical scribe whose concern is not with textual exactness or the reproduction of another's words or meanings but with the emergence of a subject (*Sache*) from a particular historical situation. According to this emphasis, the true author of a Thucydidean speech would not be its original speaker nor its subsequent scribe but the situation that called for the speech to be made. "An intention," says Wittgenstein, "is embedded in its situation" (*Philosophical Investigations*, §337). Our translation of Thucydides, which speaks of "sentiments most befitting the occasion," makes this relation of discourse to its situation sound like a relationship of aesthetic decorum, but Thucydides is plainly concerned with what, given the nature of the case, *had* necessarily to be said; that is, he is concerned with what could not have gone unsaid without leaving a hole or gap in the situation. Thus *ta deonta* should be translated not as "sentiments" that befit the occasion (a locution that belongs to after-dinner addresses) but as "essentials" that are necessary to make the situation what it is, or was. Here you can see the relevance of the hermeneutical concept of application to the problem of the Thucydidean speeches. The speeches are not epideictic or ethopoeic or dianoiac; they are not dramatic showpieces or revelations of character or exhibitions of reason; rather they are apodeictic in the etymological sense: in them the truth of history struggles to emerge every bit as much as in the narrative of the battlefield.

My second model is Plato, scribe of Socrates—not as Boswell to Johnson, however, but as, well, Thucydides to Pericles. Here I would like to give you William Chase Grene's opinion that Plato's *Apology* is "a fairly close record of the actual words of Socrates, based on *hypomnemata* written by someone who was present at the trial."[16] My own opinion would be that what Plato gives us is the truth of what Socrates said on the occasion of his trial, not perhaps in so many words, but also not just in a manner of speaking, but in order for the truth of what was said, which includes the truth of the situation and all that is contained in it, to make its appearance. Let me conclude by referring to two Platonic texts that will help to clarify the distinction at work here between giving a correct reproduction of what was said and giving the truth of it.

The first text is the *Phaedrus*, in which Socrates speaks the speech of Stesichorus, son of Euphemus (whose name means man of pious or holy speech). This is Socrates' second speech on love, but he is not the author of it, yet neither does he reproduce from memory and word for word a speech already composed by Stesichorus (indeed, memory—memory that is merely exact: memory as document—is finessed here much the way it is in Thucydides). And yet Socrates speaks the truth, not in the sense that he speaks Stesichorus' mind but in the sense that truth here is the truth or emergence of a subject (*Sache*) and not the truth of an intention.[17] The difference between false rhetoric and true might be the difference between saying what has been said and saying what must be said. Remember that in this dialogue young Phaedrus is scolded by Socrates for trying to memorize a text by Lysias—a stupid thing to do, since by memorizing a text word for word you preserve perhaps the beauty of the language but lose what is said. Phaedrus, a philologist, is intoxicated by words and will always want to get them exactly right—and remember that Socrates claims no less for himself, except that he will not get carried away by the words he loves, claiming that true philology rests not on the exact repetition of words actually spoken but upon what is said, that is, upon the subject that words allow to appear.

The second text is the *Symposium*, which seems to me plainly Thucydidean in character. This work dramatizes a round of speeches, but not directly. In fact, the *Symposium* is part of a conversation between Apollodorus, a disciple of Socrates, and an unnamed friend who although not very philosophical has just asked about what was said at a famous drinking party at Agathon's featuring those illustrious lovers, Socrates and Alcibiades. Apollodorus is happy to tell his friend what was said, because, as it happens, the matter is fresh in his mind from his having rehearsed the speeches the night before to his friend Glaucon. The surprising thing is that Apollodorus was not present at the symposium because, as he explains, the event took place many years before, when he was only a child. He was told what was said by Aristodemus, the little fellow who used to go around barefoot in emulation of Socrates—a mildly fanatical follower of Socrates, perhaps not so mildly, he hangs on every word Socrates speaks. Because Aristodemus was at the party, he can be trusted not to have missed a thing—although there is no indication anywhere in Plato that Aristodemus understands anything Socrates says. Luckily Apollodorus was later able to check some of what Aristodemus told him by interrogating Socrates himself, who confirmed the account, thus establishing it as something like an authorized version, a canonization, of what was said.

It is worth remembering that the *Theaetetus* begins the same way: Euclides, a follower of Socrates, gives an account of a conversation among Socrates, Theodorus, and Theaetetus. He cannot, Euclides says, repeat the conversation from memory, but he did make some notes—*hypomnemata*—at the time of the conversation and then later constructed a version of the conversation that he subsequently was able to correct by consulting Socrates.

The question is, of course: Why does Plato begin this way? Why doesn't he simply dramatize the speeches or conversations directly instead of presenting them as second- and third-hand versions constructed after some extended lapse of time? One answer is that Plato is simply calling his texts into question; that is, he is exposing the fictionality of his representations and thereby throwing suspicion on what is said in them in the best postmodern style. This may sound silly, but there is a sense in which Plato is waiting for us at the end of modernism because, as we know, it is already characteristic of Socrates to warn against taking anything he says (or anything anyone says) too strictly, or even too seriously. Between the serious and the frivolous in Plato's texts it is often hard to decide. They are full of Shandyisms; they are self-interfering, self-interrupting—they always hold themselves at a distance—because they are, after all, underwritten by a skepticism in which all discourse is, in a manner of speaking, just a manner of speaking: questions are the only thing we can justifiably put into words, which are always excessive in what they name because of the way they wander from thing to thing. They have to be tied down like slaves, says Socrates. Indeed, tying down words, fixing them by means of definition, is what Socrates seems always to be calling for, but since discourse always comes up short we begin to realize that the call for definition is simply a hermeneutics of suspicion, a method of unmasking rather than conceptual determination. This is why Plato says in the *Seventh Letter* that only a fool will put what matters to him into writing—and not just into writing but into spoken words as well: there really is no such thing as the *telling* of the truth, and so you must always put aside what you are told in favor of what you can see for yourself.

Another answer, however, is that Plato is just acknowledging the historicality of his texts, in disregard of their historicity as documents or documentations of Socrates. All Plato is doing in his dialogues is providing the words for what is said; the truth of what is said originates elsewhere and is never present as such, since truth is of a subject (*Sache*), not of an intention or message. Disclaimers of originality go on all the time in the dialogues, where Plato's Socrates will affirm nothing in his own name. Socrates speaks only what has been handed down to him, except for that which he puts into question. This is what occurs in the *Symposium*, in which Socrates tells the truth of love, but not because he knows the truth—he makes no claims to knowledge, hence does not speak in his own name or on his own authority; rather, he tells the truth by giving an account of the counsel or teaching of Diotima that he had undergone many years before. It is interesting that now we would be inclined to speak of *receiving* the teachings of Diotima, but

Socrates speaks in terms of initiation, not reception: he did not acquire or come into possession of a body of knowledge, a doctrine, so perhaps we ought not to speak at all of anything being handed down, as if the truth were portable and words their means of transport. This is the postal service theory of transmission that Derrida happily turns upside down with his picture of Plato dictating to his scribe, Socrates.[18] The point is that things don't make their way down from the past by means of cultural transmission or the handing on of a legacy preserved in the form of documents; they come down by a kind of translation for which we lack an adequate theory: a translation that is appropriative rather than cognate with an original.

Perhaps, however, the *Symposium* supplies a sort of theory. I'm thinking of Diotima's theory of generation:

> Mortal nature [Diotima says] always seeks as much as it can to exist forever and to achieve immortality. But it is able to do this only by means of generation [*genesei*], its way of always leaving behind another, young one against old age. It is particularly in this that each living individual is said to be alive and to be itself—just as one is described as oneself and the same person from childhood until becoming old. But in actuality one hasn't any characteristics at all whereby one can be called the same person. One is always becoming a new person, losing things, portions of hair, flesh, bones, blood and all the stuff of the body. And not only the body. In the soul as well one's habits and character, beliefs, desires, pleasures, pains, fears—none of these things remain the same in anyone—they arise and die out. But what's even stranger than these facts is that we not only gain knowledge and lose it, so that we don't remain the same people with respect to what we know, but that every single example of knowledge suffers the same thing. For a man is said to study when there is a departing of knowledge, and study, by implanting new knowledge in place of what has left, saves the memory of it, so that it seems like the same thing. It is in this way that everything mortal is preserved—not by its being utterly the same forever, like the divine, but by what is old and with-drawing leaving behind something else, something new like itself. It is by this method, Socrates, that the mortal partakes of immortality, she explained, in the body and in all other respects. (207c–208a)

On this model of tradition, that which makes its way down from the past does so according to a dialectic of loss and recuperation, as of one version of the thing standing in for another—whence "everything mortal is preserved," not exactly, that is, not empirically as a museum piece, but as something like an appropriation of what withdraws itself and refuses itself, resisting objectification. The Thucydidean speeches, like Plato's texts, are not exact renderings but recuperations of what is lost, in which the truth of what was said exhibits itself not as the same but as something else, something new that is not, however, something grown fabulous, something unheard of or sui generis, something just unrecognizable with respect to what it was; but something that is not free of these negations, either. As Gadamer says, for Plato even the *pseudos* is a way in which a thing discloses itself.

In order to make sense of this we might have to imagine something like a theory of language in which (strange to say) language is not made of words. Recall how the sophist Prodicus is treated in Plato's dialogues. Prodicus is a connoisseur of *onoma*, words or names, and he is something of a novelty or virtuoso on this matter and a bit of a comic figure, because he is always fussing about words, always insisting on nice distinctions. Prodicus represents a new way of thinking about language, call it a grammatical way of thinking, a thinking that presupposes writing and pictures language as the stuff documents are made of. A documentary approach to discourse is concerned with the exact word: its ideal is the verbatim transcription.

But Thucydides and Plato suggest a much looser, less grammatical conception of language, one might call it (absurdly) a conception that leaves language unconceptualized, which may be what Heidegger had in mind when he said that the Greeks had no word for language (*Being and Time*, p. 209). As if a theory of language would just be in the way of understanding how we understand.[19] Possibly it is no accident that in our own time both Heidegger and Gadamer have tried to disconnect the notion of truth from the notion of *adequatio ad rem* by referring us to a time when the basic component of speech was thought to be its subject matter (*Sache*). This notion of a subject matter, the what-is-said of speech, is hard to make sense of analytically: it is not reducible to a formal component of discourse, what we would call the signified; that is, it is not simply a grammatical subject or a semantic component, a meaning or linguistic entity, but an ontological subject as well, something that belongs to the world of which we speak and which makes its appearance in our speaking of it—makes its appearance, however, not as such, that is, not as an object, an apophantic entity, but rather as that which at the time always withdraws from language and renders our concepts resistant to clarification. *Die Sache,* understood in this sense, certainly testifies to the logical weakness of language, its inability to pin things down exactly or to fix them once for all. Another way to put this would be to say that in antiquity, discourse is not for framing representations at a distance, because one is always finally on intimate terms with the truth, the *Sache,* that discourse struggles to keep hold of—which is perhaps why at the end of the day the question seems our most basic form of discourse, the only form accessible to most subjects that bear down on us (time, being, death, justice). In fact most subjects cannot even be properly questioned; they merely loom before us as questions we do not even know how to formulate, or from which we do not know how to escape.

Canon and Power

in the Hebrew Bible

3

> It is not so with the man who applies himself,
> And studies the Law of the Most High.
> He searches out the wisdom of the ancients.
> And busies himself with prophecies;
> He observes the discourse of famous men,
> And penetrates the intricacies of figures.
> He searches out the hidden meaning of proverbs,
> And acquaints himself with the obscurities of figures.
> He will serve among great men,
> And appear before rulers.
> —Ben Sira, Ecclesiasticus

The first thing to be said about the Hebrew Scriptures is that we have very little evidence as to how they came into existence. Nineteenth-century textual criticism dispelled once for all the idea that Moses was the author of the sacred books; and indeed, it is now hard to see how a notion of authorship can be applied to these texts in any significant way. The British scholar Peter R. Ackroyd has summarized the current opinion as follows: "It is only rarely that we can point to individuals as authors—the author of Job, the author of Ecclesiastes perhaps, and a few more; more often we can point to compilers, single figures or schools—the Deuteronomists, the Priestly Writers, and the Chronicler whose work has undergone some substantial amplification in the same spirit."[1] The Scriptures are the heterogeneous product of various scribal traditions that flourished at odd times (beginning no later than the eighth century B.C.E.) and frequently under circumstances of great national disaster (the Babylonian Exile, the Diaspora). To put the matter as plainly as possible, all we know is that the texts we now call the Hebrew Bible are rooted in centuries of scribal activity that originated, borrowed, compiled, revised, amplified, and redacted various sorts of biblical material in ways no longer possible to describe. As Brevard Childs says, in this process "particular editors, religious groups, and even political parties were involved. At times one can describe these groups historically or sociologically, such as the reforming Deuteronomic party of Jerusalem, or the editors associated with Hezekiah's court (Prov. 25.1). But basic to the canonical process is that those responsible for the actual editing of the text did their best to obscure their own identity. [The] actual process by which the text was reworked lies in almost total obscurity."[2]

It is only very late—in the first and second centuries of the common era, as part of the development of rabbinic Judaism, and in the context of conflicting religious and cultural traditions—that it was thought necessary to cast the Scriptures into something like a canonical form of single, fixed, authoritative versions (as in the Masoretic texts, which give us the modern Hebrew Bible).[3] Prior to this we can refer only generally to Persian or Babylonian, Palestinian, Samaritan, Aramaic, and Greek textual traditions, and there are many others, as we know from the scrolls found at Qumran.[4] About the third or second century B.C.E. the Greek tradition gives us the Septuagint, which is based on lost Hebrew versions and upon which the Christian Old Testament was based until Jerome's Vulgate in late antiquity; in fact, the Septuagint remains authoritative for many Eastern churches. As for the notion of canonization, this is a patristic idea with applications of its own and is not easy to map onto earlier periods, especially not before the Scriptures had stabilized into what we would recognize as formal texts.[5] Thus, some scholars distinguish sharply between Scripture and canon, where the one is authoritative and open (that is, open to supplementation and in constant revision), and the other is closed and fixed.[6] Or, in other words, from the technical standpoint of literary or textual criticism, with its special concern for the final form of documents, canonization frequently refers simply to an official closing and fixing of texts in a form that is declared to be authoritative (for whatever particular tradition) against all prior, competing, eccentric, and subsequent books and versions.

The point of this chapter, however, is to develop the sense in which the canonization of the Scriptures has a hermeneutical as well as a textual or literary critical meaning, for what is important is not only the formation, collection, and fixing of the sacred texts but also their application to particular situations. A text, after all, is canonical not in virtue of being final and correct and part of an official library but because it becomes *binding* on a group of people. The whole point of canonization is to underwrite the authority of a text, not merely with respect to its origin as against competitors in the field—this, technically, would simply be a question of authenticity—but with respect to the present and future in which it will reign or govern as a binding text. The distinction between canonical and noncanonical is thus not just a distinction between authentic and inauthentic texts—that is, it is not reducible to the usual oppositions between the inspired and the mundane, the true and the apocryphal, the sacred and the profane, and so on. On the contrary, it is a distinction between texts that are forceful in a given situation and those that are not. From a hermeneutical standpoint, in which the relation of a text to a situation is always of primary interest, the theme of canonization is power.

The Hebrew notion of Torah greatly clarifies this aspect of canonization. The word *torah* is normally used to refer to the Pentateuch, or the first five books of the Scriptures—the "Torah of Moses" or the "Priestly Torah"—but it is frequently extended to include the books of the prophets (the *nebi'im*) and the Writings (the *ketubim*) as well. And in various subsequent traditions, the term also embraces the entire sacred literature of the Jews, including principally the Mishna, the Talmuds, and the great midrashic collections that continue down to the tenth century. What the word *torah* embraces as a body of texts, however, is not what matters. More important is the force implicit in the word, which derives from the legal and political thinking of the Deuteronomists in the seventh and sixth centuries.[7] In the third century, *torah* (meaning "directive" or "instruction") was translated as *nomos* ("law"), and since that time the characterization of the books of the Torah as Law has become commonplace, although not completely accurate, because the Scriptures contain many sorts of writing besides legal material. Nevertheless—and here is the main point—the books of the Torah have the force, if not everywhere the form, of law. The Hebrew Torah is a monumental example of a binding text; its significance lies not only in what it contains or means but also in its power over those who stand within its jurisdiction. It is precisely within such a textual jurisdiction that the true meaning of canonicity begins to emerge. To inquire into the canonization of the books of the Torah is to ask how they came to possess their power over a nation and a people. What did it mean for these books to become binding? More important, what were the conditions under which such a thing occurred? Or, to put the question in its simplest form: Torah—as opposed to what? Against what forces were the books of the Torah put into play—and by whom, and toward what end?

One way to get a sense of these questions is to consult the famous canonization story told in 2 Kings: in the eighteenth year of his reign, Josiah, king of Judah, sends Shaphan the scribe on business to Hilkiah, the High

Priest of the Temple at Jerusalem. The Temple has been undergoing repairs, and the workmen need to be paid. Unexpectedly, and apropos of nothing at all, Hilkiah mentions that he has discovered a book:

> And Hilkiah the high priest said unto Shaphan the scribe: "I have found the book of the Law [Torah] in the house of the Lord." And Hilkiah delivered the book to Shaphan, and he read it. And Shaphan the scribe came to the king, and . . . told the king, saying "Hilkiah the priest hath delivered me a book." And it came to pass, when the king had heard the words of the book of the Law, that he rent his clothes. And the king commanded Hilkiah the priest, and Ahikam the son of Shaphan, and Achbor the son of Micaiah, and Shaphan the scribe, and Asaiah the king's servant, saying: "Go ye, inquire of the Lord for me, and for the people, and for all Judah, concerning the words of this book that is found; for great is the wrath of the Lord that is kindled against us, because our fathers have not hearkened unto the words of this book, to do according unto all that which is written concerning us."
>
> So Hilkiah the priest, and Ahikam, and Achbor, and Shaphan, and Asaiah, went unto Huldah the prophetess, the wife of Shallum the son of Tikvah, the son of Harhas, keeper of the wardrobe—now she dwelt in Jerusalem in the second quarter—and they spoke with her. And she said unto them: "Thus saith the Lord, the God of Israel: Tell yet the man that sent you unto me: Thus saith the Lord: Behold, I will bring evil upon this place, and upon the inhabitants thereof, even all the words of the book which the king of Judah hath read; because they have forsaken Me, and have offered unto other gods. . . ."
>
> And the king sent, and they gathered unto him all the elders of Judah and of Jerusalem. And the king went up to the house of the Lord, and all the men of Judah and all the inhabitants of Jerusalem with him, and the priests, and the prophets, and all the people, both small and great; and he read in their ears all the words of the book of the covenant which was found in the house of the Lord. And the king stood on the platform, and made a covenant before the Lord, to walk after the Lord, and to keep His commandments, and His testimonies, and His statutes, with all his heart, and all his soul, to confirm the words of this covenant that were written in this book; and all the people stood to the covenant (2 Kings 22:8–23:3).[8]

Here one beings to understand what it means for a text to be canonical, that is, forceful in a given situation. Josiah recognizes a binding text when he sees one—and his recognition is the decisive thing. Naturally, we would like to know what it is in the text that causes Josiah to respond so deci-sively—rending his garments, a ritual act of testimony or witness to the truth—but, strictly speaking, it does not matter. The power of the text is not intrinsic to it. On the contrary, the text draws its power from the situa-tion in which it makes its unexpected appearance, because this is a situa-tion that belongs to a definite history and that is structured by this history to receive just this text as it will no other. This is a text that (whatever it says) speaks to the situation at hand.

The history to which the text belongs is the one inaugurated by the cov-enant that Moses made with Yahweh on Sinai (Exod. 19–40:38). In another situation, containing other people with a different history, this text would be mute or idle in the manner of a foreign law—an object of curiosity, some-thing eventually to be put back where it was found, or maybe put in a museum. But its applicability in the present situation cannot be escaped; this is just what Josiah recognizes in the text. What he knows is the history in which this text emerges as *the* book of the Torah, the book of the cove-nant before which Josiah is accountable, notwithstanding the disregard in which the covenant had been held by his predecessors (Solomon, for ex-ample, who set up altars to the gods of his foreign wives). Josiah, recogniz-ing the history and, therefore, the claim of the text, sets in motion a process (call it canonization) that includes the underwriting of the text by a local oracle and an impressive public reading or promulgation in which the words of the book are confirmed and in which the people are bound by the text as by an oath. The ceremony is a reenactment of the original Mosaic or Sinai covenant. It is a renewal of Israel's Yahwist faith.

The point for us to notice, however, is that canonization here is essentially a legal process in which "binding" means binding with the force of a con-tract; in fact, it means a good deal more, because binding is a political as well as a legal metaphor. The canonization story occurs at the end of a group of texts that scholars sometimes identify as the Deuteronomic History (Josh.–2 Kings). In the context of this version of Israel's history, the book said to have been discovered by the priest of the Temple would be some early edition of what is now the Book of Deuteronomy (an *Urdeuteronium*), which is a collection of laws, codes, or regulations governing the whole range of life—religious, political, military, social, ethical, domestic, and so on. Deuteronomy is a series of addresses of Moses to his people, including his last words before dying (something like a will or legacy), in which he commands his people to adhere to the covenant, here said to be the same thing as following "all the words of this law [Torah]" (Deut. 32:46). Essen-tially Deuteronomy is a retelling of the Sinai story (in which Sinai is now named Horeb) from the point of view of the monarchy and the priestly cult, institutions that came into existence long after the wilderness experience commemorated in the Exodus narrative. Deuteronomy represents Moses as the founder of these institutions, and thus it invests them with the highest authority. In this same fashion the story of Josiah's canonization of the Torah is a careful allusion to the Deuteronomic valediction of Moses; it is clearly designed to dramatize the authority of Deuteronomy or the Deuteronomic Code as *the* book of the covenant. Deuteronomy was the first of the ancient Scriptures (compare the so-called JE texts) to achieve something like canonical status.[9] Scholars can even pinpoint the date of canonization: the eighteenth year of Josiah's reign would be 621 B.C.E. Deuteronomy underwent considerable revision and amplification, however, during the period of exile, when it was assimilated along with other codes and narratives into the Pentateuch. It serves as a good example of what is sometimes called an "open canon."[10]

This initial Deuteronomic Torah was the basis of (or served to ratify) a number of wide-ranging reforms carried out by Josiah in the years prior to the catastrophe of the Babylonian conquest. These were religious reforms, to be sure, motivated by the desire to restore Israel's commitment to Yahweh against all strange gods, but their undeniable political goal was to strengthen the monarchy and the priesthood by centralizing the court and the Temple cult in Jerusalem. The first canonization of the Scriptures was a crucial part of this political movement. Hilkiah, the high priest, did not discover the book of the Torah by accident, or, if he did, it was his good fortune to be the one to bring it forward. Indeed, the Torah, more than the Temple and its sacrifices, is the real source of priestly power in ancient Judaism, because the Torah was not simply a liturgical and pedagogical document.

In an excellent book entitled *Deuteronomy and the Deuteronomic School*, Moshe Weinfeld points out that the "book of Deuteronomy appears . . . to have the character of an ideal national constitution representing all the official institutions of the state: the monarchy, the judiciary, the priesthood, and prophecy"—where prophecy, Weinfeld explains, means "official cultic prophecy and not classical prophecy."[11] This is a vital distinction, especially from a political standpoint. Huldah the prophetess, who speaks on behalf of the priestly Torah, is a cultic or court prophet and (2 Kings underscores this fact) a resident of Jerusalem, in contrast to Jeremiah, for example, whose relationship to Jerusalem is always that of an outsider and an adversary. Jeremiah is a contemporary of the Deuteronomists and their Torah, but it is no accident that Deuteronomy does not mention him (or any of the classical prophets: Elijah, Isaiah, and so on). From the Deuteronomic standpoint, Huldah is an authoritative prophet. Weinfeld's opinion is that Jeremiah was sympathetic to the Deuteronomic reforms—as we shall see, this is a highly controversial issue—but there is no doubt that he stood completely outside the "official institutions of the state" and would never have done what Huldah did.

For Weinfeld, the crucial figure in the canonization story is Shaphan, who is a good example of what is meant by a Deuteronomist or a Deuteronomic scribe. Together with Hilkiah, and evidently under Hilkiah's guidance and in service to the king, Shaphan is officially responsible for the Scriptures. The Scriptures are traditional material handed down through him, and he reshapes them and adapts them according to current exigencies. It is thus important to know, as Weinfeld says, that the scribes "regarded the institution of the monarchy as essential for the proper functioning of society. The premonarchic period, the period of the judges, is depicted by the Deuteronomist as one of religious and political anarchy. . . . This sombre depiction . . . finds expression in the formula 'In those days there was no king in Israel: every man did what was right in his own eyes' that recurs in the literary unit comprising chs. 17–21 of [Deuteronomy]" (p. 169). It is this relativism that the Deuteronomic reforms, and in particular the canonization of the Torah, were meant to overcome. As Weinfeld says, to the mind of the Deuteronomic scribe, "'the written Torah of Moses' (= the book of Deuteronomy) was designed for kings and *quasi*-regal leaders, who alone were capable of enforcing its sway over the people. It is indeed only when referring to kings and leaders of a regal type (Moses and Joshua, David and Solomon, and other kings) that the Deuteronomist alludes to the 'book of the Torah,' whereas in the anarchic period of the judges, when each man did 'as was right in his own eyes,' no mention is made of it because the 'book of the Torah' could be implemented only in a society governed by a centralized government, that is, a king" (p. 171).

It is against this Deuteronomic background, in which the Scriptures are not just sacred texts but legal and political ones as well—texts in a real, historical world in which power is grasped and put into play—that the book of Jeremiah becomes a rich and puzzling collection of writings. And it *is* a collection of writings, not a work: it is composed of heterogeneous material (sayings, sermons, various sorts of matter about Jeremiah) that we really don't know how to read. The famous crux is the following from Jeremiah:

> How do ye say: "We are wise,
> And the Law [Torah] is with us"?
> Lo, certainly in vain hath wrought

the vain pen of the scribes.
The wise men are ashamed,
They are dismayed and taken.
Lo, they have rejected the word of the Lord;
And what wisdom is with them?

(Jer. 8:8–9)

This text is important for the opposition it constructs between a written Torah and the word of Yahweh, where the acceptance of the one amounts to a repudiation of the other. How is this opposition to be understood? This is one of those great questions of biblical scholarship that will always remain open, and for this reason it provides a rich field for speculation. It is worth our reflection because, from a hermeneutical standpoint, we can learn a good deal about the nature of canonization from the topics that this question opens up.

Scholars continue to quarrel over what text Jeremiah could have been thinking of in this passage—was it canonical or was it some forgery? The general opinion is that the reference is nothing less than to Deuteronomy itself. For example, a number of years ago the famous Jeremiah scholar J. Philip Hyatt argued that "Jeremiah, in 8:8–9, 13, expressed opposition to the claim that the Torah of Yahweh is contained in some written book or books, including the original edition of Deuteronomy, and that he considered it false because it did not agree with the 'word of Yahweh' given to the prophets."[12] Jeremiah, Hyatt added, "opposed the claim of the priests that Torah was their special prerogative, and he opposed the activity of the soferim [scribes] and the tofe se hat-torah [handlers or holders of the Torah]. He also denied that true Torah was contained in some written book, probably including Deuteronomy." Indeed, what we need to understand, according to Hyatt, is that "the concept of Torah was not a very important one in Jeremiah's thinking" (pp. 394–95).

This view of the opposition between prophetic word and written Torah can be correlated in fruitful ways with Max Weber's famous distinction between charismatic and institutional authority. On the basis of this distinction, one can see in the biblical period a necessary and inevitable conflict between the Hebrew prophets and the priestly class, with its ties to the monarchy, its Temple in Jerusalem, its teaching role, and its command of the scribes and the written Torah that possesses the authority of the Law. Charismatic authority, Weber says, is highly individualistic and ad hoc; that is, "it is sharply opposed to rational and particularly bureaucratic, authority, and to traditional authority, whether in its patriarchal, patrimonial, or estate variants, all of which are everyday forms of domination."[13] The relationship of the classical prophets to Moses, the first prophet, is on this model a relationship of equivalence rather than of descent—or very nearly so: the figure of Moses is unique in the biblical period because he is represented as a charismatic or prophetic lawgiver, or *aisymnete*.[14] His relationship to Yahweh is direct, personal, and thus prophetic, but at the same time it is Moses who establishes the covenant, promulgates the law, and founds the institutions by which the law and the covenant are handed down. Thus the Deuteronomic scribes, when they write, do not do so as authors; that is, they compose not in their own names but only in the name of Moses. Their authority is Mosaic or traditional rather than authorial and is institutional rather than charismatic or prophetic—and the same is true of the priests of the Temple, especially the priests of the postexilic period or the theocracy of the Second Temple, who are represented as descendants of Aaron, the brother of Moses and the one who handled religious, legal, and political affairs. If you ask, Who speaks for Yahweh? the Deuteronomic and priestly answer is that the Torah of Moses, the "Priestly Torah," contains the message of Yahweh to his people.

By contrast, the authority of men like Elijah, Isaiah, and Jeremiah is equal to the unmediated authority of Moses himself. If you ask, Who speaks for Yahweh? the answer here is that Yahweh speaks for himself directly through his prophets, which is to say that the prophets do not themselves speak (they do not speak in their own names or in the name of Moses), but, rather, that the message of Yahweh speaks itself through them. He speaks, moreover, in ways that are entirely unpredictable and which no one can control, neither king nor priest nor, indeed, the prophet himself, who characteristically finds himself (as in Jer. 20:9) speaking the prophetic word against his own will and his own best interests. The most important point, however, is that the prophetic word is always addressed to the situation in which it is uttered, that is, to the moment at hand; it is not a traditional idea, intended as part of a permanent record. It does not bind the future but only addresses the present, which it frequently judges from the standpoint of the future. The prophetic word has something unwritable about it.

The nineteenth-century biblical scholar Julius Wellhausen, who emphasized the opposition between priest and prophet in an uncompromising way, characterized prophecy as follows: "The element in which the prophets live is the storm of the world's history, which sweeps away human institutions; in which the rubbish of past generations with the houses built on it begins to shake, and that foundation alone remains firm, which needs no support but itself. . . . They do not preach on set texts; they speak out of the spirit which judges all things and itself is judged of no man. Where do they ever lean on any other authority than the truth of what they say; where do they rest on any other foundation than their own certainty?"[15] It is this nine-teenth-century romantic and antinomian theory of prophecy that underlies Weber's distinction between charismatic and institutional authority. On this model, the authority of the prophet derives exclusively from Yahweh and is inaugurated in the prophetic call, as when God cleanses the lips of Isaiah with a burning coal (Isa. 6:6–7). Such authority is completely outside the jurisdiction of monarchy, Temple, and Torah. The prophet is bound by nothing but the necessity of speaking. The question is, What can the can-onization of a written Torah mean in the context of biblical prophecy under-stood in this way? How, for example, are we to read the canonization story in 2 Kings (and other, similar stories in the Scriptures) if we entertain the hypothesis of a fundamental opposition between Hebrew prophets and those who produced and canonized the sacred texts? And, most important, what are we to make of the production and canonization of texts like the Book of Jeremiah? What happens to the prophetic word when it is turned into a scriptural and, eventually, a canonical text? Let me try to work out some answers to these questions.

It is important to emphasize that in contrast to Wellhausen's time, the inclination of modern biblical scholars, especially those working from a strong theological base, has been to qualify or underplay (and sometimes to argue strongly against) any conflict between priestly class and prophetic oracle. This is partly because of the assumption, widely held, that in spite of the heterogeneous and frequently contradictory character of the biblical texts, these texts are to be read from the standpoint of a unified religious outlook. The strongest advocate of this principle of harmony, at least in the context of Jeremiah versus Deuteronomy, has been H. H. Rowley,[16] but the most recent persuasive voice is Weinfeld's. Weinfeld confronts the crux of Jer. 8:8–9 directly and without blinking: "Jeremiah fully identified himself with the religious ideology of the book of Deuteronomy and also appears to have supported the Josianic reforms (Jer. 11:1–8). . . . The prophet in our verse [Jer. 8:8–9] is not denouncing the book of Deuteronomy but con-demning the [scribes] for not observing the teaching that they themselves had committed to writing: the pen of the scribes has made (i.e., composed) to no purpose, the scribes have written in vein" (*Deuteronomy and the Deu-teronomic School*, p. 160).

And it is true that Jeremiah rails principally against the Judah and Jeru-salem of Jehoiakim, son of Josiah and backslider into pre-Deuteronomic idolatry. There is a wonderful story in Jer. 36:1–3, in which God commands Jeremiah, now well into his prophetic career, to "'take thee a roll of a book, and write therein all the words that I have spoken unto thee against Israel, and against Judah, and against all the nations, from the day I spoke unto thee, from the days of Josiah, even unto this day.'" Jeremiah summons Baruch, a scribe, and dictates "all the words of the Lord, which He had spoken unto him." Baruch then takes the book to Jerusalem and reads it aloud in the Temple—to the alarm of the princes of Jehoiakim, who urge Baruch and Jeremiah to go into hiding. The princes then read the book to Jehoiakim:

> And Jehudi read it in the ears of the kind, and in the ears of all the princes that stood beside the king. Now the king was sitting in the winter-house in the ninth month; and the brazier was burning before him. And it came to pass, when Jehudi had read three or four columns, that he cut it with the penknife, and cast it into the fire that was in the brazier, until all the roll was consumed in the fire that was in the brazier. Yet they were not afraid, nor rent their garments, neither the king, nor any of his servants that heard these words. Moreover Elnathan and Delaiah and Gemariah had entreated the king not to burn the roll; but he would not hear them. And the king commanded Jerahmeel the king's son, and Seraiah the son of Azriel, and Shelemaih the son of Abdeel, to take Baruch the scribe and Jeremiah the prophet; but the Lord hid them. (Jer. 36:21–26)

This is another canonization story, with its own variation on the theme of power; but what is interesting is that no priests are mentioned in the story, and the scribes are on the side of Jeremiah (and Yahweh) against the idolatrous Jehoiakim. Jehoiakim does not rend his garments when he hears what is said in the book; he refuses to be bound by the text—even as he refuses to be bound by the Deuteronomic Torah and the reforms of his father. But Yahweh brushes Jehoiakim aside and commands Jeremiah to produce another prophetic text: "Then took Jeremiah another roll, and gave it to Baruch the scribe, the son of Neriah; who wrote therein from the mouth of Jeremiah all the words of the book which Jehoiakim king of Judah had burned in the fire; and there were added besides unto them many like words" (Jer. 36:32)—the second version, in other words, is an amplification of the first.

This story of the production of a Jeremianic Torah needs to be read in conjunction with Jer. 11:1–5, which Weinfeld cites in support of the view of Jeremiah's allegiance to Deuteronomy:

> The word that came to Jeremiah from the Lord, saying: "Hear yet the words of this covenant, and speak unto the men of Judah, and to the inhabitants of Jerusalem; and say thou unto them: Thus saith the Lord,

the God of Israel: Cursed be the man that heareth not the words of this covenant, which I commanded your fathers in the day that I brought them forth out of the land of Egypt, out of the iron furnace, saying: Hearken to My voice, and do them, according to all which I command you; so shall ye be My people, and I will be your God; that I may establish the oath which I swore to your fathers, to give them a land flowing with milk and honey, as at this day." Then answered I [Jeremiah], and said: "Amen, O Lord."

This passage expresses the central motif of Deuteronomic covenant theology, together with the allegiance to Torah and nationhood that such a motif presupposes. There is no conflict in this passage between prophetic word and written text; on the contrary, the prophetic word (like the word of Huldah in 2 Kings) clearly underwrites the authority of Deuteronomy and the covenant tradition.

From the standpoint of a romantic theory of prophecy, however, we are compelled to ask: Who produced this passage? Here we must remind ourselves that little or nothing in the Scriptures is an authored text. What we have in Jer. 11:1–5 appears to be the result of an unseen Deuteronomic hand, writing as if in Jeremiah's name but secretly on behalf of covenant, law, and priesthood. This was, for example, Hyatt's view: "The Book of Jeremiah as we now have it . . . has received expansion and redaction at the hands of 'Deuteronomic' editors, whose purpose in part was to claim for Deuteronomy the sanction of the great prophet."[17] Thoughts naturally fly to Baruch the scribe: Was he a Deuteronomist or a disciple of the prophet— or perhaps someone friendly to both sides?[18]

Deuteronomic recension of Jeremianic material is generally acknowledged by scholars, but it is hard to reach a final opinion as to how this recension is to be understood. Childs explains that the Book of Jeremiah is the product of three sources or traditions: an original poetic tradition made up of sayings or oracles handed down by the prophet's disciples; a secondary prose tradition containing sermons and stories about Jeremiah, including the one about Baruch and the making of a prophetic text; and a Deuteronomic redaction investing this prophetic material with a priestly understanding.

Childs, for his part, stresses the hermeneutical nature of this redaction: "From a historical critical perspective," he says, "the authentic poetic tradition of Jeremiah was transformed by cloaking the prophet's message in the later, prose language of the Deuteronomic tradition. From the perspective of the tradition, a new understanding of Jeremiah emerged from the events of history, which, far from being a distortion, confirmed the prior

word of Scripture. The canonical shaping of the Jeremianic tradition accepted the Deuteronomic framework as an authentic interpretation of Jeremiah's ministry which it used to frame the earlier poetic material"
(*Introduction to the Old Testament as Scripture*, p. 346). From the purely
analytical standpoint of literary criticism, with its concern for authorship
and authenticity, the Book of Jeremiah is a doctored text. But from a hermeneutical standpoint this doctoring was an attempt of the Deuteronomists
to make sense of the prophetic message in order to understand and account
for their own situation, particularly after the failure of the Josianic reforms
under Jehoiakim and, subsequently, the destruction of Jerusalem and the
exile in Babylon. Similarly, Ernest Nicholson has argued that the reshaping
of the "Jeremianic prose tradition" by the Deuteronomists was an attempt
not only to interpret Jeremiah within the context of national catastrophe
but also to apply Jeremiah's message as a way of understanding this catastrophe. The Book of Jeremiah, as we now have it, reflects the understanding
of Jeremiah by the exiles in Babylon.[19]

Understanding here is clearly a mode of appropriation, where the text is
taken not simply in itself but also in the way it speaks to the situation of
the interpreter. A canonical text is canonical, after all, precisely in virtue of
its present application, which is perhaps only another way of saying that
canonization is a species of appropriation. Childs calls such understanding
actualization (*Vergegenwärtigung*) or the "process by which an ancient historical text . . . derives chiefly from a need to 'update' an original tradition."
The whole canonical process by which the Scriptures reached their final
form is governed by this principle of actualization. For Childs, "it is constitutive of the canon to seek to transmit the tradition in such a way as to
prevent its being moored in the past. Actualization derives from a hermeneutical concern which was present during the different stages of the book's
canonization. It is built into the structure of the text itself, and reveals an
enormous richness of theological interpretation by which to render the text
religiously accessible" (p. 79). As a redacted rather than an authored text,
the Scriptures are structurally orientated away from an original intention
toward the manifold possibilities of future understanding. They possess the
openness to the future interpretation that is characteristic of, for example,
a good law. Thus, according to this argument, what we have in the Book of
Jeremiah as a canonical text is not what Jeremiah said in his own historical
moment but the way his words were received and understood by those who
heard them in circumstances radically different from those in which Jeremiah originally spoke. The Book of Jeremiah as a canonical text is a fusion
of prophetic and Deuteronomic horizons.[20]

However, let me now give an equally compelling but considerably less benevolent version of this hermeneutical view of the canonical process. The thesis here is that canonization is the priestly appropriation of prophetic authority by means of the superior forces of writing and textuality; in other words, writing, in this case, was a way of getting rid of prophecy. This had been Wellhausen's thesis in the nineteenth century. He wrote: "With the appearance of the law came to an end the old [prophetic] freedom, not only in the sphere of worship, now restricted to Jerusalem, but in the sphere of religious spirit as well. There was now in existence an authority as objective as could be [namely, the Priestly Torah]; and this was the death of prophecy" (*Prolegomena to the History of Israel*, p. 402).

In a valuable book, *Prophecy and Canon*, Joseph Blenkinsopp has made a bold attempt to rehabilitate Wellhausen's thesis (relieving it, meanwhile, of some of its romantic melodrama). Blenkinsopp follows the canonical arguments of Childs, but he does so explicitly within the context of Weber's analysis of the structural incompatibility of prophetic oracle and written Torah. Blenkinsopp's view is that Jeremiah would not necessarily have opposed the *message* of a written Torah; or, more accurately, there is no reason to suppose that Jeremiah would not have supported the Mosaic covenant as this was understood in Deuteronomic theology and in the Josianic reforms—the difficulty is that we really don't have the evidence to answer this question one way or the other. What we can say is that prophecy and priesthood are intrinsic to Israel's Yahwist traditions, but they are political as well as religious phenomena, and on political grounds it is easy to see how it would have been in the interest of a prophet like Jeremiah to oppose the institution of a written Torah as the canonical form of the Yahwist tradition. The crux of Jer. 8:8–9—

> How do ye say: "We are wise,
> And the Law [Torah] of the Lord is with us"?
> Lo, certainly in vain hath wrought
> The vain pen of the scribes.

—does not demand a choice between written law and prophetic word; rather, according to Blenkinsopp, Jeremiah's attack is aimed "at a misplaced confidence arising out of possession of a law written down, edited and authoritatively interpreted. This confidence, he is saying, blinds the official political and religious leadership, including priests, scribes and stipended prophets [like Huldah], to what is actually taking place or, to put it more prophetically, to what God is doing in the world."[21] A written text is an agent of fixity and rule; it sets boundaries and establishes precedents that can only constrict the improvisation that characterizes Hebrew prophecy. Jeremiah's basic insight, in fact, is that writing is a force superior to prophecy in establishing a claim to Yahwistic authority; in Blenkinsopp's words, "writing is a way of making a claim stick," in contrast to the prophetic word, which has to reassert its claim again and again on every occasion of its utterance (p. 38).

Thus it would not be the content or meaning of a written Torah that Jeremiah would attack; rather, it would be the Deuteronomic "claim to final and exclusive authority *by means of writing*" (pp. 38–39). Jeremiah's problem is political rather than theological. He knows that writing is more powerful than prophecy and that he will not be able to withstand it—and he knows that the Deuteronomists know no less. As Blenkinsopp says, "Deuteronomy produced a situation in which prophecy could not continue to exist without undergoing profound transformations" (p. 39)—that is, without ceasing to be "free prophecy," or prophecy unbound by any text, *including its own.* "It might be considered misleading or flippant to say that for [Deuteronomy], as for rabbinic orthodoxy, the only good prophet is a dead prophet. But in point of fact the Deuteronomic scribes, despite their evident debt to and respect for the prophets, contributed decisively to the eclipse of the kind of historically oriented prophecy (*Geschichtsprophetie*) represented by Jeremiah and the emergence in due course of quite different forms of scribal prophecy" (pp. 38–39; see also pp. 119–20).

At this point we reach a sort of outer limit of biblical criticism—a threshold that scholars, with their foundation in literary criticism, their analytical attitude toward texts, and their theological concerns, are not inclined to cross. In any case, it is no accident that the political meaning of the conflict of prophecy and canon has received its most serious attention not from a biblical scholar but from a radical historian, Ellis Rivkin. In *The Shaping of Jewish History* Rivkin proposes to treat the question of canon formation and the promulgation of canonical texts of the Scriptures according to *power* criteria rather than literary criteria. For Rivkin, the production of the Hebrew Scriptures "was not primarily the work of scribes, scholars, or editors who sought out neglected traditions about wilderness experience, but a class struggling to gain power."[22]

Rivkin's "power hypothesis" is squarely in the Wellhausen-Weber tradition: the theological unity of ancient Yahwism that the Scriptures exhibit conceals a politically unstable situation in which there was not one but several rival versions of Yahwism. "There was the Yahwism of the tribal phase; the Yahwism of the wilderness phase; the Yahwism of the premonarchical agricultural and urban phase; the Yahwism of cult and priesthood; and the

Yahwism of the new [post-Mosaic or classical] prophecy" (pp. 16–17). For
Rivkin, the canonization of Deuteronomy in 621 B.C.E. was an attempt by
the Jerusalem coalition of Court and Temple to resolve the conflict of interpretations and consequent crisis of authority that the heterogeneous nature
of Yahwism entailed. In particular, the institution of an authorized version
of Yahwism centered in Jerusalem meant that, above everything else, prophetic power had to be brought under control. "So long as prophets had
the freedom to speak out in Yahweh's name," Rivkin says, "no institution
was sage, and no authority, other than prophecy, sacrosanct" (p. 20). Deuteronomy, in other words, was promulgated as an official countertext to
prophecy. It was not only a political and religious constitution enshrining
the monarchy and the Temple priesthood, with its scribes and oracles; it
also proclaimed unambiguously that true charismatic prophecy had begun
and ended with Moses. Deuteronomy concludes dramatically with the statement, inscribed with the force of law, that "there hath not arisen a prophet
since in Israel like unto Moses, whom the Lord knew face to face" (Deut.
34:10). As Rivkin says, "Prophetic authority, though recognized [by Deu-
teronomy], was curbed. It was not permitted to challenge the Mosaic laws,
or the legitimacy of the priesthood or the monarchy. The authenticity of a
prophet was not to be measured against the Book of Deuteronomy. In case
of conflict, the book would prevail" (p. 18).

And prevail it did, but not in its Deuteronomic form. The backsliding of
Jehoiakim, Nebuchadnezzar's conquest of Judah, the destruction of Jerusalem and the Temple, and the subsequent exile exploded the Deuteronomic
program. "Prophets such as Jeremiah and Ezekiel refused to give up their
prophetic freedom," Rivkin says. "They continued to exercise their prophetic prerogative as though Deuteronomy had never been promulgated"
(p. 19). Nevertheless, the years of exile were evidently a time of furious
scribal activity. We know virtually nothing about this period, but when it
came to an end with the return to Jerusalem and the restoration of the
Temple (anywhere from the middle of the fifth century to the beginning of
the fourth), there, suddenly, stood a monumental Torah: the Pentateuch. For
Rivkin, the appearance of the Pentateuch is decisive. The monarchy is no
more, nor are there any prophets. "Before the canonization of the Pentateuch, even as late as the time of Nehemiah's visit to Judea about 445 B.C.E.,
prophecy is still alive. And then, in the fourth century, there is the Pentateuch and prophecy has evaporated." Never again is there an Elijah, Isaiah,
Jeremiah, or Ezekiel. "Exercising authority in [their] stead is a priestly class
of Aaronides, unknown to Moses, unmentioned in Deuteronomy, unheard
of by Ezekiel, and outside the ken of even so late a prophet as Malachi" (p.

23). The Aaronides are priests of the Second Temple and the founders of the theocracy that resolved the crisis of Yahwism once and for all by centering Yahwism in a book. "The Aaronides succeeded," Rivkin says, "where Deuteronomy had failed. They saw Yahwism threatened unless they wielded absolute authority. They therefore designed the Pentateuch to attain this end, arrogating to themselves not only altar rights but also control over the expiation from sin. They broke prophetic authority by having Moses invest Aaron and his sons with the priesthood forever (p. 31).

The great legendary figure in this political drama is Ezra, priest and ruler, who embodies the characters of prophet and scribe and is sometimes called the Second Moses, since it was he whom God commanded to rewrite the Torah after it had been lost in a fire. The story of the rewriting of the Torah is preserved in a very late text, 2 Esdras, which does not exist in a Hebrew version and is so placed among the apocrypha, which refers not to bogus texts and discredited stories but (among other things) to writings set aside for private study rather than liturgical texts. In 2 Esdras, Ezra is represented as a prophetic figure, but he is plainly an *aisymnetic* rather than charismatic figure: a prophet in the manner of Moses or, more accurately perhaps, a scribal prophet of the sort described by Blenkinsopp. Here is part of the account of Ezra's call:

> "Ezra [God says], open your mouth, and drink what I give you to drink."
> And I opened my mouth, and, behold, a full cup was offered me. It was full of what looked like water, but the colour of it was like fire. And I took it, and drank, and when I had drunk it my heart gushed forth understanding, and wisdom grew in my breast, for my spirit retained its memory, and my mouth opened and was no longer closed. Moreover, the Most High gave understanding to the five men [Ezra's scribes], and they wrote what was said, one after another, in letters that they did not know. (2 Esd. 13:40–48)[23]

Ninety-four books are composed in only forty days of dictation, at which point God instructs Ezra to "publish the twenty-four books that you wrote first, for the worthy and the unworthy to hear, but keep the seventy books that were written last to hand down to the wise men among your people, for in them is the source of understanding, the spring of wisdom, and the steam of knowledge" (2 Es. 14:45–48). This is important for the way it implies the existence of a double canon, one public and the other hidden, one for all the people to hear and one for the wise or for those who can understand what is written.

Who were these people of understanding? In later years they are easily
identified as the sages, or *soferim,* described by Ben Sira in the epigraph to
this chapter, ancestors of the great rabbinical scholars of the Diaspora, who
were able to maintain Judaism as a living tradition in defiance of every
conceivable worldly catastrophe. In Ezra's time, however, they are not sages
but priests. The last canonization story told by the Hebrew Scriptures is in
Nehemiah, in which Ezra promulgates his Second Torah, doing so, we
should notice, on the Deuteronomic model of 2 Kings:

> And Ezra the priest brought the Law [Torah] before the congregation,
> both men and women, and all that could hear with understanding. . . .
> And he read therein before the broad place that was before the water
> gate from early morning until midday, in the presence of the men and
> women, and of those that could understand; and the ears of all the
> people were attentive unto the book of the Law. And Ezra the scribe
> stood upon a pulpit of wood, which they had made for the purpose;
> and beside him stood Mattihiah, and Shema, and Anaiah, and Uriah,
> and Hilkiah. (Neh. 8:2–4)

Hilkiah! The name is an allegory of priestly power. He is listed along with
those who stood beside Ezra as he read and who walked among the people,
"[causing] the people to understand the Law." One senses that the occasion
would be incomplete, and the status of the Torah less than certain, without
him.

The lesson of Hilkiah is that the canon is not a literary category but a
category of power; or, in Blenkinsopp's words, "what we call 'canon' is
intelligible only in the context of conflicting claims to control the redemptive media and, in particular, to mediate and interpret authoritatively the
common tradition" (*Canon and Prophecy,* p. 96). One can see how the
canonization of books of the prophets would naturally follow the promulgation of the Pentateuch, because the process of turning prophecy into text
would only be complete when fugitive texts become bound to the Torah as
an integral part of its canonical domain. Henceforward, when the prophet
speaks, it will only be to disclose a prior, written Torah. Let me conclude
by quoting my favorite canonization story, which is part of the account of
Ezekiel's call to prophetic utterance:

> "And thou, son of man, hear what I say unto thee: be not thou rebel-
> lious like that rebellious house; open thy mouth, and eat that which I
> give thee." And when I looked, behold, a hand was put forth unto me;
> and lo, a roll of a book was therein; and He spread it before me, and

it was written within and without; and there was written therein lamentations, and moaning, and woe.

And he said unto me: "Son of man, eat that which thou findest; eat this roll, and go, speak unto the house of Israel." So I opened my mouth, and He caused me to eat that roll. And He said unto me: "Son of man, cause thy belly to eat, and fill thy bowels with this roll that I give thee." Then did I eat; and it was in my mouth as honey for sweetness. (Ezek. 2:8–3:3)

Allegory as

Radical Interpretation

4

> As an empiricist I continue to think of the conceptual scheme
> of science as a tool, ultimately, for predicting future experience
> in the light of past experience. Physical objects are imported
> into the situation as convenient intermediaries—not by
> definition in terms of experience, but simply as irreducible
> posits comparable, epistemologically, to the gods of Homer.
> For my part I do, qua lay physicist, believe in physical objects
> and not in Homer's gods; and I consider it a scientific error to
> believe otherwise. But in point of epistemological footing the
> physical objects and the gods differ only in degree and not in
> kind.
> —W. V. O. Quine, "Two Dogmas of Empiricism"

"Radical interpretation" means the redescription, in one's
own language, of sentences from an alien system of concepts and beliefs.
My thought is that this idea describes, in a rough, preliminary sort of way,
the logic of allegorical interpretation, at least in the case of someone like
Philo Judaeus, who lived in Alexandria about the time of Christ and produced a number of commentaries on the Septuagint, the (almost legendary)
Greek translation of the Hebrew Bible, in order to make sense of it in terms
of the concepts and beliefs of Hellenistic culture. In this context making
sense does not mean recovering or preserving an original message, or at least
not just that; rather, it means integrating a text (and its meanings) into a
radically new cultural environment. One might say that in radical interpretation what matters is not meaning but truth; that is, the question is not,
What does this sentence mean? but How would this sentence have to be
construed so as to be held true in our language?

I borrow the term "radical interpretation" from Donald Davidson, who
adapted it from Quine's "radical translation," or translation between two

languages not joined by cognate values.[1] This idea belongs to Quine's effort to determine whether there is any sense to be made of the concept of meaning. If meaning is anything, it is what survives translation from one language to another. In Edmund Husserl's theory, for example, meaning is an ideal object like the Pythagorean theorem, which can be transported without loss across every boundary of historical and cultural difference; if we follow Plato's *Meno*, even uneducated slave boys can be made to recognize the rudiments. Linguistic meanings are not so ideal as geometrical ones, being internal to life-worlds in more material and ungovernable ways, but under the right (scientific) conditions certain propositions, which it is the task of philosophy to identify, can achieve a pure translatability.[2]

Quine the empiricist does not believe in ideal objects that are external to language. For him, meaning and truth are, rather, a function of how things hang together logically in a conceptual framework. In "Two Dogmas of Empiricism" (1951) Quine characterizes such a framework this way:

> The totality of our so-called knowledge or beliefs, from the most casual matters of geography and history to the profoundest laws of atomic physics or even of pure mathematics and logic, is a man-made fabric which impinges on experience only along the edges. Or, to change the figure, total science is like a field of force whose boundary conditions are experience. A conflict with experience at the periphery occasions readjustments in the interior of the field. Truth values have to be redistributed over some of our statements. Reevaluation of some statements entails reevaluation of others, because of their logical interconnection—the logical laws being in turn simply certain further statements of the system, certain further elements of the field. Having reevaluated one statement we must reevaluate some others, which may be statements of logical connections themselves. But the total field is so underdetermined by its boundary conditions, experience, that there is much latitude of choice as to what statements to reevaluate in the light of any single contrary experience. No particular experiences are linked with any particular statements in the interior of the field, except indirectly through considerations of equilibrium affecting the field as a whole.[3]

Sometimes Quine's is called a holistic theory of meaning, which is, in a way, a logical empiricist's version of the hermeneutical circle. The truth of most statements is not determined by direct experience; rather, truth is a product of the law of noncontradiction. It is what is warranted in view of what has already been certified. If a statement fits in with others held to be true, it stays, possibly after some readjustment to the whole. Indeed, we must imagine the "man-made fabric" as being in a constant state of reweaving so as to maintain its coherence with itself. So "it is misleading to speak of the empirical content of an individual statement—especially if it is a statement at all remote from the experiential periphery of the field" (LPV, p. 43). Every conceptual scheme is underdetermined by experience, which means that reality can, in principle, be (said to be) made of gods or objects or numbers without being contradicted by brute facts; no one's metaphysics is superior to another's on the basis of how it connects up with reality. This also means that in translating, say, from the language of gods to the language of objects a number of equally supportable versions of the original may be possible, although chances are no two will square with one another. This is Quine's famous thesis about the "indeterminacy of translation."[4]

With respect to allegory, it seems to me that Quineans will have an easier time of it than Husserlians. At all events it is against this crudely sketched Quinean background that I want to give an account of Philo's interpretive practice. Allegory is, crudely, the squaring of an alien conceptual scheme with one's own on the charitable assumption that there is a sense (which it is the task of interpretation to determine) in which they are coherent with one another. In a later chapter I will want to suggest that the opposite of allegory might be something like an epistemological crisis or the shattering of one's conceptual scheme in its encounter with a radically different or stubbornly resistant text or tradition. But for now I only want to suggest the Quinean nature of allegory, which is, borrowing Davidson's language, a way of assigning "truth conditions to alien sentences to make speakers right when plausibly possible according, of course, to our view of what is right" (p. 137). Davidson calls this the principle of charity, which, he says, "directs the interpreter to translate or interpret so as to read some of his own standards of truth into the pattern of sentences held true by the speaker."[5] This same principle applies in cases of metaphor, where a sentence that seems, on the face of it, false or absurd is to be taken in a sense that makes it come out right, that is, coherent with other sentences held true.[6]

Moreover, allegory is also the squaring of a field with itself—the reweaving of a text or a context that Quine calls "readjustments in the interior of the field." As Davidson says, "The problem of interpretation is domestic as well as foreign: it surfaces for speakers of the same language in the form of the question, how can it be determined that the language is the same?" (p. 126). Sameness of language is a concept with some application in geometry, less so perhaps in physics, but natural languages are heterogeneous, stratified, historical, opaque, hardly resembling anything we could imagine as a logically correct language. "Speakers of the same language," says Davidson, "can go on the assumption that for them the same expressions are to be interpreted in the same way, but this does not indicate what justifies the assumption. All understanding of the speech of another involves radical interpretation." Which would be to say that all understanding is allegorical.

I think of Philo as the greatest allegorist in antiquity, one of history's great masters of commentary and in many ways foundational for the history of interpretation, but I'm not sure anyone agrees with this. As an interpreter of texts, Philo has never aroused much interest or attention.[7] Classicists ignore him because his interpretations are not of classical texts.[8] Christian biblical scholars note his obvious influence on the Letter to the Hebrews and on Church Fathers like Origen, but his commentaries are without a ghost of typology or figural prophecy, and his theology is a melange of Judaism, Plato, and unsifted Hellenistic lore.[9] Jewish scholars meanwhile dismiss him as a mere Hellenizer. Moreover, scholarly tradition, in both its positivist and postmodern modes, understands itself as having got beyond interpretation, and so commentators like Philo routinely get brushed aside with a superior gesture—in their general introduction to the Loeb edition of Philo, F. H. Colson and G. H. Whitaker, Philo's translators, remark that "his purpose was the same as Bunyan had in *The Pilgrim's Progress* and *The Holy War*, and Dante to some extent in his *Divine Comedy*, namely, to set forth an allegory of the human soul and its relations to God. But while Scripture to Bunyan and mediaeval eschatology to Dante were merely foundations on which they could rear the fabric which their own imagination created, Philo, entirely devoid of creative genius, could never get away from the role of interpreter."[10] In a different style, but in much the same spirit, Joel Fineman says that "the motive to allegoricize emerges out of a recuperative originology"—that is, a conservative desire to recover original utterances and restore lost presences—and accordingly "with Philo we note a self-conscious and sacralizing nostalgia in response to authoritative but in some sense faded origins."[11]

Harry Austryn Wolfson, the great commentator on Philo as a philosopher and his strongest champion, is frankly embarrassed by Philo's allegorizing and argues as much as he can that nowhere does Philo reject the Scriptures as history.[12] And, indeed, along with Wolfson, scholars and critics are inclined to side against allegory with the modern tradition of Aquinas, Luther, Spinoza, Schleiermacher, and Husserl, which one could very well summarize with some lines from Morton Bloomfield's essay "Allegory as Interpretation": "I should say that the greatness of any work of art lies with the literal sense: that which gives it shape and being. It is the literal sense which is by far the most profound, because it always provides us with a new possibility of interpretation. Any particular signification is unchanging. In order to extend signification we must go back to the literal sense. The literal gives life and continuity to the text. It acts as a corrective force to misinterpretation."[13] To be sure, the *sensus litteralis* is a variable concept. Bloomfield's idea implies a text (in this case a context-free or autonomous work of art) whose meaning can be derived analytically from the composition of its parts. The text is, in Luther's phrase, self-interpreting and authoritative in itself. But of course by "literal" Bloomfield means mostly that a text just means what it says, and it is easy to take his point. There can be no allegorical (nor any sort of) reading of, say, the Cain and Abel story until there first *is* a Cain and Abel story in which, among other things, it is stated as a fact of the matter that Cain rises up and slays his brother, Abel; and this is just to say that the narrative fact that Cain kills Abel is not open to interpretation.[14] It is what happened, the *pragma* or res of the narrative.[15] The question is then how to take what happened: *Littera docet gesta*—but how do we read the facts (the literal sense) of Cain's case?

It happens that in antiquity the literal is not always foundational in Bloomfield's sense but floats rather freely among other, sometimes more powerful distinctions. For example, in book 2 of Aristotle's *Rhetoric* the ruling distinction is not between the literal and other sorts of sense but rather between *kurios* and *xenos* (1404b), that is, between the near and the remote, the familiar and the strange, the proper and the foreign, that which is binding on us and that which remains unruly or out of bounds: even, as Aristotle elaborates it, between the urban and the rustic (1419b). In place of the literal we have the idea of speaking correctly; or, as Aristotle puts it, *esti d' archē tēs lexeōs to hellēnizein:* speaking like the Greeks is the foundation of lexis or style (1407b)—and for all of that it is the foundation of meaning as well, since there is no making sense of what we cannot understand: as if Aristotle had anticipated Heidegger's idea, or Wittgenstein's, that understanding is a condition of belonging to a familiar world or form of life; or had, much to the same point, anticipated Quine, that meaning is internal to a conceptual scheme. At all events it is here, at the boundary of the Greek and the non-Greek, *kurios* and *xenos*, the proper and the foreign, the (already) intelligible and the strange, that allegory as radical interpretation is to be found.

It is doubtful, however, whether Aristotle or any classical Greek could have imagined such an event as the production of the Septuagint. What sort of xenotic text would ever, under any circumstances, get rendered into Greek? One might as well reverse the flow of a river to its source. Not that the Greeks could not imagine an "alien wisdom," in Arnaldo Momigliano's phrase.[16] On the contrary, among the Greeks the Jews had an enormous reputation as lawmakers and wise men. The legend of the Septuagint translation, given in the *Letter of Aristeas* (c. 100 B.C.E.) and repeated by Philo in his "Life of Moses," is a sort of monument of Jewish intellectual mystique, although its main purpose was probably to underwrite the authority of the Septuagint as a Jewish Torah. So great (so the letter goes) was the Torah's reputation for wisdom that Ptolemy of Alexandria summoned seventy (actually, seventy-two) Jewish scholars from Palestine to produce a translation for his library, which they did under inspired circumstances, as if producing a second revelation. Unfortunately, the Septuagint made no impression on the Greeks. As Momigliano says, "The Greeks expected the Jews not to translate their holy books, but to produce an account of themselves according to the current methods and categories of ethnography" (AW, p. 92). It is doubtful whether the Septuagint ever made it into the great library at Alexandria, but it is plain that it placed a special burden of exegesis on the Jewish community at Alexandria, especially among intellectuals like Aristobulus (second century B.C.E.) and later Philo, namely, to justify both legend and text by reading the Septuagint as a philosophical text worthy of inclusion in a Greek canon. Yet how to accomplish such a Greek reading (just to call it that) and at the same time remain faithful to the text as a Jewish Torah?

Philo's hermeneutical task, in other words, runs in two directions, or (let us say) requires him to satisfy two sets of truth conditions, one Jewish and one Greek. Perhaps we can begin to get some sense of the complications of this task by asking what counts as "literal" for Philo, because this is an open-ended question. There is, first of all, literal in the sense of exact, word-for-word (as against loose) translation, as in Philo's account of the Septuagint legend:

> Sitting there in seclusion with none present save the elements of nature, earth, water, air, heaven, the genesis of which was to be the first theme of their sacred revelation, for the law begins with the story of the world's creation, they [the Seventy] became as it were possessed, and, under inspiration, wrote, not each several scribe something different but the same word for word [*onomata kai rhēmata*], as though dictated to each by an invisible prompter. Yet who does not know that every language, the Greek especially, abounds in terms, and that the same thought can be put in many shapes by changing single words and whole phrases and suiting the expression to the occasion [*allote allas epharmozonta*]? This was not the case, we are told, with this law of ours, but the Greek words used corresponded literally with the Chaldean,

exactly suited to the things they indicated [*sunenechthēnai d' eis tauton kuria kuriois onomasi, ta tois Chaldaikois, enarmosthenta eu mala tois dēloumenois pragmasin*]. For, just as in geometry and logic, so it seems to me, the sense indicated [*sēmainomena:* the sign given] does not admit of variety in the expression which remains unchanged in the original form, so these writers, as it clearly appears, arrived at a wording which corresponded with the matter, and alone, or better than any other, would bring out clearly what was meant [*emphantikōs ta dēloumena:* the phrase "what was meant" is the Loeb translator's interpolation]. ("The Life of Moses," 2.38.1–39.7)

This passage suggests something like an antique distinction between a philosophical and a natural language, where the one is a tightly knit fabric of original names and the other a loosely woven surplus of signifiers. Not surprisingly, the justification of the Septuagint calls for a Husserl-like theory of translation, or of pure translatability without remainder, as if the Mosaic Law had the universality and univocality of geometry and logical form. Certainly the Greek Scriptures are a translation like no other—both literal in the sense of word for word (*kuria kuriois onomasi*) and also literal in the sense of an exact rendering that preserves the correctness of names, or what things are properly so-called—in other words, the primordial identity of words and things. What we have in the Septuagint is translation without transference, in which the Greek participates in the self-identity of the first language. There is no difference (nothing foreign) intruding between them: their relation is *kurios-kurios* rather than *kurios-xenos*. So it is not, as a Greek might have it, that Hebrew is already, in some sense, Greek (that is, capable, as Greek alone is, of inscribing a wisdom text), as it is that Greek has, in this special and miraculous instance, been restored to the status of a pre-Babel language in which words are exactly suited to things instead of being rhetorically altered to fit the occasions of their use.

In this ideal case literal means proper and exact, but things loosen up when Philo confronts the Scriptures himself, because although they are theoretically one systematically coherent Law, they are not of a piece. They belong to different sorts of hermeneutical situation, each with its own definition of the literal. So more than one word for literal is needed. The word that is frequently chosen is *rhētos* or *rhētē* (whence "rhetoric"), a word for the said or the spoken or the (expressly) named: in other words, whatever a text appears to say. In the commentary "On the Posterity of Cain" there is also the expression *onomasi procheirou* (1.5), or words that are common, easy, ready-to-hand, that is, familiar or ordinarily accepted. Elsewhere it is called *mēdeis oun tēn procheiron ekdochēn tou logon:* "the way of understanding language that first presents itself" ("The Worse Attacks the Better," 155.3–4). There are other expressions as well—most obviously *kuriolegetai*, what is properly said. In many of these cases the "literal" is not so much a category of meaning as it is a moment when the text foregrounds itself as a *skandalon*, or stumbling block, that makes it difficult for reading to continue, as in the frequent cases of anthropomorphism. "Thus even the phrase 'as a man' (Deut. i.31) is not used of God in its literal sense [*kuriolegetai*], but is a term used in a figure [*katachrēsis*], a word to help our feeble apprehension" ("On the Birth of Abel," 101.6–9). That is, what the text says cannot properly be said of God but is to be taken as a way of saying the unnameable or unsayable, as in Plato's *Phaedrus* (246a), where Socrates in his second speech on love is forced to speak of the soul as a pair of winged horses and a charioteer because to say what it is in itself would require a long speech in a divine language. Catachresis is a figure for the limits of language. Technically it is not so much "another sense" as it is a way of placing the unacceptable text in quotation marks, as if to open up an indeterminate space between the literal and the figurative: the literal is not to be taken literally, even though there is, properly speaking, no other way to take it owning to the weakness of the logos or the shortfall of human understanding.

In other contexts, however, the literal has the force of Torah itself. This is obvious in the case of explicitly legal texts, which have to be construed differently from narratives because they entail the question of how literally (in the sense of strictly or loosely) they are to be observed. There is an obvious sense in which commandments and prohibitions always mean what they say and are not to be fooled with. In his commentaries on the Decalogue and particularly in the more extensive and detailed text "On the Special Law Books," which concerns specific Jewish practices—circumcision, Sabbath observance, the prohibition of images, dietary laws, ordinances governing temple sacrifice, the observance of feasts, and so on—Philo makes it clear that what is said is binding and, in regard to practice, open to interpretation mainly with respect to its reasonableness and point. Indeed, Philo has a sharp sense of the different claims on theory and practice that the Torah makes. He objects to those who do away with difficult observances by taking everything in a purely symbolic way, as if circumcision, for example, were not anything actually to be performed but only a sort of general warning against fleshly indulgence ("On the Migration of Abraham," 89.1–2). To be sure, the law can be taken in this abstract way, but "let us not on this account repeal the law" (92.7–8). The symbolists, says Philo, are too transcendental: "as though they were living alone by themselves in a wilderness, or as though they had become disembodied souls, and knew neither city nor village nor household nor company of human beings at all, overlooking all that the mass of men regard, they explore reality in its naked absoluteness" (90.1–6).

But at the same time, Philo is scornful of those who take the law rigidly without thought to what is reasonable—*tēs rhētēs pragmateis sophistas*, he calls them: roughly, experts of the literal ("On Dreams," 1.102.2). For Philo, the law, where reasonable (and he means to show its reasonableness), is normative and binding, but for all of that it is not reducible to the concept of rule. The legal text is not to be loosely interpreted; it is fixed and immovable, but it has bearing upon other contexts and so remains open to further reflection. At the outset of his commentary on the Decalogue Philo says that his purpose will be to give accurate representations (*tas ideas akriboso*) both of the Ten Commandments and of the special ordinances that, on his reading, follow systematically from them; but he adds that "if some allegorical interpretation should appear to underlie them [*ei tis hupophainoito tropos allēgorias*], I shall not fail to state it. For knowledge loves to learn and to advance to full understanding and its way is to seek the hidden rather than the obvious [*ē pro tōn emphanōn ethos ta phanē zētein*] ("On the Decalogue," 1.5–8). The law is wisdom and an oracle as well as a code; it has a claim upon the contemplative as well as on the practical life, and so it is to be studied for what it teaches as well as for what it requires in the way of conduct and action.

The notion of teaching seems crucial. One might well say that for Philo the literal is not primarily a grammatical or textual concept but is how the law is to be taken insofar as it commands and prohibits; whereas to go beyond the literal is to recognize those instances in which the law, whatever it might explicitly call for in the way of observance, is also coherent with an authoritative body of teachings, or, say, with prevailing systems of lore, theory, and tradition. The task of interpretation (or, more accurately, of study and commentary) is to bring out these coherences. The text is of some help in this, because although not always expressly legal, it is heterogeneous in its genres—made up, one might say, of endlessly provocative bits and pieces of every sort of discourse. So the text is, in a sense, always in advance of itself, or always open or porous with respect to what it discloses.

In Philo's practice this means several things, depending on whether he treats the text in its parts or as a whole. Generally speaking, the coherence of text and teaching occurs for Philo at the level of the proper name. In rendering Hebrew names into Greek a good deal more is at stake than transliteration because names are, in their nature, never simply literal but are always heavy with conceptual weight. In modern theory the idea is to reduce names to the pure designation of existing entities as a way of satisfying our sense of how words hook empirically onto the world. Saul Kripke has a wonderful idea whereby objects or persons undergo original "baptisms," such that we get a name right when we can trace its use back to the original moment of dubbing. This is the causal theory of naming, or hardcore designation. As Kripke explains, "The object may be named by ostension, or the reference of the name may be fixed by a description. When the name is 'passed from link to link,' the receiver of the name must, I think, intend when he learns it to use it with the same reference as the man from whom he heard it. If I hear the name 'Napolean' and decide it would be a nice name for my pet aardvark, I do not satisfy this condition."[17] Natural kind names work a bit like this as well. A thing is called gold, for example, because it coincides, in its deep or hidden structure, with a paradigm instance that scientific procedures can identify. Meanwhile for the rest of us a spade is a spade, a smile is just a smile, and so on.

But for Philo names seem to inhabit a different order of discourse in which it makes sense to ask what's in a name? This is, after all, what Socrates wants to know in the *Cratylus*, with its bewildering inventory of etymologies. The *Cratylus* takes up the hoary topic of the "correctness of names [*onomatōn orthotēton*]," and it must be that its purpose is to arouse our suspicions against language ("surely no man of sense can put himself and his soul under the control of names" [440c.5–7]), but perhaps all this means is that there is no coherent way to contain names within a purely designative theory; rather, names presuppose elaborate contexts of discourse that give their use some point besides designation, as if names were inherently allegorical, always coming with stories attached to them. What matters is how names fit in with these stories, as in the famous case of Tantalus. As Socrates says, "Anyone would think the name of Tantalus was given rightly and in accordance with nature, *if the stories about him are true*" (395d.3–5; my emphasis):

> The many terrible misfortunes that happened to him both in his life, the last of which was the utter overthrow of his country, and in Hades, after his death, the balancing [*talanteia*] of the stone above his head, in wonderful agreement with his name; and it seems exactly as if someone who wished to call him most wretched [*talantaton*] disguised the name and said Tantalus instead; in some such way as that chance seems to have affected his name in the legend. And his father also, who is said to be Zeus, appears to have a very excellent name, but it is not easy to understand; for the name of Zeus is like a sentence; we divide it into

two parts, and some use one part, others the other; for some call him Zena (*Zena*), and others Dia (*Dia*); but the two in combination express the nature of the god, which is just what we said a name should be able to do. (395d.7–396a.6)

The story of Tantalus suggests that names are conferred allegorically, as if character were fate and one's name were allegorical of one's nature to the extent that nature is entailed by destiny. In any case, this is how ancient stories frequently seem to go, as if it were the task of stories to show, among other things, the origin of names. Socrates seems bothered, Kripke-like, by the contingency of naming, but one could say just as well that names are prophetic, as we know from the stories of Odysseus and Oedipus; or, to put it another way, there are names that are fixed beforehand (*tithēmi*), as if of necessity, and whose significance emerges unavoidably in time, like the terrible meaning of Oedipus' lame foot; and then there are those names that are added later (*epithēmi*), or contingently, depending on how the story unfolds.[18] In either case, however, whether proper name or epithet, what matters is the coherence of name and life. It is this coherence that gives names their seemingly awful magical power. Socrates may distrust names, but he knows very well the force of this coherence. Plato's dialogues are regularly satirical in the way they show how people fail to live up to their names, with Euthyphro, for example, lacking the good sense or right-mindedness his name suggests. Or, where not satirical, names are frequently ironic, even if mildly, as in the *Phaedrus,* where Socrates speaks the speech of Stesichorus, son of Euphemus, "man of pious speech" (244a.5).[19] Behind every name there's a story.

Philo at any rate follows the Cratylus theory in showing how biblical narratives disclose the fitness or correctness of names, or, much to the same point, how names show the many ways a story can be understood and interpreted.[20] Philo probably had beside him something like a manual of translation showing how Hebrew names can be refigured as Greek concepts:[21]

Adam = Mind	Egypt = Body
Eve = Senses	Eden = Right Reason
Israel = One who sees God	Judah = He who confesses
Moses = Wisdom	Aaron = Speech (Eloquence)

What's in a name? "A name," says Socrates, "is an instrument of teaching [*didaskalikon*] and of separating reality, as a shuttle is an instrument of separating the web" (*Cratylus,* 338c). This defines very well Philo's approach, as in the Cain and Abel story in which names are analytical of the soul, that is, they separate the soul into its elementary principles:

> In case these unfamiliar names [Cain and Abel] may cause perplexity to many, I will attempt to give as clear an account as I can of their underlying philosophical thought [*tēn emphainomenēn philosophian*]. It is a fact that there are two opposite and contending views of life, one which ascribes all things to the mind as our master, whether we are using our reason or our senses, in motion or at rest, the other which follows God, whose handiwork it believes itself to be. The first of these views is figured [*ektupōsis*] by Cain, who is called Possession [*ktēsis*], because he thinks he possesses all things, the other by Abel, whose name means [*ērmeneuetai*] "one who refers all things to God." Now both these views or conceptions [*doxas*] lie in the womb of the single soul. ("On the Birth of Abel," 1.7–3.2)

The "underlying philosophical thought," which elsewhere goes by the name of *huponoia*, ought not to be thought of as a latent content or deep semantic structure but as an expression of the text's openness or accessibility to various contexts and schemes of thought, in this case Hellenistic moral and psychological theory. The notion implied here is that meaning means belonging to a whole, and that multiple meanings derive from a text's ability to occupy many contexts or join many patterns. A Bloomfieldian would want to say that the hermeneutical circle is internal to the text itself, whose parts and wholes are mutually determining to the exclusion of other readings—whence we get our distinction between the intrinsic meaning of the object and its subjective significance; but for Philo the text is not sealed off in this way from other situations and contexts of discourse. It is not a fixed object identical only with itself but can be transferred across many textual and intellectual boundaries and fitted into many coincidences. So in "On the Birth of Abel" the Cain and Abel story is coherent not only with itself but also, as the names indicate, with a moral narrative about the soul's internal conflict and about how self-love destroys the love of God. It is also, Philo points out, coincident with other biblical narratives, like the stories of Jacob (practical wisdom) and Esau (folly) or of the two wives mentioned in Deut. 22:15–27, which Philo glosses with an elaborate debate, running to several pages, between Pleasure and Virtue (*aretē*)—an allegorical construction of Philo's own making that includes a wonderful Rabelaisian catalog of epithets that Virtue attaches to all pleasure seekers:

> Know then, my friend [says Virtue], that if you become a pleasure-lover [*philodonos*] you will be all these things:

unscrupulous	without city	braggart
impudent	seditious	conceited
cross-tempered	disorderly	stubborn
unsociable	impious	mean
intractable	unholy	envious
lawless	wavering	censorious
troublesome	unstable	quarrelsome
passionate	excommunicate	slanderous
headstrong	profane	vainglorious
coarse	accursed	deceitful

And so on, through 144 predicates, concluding with "a mass of misery and misfortune without relief" (32.1–33).

The story is accessible to other contexts as well. In "The Worse Is Wont to Attack the Better," the opposition between Cain and Abel is a version of the quarrel between rhetoric and philosophy, or, more exactly, between rhetoric and a species of impractical wisdom that is helpless against sophistry. Cain is your basic streetwise urban wrangler who has nothing to say but speaks only to win, snaring his adversaries with colorful and intricate language, whereas Abel is the tongue-tied contemplative filled with wisdom but a solitary shepherd unpracticed in speech—rather like Moses without Aaron, who is a figure of philosophical eloquence, in contrast to Cain-like Joseph, a figure of the pure pragmatist, whose coat of many colors shows that "he is the promulgator of a doctrine full of mazes and hard to disentangle. He is one who moulds his theories with an eye to statecraft rather than to truth" (6.11–7.1). Moses and Aaron represent the ideal of theory and practice that Abel falls short of—"It would have been well . . . for Abel to have exercised caution, and to have stayed at home taking no notice of the challenge to the contest in wrangling" (45.1–4). Indeed, the commentary contains defense of a philosophical rhetoric and a theory of speech as *hermēneia*, that is, not as exoteric expression but as esoteric reflection that sheds light on the inventory of the mind: "For just as things laid up in darkness are hidden, until a light shine on them and show them, in the same way conceptions [*enthumēmata*] are stored in the understanding [*dianoia*], a place that is out of sight, until the voice illumine them like a light and uncover them all" (127.8–128.2). On this view, the interpretation of the text would be not an exegesis of what the text contains but an event in which the text throws its light on the mind of the interpreter and brings what is known into the open. We can come back to this point in a moment.

"The Posterity and Exile of Cain" is essentially a commentary on the names in the genealogy of Cain's descendants (Gen. 4:17–24), where each name is a conceptual extension of Cain's—a fact that helps to resolve a problem about those names that also turn up in the genealogy of Seth's descendants (Gen. 5:6–34):

> Now since Cain is said to have begotten Enoch, and there is afterwards a descendent of Seth with the name of Enoch (Gen. iv.17, v.18), we must consider whether they were two different persons or the same person. While we are engaged with these, let us investigate also the difference between others who have the same name. Like Enoch, Methuselah and Lamech appear as descendents of Cain, and descendents no less of Seth (Gen. iv.18, v.21, 25). It is important . . . that we should know that each of the names mentioned has a meaning that can be taken in two ways [*tōn lechthentōn ekaston onomatōn ermēneuthen diploun estin*]. "Enoch," as I have already said, means [*ermēneuetai*] "thy gift," "Methuselah," "a sending forth of death," and "Lamech," "humiliation." Take the first. Thy gift is, on some people's lips, an address to the mind within us; on the lips of the better kind of men it is addressed to the universal Mind. Those who assert that everything that is involved in thought or perception or speech is a free gift of their own soul, seeing that they introduce an impious and atheistic opinion, must be assigned to the race of Cain, who, while incapable even of ruling himself, made bold to say that he had full possession of all other things as well. But those who do not claim as their own all that is fair in creation, but acknowledge all as due to the gift of God, being men of real nobility, sprung not from a long line of rich ancestors but from lovers of virtue, must remain enrolled under Seth as the head of their race (41.1–42.11).

Similarly, as Cain is a figure of rhetoric and sophistry (a progenitor, in fact, of Protagoras [35.3–4]), so his descendant Jubal becomes a figure of indeterminacy, since his name "means 'inclining now this way now that,' and . . . is a figure for the uttered word. . . . It is a most appropriate name for the utterance of a mind that alters the make of things, for its way is to halt between two courses, swaying up and down as if on a pair of scales, or like a boat at sea, struck by huge waves and rolling towards either side. For the foolish man has never learned to say anything sure or well-grounded" (100.2–10). Interestingly, the verse "This Jubal is a father who invented psaltery and harp" (Gen. 4:21) becomes the occasion for a brief essay on the relation of music and rhetoric or the adaptation of expression to the audience, for "just as instruments are tuned to vary in accordance with the infinite number of combinations of the music which they have to give forth, so speech proves itself an harmonious interpreter of the matters dealt with and admits of endless variations. For who would talk in the same way to parents and children . . .? Who would speak in the same way to brothers, cousins, near relatives . . . and to those only distantly connected with him? . . . What need to make a list of the innumerable sorts of persons, in our conversation with whom our talk varies, taking one shape at one time, another at another?" (108.4–110.11).

In texts without characters, like the account of creation in Genesis, Philo fastens on the names of numbers. His purpose in his commentary "On the Creation" is to show that God's creation of the world is systematic (in fact Philo regularly figures the cosmos as a city and God as a geometrician and architect [for example, 19.1–22.7]): everything proceeds according to a process of deductive reasoning; nothing happens without a reason, that is, there is nothing random in the universe, nothing uninterpretable or lacking point, whence the number of days required for creation can be taken as key to the coherence of the whole:

> Order involves number, and among numbers by the laws of nature the most suitable to productivity is 6, for if we start with 1 it is the first perfect number, being equal to the product of its factors (i.e., $1 \times 2 \times 3$), as well as made up of the sum of them (i.e., $1 + 2 + 3$), its half being 3, its third part 1, its sixth part 1. We may say that it is in its nature both male and female, and is a result of the distinctive power of either. For among things that are it is the odd that is male, and the even female. Now of odd numbers 3 is the starting-point, and of even numbers 2, and the product of these two is 6. For it was requisite that the world, being most perfect of all things that have come into existence, should be constituted in accordance with a perfect number, namely six; and, inasmuch as it was to have in itself beings that sprang from a coupling together, should receive the impress of a mixed number, namely the first in which odd and even were combined, one that should contain the essential principle both of the male that sows and of the female that receives the seed. (13.5–14.7)

"On the Creation" contains extensive analyses of the numbers four and seven—in fact, Philo's commentary on the number seven covers some fifteen pages in the Loeb volume ("I doubt," Philo says, "whether anyone could adequately celebrate the properties of the number 7, for they are beyond all words" [89.4–6]). Given Philo's impressive mastery of numerology, it is not surprising that he seldom lets a number pass unremarked—as if allegory were something like a hermeneutics of recognition, where interpretation is called into play not just by what is scandalous or offensive to reason but, on the contrary, by those instances in which a text coincides with what the interpreter already knows or holds to be true.[22] The understanding of a text is, in this sense, a species of recognition; that is, we ought to think of the text not as a self-contained object that requires to be unpacked but as something that sheds its light on the mind of the interpreter, where the mind is a vast inventory of remembrance, a "vast storehouse [that] has ample room for the conceptions of all substances and all circumstances" ("The Worse Attacks the Better," 68.8–9).

Philo's approach to names, numbers, and other particles and details of the text like flaming swords and burning bushes suggests that what motivates interpretation is not nostalgia for origins but an abhorrence of randomness and contingency. This is a motivation that one encounters frequently in antiquity—in Porphyry's famous commentary on the Cave of the Nymphs in the *Odyssey*, the rejection of contingency is axiomatic: "Since the cosmos did not come into existence in vain or randomly, but exists as a result of the thoughtfulness and intention of god and of noetic nature, the olive, a symbol of god's thoughtfulness, grows next to the image of the world, which is the cave."[23] A random object in the world is as unthinkable as a number that has no place in arithmetic, and this principle of sufficient reason or plenitude applies to names and to whole narratives as well.

Philo holds to this principle by frankly embellishing the biblical narratives, as when he retells the lives of the patriarchs and of Moses, "interweaving," as he puts it, what he reads in the Scriptures themselves with what he has learned otherwise, raising both text and teaching to higher levels of systematic coherence ("Life of Moses," 1.4.6). In effect, Philo rewrites the biblical stories as ethical narratives in the Aristotelian mode, where each patriarch is an ethical type or type of human soul: Abraham is the man who achieves *aretē* through teaching; Isaac comes by this sort of thing naturally, whereas Jacob achieves it painstakingly through practice ("On Abraham," 52.4–7).[24] Interestingly, in his life of Joseph, Philo characterizes Joseph differently than he figures him in his Cain and Abel commentaries. Here he is the Aristotelian statesman rather than the Platonic Gorgias. Moses, meanwhile, is the complete man of wisdom—king, lawgiver, priest, and prophet. The "Life of Moses" is a two-part narrative, the second of which gives us the theory of these types (law giver, and so on), but perhaps more important is the first part in which Philo concentrates on the education of Moses, which turns out to be a sort of *translatio studii*, or transference, of the prevailing empires of learning to Moses and thus to the Jews. The upshot of this transference is a sort of prophetic appropriation of human wisdom.

A foundling at pharaoh's court, Moses "received as his right the nurture and service of a prince," with the result that "teachers at once arrived from different parts, some unbidden from the neighboring countries and provinces of Egypt, others summoned from Greece under promise of high reward [a nice touch, that: Philo rather regularly represents the Greeks as Sophists]. But in a short time he advanced beyond their capacities; his gifted nature forestalled their instruction, so that he seemed a case of recollection rather than of learning, and indeed he himself devised and propounded problems that they could not easily solve. For great natures [*megalai phūseis*] carve out much that is new in the way of knowledge" (1.21.1–22.1). Not to put too fine a point on it, "when he had mastered the lore of both nations [Egypt and Greece: or, in other words, the world]," Moses reduced it to systematic order, weeding out every falsehood, resolving every internal disagreement, in short producing something very like a coherent conceptual scheme where before there had been only a history of heterogeneous opinion. At the same time, he was "zealous for the discipline and culture of his kinsmen and ancestors" (1.32.6–7) and soon became the leader of the Jewish exiles. Forced to flee pharaoh's court, he withdrew to Arabia, where, Abel-like, he pursued the life of a philosopher-shepherd. Even while tending his sheep, Philo says, "[Moses] was ever opening the scroll of philosophic doctrines, digest[ing] them inwardly with quick understanding, commit[ting] them to memory never to be forgotten, and straightaway [bringing] his personal conduct . . . into conformity with them; for he desired truth rather than seeming, because the one mark he set before him was nature's right reason [*ton orthon tēs phūseōs logon*]" (1.48.5–12). When Moses encounters the burning bush, it is as if the whole of human wisdom were suddenly subsumed into a higher order where philosophy and the prophetic experience of God are joined.

Philo takes recourse to this model in almost all of his writings: traditional learning, the wisdom of the schools, whatever comes down to us from the past or more generally goes by the name of lore, must always be appropriated and then transcended by the reflection, insight, and prophetic experience of the individual soul. In "On the Birth of Abel," Philo says that "we must not indeed reject any learning that has grown gray through time, nay, we should make it our aim to read the writings of the sages and listen to proverbs and old-world stories from the lips of those who know antiquity, and ever seek for knowledge about the men and deeds of old. For truly it is sweet to leave nothing unknown. Yet when God causes the young shoots of self-inspired wisdom [*autodidaktou sophias*] within the soul, the knowledge that comes from teaching must be abolished and swept off" (79.4–15). In many places Philo distinguishes between Abraham's two wives, where Hagar is school-knowledge, or the Encyclia, and Sarah is philosophy—except that philosophy no longer consists in doctrines or teachings but is, rather, a virtue, or *aretē*, of the soul. What this means is spelled out quite clearly in a commentary "On the Migration of Abraham," which is about the soul's withdrawal from common knowledge into self-contemplation. Abraham's migration from Chaldea to Haran is essentially a movement from what everyone knows (in this case astrology, the specialty of the Chaldeans) to the world of immediate experience, or perhaps natural philosophy—in any case, Haran is the "place of sense-perception"—but philosophy as a condition of wisdom occurs only in the soul's study of its own *nous,* or of mind itself:

> Come down therefore from heaven [i.e., abandon astrology], and, when you have come down, do not begin in turn to pass in review earth and sea and rivers, and plants and animals in their various kinds; but explore yourselves only and your own nature, and make your abode with yourselves and not elsewhere: for by observing the conditions prevailing in your own individual household, the element that is master in it, and that which is in subjection, the living and the lifeless element, the rational and the irrational [*to logikon, to alogon*] the immortal and the mortal, the better and the worse, you will gain forthwith a sure knowledge of God [*euthus epistēmēn theou*] and of His works. Your reason will show you that, as there is mind [*nous*] in you, so is there in the universe, and that as your mind has taken upon itself sovereign control of all that is in you, and brought every part into subjection to itself, so too He, that is endued with lordship over all, guides and controls the universe by the law and right of an absolute sway. (185.1–186.7)

Not surprisingly, sleep provides a sort of equivalence of this philosophic state: "In deep sleep," Philo says, "the mind [*nous*] quits its place, and, withdrawing from the perceptions and all other bodily functions, begins to hold converse with itself, fixing its gaze on truth as on a mirror, and, having purged away as defilements all the impressions made upon it by the mental pictures presented by the senses, it is filled with Divine frenzy [*enthousia*] and discerns in dreams absolutely true prophecies concerning things to come" (190.4–10).

This idea of the mind's conversion toward itself accounts for a prominent feature of certain of Philo's commentaries, namely, that he addresses them to his own mind or soul, as though commentary were a species of contemplation that aims (ultimately) at prophetic experience. This comes out dramatically in Philo's commentary on Gen. 3:24: "And he cast forth Adam and set [him] over against the Garden of Pleasure [and posted] the Cherubim and sword of flame which turns every way, to guard the way of the Tree of Life" ("On the Cherubim," 1.1–3). Philo offers three interpretations of this figure of the angels and the flaming sword. The first two are cosmological (the angels represent the revolution of the spheres and also the hemispheres above and beneath the earth). "But there is," he says, "a higher thought [*spoudaioterou logou*] than these. It comes from a voice in my own soul [*para psuchēs emēs eiōthuias*], which oftentimes is god-possessed and divines where it does not know. This thought I will record in words if I can. The voice told me that while God is indeed one, His highest and chiefest powers are two, even goodness and sovereignty. . . . And in the midst between them there is a third which unites them, Reason, for it is through reason that God is both ruler and good. Of these two potencies sovereignty and goodness the Cherubim are symbols, as the fiery sword is the symbol of reason" (27.1–28.5). Here again the movement is from the contemplation of the cosmos to the contemplation of the soul, or reason's contemplation of itself, which is mirrored in Philo's self-apostrophe, in which the teaching of the text finds application in his own life: "O then, my mind [*hō dianoia*], admit the image unalloyed of the two Cherubim, that having learnt its clear lesson of the sovereignty and beneficence of the Cause, thou may reap the fruits of a happy lot. For straightaway thou shalt understand how these unmixed potencies are mingled and united. . . . Thus thou may gain the virtues begotten of these potencies, a cheerful courage and a reverent awe towards God. When things are well with thee, the majesty of the sovereign king will keep thee from high thoughts. When thou suffer what thou would not, thou wilt not despair of betterment, remembering the loving-kindness of the great and bountiful God" (29.1–5).

One is tempted to say that "On the Cherubim" is the most mystical of Philo's commentaries, and in a sense this is certainly the case. Philo draws freely from the vocabulary of the mystery traditions in which the understanding of a text presupposes initiation into a special community and a special wisdom ("For this is a divine mystery and its lesson is for the initiated who are worthy to receive the holiest secret" [42.3–5]). But because there are many communities (Chaldeans, Greeks, Egyptians, Jews), there are many sorts of wisdom, so that understanding is inevitably richly layered, or many-sided and open-ended in the manner of Philo's understanding of the Cherubim and the flaming sword. In this case there can be no easy or gross distinction between the exoteric and the esoteric, the literal-minded and the wise, exegesis and eisegesis—nor, in the end, any difference between prophecy and understanding.[25] Instead, it appears that for Philo understanding has many gradations and proceeds infinitely, as if through increasingly narrow hermeneutical circles, in the direction of an illumination that leaves even the teachings of the wise in the shadows and brings one face-to-face with reason itself. The hermeneutical point would be that the circularity of understanding is ontological rather than purely formal.[26] That is, understanding starts out from the condition of belonging to what is already understood. In Philo's language, this means that understanding is a form of recognition, of being turned toward and received into what before had been hidden or strange. Understanding is thus a form of participation within the mysteries, not a grasping of them from some external standpoint. "I myself," Philo says, "was initiated under Moses the God-beloved into his greater mysteries [ta megala mustēria], yet when I saw the prophet Jeremiah and knew him to be not only himself enlightened, but a worthy minister of the holy secrets, I was not slow to become his disciple" (49.1–6). Or, in other words, it was Philo's prior understanding of Moses that enabled him to recognize Jeremiah as belonging to the same prophetic circle—and, more important, to recognize himself as belonging to Jeremiah, not (interestingly) as an exegete who is in some sense external to Jeremiah's text, outside the circle, but as a disciple who has been taken up or appropriated by prophetic teaching. Philo in this respect is a part of what he understands.

Indeed, from the standpoint of a disengaged, solitary ego, allegorical interpretation is probably incomprehensible. And insofar as it presupposes belonging and participation, interpretation is not something that such an ego can intelligibly perform. It can hardly be an accident that allegory did not survive the onset of modernity, with its definition of the self as a subject external to everything but itself. The postmodern question is, perhaps, Which is more implausible, allegory or the theory of the disengaged punctual ego? But for our present purposes it is enough to see that Philo's practice presupposes a hermeneutical situation in which text and interpreter are not sealed off from each other but are caught up in a complicated mutual appropriation. On the one side the Mosaic text has been made intelligible in terms of the concepts and beliefs of Hellenistic teaching and of Alexandrian philosophy and its prevailing theory of wisdom; on the other, the Alexandrian Jewish community has appropriated its cultural environment and reinscribed its teachings with a new prophetic authority—rewritten Hellenism, so to speak, in the name of God and Moses.

But appropriation here seems almost too technical a concept. Philo's hermeneutics presupposes a relationship of meditative intimacy with the text. It is all very well to talk of the conflict and interplay of conceptual schemes, but one ought not to let this language obscure the singularity of Philo's practice, which is closer to being a way of life than a method of resolving the conflict of interpretations. Perhaps we should imagine that the goal of Philo's hermeneutics is not the production of interpretations but just the living of the contemplative life to its proper end, call it "abiding in wisdom." Then the lesson we might learn from Philo is that, whatever else it may be, hermeneutics is never less than this; or anyhow that's the moral of the story so far.

The Hermeneutics
of Midrash

5

The words of Torah are fruitful and multiply.
—Talmud, Hagigah, 3b

In this chapter I want to examine in some detail a midrashic text that, from a hermeneutical standpoint, seems to articulate most
fully the ancient rabbinical conception of what it means to interpret the
Scriptures. In spite of its reputation, midrash is not just a sort of edifying
companion to the Bible that goes off by itself; it is a genuinely hermeneutical
practice in the sense that its purpose is to elucidate and understand scriptural text as such.[1] But what counts as understanding in this case? In Philo
we saw that understanding and interpretation are internal to the practice of
wisdom. How does it stand with midrash?

In general *midrash* is simply the ancient Hebrew word for interpretation.
It is the word for the relationship of Judaism to its sacred texts (Torah), and
one could say that it covers the relationship of one sacred text to another
as well. Midrash is a rabbinical concept or practice, but it is certainly as old
as writing itself. The word derives from *darash,* meaning "to study," "to
search," "to investigate," "to go in quest of." Midrash is preoccupied with
wisdom, where wisdom is not just what is contained in the head. More

loosely, midrash can be taken to mean "account," in the sense of giving an account of what is written. "Giving an account" could mean simply "telling" but also "accounting for," in which case the task is to address whatever becomes an issue when the Torah is studied or recited or when the understanding of Torah is called for. Insofar as there is never, in Jewish tradition, a situation in human life in which such understanding is not called for, midrash can be said to have a great range of application.

"This book of the law must ever be on your lips; you must keep it in mind day and night so that you may diligently observe all that is written in it" (Josh. 1:8 [New English Bible]). This text summarizes very well the midrashic incentive. At all events, my argument would be that we ought to think of midrash as a form of life (in Wittgenstein's sense) rather than simply as a form of exegesis (in the technical sense); midrash is concerned with practice and action as well as with (what we think of as) the form and meaning of texts. There is a venerable distinction between midrash *halakhah* and midrash *aggadah,* that is, between an account given of a legal text and an account of every other sort of text—narratives (on rare occasions), verses, words, letters of the alphabet, as well as textual or diacritical embellishments such as the *tagin* and *te-amim* that adorn words and letters. It is not obvious that this distinction covers actual practice, however, because, as suggested in chapter 3, the Torah is everywhere a binding text. That is, midrash is concerned to tell about the force of the text as well as to address its problems of form and meaning. The sense of Torah is the sense in which it applies to the life and conduct of those who live under its power, and this principle of application applies to homiletic aggadah as well as to the explicitly legal constructions of *halakhah.* Indeed, this was the upshot of Joseph Heinemann's study of *aggadah:* "While the rabbinic creators of the Aggadah looked back into Scripture to uncover the full latent meaning of the Bible and its wording, at the same time they looked forward into the present and the future. They sought to give direction to their own generation, to resolve their religious problems, to answer their theological questions, and to guide them out of their spiritual complexities. . . . The aggadists do not mean so much to clarify difficult passages in the biblical texts as to take a stand on the burning questions of the day, to guide the people and to strengthen their faith."[2] And as we shall see, this emphasis on application entails the political meaning of midrash as well as its spiritual purpose.

So what matters in midrash is not only what lies behind the text in the form of an originating intention but what is in front of the text where the text is put into play. The text is always contemporary with its readers or listeners, that is, always oriented toward the time and circumstances of the interpreter. It lays open paths to the future. "Let the Torah never be for you an antiquated decree, but rather like a decree freshly issued, no more than two or three days old. . . . [Indeed,] Ben Azzai said: not even as old as a decree issued two or three days ago, but as a decree issued this very day."[3] Moreover, this orientation toward the present and future helps at least in part to explain the legendary extravagance of midrash, where typically a single verse or word or letter will be given not a single, settled, official construction but a series of often conflicting and disputed expositions. This hermeneutical openness to the conflict of interpretation cannot be accommodated within modernist doctrines of romantic hermeneutics or Husserlian concepts of the primacy of intentional experience where understanding a text means understanding its author at least as well as she understood herself. Interpretation on the Husserlian view means reconstruction of intentional experience as this is reflected in the formal properties and historical background of the text. Here interpretation is a working backward rather than a taking forward. Yet we know that it is never enough to construe texts just in this way—as historical documents and formal objects. A legal text, to take the obvious example, cannot simply be construed in relation to itself but must be understood in relation to the situations in which it is applied. These situations always differ in particular ways from the one in which the text was originally handed down. Each situation will command its own sense of how the text has to be taken, which is why a legal text has to be open and loosely textured, not indeterminate but not a calculus of rules, either. Midrash applies roughly this same textual principle to the Scriptures and so presupposes that interpretation cannot mean simply giving uniform representations of a text that is sealed off from the heterogeneity of human situations. Midrash understands that if a text is to have any force, it must remain open to more than the context of its composition.

Something like this idea underwrites the rabbinical gloss on 1 Kings 4:32 (1 Kings 5:12 in the Hebrew Bible), "And he spoke three thousand proverbs, and his songs were a thousand and five": "This teaches," the Talmud says, "that Solomon uttered three thousand proverbs for every single word of the Torah and one thousand and five reasons for every single word of the Scribes."[4] This reading shows how the rabbis conceived the spirit of midrash. To get into this spirit we need to understand that midrashic interpretation is not just something going on between a reader and a text with a view toward intellectual agreement between them. We need to get out from under the model of methodical solipsism that pictures a solitary reader exercising strategic power over a text. Certainly the ancient midrashists are not pictured this way. The midrashic collections that come down to us (say, from the fifth through the tenth centuries C.E.) figure interpretation as something social and dialogical. Indeed, on this social point the Talmud is very clear: "Make yourselves into groups [*kittoth*] to study the Torah, since the knowledge of the Torah can be acquired only in association with others" (Berekoth, 63b).[5] The idea is that Torah speaks to a public, communal situation, not to the solitary, single-minded, private reader. Under these conditions—which are very different from those produced by the printing press and which led Luther to restructure hermeneutics around the individual reading subject—interpretation is bound to be many-sided and open-ended, as in the following example, which concerns Eccl. 12:11: *"The words of the wise are as goads, and as nails well fastened (literally, 'planted') are those that are composed in collections; they are given from one shepherd."*

> Once R. Johanan b. Beroka and R. Eleazar Ḥisma went to welcome R. Joshua at Peḳi'im, and he asked them: "What new thing has been said in college [the beit midrash, or house of study] to-day?" They replied: "We are your disciples and it is your water that we drink" [i.e., we follow your interpretations]. Said he to them: "Nevertheless one cannot imagine a college where something new has not been said. Whose Sabbath was it?" "The Sabbath of R. Eleazar son of 'Azariah," they replied. "And on what topic was the exposition to-day?" They told him: "On the section, '*Assemble.*'" [Deut. 21:12]. . . . He also opened a discourse on the text, *"The words of the wise are as goads."* Why were the words of the Torah likened to a goad? To tell you that as a goad directs the cow along the furrows, in order to bring life to the world, so the words of the Torah direct the heart of those who study them away from the paths of death and long the paths of life. Should you assume that as the goad is shifted about so the words of the Torah can be shifted about, Scripture states: *"And as nails well fastened."* Should you assume that as a nail contracts but does not expand, Scripture states, *"fastened (lit. 'planted')"*; to signify that as a plant is fruitful and increases, so the words of the Torah bear fruit and multiply. *"Those that are composed in collections (ba'ale asufoth)." "Ba'ale asufoth"* applies to the scholars, who sit in groups and study the Torah, some of them declaring a thing unclean, others declaring it clean; some pronouncing a thing to be forbidden, others pronouncing it to be permitted; some disqualifying an object, others declaring it fit. Lest a man should say, Since some scholars declare a thing unclean and others declare it clean; some pronounce a thing to be forbidden, others pro-

nouncing it to be permitted; some disqualify an object while others uphold its fitness, how can I study Torah in such circumstances? Scripture states, *"They are given from one shepherd"*: One God has given them, one leader (Moses) has uttered them at the command of the Lord of all creation, blessed be He; as it says, *And God spoke all these words* (Ex. XX, I). Do you then on your part make your ear like a grain-receiver and acquire a heart that can understand the words of the scholars who declare a thing unclean as well as of those who declare it clean; the words of those who declare a thing forbidden as well as those who declare it permitted; the words of those who disqualify an object as well as those who uphold its fitness.[6]

There is considerably more to this text, as we shall see, but we might rest here a moment to place it in hermeneutical context.[7] What we have here is a midrash on the conflict (and not just the plurality) of midrashes. The text is a narrative report of a Sabbath performance by Rabbi Eleazar son of 'Azariah, a master of the beit midrash (the house of study where the rabbis and their students gather to expound and dispute concerning the Torah), and it is important to notice that the report is given by disciples of Rabbi Joshua, who was not present on this particular Sabbath. The allusion here is to a historic controversy that resulted in a revolt of a number of rabbis against the Patriarch, Rabban Gamaliel II (d. 110 c.e.), who had tried to bring halakhic interpretation under a central administrative authority.[8] The beit midrash is not to be imagined as a preserve of serene logic, where a liberal pluralism neutralizes the force of disagreement; it is a place where power flows in multiple directions and the struggle for control between the Patriarch and the rabbis, as well as among schools and factions (and not infrequently between masters and disciples), is fierce and sometimes laced with insult.[9] Significantly, the focus of Rabbi Eleazar's midrash is on an outsider or newcomer who finds this conflicted environment bewildering and intolerable: "How can I study the Torah in such circumstances?" How indeed? What is it to do such a thing? And what is the point of Rabbi Eleazar's reply, which counsels the study not just of the scriptural texts but of their competing interpretations as well? To be able to cope with these questions, we need to read further. The midrash continues as follows:

Another exposition of the text, *"The words of the wise are as goads."* R. Tanḥuma b. Abba said: As the goad directs the cow how to plough in the proper furrow, so do the words of the wise direct a man in the ways of the Holy One, blessed be He. The Mishnah, observed R. Tanḥuma, calls the goad *mardea'*, while the Scripture calls it *darban* and

malmad, as may be inferred from the text, *With an ox-goad*—bemal-
mad (Judg. II, 31), and also from, *To set the goads*—haddarban (I Sam.
XIII, 21). R. Nathan asked: Why was it called *"mardea' "*? Because it
teaches the cow knowledge (*moreh dea'*). Why was it called by the
name of *darban*? Because it causes understanding to take up its abode
(*dar binah*) in the cow. And why was it called *malmad*? Because it
instructs (*melammed*) the cow how to plough in the proper furrow. It
is so with the words of the wise. They implant understanding in the
minds of men, they teach them knowledge and instruct them in the
ways of the Holy One, blessed be He. *"And as nails* (masmerim) *well
fastened* (netu'im)." They are implanted (*netu'im*) in man when he ob-
serves them (*meshammerem*). Why were they compared to a planting?
Because in the same way that the roots of a tree penetrate in all directions, so the words of the wise enter and penetrate into the whole body.

This midrash gives, one might say, the "theory" of midrash—gives its "formal operations" (shows us how it works). As the rabbis themselves put it,
midrash works by "linking up words of Torah with one another" (*Midrash
Rabbah*, Hazita [Song of Songs], 1.10.2). Linking, however, means several
things, beginning with the common philological practice of tracking the
words of the Scriptures, counting them, noting how each one turns up—
how often, in what contexts, and with what internal differences. Scripture
is one, but it is also a nonlinear text whose letters and words can be discovered in heterogeneous combinations. Linking also means using one text (a
letter, a word, a phrase, a verse, a piece of narrative, in principle a whole
book like the Song of Songs) to elucidate another. Indeed, the rabbis treated
the Scriptures as a self-interpreting text, on the (again) ordinary philological
principle that what is plain (that is, understood) in one place can be used to
clarify what is obscure or in question in another. "Words of Torah need
each other. What one passage locks up, the other discloses" (*Midrash Rabbah*, Bemidbar, 19, 7). In most cases this means using later texts to comment
on earlier ones. In principle, one needs nothing but Scripture to interpret
Scripture, as both Augustine and Luther would later argue (asserting, however, as Christians do, that one needs only the New Testament to interpret
the Old). But the rabbis also read the Scriptures as being already hermeneutical, that is, as works of interpretation as well as Scripture: the prophetic books and wisdom writings, for example, are characterized as texts
composed specifically for the elucidation of the first five books of Moses.
The rabbis seem not to have distinguished as we do between literary and
hermeneutical categories of writing (did not, as we try to do, filter out the
hermeneutical in order to keep literature pure). A midrash on the Song of

Songs says of Solomon that "he pondered the words of the Torah and investigated the words of the Torah. He made handles to the Torah"—where "handles" means parables and sayings, basic forms of rabbinical exegesis (ways of coming to grips with Torah). "So till Solomon arose," the midrash says, "no one was able to understand properly the words of the Torah, but as soon as Solomon arose all began to comprehend the Torah" (1.1.8). What this comes down to, however, is the rabbinical version of the principle of the hermeneutical circle: "linking up the words of the Pentateuch with those of the prophets and the prophets with the Writings" simply means making sense of the whole by construing relations among the parts, if not exactly vice versa (1.10.2). Exactly what the whole amounts to, however, is a question the rabbis seem deliberately to leave open. Indeed, what seems to distinguish a scribal from a print culture is how narrow the analytical distance between text and exegete remains when the text exists in memory instead of in a small portable book. We probably do not have a very good idea of what the rabbinical textual imagination looks like. Certainly it is far from clear what sort of concept of parts-and-whole a reader of scrolls (versus codices, not to say printed books) might have. In any event, midrashic interpretation is mediated by painstaking attention to the smallest details of the text and to the intricacies of their combination; taking a view of the whole—using it as a hermeneutic standpoint—just doesn't seem to be part of midrashic practice.[10] What counts as a context in midrash? There is no firm or ready answer. What we would call the "sense of the whole" seems to be highly fluid and variable, and it is this fluidity—this lack of fixed views as to where the hermeneutical circle should be drawn—that makes multiple, open-ended interpretation possible.

In the long midrashic text from which I have been quoting, for example, "linking up words of Torah with one another" also means vigorous punning (*mardea': moreh dea'*), that is, picking up on the way the words of the Scriptures are filled with echoes of other words (a practice underwritten by the fact that a consonantial text like the Hebrew Bible can be sounded or vocalized in multiple ways). Openness to the pun allows words of the text to be taken now one way, now another, so that the working out of a hermeneutical question ("Why are the words of the wise as goads?") can be carried on at considerable length, or in several directions, and to no determinate end. This open-endedness suggests that the rabbis did not think of interpretation as problem solving, settling things once and for all, or working toward a final agreement as to how the text is to be taken. Agreement or universal consensus does not appear to be the goal of argument (as it is for John Stuart Mill, for example). Midrash is more reflective than de-

The Hermeneutics of Midrash   111

monstrative, divergent rather than convergent. Indeed, the text is treated as something moving rather than fixed, something that is always a step ahead of the interpreter, always opening onto new ground, and ("lest you assume" that you finally have a handle on it) always calling for interpretation to be begun anew. And so, characteristically, our midrash continues:

> Another interpretation of the text, *"The words of the wise are like goads* (kedarbanoth)." R. Berekiah the priest explains the metaphor to mean *"kaddur shel banoth,"* "like a little children's ball," which they pick up and throw about, this way and that. It is the same with the words of the wise: One Sage gives his view and another gives his. Lest it be imagined that since one gives one opinion and another gives another their words merely fly about in the air, Scripture states, *"And as nails well fastened* (netu'im: planted)." It does not say, "As nails well fixed (kebu'im)" but *"As nails well fastened* (netu'im)." Why? Because Scripture compares the Sages' words to nails, and a nail that has a head is easy to draw out. Accordingly, it says, *"As nails* netu'im," for the roots of a tree that are implanted *(netu'im)* are hard to pull out. Why were their words compared to a nail? Because an iron nail that has a head, although hard, can be easily pulled out, while the roots of a tree that are implanted, even though they are hard to pull out, have not the same strength as the iron has. For this reason it says, *"And as* nails *well* planted," thus giving the words of the Torah the strength of iron and the resistance of the well-planted roots of a tree.

The midrash continues for several more pages, turning the words of the text (and words that sound like words of the text) this way and that, going backward and forward over the text again and again, each time picking up on some element or inflection not sounded before—all according to no discernible plot that would bring the whole to a close. Midrashic interpretations stop but do not end.

But all this means is that midrash is not linear exposition—not a species of monological reasoning but exegesis that presupposes or starts out from alternative readings and anticipates and, indeed, encourages or provokes them in turn. The text from which I have been quoting gives us an excellent insight into the dialogical nature of midrash. Midrash is not the work of the isolated reader but an endless give-and-take between the text and its exegetes and above all among the rabbis who gather together to expound and dispute. Thus the pun in the text above which turns a goad into a ball that children play with opens the way to the characterization of midrash as multiple, heterogeneous, and conflicting. The version of this midrash preserved in the *Pesikta Rabbati* puts it this way: "so words fly back and forth when the wise come into a house of study and discuss Torah, one stating his view, and another stating his view, still another stating another view, and another stating a different view" (Piska 3.2).

The main question, of course, is: How is this stratified, open-ended form of contested interpretation to be understood?

Customarily we understand the conflict of interpretation as a defect of interpretation itself, part of the logical weakness of hermeneutics. It is what prompts the desire to get beyond interpretation to the meaning itself, settling things once and for all. This appears to be the desire of the bewildered fellow who asks: "How can I study Torah in such circumstances?" How can one know for sure what the Torah says when what it says is constantly in the air, endlessly open to dispute (open, indeed, to radical and not often friendly disagreement)? My thought is that this very question implies a transcendental outlook that has, in Western culture, never been able to accept the finite, situated, dialogical, indeed political character of human understanding and that even now finds midrash to be irrational and wild. Our ideal is an uncontested grasp of the text. We want to say: All interpretation aside, what does the text really mean? The transcendental desire is unsatisfiable with respect to the historicality and social heterogeneity of understanding. It is a desire that seems always to end in a contempt for interpretation and a suspicion concerning the whole idea of dialogue as relativistic and empty, or what analytic philosophers refer to as "just talk." One can read the history of interpretation as a history of hermeneutical conflict highlighted by repeated efforts to get beyond hermeneutics, that is, to bring the history of interpretation to an end or to regard it as a history of error from which we must emancipate ourselves before knowledge can begin. Our current desire to get beyond hermeneutics, for example, is very much a part of our Cartesian heritage (recall Descartes's contempt for controversy and his effort to seal thinking off from whatever is not itself).

What is especially interesting about our midrashic text is that its subject appears to be just this overarching and irresolvable conflict between transcendental and dialogical attitudes and the breakdown that always threatens the institution of midrash (or any institution of interpretation) as a consequence. It would not be too much to say that interpretation generally is always in crisis; this is part of what its historicality means. In the case at hand the question seems to be (very roughly) whether the beit midrash should be structured as a dogmatic system in which certain interpretations will be formally instituted while others are ruled out beforehand, or as an agonistic forum in which argument and dispute constitute exactly the medium in which interpretations are to be developed and preserved. As we have seen, our midrash is framed by a narrative that situates the midrashic conversation in a highly conflicted social environment. In this context the heterogeneous glosses on Eccl. 12:11 add up to an argument for open-ended dialogue and the need to study midrash in *all* of its multiple and contested cases. This seems directed against the dogmatic attitude implied in the line, "We are your disciples and it is your water that we drink." So even Rabbi Joshua directs his disciples' attention away from himself and his own teachings back to the house of study. The antidogmatic principle is that "the words of these and of the other Sages, all of them"—that is, all the heterogeneous and even contradictory things said about these texts—"were given by Moses the shepherd from what he received from the Unique One of the Universe" *(Pesikta Rabbati,* Piska 3.2). This is, in effect, an argument against collapsing the conflict of interpretation into a conflict of authority. There is (so the argument goes) no conflict of authority in midrash because in midrash authority is social rather than methodological and thus is holistic rather than atomic or subject-centered: the whole dialogue, that is, the institution of midrash itself—rabbinic practice—is authoritative, and what counts is conformity with this practice rather than correspondence to some external rule or theory concerning the content of interpretation as such. Here the question is: What does this practice call for or allow for? What if puns and parables and open-ended dispute are the rule rather than systematic closure or even decision by majority rule?[11] Here one's own individual commentary is forceful by being part of the ongoing dialogue rather than by connecting up with something outside of it. No interpretation can be isolated from the whole and set up on its own ground, not without (in effect) setting up a new conversation or new community—or new Torah.[12] At the basis of Rabbi Eleazar's thinking on this score is almost certainly a midrash on Deut. 14:1 ("You are the sons of the Lord your God: you shall not cut yourselves [*titgodedu*]"): i.e., "Do not split yourselves into factions (*'aguddot*) but rather be one faction, as it is said, *It is He that buildeth His upper chambers in the heaven, and hath founded His (single) vault* (aguddato) *upon the earth* (Amos 9:6)" *(Sifre on Deuteronomy,* Piska 96).[13]

To be sure, one can understand the outsider's puzzlement and reluctance to join the argument. From a transcendental standpoint, this theory of authority is paradoxical because it is seen to hang on the heteroglossia of dialogue, on speaking with many voices, rather than on the logical principle of univocity, or speaking with one mind. Instead, the idea of speaking with one mind ("it is your waters that we drink") is explicitly rejected; singlemindedness produces factionalism. The dialogical point seems (like the hermeneutical circle) logically weak, but it is hermeneutically sound, because it is hard to see how one could make any sense at all of an individual midrash, with its scrupulous and sometimes exotic attention to detail, except by situating it in the context of an ongoing discussion in which just such attention is called for—in which details of the text are endlessly disseminated as if in the absence of established contexts. Context, in other words, is social rather than logical and is therefore alterable and variable, as in the case of a conversation, where no statement is likely to make much sense when taken in isolation from the whole, even though the whole is not an internally coherent system superior to its parts but a chaotic system in perpetual transition back-and-forth between order and turbulence. In such a system parts tend to be random rather than constitutive of a settled whole. Hence the principle that the conversation itself is the true author of all that is said in it; no one participant in the conversation can claim original authorship or final authority, because what one says derives from the give-and-take of the conversation itself, not from one's own subjective intention. This principle surely guided the compilers of the midrashic texts, but it also seems basic to the midrashic tradition itself. Each rabbi's interpretation is, strictly speaking, ungrounded: it derives its meaning and authority not from its separate correspondence—at a distance—to a piece of original textual evidence but from its participation *in* the original, that is, from its place in the dialogue inaugurated on Sinai when God addressed the Torah to Moses. Midrash presupposes not ultimate ground (*Letztbegrundung*) but common ground; it presupposes belonging and participation rather than logical foundation. Midrash is not method but form of life.

This line of thought tempers somewhat the seeming indifference of midrashists to the principle of noncontradiction ("some scholars declare a thing unclean and others declare it clean"). Interpretations are not to be figured on the propositional model as (mono-)logical assertions seeking their own separate validity; rather, they are the mode of participation in dialogue with Torah itself. Midrash is not a method for resolving hermeneutical disputes (even the principle of majority rule was rejected by many rabbis as alien to the whole idea of midrash); it is the place where disputes are meant to go on, where there is always room for another interpretation or for more dialogue, where interpretation is more a condition of being than an act of consciousness. We need to shake the idea that midrash is (just) a mental process. The point is not to try to hold its multiple interpretations simultaneously in mind as if they constituted a logical system, a canon of internally consistent teachings to be held true for all time or tested against a rule or deposit of faith. On the contrary, to say that midrash is dialogical rather than systematic is to say that it is closer to the rhetorical inventory than to logical organon; it is to say that it is structured discursively according to the principle of "now one, now another," as within the open indeterminacy of the question rather than in the closure of the proposition. Indeed, if the task of midrash is to speak to concrete human situations in which something needs to be decided—situations that are themselves discursively structured ("now one thing, now another," in no predictable order, open-ended)—then midrash must always seek to nourish the conflict of interpretation, not to shut it down. Hence the danger of factionalism, or the dogmatism of schools: "We are your disciples, and it is your water that we drink" is a scholastic motto whose subtext is, "There is no more to be said." Closing down the dialogue by means of a final interpretation, a last word or final appeal to a rule of faith, would be to close interpretation off from human life. It would turn Torah into a dead letter, a museum piece, a monument to what people used to believe. If the Torah is to have any force as a text, it must always be situated in a culture of argument. One imagines that this would be true of any text.

Earlier I remarked that it is difficult to know what sort of concept of part-and-whole guides midrashic interpretation; the rabbis seemed not to have any recognizable sense of wholeness. Now we see that they imagined themselves as *part* of the whole, participating in Torah rather than operating on it at an analytic distance. A participatory point of view undermines any formal sense of wholeness. And if participation replaces foundation in this way, it follows that the words of interpretation cannot be isolated in any rigorously analytical way from the words of Torah itself. This is consistent with the fact that the rabbis do not possess (beyond a few formulas like the *Ketib-Kere'*) a technical interpretative vocabulary but apply to the text the words of the text itself, using one verse as commentary upon another. It is this dialogical principle that underlies the picture of Solomon as an interpreter as well as author of sacred writings like the Psalms. It is this principle that underlies the rabbinical claim concerning the unity of written and oral Torah, which is not so much a formal, logical, or aesthetic unity as a continuity of authority—the sort of unity entailed in speaking in another's name, which is how the rabbis regularly characterize their own discourse. Both written and oral Torah are given from one shepherd, meaning that everything (including unheard-of ideas and spontaneous puns) is spoken in the name of God and Moses and the lines of interpreters descending from them. The idea is *not* that midrash is repetition or a postal service. The word Torah, and therefore its power and authority, extends itself to include not only the original books of Moses but also the Mishnah, the Talmuds, and

Aggadot as well. In other words, the Torah is constituted as an open canon. To be sure, the letters of the original Scriptures are fixed, but they are not dead. Openness here has to be construed as the openness of what is written, that is, its applicability to the time of its interpretation, its need for actualization. What is important is that interpretation not be fixed—an idea that is reflected in the controversy (extending from at least the quarrel between the Pharisees and Sadducees to the beginnings of the midrashic collections) over whether the words of the Sages should be written down. "Of the making of books there is no end" (Eccl. 12:12). Openness in this respect means openness of the written word to the spoken (an indispensable principle in the interpretation of a consonantal text).

Perhaps now we are in a position to situate properly the question, "How can I study Torah in such circumstances?" To study Torah is clearly not to study a text independently of the interpretations through which it is handed down from the past. Study is not the activity of a private, sealed-off, monological subject. When Rabbi Eleazar tells the bewildered fellow to "make your ear like a grain receiver and acquire a heart that understands the words of the scholars who declare a thing clean as well as of those who declare it unclean," he is saying, in effect, get into the spirit of dialogue. One understands by getting into the game, not by applying techniques. Do not think of yourself as an analytical spectator situated outside the text; think of yourself as belonging to the text. Only now you must picture the text not as a formal object (so many fixed letters) but as an open canon whose boundaries are shaped and reshaped by the give-and-take of midrashic argument. This means studying not just an original text but also midrash itself, for the words of the Sages constitute Torah, make it what it is, and above all open it to the present and future. The words of the wise are not added to the text; they are the text as well, linking its words to form not an integrated, hierarchical system but an ongoing tradition, a structure of mutual belonging. The Torah emerges as what it is and comes into its own only in the dialogue it generates; and only by entering into the dialogue can one enter the Torah. To belong to the dialogue is to belong to Judaism. This is why the rabbis insist that the words of the wise, which are as goads, include not only the words of Rabbi Akiba and his colleagues but also the words of Solomon and Moses, and not of Moses only but of God himself, who is frequently pictured studying his own texts.

But where exactly does the line of power and authority get drawn? Who has the right to interpret? Who has access to the discourse of midrash? One view is that Torah is not the exclusive possession of an interpretive community defined as those who come into the beit midrash, together with the whole ancestry of official midrashists extending from Solomon to Moses to God. Torah belongs to all, and all to Torah. A midrash on the text from Ecclesiastes we have been studying pictures it as follows:

When are the words of Torah spoken in their most correct form? When they who are versed in them hear them in assemblies. Whence do we know that if one heard (a teaching) from the mouth of an ordinary Israelite, he must regard it as though he heard if from the mouth of a Sage? There is a text, *Which I command thee this day* (Deut. vi.6); and not only as though he heard if from the mouth of one Sage but as though from the mouth of (many) Sages, as it is said, THE WORDS OF THE WISE ARE AS GOADS: and not only as though he heard it from the mouth of (many) Sages but as though from the mouth of the Sanhedrin, (as it is said), *Gather unto Me seventy men* (Num. xi.6); and not only as though he heard if from the mouth of a Sanhedrin, but as though from the mouth of Moses, as it is said, THEY ARE GIVEN FROM ONE SHEPHERD(XII.11), i.e., Moses; and not only as though he heard it from the shepherd Moses but as though from the mouth of the Holy One, blessed be He, as it is said, FROM ONE SHEPHERD, and SHEPHERD denotes none other than the Holy One, blessed be He, as it is said, *Give ear, O Shepherd of Israel* (Ps. lxxx.2), and ONE denotes none other than the Holy One, blessed be He, as it is said, *Hear, O Israel, the Lord our God, the Lord is One* (Deut. vi.4). (*Midrash Rabbah*, Eccl. XII. 11, 1).

Here is a text that sets itself squarely against the scholastic or dogmatic outlook. It is, in effect, a further extension of the rule of *lo' titgodedu:* "Do not cut yourselves into factions." The interpretive community is nothing less than Israel herself, and all who belong to Israel belong to the ongoing dialogue in which the Torah is understood. No one, in other words, not even the "ordinary Israelite," is without authority to say what the text means. So it is by no means just metaphorical to call midrash a form of life rather than a technique of exegesis. Midrash is the mode of identity of Torah and Israel. In rabbinic terms, it is the form of God's covenant with his people. "Even though Israel be in exile among the nations, if they occupy themselves with Torah, it is as though they were not in exile."[14]

Adopting Wittgenstein's phrase "form of life" provides a short way of explaining why midrash, like interpretation generally, is irreducible to a logic of validation. Or, as Stanley Cavell says, the search for criteria always ends up being a search for society.[15] This means figuring the question of what counts as a good interpretation in terms of what Charles Taylor calls "mattering."[16] Say that interpretation is an act performed by a person to whom things matter, not by a consciousness primed to produce pictures of how things are in the world or in the text or in whatever state of affairs is put before it for analysis. The Torah is a text that makes things matter; it preserves the smallest details of life from inconsequence and triviality. Mattering at all events is what the midrashic text I have been quoting from presupposes with respect to interpretation. Midrash is not a formal operation but a form of life lived with a text that makes claims on people. A text that makes claims upon people turns them into respondents: they are answerable to the text in a way that is qualitatively different from the answerability of disengaged observers to the scenes they wish to depict. This is why, as in legal hermeneutics, you find in the foreground of midrash the idea that interpretation is inseparable from application to a situation that calls for action.

In the midrashic texts themselves this idea takes the form of a relentless preoccupation with the *force* of interpretation. The text from Ecclesiastes—"The words of the wise are like goads," and so on—is a favorite of the rabbis because it concerns the point of midrash, its practical as against merely academic context. Midrash is not just talk. In the *Pesikta Rabbati* version, Rabbi Berechiah asks: "Now since one states one view and one states another view, do their words merely fly aimlessly in the air? Indeed not!" (Piska 3.2). The words of the wise are *situated;* their meaning is embedded in their situation. This comes out in the careful unpacking of the mixed metaphor that has nails being planted like trees in the bodies of those who understand. The words of the wise "impart sense" (Piska 3.2: *moreh de'ah*). But imparting sense does not mean producing concepts in someone's mind. It is more like getting under someone's skin. The task of imparting sense cannot be separated from the task of getting someone (oneself or another) off his or her feet; imparting sense means moving the one who understands along a certain path. Moreover, understanding means moving in just this wise. Understanding is not a form of mental agreement with a textual object but a mode of being that can only show itself in action—call such action, in this context, walking in "the ways of the Holy One, blessed be He." Midrash on this theory is wisdom rather than know-how with respect to what the Torah says, knowing how to take it rather than just knowing how its words work. Midrash is *phronēsis* as well as *technē* because what matters in midrash is our responsiveness to the claims of the text, where responsiveness means knowing not only how the words of the text work but also how they are to be applied in this or that situation, how they are to be internalized and put into practice: "the purpose is *to do it*" (*Sifre on Deuteronomy,* Piska 48). This is what it means to say that the concern of midrash is to make every jot and tittle of the Torah *matter* to human life, every moment of it. Nothing in the text is without consequence; nothing is to be overlooked or brushed aside. The whole point of midrash is to embed the sacred text in human life, and so to alter it or, say, channel it or indeed define it in a certain utterly distinctive way. What midrash finally concerns itself with is the question of what it is to be a Jew. In the political and cultural turmoil and heterogeneity of the Diaspora, to say that understanding is a mode of being is no longer an abstract principle. Call it the criterion of a form of life.

One can take this point in a slightly different direction, of course, because a form of life is always a capillary system through which power circulates in potentially disruptive ways. Imparting sense means taking hold of this power, using it. I mentioned earlier that Rabbi Eleazar's midrash tries to keep the conflict of interpretation from collapsing, or erupting, into a conflict of authority. Hence the broad principle that every Jew has the right to interpret the text. But the framing narrative of our midrash suggests how controversial this question of authority is. Indeed, insofar as what matters in midrash is the *force* of interpretation, authority is the whole issue. Authority is what is always (tacitly, and sometimes explicitly) in dispute. Our midrash seems concerned to sort out the several strata of this issue in order to affirm rabbinical power and to affirm it absolutely, as in the following:

R. Johanan used to recite on the first day of the Tabernacles festival the benediction, "Blessed art Thou, O Lord our God, the King of the Universe, who hath sanctified us with His commandments and hath commanded us concerning the taking of the *lulab*," while during all the remaining days he ended with, "Concerning the commandment of the elders." R. Joshua recited each day the blessing, "Concerning the taking of the *lulab*." R. Joshua does not admit R. Johanan's contention that according to the Torah the *lulab* is obligatory only on the first day of the festival, since it says, *And ye shall take you on the first day*, etc. (Lev. XXIII, 40), but that on all the remaining days the obligation has only the force of Rabbinic authority. R. Simeon bn. Halafta in the name of R. Aha said that R. Joshua actually held the same view as R. Johanan, and the reason why he acted differently was because it is written, *"The words of the wise are as goads . . . They are given from one shepherd"*; that is, the words of the Torah and the words of the Sages have been given from the same shepherd. *And more than of them, my son, be careful; of making many books there is no end; and much study is a weariness of the flesh* (Eccl. XII, 12). "And more than of them, my

son, be careful," means: More than of the words of the Torah be careful
of the words of the Scribes. In the same strain it says, *For thy beloved
ones are better than wine* (S. S., I, 2), which means: The words of the
beloved ones (the Sages) are better than the wine of the Torah? Why?
Because one cannot give a proper decision from the words of the Torah,
since the Torah is shut up and consists entirely of headings. . . . From
the words of the Sages, however, one can derive the proper law, because
they explain the Torah. And the reason why the words of the Sages are
compared to goads (*darbanoth*) is because they cause understanding to
dwell (*medayerin binah*) in men.

The dispute here between Rabbis Johanan and Joshua is over the force of
rabbinical authority vis-à-vis the force of Torah. Rabbi Joshua contends—
this is certainly what put him in contention with the Patriarch, Rabban
Gamaliel—is that there is no difference of power and authority between
Torah and Sage. This (he argues) is what the Torah itself says when it compares the words of the wise to goads. The difference between Torah and
Sage is that the words of the one are dark and powerless by themselves,
whereas the words of the other are as goads: there is no mistaking them,
nor escaping their import. And to underscore this the midrash construes a
text from the Song of Songs as saying, "The words of the beloved ones (the
Sages) are better than the wine of Torah." This is a powerful claim, and a
trenchantly political one. The relation between Torah and Sage, text and
interpretation, is one of *appropriation;* the claim of the one is answered by
the other in the form of an appropriation of what is written, a taking of it
that amounts to taking it over, bringing its power under one's own control,
putting it into play, inscribing it within one's self-understanding so that text
and interpretation are constituted as a single political entity.

It would be a mistake, however, to reduce the political nature of midrash
to power criteria or to characterize power purely in terms of domination
and control, because it remains the case that midrash is constitutive of rabbinical Judaism, that is, culturally constitutive of Judaism itself in the period
following the destruction of Jerusalem and extending at least until the time
of Maimonides and even, in some circumstances, to the present time. The
politics of interpretation is not exhausted by the theme of coercion. At all
events, a hermeneutics of midrash needs to take into account the full range
of social and political consequences of interpretation and cannot simply
map onto midrash the categories of instrumental reason. The argument here
has been that midrash is not simply a technique of polysemic exegesis. Nor,
for the same reason, is it enough to characterize midrash as simply an instrument of social control exercised by a particular class within Judaism; it

is also a powerful medium of cultural and religious difference, a cultural practice that enables Judaism to set itself apart and articulate its identity against traditionally hostile cultural forms that have their own strategic (and frequently single-minded) picture of what the consequences of interpretation should be. Here the task for study would be the ways in which midrash in itself constitutes a form of resistance within larger and more violent conflicts of interpretation. In this case the irreducibility of midrash to single-mindedness and logical rule, its unpredictability and uncontainability within dogmatic frameworks, its bewildering playfulness ("how can I study Torah in such circumstances?"), becomes an allegory of the resistance to dominant cultures that characterizes the history of Judaism itself.

APPENDIX
FROM THE TALMUD, BERAKOTH, 27b–28a

THE EVENING PRAYER HAS NO FIXED LIMIT. What is the meaning of NO FIXED LIMIT? Shall I say it means that if a man wants he can say the *Tefillah* in the night? Then let it state, "The time for the evening *Tefillah* is the whole night"!—But what in fact is the meaning of HAS NO FIXED LIMIT? It is equivalent to saying, The evening *Tefillah* is optional. For Rab Judah said in the name of Samuel: With regard to the evening *Tefillah*, Rabban Gamaliel says it is compulsory, whereas R. Joshua says it is optional. Abaye says: The *halachah* is stated by the one who says it is compulsory; Raba says the *halachah* follows the one who says it is optional.

It is related that a certain disciple came before R. Joshua and asked him, Is the evening *Tefillah* compulsory or optional? He replied: It is optional. He [the disciple] then presented himself before Rabban Gamaliel and asked him: Is the evening *Tefillah* compulsory or optional? He replied: It is compulsory. But, he said, did not R. Joshua tell me that it is optional? He said: Wait till the champions enter the Beth ha-Midrash. When the champions came in, someone rose and inquired, Is the evening *Tefillah* compulsory or optional? Rabban Gamaliel replied: It is compulsory. Said Rabban Gamaliel to the Sages: Is there anyone who disputes this? R. Joshua replied to him: No. He said to him: Did they not report you to me as saying that it is optional? He then went on: Joshua, stand up and let them testify against you! R. Joshua stood up and said: Were I alive and he [the witness] dead, the living could contradict the dead. But now that he is alive and I am alive, how can the living contradict the living? Rabban Gamaliel remained sitting and expounding and R. Joshua remained standing, until all the people there began to shout and say to Huzpith the *turgeman,* Stop! and he stopped. They then said: How long is he [Rabban Gamaliel] to go on insulting him

[R. Joshua]? On New Year last year he insulted him; he insulted him in the matter of the firstborn in the affair of R. Zadok; now he insults him again! Come, let us depose him! Whom shall we appoint instead? We can hardly appoint R. Joshua, because he is one of the parties involved. We can hardly appoint R. Akiba because perhaps Rabban Gamaliel will bring a curse on him because he has no ancestral merit. Let us then appoint R. Eleazar b. Azariah, who is wise and rich and the tenth in descent from Ezra. He is wise, so that if anyone puts a question to him he will be able to answer it. He is rich, so that if occasion arises for paying court to Caesar he will be able to do so. He is tenth in descent from Ezra, so that he has ancestral merit and he [Rabban Gamaliel] cannot bring a curse on him. They went and said to him: Will your honour consent to become head of the Academy? He replied: I will go and consult the members of my family. He went and consulted his wife. She said to him: [28a] Perhaps they will depose you later on. He replied to her: [There is a proverb:] Let a man use a cup of honour for one day even if it be broken the next. She said to him: You have no white hair. He was eighteen years old that day, and a miracle was wrought for him and eighteen rows of hair [on his beard] turned white. That is why R. Eleazar b. Azariah said: Behold I am *about* seventy years old, and he did not say [simply] seventy years old. A Tanna taught: On that day the door-keeper was removed and permission was given to the disciples to enter. For Rabban Gamaliel had issued a proclamation [saying], No disciple whose character does not correspond to his exterior may enter the Beth ha-Midrash. On that day many stools were added. R. Johanan said: There is a difference of opinion on this matter between Abba Joseph b. Dosethai and the Rabbis: one [authority] says that four hundred stools were added, and the other says seven hundred. Rabban Gamaliel became alarmed and said: Perhaps, God forbid, I withheld Torah from Israel! He was shown in his dream white casks full of ashes. This, however, really meant nothing; he was only shown this to appease him. . . .

[There follows a dispute in the beit midrash between Rabban Gamaliel and R. Joshua in which R. Joshua proves to have the better argument.] Rabban Gamaliel thereupon said: This being the case, I will go and apologize to R. Joshua. When he reached his house he saw that the walls were black. He said to him: From the walls of your house it is apparent that you are a charcoal-burner [a blacksmith]. He replied: Alas for the generation of which you are the leader, seeing that you know nothing of the troubles of the scholars, their struggles to support and sustain themselves! He said to him: I apologize, forgive me. He paid no attention to him. Do it, he said, out of respect for my father. He then became reconciled to him. They said:

Who will go and tell the Rabbis? A certain fuller said to them: I will go. R. Joshua sent a message to the Beth ha-Midrash saying: Let him who is accustomed to wear the robe wear it [let Rabban Gamaliel be master of the house of study]; shall he who is not accustomed to wear the robe say to him who is accustomed to wear it, Take off your robe and I will put it on? Said R. Akiba to the Rabbis: Lock the doors so that the servants of Rabban Gamaliel should not come and upset the Rabbis. Said R. Joshua: I had better get up and go to them. He came and knocked at the door. He said to them: Let the sprinkler son of a sprinkler sprinkle [let the priest, son of a priest, sprinkle the water of purification]; shall he who is neither a sprinkler nor the son of a sprinkler say to a sprinkler son of a sprinkler, Your water is cave water and your ashes are oven ashes? Said R. Akiba to him: R. Joshua, you have received your apology, have we done anything except out of regard for your honour? Tomorrow morning you and I will wait on him. They said: How shall we do? Shall we depose him [R. Eleazar b. Azariah]? We have a rule that we may raise an object to a higher grade of sanctity but must not degrade it to a lower. If we let one Master preach on one Sabbath and one on the next, this will cause jealousy. Let therefore Rabban Gamaliel preach three Sabbaths and R. Eleazar b. Azariah one Sabbath. And it is in reference to this that a Master said: "Whose Sabbath was it? It was the Sabbath of R. Eleazar b. Azariah."

Ṣūfiyya

THE MYSTICAL HERMENEUTICS

6

OF AL-GHAZĀLĪ

> The story begins in the 1950s. It was during those years that I
> began to be burdened with concern for the future of the Koran.
> Toward the end of that decade I had the opportunity to attend,
> on a regular basis, some of the foremost "recitation" sessions
> (*maqāriʾ*) in Cairo and to listen to the chanting of some of the
> most accomplished Koran-readers of the time. As I listened, I
> could not but contemplate remorsefully the tremendous loss
> that the passing away of these readers, so skilled and so
> learned, yet not likely to be succeeded by readers of equal
> stature, would mean to the world of Islam. Whenever I learned
> of the death of a famous reader, I was deeply saddened, for I
> knew that the vocal treasures of the great readers were in many
> cases not passed on to successors, but were buried with them
> in their graves, forever lost. The art of chanting the Koran was,
> in short, in danger of extinction.
> —Lābib al-Saīd, *The Recited Koran*

Not all texts are for reading. Of course, the word *text* itself
contradicts this idea. Discourse from a textual standpoint is not so much
expression as ciphering and concealing, that is, plotting and weaving, lay-
ering and folding, structuring and packing; and these are metaphors that
call for reading in the strong modernist sense of analytical action. Texts
impose tasks that it seems natural for us to characterize in the language of
instrumental reason—of grasping and penetrating, getting on top of and
breaking down, unpacking and laying bare. The text is an object defined by
our ability to reduce and explain it, to command its processes and results,
to weave and reweave it as we will. Whereas, by contrast, there was a time
when it seemed natural to conceive the hermeneutical task as a quest ro-
mance, with the reader at risk in a world made up of impenetrable walls,
secret caves, dense forests, mystic gardens, disembodied voices, whirlpools,
labyrinths, mists, crypts, knots, veils, dreams, riddles, curses, and coats of
many colors. The Qurʾān, for example, is "a sea without a shore."[1] One
cannot become the master of such a text.

124

In fact, it is not enough to speak of the Qurʾān as a text. Rather, it is the recitation (qurʾān) of a text that only God has seen, the umm al-kitāb, literally, "Mother of the Book."² God sent the Angel Gabriel (Jabraʾil) to recite this heavenly book to Muhammad, who received it in bits and pieces over a period of more than twenty years (610–32), committing it to memory and perhaps recording some of it in writing, for although the Prophet (it is said) could not read or write he had an amanuensis named Zaid ibn Thābit. Muhammad recited in turn to his Companions, who also memorized the recitation and likewise had portions of it written down, but after the Prophet's death many of the Companions were slain in battle and there was a real possibility that the Qurʾān would be lost. So Zaid ibn Thābit was ordered by Muhammad's successor, Abū Bakr, to gather together the various surviving fragments of memory and text and to produce a compilation. ("I wrote it," Zaid says, "on page-size pieces of hide, small pieces of scapula and palm leaves.")³ But there were other compilations in circulation as well, and discrepancies among them led to uncertainty as to what counted as the true Qurʾān. Accordingly, Abū Bakr's successor, the Caliph ʿUthman, instructed Zaid to compare the different versions with the Abū Bakr collection and to produce from all available materials an official text, the so-called "ʿUthmānic Recension." ʿUthmān then ordered all unofficial copies destroyed.

As a consonantal text, however, the ʿUthmānic Qurʾān left open the question of how it was to be vocalized; in fact, because not all consonants could be distinguished from one another, different traditions of reading developed—where, crucially, reading means qirāʾa, or recitation. In 322 A.H. (932 C.E.) Abū Bakr ibn Mujāhid reduced the various systems of vocalization to an official seven, one each from Medina, Mecca, Damascus, and Basra, and three from Kūfa. Two versions of these seven were handed down, and there are other variations allowed as well, but basically there remain seven authorized modes of recitation, in keeping with the idea that God sent down the Qurʾān in seven dialects of Arabic. These traditions of quirāʾat, preserved in formal schools that trace their lineage back to the second and third centuries A.H., are more authoritative than any text for determining the official version of the Qurʾān.⁴ Thus when the standard or authorized version of the Qurʾānic text was produced in Egypt in 1923–24, it was based, against all rules of bibliographical method, on the "science of recitations" (ʿilm al-quirāʾat) rather than on reigning manuscript traditions. Moreover, the text itself does not determine how it is to be vocalized, that is, its points and diacritical marks are not themselves canonical, which is why, when committing the Qurʾān to memory, one must memorize not the written text but one or more of the authoritative recitations. In addition,

Qur'ānic recitation is governed by a discipline known as *Tajwīd,* or rules for the articulation of sounds, including nasality, breathing, pauses, beginnings and endings, duration of syllables, and so on. And there are further disciplines still, depending on whether one's recitation is melodic or chanted.[5]

To speak strictly, the *qirā'at* constitute the mode of existence of the Qur'ān; as a text the Qur'ān exists only within quotation marks. The Qur'ān cannot be fixed as a text, even though the texts (*muṣḥafs:* roughly, written versions or copies) are fixed and remarkably consistent with one another. The hermeneutical consequences of this fundamental orality are many and complex. For example, the translation of the Qur'ān is not so much forbidden as it is materially or, say, ontologically impossible. Arabic is not only a literary language but a living vernacular from which the Qur'ān cannot be extracted. In a similar way, Qur'ānic exegesis (*tafsīr, ta'wīl*) is quintessentially an exegesis of the ear, since the eye alone cannot know what it is reading. This does not mean that the Qur'ān is not for study and that one should not search the text and meditate upon its smallest detail; but each detail is accessible only through listening. The question of what a critical reading of the Qur'ān might look like is therefore hard to formulate. A critical reading presupposes interrogation rather than listening; that is, in a critical reading one reflects oneself out of the space of the text and places it in a space of one's own, before one's gaze, under one's scrutiny—makes it, literally, a suspect. But one cannot, strictly speaking, hold the Qur'ān in one's hands (away from oneself) in this way; rather, as a recitation the Qur'ān surrounds us with itself, fills the space we inhabit, takes it over and ourselves in the bargain. The whole movement of reading as an appropriation or internalizing of a text is reversed. Here there is no grasping and unpacking and laying the text bare. On the contrary, reading is participation. To understand the Qur'ān is to disappear into it.

One can begin to get a sense of what this means from Abū Ḥāmid Muḥammad al-Ghazālī's hermeneutics, which he developed in the eighth book of his *Iḥyā' 'ulūm ad-dīn* ("The Revival of the Religious Sciences").[6] Al-Ghazālī (d. 505 A.H. / 1111 C.E.) was an Islamic legal scholar and theologian who is perhaps best known in the West for having mastered Greek philosophy expressly to refute it, which he did in a famous text, the *Tahāfut al-Falāsifah,* or *Incoherence of the Philosophers.*[7] Al-Ghazālī's life is the classic tale of the wise man who experiences the groundlessness of school-knowledge and abandons an illustrious career as a teacher for a life of solitude, meditation, and pilgrimage. In his autobiographical *al-Munqid min aḍalāl* ("Error and Deliverance"), al-Ghazālī gives an account of his spiritual crisis and journey from theology, philosophy, and authorized religious instruction (ta'līm) to the "mystic way [tarīqa]" of Sufism, where the goal is a pure, unmediated relationship with God, in which one enters into the experience of God's absolute self-identity (the so-called Doctrine of Unification, or tawḥīd).[8]

The centerpiece of al-Munqiḏmin aḏalāl, however, is an account of prophecy that characterizes the prophetic calling as a life of the Good Physician who cures the diseases of the mind and spirit. Like one of Plato's visionaries, al-Ghazālī saw that his obligation was not to repudiate the world but to return to it and restore it to health; specifically, this meant a return to academic life and an attempt to renew philosophy and religion by linking them prophetically or mystically to "a sphere beyond reason."[9] Basic to the Ṣūfī way is the idea that knowledge is empty unless it is connected internally with what is known. Reason always means knowledge at a distance, across the mediation of language and concepts; but wisdom presupposes something like the intimacy of becoming what one knows. "What a difference there is," al-Ghazālī writes in his autobiography, "between *knowing* the definition of health and satiety, together with their causes and presuppositions, and *being* healthy and satisfied!" (p. 55). Only the mystics can raise knowledge to the level of gnosis (ma'rifa), in which one experiences what one knows with all the intimacy of being, and this means above all the unmediated experience of God, where one no longer retains any sense of one's self (a condition of self-annihilation or self-abandonment known as fanā') but is absorbed completely into God's being (baqā').[10] But al-Ghazālī's idea was that this experience is meant not to replace philosophy and religion but to fulfill them, to provide their foundation and purpose. And the same is true for hermeneutics, where the point is not simply to understand the Qur'ān in the usual exegetical style but to achieve a gnostic experience of it.

The basic structure of al-Ghazālī's hermeneutics derives from his intellectual journey away from received philosophy and authorized teaching toward the condition of seeing with one's own eyes, that is, toward the primacy of mystical experience as against the authority of established exegesis. Nothing is more reprehensible to al-Ghazālī than the blind following (taqlīd) of what others have taught. At the same time, however, mysticism is not subjectivism or antinomianism, that is, it is not simply the substitution of one's own exegesis for what is established and authoritative; rather, it is an encounter with the text that is unmediated by any construction of meaning, whether traditional or otherwise. In the mystical event, there is no longer any subject separated from its object; there is no self left to assert against tradition. This last point is an important one, because al-Ghazālī's purpose is to square his hermeneutics with what appears to be the Qur'ān's prohibition against overinterpretation and readings that turn the text against itself. The Qur'ān is unique among sacred texts for the way it repeatedly insists on its vernacular clarity and expressly condemns those who concern themselves with what is esoteric and obscure.[11] It is a text for the many rather than for the few. A long-standing tradition distinguishes, for example, between two sorts of exegesis: *tafsīr bi'l-ra'y*, or interpretation by the use of reason or according to personal opinion, and *tafsīr bi'l-ma'thūr*, interpretation according to what has been handed down in *ḥadīth*, or collections of material concerning Muhammad, which include sayings, anecdotes, and narratives about his life (especially concerning episodes of revelation), the Prophet's own explanations of words and verses, reflections and comments by his Companions, and so on. This material was produced during the first two centuries or so after the Prophet's death and handed down through a series of *isnāds*, or transmitters.[12] Essentially the *ḥadīth* constitute a vast library of contexts—the foreground or forestructure—within which the understanding and interpretation of the Qur'ān is to take place. Interpretation that falls outside this framework is liable to the charge of "innovation" (*bi'l-ra'y*).

Al-Ghazālī wants not so much to introduce innovations as to reformulate the concept of *tafsīr bi'l-ra'y* in order to locate hermeneutics explicitly at the level of experience rather than at the level of formal exegesis or in the archive of received interpretation. In his *Jawāhir al-Qur'ān,* for example, al-Ghazālī distinguishes between two Qur'ānic disciplines, the sciences of the shell and the sciences of the pith. The first includes grammar, philology, the science of recitations (*'ilm al-quirā'at*), as well as the so-called "science of outward exegesis," or knowing what the words of the text mean, and the "science of Traditions," or knowledge of the commentaries (*ḥadīth*) handed down from the earliest centuries. The sciences of the pith are of two sorts: the lower sciences of theology and law, and the science of *gnosis* (*'ilm al-ma'rifa*), or knowledge of God and of the last day and the world to come.[13] The scholar mulling over parchment and ciphers in the privacy of a library is occupied with the shell of the Qur'ān. The theologian and the legal scholar meanwhile are concerned with what the text says in the context of questions concerning conduct and belief. But *gnosis* is an event. It is not a product of reading, that is, its aim is not to know what the text means but to experience what it is—namely, God's own speech.[14] The eighth book of al-Ghazālī's *Ilḥa' 'ulūm ad-dīn* is to all appearances entirely traditional.[15] In strict pedagogical style it sets down ten external and ten internal rules (or "mental tasks") for Qur'ānic recitation. The external rules concern the disposition of the body during recitation. For instance, the reader of the Qur'ān should be in a state of ritual purity, should practice politeness and quietness, and whether standing or sitting should be facing the *qibla* (in the direction of Mecca) with the head downcast. One should neither sit cross-legged nor lean against anything; nor should one sit in a manner of self-importance but, instead, as if in the presence of one's teacher. Better to stand in a mosque, moreover, than to recline on one's side in a bed. Other rules concern how much of the Qurʾān to read (whether to read it once a day or to spread the reading over a week or a month) and how one's readings should be divided. Rule four is scribal: letters should be clear and distinct, points and diacritical marks may be in color. There is some question, however, as to whether the written text should be divided into sections. Some scholars, al-Ghazālī says, are against "the opening of this door, fearing that it would lead to the creation of superfluous things [in the Qurʾān]. They wanted to close this door completely, and to encourage the protection of the Qurʾān from any change that may penetrate into it. Since the opening of this door has not in practice led to any forbidden thing, and since it has been established by the Islamic community that it is something by which added acquaintance [with the Qurʾān] may be achieved, there is no sin in it" (pp. 39–40). To which al-Ghazālī adds: "The fact that it is a new thing introduced in Islam [*muḥdath*] does not mean that it should be forbidden, for many a newly introduced thing is good" (p. 40).

The fifth rule says that one should read slowly and distinctly in order to be able to reflect as one reads. But reflection does not imply cool detachment, as we learn at once: "The sixth rule is for weeping." In Islamic tradition grief is something like a hermeneutical emotion. "The Messenger of God (may God bless him and greet him!) commanded, 'Recite the Qurʾān and weep. If you do not weep naturally, then force yourself to weep'" (p. 43). With weeping goes prostration (rule seven) and supplication (rule eight). According to the ninth rule, the Qurʾān is to be read aloud. "There is no doubt," al-Ghazālī says, "that it is necessary to read the Qurʾān loud enough so that the reader can hear it himself because reading means distinguishing clearly between sounds; thus sound is necessary, and the smallest degree of it is that which he can hear himself" (p. 49). Silent reading is not forbidden and is even admirable so long as it is without ostentation, for one should never disturb another with one's reading, but reading aloud awakens the mind of the reader and drives away distractions. In Western (or, more accurately, Latin) tradition silent reading implies a private, solitary relationship with the text, but for al-Ghazālī it is in reading aloud that one enters into an exclusive relationship with the Qurʾān. Interestingly, al-Ghazālī says that "reading the entire Qurʾān once from the *muṣḥaf* [copy or text] is equal to reading it in its entirety seven times from memory, because looking at a *muṣḥaf* is also an act of devotion to God" (pp. 52–53). But the Qurʾān is not therefore a textual object. It is only accessible through the mediation of the voice, not through the eye. Hence the tenth rule, which is "to read the Qur'ān beautifully and in a slow and distinct manner, by controlling the voice though not with that excessive stretch which changes the prose order [*nazm*]" (p. 53).

But in another sense, it is misleading to speak of the voice as mediation, because the whole orientation of al-Ghazālī's hermeneutics is to overcome mediation so that nothing stands between the reciter and God. The internal rules or mental tasks to be performed during recitation make this explicit. When we begin to read, for example, we must "magnify" the Qur'ān by meditating on parables and figures that emphasize the transcendence and power of divine speech. "At the start of Qur'ān recitation the reciter should bring to his mind magnification of the One Who Speaks, and should realize that what he is reading is not the speech of a human being, and that in the recitation of the speech of God (great and mighty is He!) there is an extreme danger, because God (exalted is He!) said, 'Only those who are clean can touch it [Sura 56:79]'" (p. 60). And as we magnify the Qur'ān, so we must diminish ourselves. "The third mental task is to pay attention and abandon the inner utterances of the soul" (p. 61). Here the process of self-abnegation that is crucial to al-Ghazālī's hermeneutics becomes explicit. One must empty oneself of one's own interior monologue so that one can be completely absorbed into the language of the Qur'ān. The speech of God is transcendent, powerful, and dangerous, but our relations with him are meant to be warm and intimate. And so the very letters of the Qur'ān are like openings onto paradise:

> It is said that in the Qur'ān are to be found fields, gardens, closets, brides, brocades, meadows, and khans. All *mīms* are the fields of the Qur'ān; all *rā's* are the gardens; all *hā's* are its closets; all suras starting with the glorification of God are its brides, all suras starting with the letters *hā mīm* are its brocades, all the suras in which laws, stories, etc. are expounded are its meadows, and all the other parts of it are its khans. When the Qur'ān reader enters into the fields of the Qur'ān, plucks different types of fruits from its gardens, enters into its closets, views the brides, wears the brocades, is relieved of cares, and dwells in the khans, then all these absorb him wholly and keep him from things other than these; consequently his mind cannot be inattentive, nor can his thought be separate. (p. 62)

But it is not enough merely to pay attention. Self-abnegation is not passivity. "The purpose of reading the Qur'ān is to ponder over it" (p. 62)— not to elucidate the text but to understand those things on which it sheds its light. Like all sacred texts, the Qurʾān is to be read as a book of teach-ings—"One who wants to acquire the knowledge of the ancients and mod-erns should deeply study the Qurʾān" (p. 66)—but it is very far from being the dark text of esoteric wisdom. Rather, it is a light that illuminates all the works of God, and the task of hermeneutics is to stand within this light in order to serve as its reflection. Or, again, one must recite the Qurʾān thoughtfully, in a philosophical spirit of reflection, but one need not be a philosopher. "To fathom it is not the coveted thing in this respect" (p. 69), but simply to understand what is said according to one's capacities ("It is lawful for everyone to elicit meaning from the Qurʾān commensurate with his understanding and the limit of his intelligence" [p. 92]). God sent down a lucid and Arabic Qurʾān; one does not need to add one's own brilliance to it. One simply needs not to get in the way.

> Those who conceal the clear signs and the guidance
> that We have sent down, after We have shown them
> clearly in the book—they shall be cursed by God.
> (2.150)

Just so, the text is not dark, but our minds are—although this darkness is not an absence of wit or learning. On the contrary, there are, al-Ghazālī says, four veils that obstruct our understanding, and these have nothing to do with how bright or dull we are. The first veil is a kind of aestheticism in which one makes a fetish of pronunciation (p. 69). The second is dogmatic adherence to a school, where one simply accepts what one is taught "with-out arriving at it by spiritual insight and mystical vision" (p. 70). The third veil, al-Ghazālī says, is sin, which is like "dirt accumulating on a mirror" (p. 71).[16] The fourth is nothing less than adherence to the hallowed distinc-tion between *tafsīr biʾl-maʾthur* and *tafsīr biʾl-raʾy*. "The fourth veil is pres-ent," al-Ghazālī says, "when a man has read the outward exegesis of the Qurʾān and has formed the belief that Qurʾānic sentences have only those meanings which have come down by tradition from Ibn ʾAbbas, Mujāhid, and other exegetes, that meanings going beyond them are interpretations of the Qurʾān by personal opinion (*tafsīr biʾl-raʾy*), and that 'he who has ex-plained the Qurʾān by personal opinion has taken his place in Hell'" (p. 72).

There are two ways of transcending this distinction. The first is practical and affective. The seventh mental task "is to render the Qurʾān specific" (p. 72), that is, it is the application of the Qurʾān to one's own situation. The Qurʾān is a legal text and a work of moral authority; it is a binding text, and this is so not in the aggregate or in the abstract; rather, the Qurʾān speaks to me alone in the particularity of my condition. I am everywhere internal to the embrace of its utterances, and this is so not only morally and legally but also emotionally and, one might even say, ontologically. "The eighth mental task," al-Ghazālī says, "is to feel the Qurʾān. This means that the mind of the Qurʾān-reader will be affected by different feelings according to the different verses recited. Thus in accordance with what his mind understands, he will be in a state of grief, fear, hope, and so on" (p. 75). So the Qurʾān-reader is never "a mere narrator" (p. 76), that is, never simply an agent of recitation but, one might say, the point of it, the place where the Qurʾān brings itself most forcefully and concretely to bear upon human existence. Hence al-Ghazālī speaks of the reader as being "included in the verse" (p. 77)—internal to the text, consumed by it, not working on it at a distance but, on the contrary, worked on and actualized by it, as if one could be the work of the Qurʾān, its creation, a being brought fully to being in the way of action and feeling.

The second way of transcending the distinction between traditional and personal exegesis is explicitly mystical. Here it is no longer adequate to speak of exegesis. Rather, for al-Ghazālī the whole purpose of the recitation of the Qurʾān is to go beyond interpretation to the experience of God's speech itself:

> The grades of Qurʾān-reading are three in number. The lowest grade is when a man supposes that he is reading the Qurʾān to God (great and mighty is He!), standing in front of Him, and He is looking at him and listening to what he is reading. In this case his mental condition is one of begging, praising and entreating Him and supplicating Him.
>
> The second grade is when a man views with his mind that God (great and mighty is He!) is seeing him, addressing him with his kindnesses, and secretly conversing with him with his gifts and beneficence. So his station is one of modesty, magnification, listening and understanding.
>
> The third grade is when a man is seeing the Speaker in the Speech and His attributes in its sentences. He does not think of himself, nor [of] his Qurʾān-reading, nor [of] the relation of divine gifts to him as the one upon whom they are bestowed; rather he confines his care to the Speaker, and concentrates all his thought on Him as if he were engrossed in the vision of the Speaker, being divested of thought of anything other than Him. This is the grade of those drawn near to God [al-muqarrabūn], while the grades preceding it constitute the grades of people on the right [aṣḥāb al-yamīn]; all grades other than these form the grades of inattentive people [al-ghāfilūn]. (pp. 80–81)

Supplication, conversation, vision—or perhaps not quite vision, or not yet:

at the third grade one concentrates one's thought on God *as if* engrossed in a vision, but one is still in a reflective condition in which one's relationship with God is mediated by a meditative rehearsal of his speech and his attributes. What remains is the event of self-annihilation in which one will be taken up entirely into God's self-identity, thus to see what God sees, know what He knows.

Hence the "tenth mental task consists in the Qur'ān-reader's getting rid of any sense of his ability and power" (p. 82), or in other words the attainment of *fanā'*, in which one transcends subjectivity or the experience of one's separate existence. "Whenever a man sees himself with the eye of satisfaction," al-Ghazālī says, "he becomes veiled from God by himself. When, however, he crosses the limit of looking at himself and does not see in his Qur'ān-reading anything except God (exalted is He!), then the secret of the invisible world is revealed to him directly" (p. 83).

It is perhaps important to notice that al-Ghazālī speaks not of seeing God face-to-face but only of hearing his speech and experiencing "mystical intuitions" that are coherent with what God's speech happens to be about in this or that verse of the Qur'ān:

> These mystical intuitions can only occur after one gets rid of one's self and does not look at one's self with a sense of satisfaction and purification, nor at one's passion. Then these intuitions become specific in accordance with the mental state of the man receiving them. Thus when he recites verses on hope, and his mental state is dominated by a good omen from them, the image of paradise comes to him through mystical intuition . . . and he views it as if he sees with his eyes. But if fear dominates him [as a result of reading verses on punishment], then Hell is shown to him through intuition so that he sees its different types of punishment. This is because the speech of God (great and mighty is He!) includes those verses which are kind and witty as well as those which are violent and forceful, and those which inspire hope as well as those which are frightening. And this is in accordance with God's attributes, since among His attributes are mercy and kindness as well as revenge and violence. Then, in accordance with the Qur'ān-reader's view of Qur'ānic sentences and of divine attributes, his mind alternates in different mental states, and, according to each of these mental states, the mind is prepared for a mystical intuition appropriate to it and approaching it. (pp. 84–85)

This passage helps to clarify al-Ghazālī's distinction between outward and inner exegesis. This distinction does not derive from the usual doctrine of hidden meanings. Rather, in external exegesis one's understanding of the text is mediated by words and meanings, both of the text of the Qurʾān and of what has been handed down in tradition, whereas inward exegesis means that one *sees* (quite literally) what the text says. To put it another way: to the eye cleansed of whatever might darken it, God's speech *is* what it is about, so that one does not just understand what is said but sees it, knows it, so to speak, by experience. From which it would follow that understanding the Qurʾān becomes a condition for understanding God's creation.

There remains, of course, the question of what sort of exposition someone would give of a verse of the Qurʾān *after* having had a gnostic encounter in which what the Qurʾān is about is experienced firsthand, as if seen with one's own (or God's own) eyes. Perhaps the answer to this lies in the idea that one knows the meaning of something (grief, love, friendship, fatherhood) only after having lived through it, and that what al-Ghazālī's hermeneutics gives us is an itinerary for living through the Qurʾān and, therefore, being in a position to say what it means. Simply to borrow interpretations from the archive handed down in tradition is not enough, no matter how authoritative these interpretations are in themselves or in consequence of their origin and transmission. One has to have lived through an experience of the Qurʾān in order to be able to say what these interpretations amount to or what they might be getting at. "Energy and awakening on your own account," al-Ghazālī says, "is greater than the joy achieved by awakening caused by others."[17]

It is possible, therefore, to think of mystical hermeneutics as a kind of appropriation, not of the sacred text but of the archive of interpretation that surrounds it. One's understanding of the text is not mediated by tradition; rather, one's understanding of tradition is mediated by one's experience of the text. Mystical hermeneutics is a hermeneutics of experience—only we should understand that experience here must be taken, if at all possible, in a nonsubjectivist sense; experience is not an event that sets the individual subject up as an institution of its own the way the Cartesian *ego cogito* supersedes whatever has preceded it and underwrites whatever follows. Quite the contrary, experience as al-Ghazālī conceives it subsumes the subject, who can no longer be thought of as a self-possessed, self-contained agent. Indeed, the very idea of mysticism is incompatible with a modern theory of the subject. Having said this, however, it remains the case that what this experience wins for the individual is something like a free interpretive space or, more accurately, a region of meditation, an open place of study, where one is able to abide with the text in what amounts to a condition of personal intimacy. So we should take it that the purpose, or effect, of hermeneutical experience is not to produce new interpretations that would replace tradition—this would be to impose a Cartesian model on al-Ghazālī's hermeneutics. Rather, the point is simply to open up this place of intimacy, this intimate dwelling place with the Qur'ān. We have already seen this sort of hermeneutical intimacy both in the case of Philo's hermeneutics and in midrash. Hermeneutics in these instances is not a *technē* of interpretation but a *praxis,* a form of life. Its task is not the unveiling of the meaning of the text—"As for the full unveiling of all the secret meanings," al-Ghazālī says, "there is no coveted object in it" (p. 103)—but meditation throughout one's life upon what the text discloses.

A comparison between al-Ghazālī's hermeneutics and Kabbalist hermeneutics of Abraham Abulafia (1240–91 C.E.) might be instructive here, in spite of the enormous differences between them, not the least of which is the difference between Qur'ān and Torah as texts, where the one exists only in (or as) recitation, while the other is constituted entirely in (or as) its letters and diacritical forms. In Kabbalah, the inscriptions of Torah have a meaning and purpose of their own quite apart from their grammatical function within the Bible as a book of narratives and laws, so that whereas the Qur'ānist will recite the Qur'ān as it is handed down liturgically in tradition, Kabbalists (of a certain sort) will recite separately the individual letters of the text on the principle that each letter by itself and in combination with others is a name of God.[18] For Abulafia, says Moshe Idel, "the 'highest' hermeneutic method . . . consists of atomizing or monadizing the biblical texts," that is, breaking the text down into its letters and then recombining them according to various permutations. The point of this practice seems analogous to al-Ghazālī's third mental task, which is to empty one's mind of human language so as to provide a pure interior space for the recitation of the Qur'ān. As Idel says, for Kabbalists like Abulafia, "language is a powerful instrument for understanding natural reality, and even the spiritual world is adequately projected onto the structure of linguistic material. When a man strives for an ultimate mystical experience, however, he must break the structured language, as he needs to efface the forms inscribed in his mind in order to make room there for higher entities to dwell."[19] Moreover, the letters themselves must undergo a process of purification from their material form by being first recited on the tongue and then transferred to the heart or memorized. Once internalized, the letters are then combined and recombined, sometimes randomly, sometimes systematically—not, however, to produce a new text, nor even to produce new or unprecedented interpretations of the Torah. Rather, like al-Ghazālī's hermeneutics, Kabbalistic hermeneutics is a hermeneutics of experience rather than of exegesis. Idel calls it "an experiential study of Torah": "For the Kabbalist, the understanding of the inner sense of the text or of the tradition is more than simply the comprehension of some additional details; it implies a radical change in the perception of the Torah, as well as of the personality and status of the Kabbalist himself. No longer an outsider, he becomes the lord of the palace—*heikhal*—a word alluding to the location of the Toral Scroll in the synagogue. He actualizes his uniqueness by leaving the surrounding ignoramuses in order to become one of the *perfecti*—an overwhelming experience, which goes beyond the passive contemplation of the symbolic sense of the text. More than an interiorization of specific contents, this study entails the establishment of a close relationship [with the Torah or, what amounts to the same thing, with God]."[20]

Al-Ghazālī's hermeneutics, however, is clearly not esoteric in the Kabbalistic sense but remains within the horizon defined by the public, liturgical character of the recited Qur'ān. There is no internalization and reinscription of the Qur'ānic text—on the contrary, the text internalizes the one who recites it, so to speak. Moreover, for al-Ghazālī the mystical experience of the text is not an event that is to be set apart from the rest of life. There is no withdrawal into a community of *perfecti*. Rather, as al-Ghazālī's own life indicates, the hermeneutical task entails a return from the experience of text to the social world of argument and teaching, as if to bring even the most remote periphery of the secular world within the experience of divine intimacy. This exoteric dimension of al-Ghazālī's hermeneutics is perhaps unique in antiquity but is not surprising, because, after all, the distinction between the esoteric and exoteric is essentially a philosopher's distinction and therefore part of what al-Ghazālī would be determined to obviate or refute. We'll see a similar exoteric turn in the next chapter.

The Moderns

11

Scriptura sui ipsius interpres   7

LUTHER, MODERNITY, AND THE

FOUNDATIONS OF PHILOSOPHICAL

HERMENEUTICS

> One should also understand that the literal sense of the text
> has been much obscured because of the manner of expounding
> the text commonly handed down by others. Although they
> have said much that is good, yet they have been inadequate in
> their treatment of the literal sense, and have so multiplied the
> number of mystical senses that the literal sense is in some part
> cut off and suffocated among so many mystical senses.
> Moreover, they have chopped the text into so many small
> parts, and brought forth so many concordant passages to suit
> their own purpose, that to some degree they confuse both the
> mind and memory of the reader and distract it from
> understanding the literal meaning of the text.
> —Nicholas of Lyra (c. 1270–1340), *Literal Postill on the Bible*

The Bible studied in the medieval schools was, we know, a
glossed text, the *Glossa Ordinaria,* in which each verse is surrounded by
notes and commentaries handed down from the Church Fathers.[1] In effect,
the biblical text was materially embedded in the history of its interpretation.
If one were to look for a symbolic moment of transition between ancient
and modern hermeneutics, one might choose the winter semester of 1513–
14, when Martin Luther began preparing his first lectures as professor of
theology at the University of Wittenberg. He was to lecture on the Psalms
and wanted each of his students to have a copy of the scriptural text to
consult. Luther therefore instructed Johann Grunenberg, the printer for the
university, to produce an edition of the Psalter with wide margins and lots
of white space between the lines. Here the students would reproduce Luther's own glosses and commentary, and perhaps (who knows?) they would
have room for their own exegetical reflections as well. At all events Luther
produced for his students something like a modern, as opposed to medieval,
text of the Bible—its modernity consisting precisely in the white space

139

around the text. In a stroke Luther wiped the Sacred Page clean as if to begin the history of interpretation over again, this time to get it right.

It may be, of course, that interpretation has always tried to go beyond itself, that is, to free itself from its accumulated history and to lose itself, in some fashion, in whatever there is to be understood. Historically we can distinguish two ways in which this is accomplished. The short way would be through a form of mystical exegesis, in which the hermeneutical experience of the interpreter bypasses the archive of authorized commentary. This is the way of al-Ghazālī and also the medieval monastic tradition of Bernard of Clairvaux (c. 1090–1153), where the point is not just to interpret the text but to experience it and be transformed by it. Here the word of God is no longer a text but an event that one lives through. As in Qurʾānic recitation, the monk reads with his ears in order to hear the "voices of the page" and to reexperience the moment of their inspiration.[2] In certain respects, one of the things we will be concerned with in this chapter is the survival of this tradition into our own time.

The long way seems to be through some version of literalization in which the interpreter (so it appears) steps out of the hermeneutical scene and allows the text to speak for itself. In the Jewish tradition—most dramatically, in the commentaries of Rashi (1040–1105)—this took the form of an effort to subordinate rabbinic midrash to *peshat,* the practice of situating the biblical text within its own linguistic, literary, and historical contexts.[3] In the Christian tradition this has often meant a repudiation of allegory, starting perhaps with Diodore of Tarsus (d. 390 C.E.) and, more important, Theodore of Mopsuestia, the fifth-century bishop of Antioch who rejected not only Alexandrian allegorical practices but "any interpretation that denies the historical reality of what the biblical text records."[4] Indeed, by emphasizing the scholastic tradition (as against the monasteries), scholars like Beryl Smalley and James Preus have had no trouble writing the history of interpretation during late antiquity and the Middle Ages as one of increasingly coherent literalism in which the celebrated fourfold method of exegesis proves to be a theory without any interesting adherents.[5] On this reading, medieval hermeneutics appears to be less a method of polysemy than a critique of it in the sense summarized by Gerhard Ebeling: "Instead of taking the fourfold sense of the Scriptures as an offspring of a licentious exegetical practice, as is usually done, the distinction of the three spiritual dimensions of interpretation must be understood as an effort to stop, through regulation by church dogma, the danger of an allegorical fantasy which would digress into the heretical."[6]

The control of interpretation is clearly the motive of scholastic hermeneutics, where the fourfold scheme is made to stand squarely on a theory of the univocality of the Scriptures. Drawing on Augustine's theory of signs, Thomas Aquinas produced a formulation that remains authoritative for many Christian theologians to this day:

> The multiplicity of the senses does not produce equivocation or any other kind of multiplicity, seeing that these senses are not multiplied because one word signifies several things, but because the things signified by the words can be themselves signs of other things. Thus in Holy Scripture . . . for all the senses are founded on one—the literal—from which alone can any argument be drawn, and not from those intended allegorically, as Augustine says. Nevertheless, nothing of Holy Scripture perishes because of this, since nothing necessary to faith is contained under the spiritual sense which is not elsewhere put forward clearly by the Scripture in its literal sense.[7]

Polysemy is of things, not words, so that if senses are multiple, they are not therefore secret or hidden; or if they are, they are concealed by time, not by the words of the text.

Or, in other words, what needs to be interpreted are not words (*verba*) but things (*res*), which was roughly the idea of Augustine's rhetorical approach to the Scriptures. Augustine gave only a polite nod to the mystery tradition, in which Eastern antiquity had situated the Bible as a dark text filled with esoteric wisdom. For him the obscurity of the scriptural texts is a rhetorical rather than philosophical problem. Thus he redescribes the old distinction between the plain and obscure as a distinction between the plain and the adorned, or between that which is expressed openly (namely, the doctrine of charity) and that which is dressed or concealed in the artful vocabulary of figures.[8] Whereas for Philo, Origen, and Maimonides the function of obscurity is to preserve a sacred teaching from falling into the wrong hands, for Augustine it is to disarm the cultured despisers of the Scriptures and to move the reader in heart as well as in mind, that is, to delight as well as teach. For "no one doubts that things are perceived more readily through similitudes and that what is sought with difficulty is discovered with more pleasure. . . . Thus the Holy Spirit has magnificently and wholesomely modulated the Holy Scriptures so that the more open places present themselves to hunger and the more obscure places may deter a disdainful attitude." The main point, however, is that the plain sense of the text is foundational. As Augustine says, "Hardly anything may be found in these obscure places which is not found plainly said elsewhere."[9] So let the Scriptures interpret the Scriptures—let the New Testament, for example, shed its light on the Old. Let words always be construed in light of the thing itself, namely, the light (or rule) of faith: "whatever appears in the divine Word that does not literally pertain to virtuous behavior or to the truth of faith you must take to be figurative. [For] Scripture teaches nothing but charity, nor condemns anything but cupidity, and in this way shapes the minds of men" (p. 88).

Notice that for Augustine the plain sense of the text is not so much a *sensus litteralis* as the *sensus spiritualis;* but strictly speaking this spiritual sense ought not to be thought of as a meaning; it is not reducible to the grammar of the text. It is rather the spirit or fore-understanding in which the text is to be studied. "He is a slave to a sign," Augustine says, "who uses or worships a significant thing without knowing what it signifies. But he who uses or venerates a useful sign divinely instituted whose signifying force he understands does not venerate what he sees and what passes away but rather that to which such things are to be referred" (pp. 86–87). For Augustine, the understanding of things logically precedes the understanding of words, so that one must already have understood a text (in the sense of understanding its res, the thing that it teaches) to be able to interpret its language. This is the task of faith, which makes both things and words transparent.[10] (Of course, in practice, as the treatise *On Christian Doctrine* takes for granted, this means that only doctors of the Church are in a position to interpret the text, and it is these interpretations that faith enables the rest of us to understand.)

To put it another way, the distinction between letter and spirit refers to two different ways of inhabiting a specific (in this case, historically Christian) hermeneutical situation and not simply to two ways of interpreting a text. The question is: In what spirit is the letter to be approached? "Hardly anything may be found in these obscure places which is not found plainly said elsewhere," but before this can happen we need to be turned toward the text in the proper way, and this turning is the main concern of *On Christian Doctrine*. In book 2, for example, Augustine speaks of the steps we must take in order to be in a position to understand what we read. Each of these steps identifies a feature of the state of mind or spirit in which one is to take the text: fear, piety, knowledge, fortitude, mercy—and finally "the sixth step, where [the interpreter] cleanses that eye through which God may be seen insofar as He can be seen by those who die to the world as much as they are able. For they are able to see only insofar as they are dead to this world; insofar as they live in it, they do not see" (p. 40). As in mystical tradition, the cleansing of the eye is the crucial event. It is a metaphor of initiation and spiritual transformation.

Or take it as a metaphor of the hermeneutical circle, like the counsel of Mark 4:9: "If you have ears to hear, then hear." As Heidegger says: "What is decisive is not to get out of the circle but to come into it in the right way." Augustine's *On Christian Doctrine* gives the Christian theory of the right way, call it a Christian allegory of reading. Allegory is a mode of appropriation in which one reinterprets another's text as if it were one's own. Thus the rule of faith appropriates the Old Testament to the New. But appropriation is of readers as well as of texts. Augustine's hermeneutics implies a process in which one reinterprets oneself in order to enter into the conceptual scheme of another. Understanding, in effect, presupposes conversion. As Augustine says in the *Confessions,* his first experience of the Scriptures was to be repelled by them. Approached in a Ciceronian spirit, they are an absurd and garbled text, a book without reason or eloquence. Augustine had to learn to read them with the eyes of St. Ambrose. His conversion enabled him to enter into the spirit, or the intelligibility, of the Scriptures, which explains why the *Confessions* conclude with Augustine's commentary on Genesis, in which he offers a practical demonstration of what it means to be (at last) in a position to understand and expound the sacred text.

It is this Augustinian theory of spirit and letter (although not, obviously, Augustine's practice) that Luther follows in his controversies with Rome when he asserts the clarity and self-sufficiency of the Scriptural texts against the idea that the Scriptures, being obscure, can be understood not in themselves but only through the interpretations handed down from the Church Fathers. Luther's position emerges most completely in the so-called Leipzig debates (1519–21), which culminated in a splendid polemic, *Answer to the Hyperchristian, Hyperspiritual, and Hyperlearned Book by Goat Emser in Leipzig—Including Some Thoughts Regarding His Companion, the Fool Murner* (1521). "The Holy Spirit," Luther says, "is the simplest writer and speaker in heaven and on earth. This is why his words can have no more than the one simplest meaning which we call the written one, or the literal meaning of the tongue. But words and language cease to have meaning when the things which have a simple meaning through interpretation by a simple word are given further meanings and thus become different things so that one thing takes on the meaning of another. This is true for all other things not mentioned in Scripture because all God's creatures and works are sheer living signs and words of God, as Augustine and all the teachers say. But one should not therefore say that Scripture or God's word has more than one meaning."[11] Luther's motto is, "Let Aaron be just Aaron in the simplest sense, unless the Spirit interprets him in a new literal sense—as when St. Paul makes Christ out of Aaron for the Hebrews [Heb. 9:10]."[12]

It is not that St. Paul alters the meaning of Aaron's name; it is that Aaron himself is altered so that he himself becomes, literally, a figure of Christ. However, the "'literal meaning' is not a good term. . . . Those who call it 'grammatical, historical meaning' do better."[13] Luther is a literalist but not literal-minded. The Bible is often literally (that is, grammatically) figurative in its language, as anyone who knows how to read can see. The question is, what does one need beyond grammar to arrive at the plain sense of the text?

In his quarrel with Emser Luther glosses St. Paul's line on letter and spirit exactly in the direction laid out by Augustine. Letter and spirit are construed not according to the scholastic categories of literal and spiritual senses but as a distinction between law and gospel—which is not quite the same as a distinction between Old and New Testaments. Law and gospel are not textual categories, neither are they exegetical categories of meaning.[14] Better to think of them as categories of self-understanding, where the question is, for example, not What does the law mean? but How do we stand with respect to it? There is no mystery as to what the law means, nor any as to how we appear in its eyes (not good). In the light of the law, we can only see ourselves as miserable sinners. We stand convicted before the law. "There is no just man" (Rom. 3:10). Understanding the Scriptures as law means acknowledging, confessing, just this fact about ourselves, and there is nothing we can say in our defense. Understanding the Scriptures as gospel, however, means understanding that our relation to the law has been altered by the advent of Christ; the law is not to be read differently—it is still as binding as ever, we are still answerable to it—but now we can answer differently: now, because of Christ, we are able to justify ourselves before the law. Here understanding the Scriptures as gospel becomes indistinguishable from faith, or that which alone (according to Luther's reading of Rom. 1:17) justifies us, makes us righteous before the law, saves us as if at the last minute.[15]

"Scripture," Luther says in his dispute with Emser, "does not tolerate the division of letter and Spirit."[16] Rather, "spirit" means the spirit in which one reads; it is the spiritual state of the reader—and also the Holy Spirit who informs the one who reads. "This Spirit," Luther says, "cannot be contained in any letter, it cannot be written with ink, on stone, or in books as the law can be, but is written only in the heart [of the one who reads], a living writing of the Holy Spirit."[17] In other words, spirit is mystical as well as textual: it is the condition of faith or state of grace, which is to say the condition of understanding the gospel message, where understanding is not simply of a text (of a letter) but, prior to this, of a mode of being: not a mental state or state of conceptual agreement with what the text says (not a philosophical state of knowledge or theological state of doctrinal assent) but a state of union with God, in which you live in his Spirit, and his Spirit lives in you.

It is important to stress that Luther is more monk than schoolman. He is a university professor of theology, but in the tradition of Augustine and monastic exegesis he is concerned before everything else with what happens in the reading of the text, not (or not just) with what reading produces in the way of interpretation. In this tradition the understanding of the Scriptures is not the product of interpretation but is prior to interpretation as an event that one lives through and which carries one forward into the future.[18] Call it a hermeneutical experience that interpretation, as a form of exegesis, cannot contain, an experience that spills over into the life of the interpreter, altering *its* meaning and direction.[19] Here the text is not so much an object of understanding as a component of it; what one understands when one understands the Scriptural texts is not anything conceptual and extractable as a meaning. Rather, what one understands (that is, enters into) is the mode of being or life of faith informed by the text in much the way a plot informs a work as its soul or shaping spirit.

This emphasis on experience as against formal exegesis or the construction of meaning helps us to get clear about what it might be for a text to be self-interpreting in the sense that Luther understands this term. He means, of course, what has always been meant, namely, that what is intelligible in the text must be used to clarify what is obscure.[20] But he means more. The classic statement is as follows:

> Scripture is to be understood alone through that spirit who wrote it, which spirit you cannot find more surely present than in these sacred Scriptures, which he himself wrote. Our endeavor must, therefore, not be to put aside Scripture and to direct our attention to the merely human writings of the Fathers. On the contrary, putting aside all human writings, we should spend all the more persistent labor on the Holy Scriptures alone. . . . Or tell me, who is the final judge when statements of the Fathers contradict themselves? In this event, the judgment of Scripture must decide the issue, which cannot be done if we do not give Scripture first place. . . . We must recognize that it is in itself the most certain, most easily understood, most plain, is its own interpreter, approving, judging, and illuminating all statements of all men. . . . Therefore nothing but the divine words are to be the first principles of all Christians; all human words are conclusions drawn from them and must be brought back to them and approved by them. . . . I do not wish to boast that I am more learned than all, but that Scripture alone

should reign, nor do I pretend that it is to be interpreted by my spirit or that of other men. But I wish to understand it by its spirit.[21]

This is Luther's formulation of the great reform principle of *sola scriptura*, which is less a theory of the biblical text as such than a description of a kind of hermeneutical situation in which the reader is not so much the interpreter as the interpreted. If we take allegory as the redescription of an alien text in one's own language, what would it be for this movement to reverse itself? What is it to be appropriated by a text and understood in its terms? Scripture, Luther says, "is in itself the most certain, most easily understood, most plain, is its own interpreter": and, what is more, it interprets not only itself but everything in its path or whatever is placed before it—not just other texts (the Fathers, say) but also, most important, the one who reads. Scriptural interpretation here is analogous to legal interpretation in the sense that one is subject to the text, under its jurisdiction and its power, exposed to it, answerable to it for one's conduct, defined by its meanings. But all this means is that one's relation to the text is ontological rather than simply exegetical. Luther's distinction between law and gospel is a way of extending this ontological relation from the notion of a legal indictment to that of a spiritual one in which one's self-understanding or self-identity is reconstituted by the text.[22] To understand the Scriptures is to see oneself in its light; to understand the Scriptures as Gospel means to see oneself in the light of Christ and his redemptive power.

But if understanding means self-understanding in this sense, how is the question of authority in interpretation to be framed? Luther's response to this question is where the essence (and, one might also say, the modernity) of Reform hermeneutics is to be found. With Luther, the Church is now centered not in Rome and in university doctors but in the hermeneutical situation in which the Scriptures are encountered. What is important is that Luther insists that this situation is *not* an allegorical one; it is not one in which the reader appropriates the text but, on the contrary, one in which the reader is exposed to the text, vulnerable to it, yet is also capable of being illuminated and transformed by its light.[23] For Luther, this light is not merely metaphorical. The lucidity of the Scriptures is more than a matter of their transparency with respect to words and meaning; it is also mystical— as Luther explains in his controversy with Erasmus. Whereas Erasmus sided with the theory of scriptural obscurity and the consequent primacy of received interpretation, Luther speaks of the double clarity of the Scriptures, which are self-illuminating and at the same time dispel the internal darkness of the human heart.[24] Erasmus, the scholar and intellectual, speaks for the scholastic tradition of exegetical control when he asks how understanding according to the spirit can be tested: "If we grant that he who has the Spirit is sure of the meaning of the Scriptures, how can I be certain of what he finds to be true for himself? What am I to do when many bring diverse interpretations, about which each swears he has the Holy Spirit? And since the Spirit does not furnish the whole truth to anyone, even he who has the Spirit may be mistaken or deceived in some single point. So much for those who easily reject the interpretation of the Fathers in Holy Scripture and oppose their views to ours as if delivered by an oracle."[25] Luther, the Augustinian monk, speaks for the monastic tradition of Bernard of Clairvaux, with its emphasis on contemplative solitude and the spirituality of the scriptural encounter. In this tradition, taking the text in the spirit in which it was written does not mean producing an objective exegetical reading that can be reproduced and tested; it means being informed or consumed or even exalted by the spirit of the text. The Scriptures are a pneumatic text in which the meaning of a word is its force. As Luther says, "Scripture is not understood, unless it is brought home, that is, experienced."[26] Objectivity is achieved not by reflecting oneself out of the space in front of the text but by opening oneself and exposing oneself, laying one's heart bare; it is, as Ebeling puts it, "a surrender of the mind of the interpreter to the mind of Scripture."[27] For Luther, interpretation is reducible to neither exegesis nor eisegesis because it is concerned not with deciphering meanings but with the event of interpretation itself. The reader is not so much a productive agent acting on the text as one who listens and responds—who reads with the ear and is overtaken and possessed by the text, and indeed transformed by it.[28] Hence the need to wipe the Sacred Page clean, to remove everything that stands in the way of one's experience of the text, and this means above all the ready-made interpretations enshrined in the archive of fourfold meaning.

A pneumatic text? Luther's hermeneutics presupposes a relationship to the Scriptures that is not a grammarian's relationship to a textual object but that of a listener to a voice. Think of Petrarch's hermeneutics, as Thomas Greene reconstructs it, which seeks to recover pagan antiquity rather than to allegorize it. As Greene says, reading for someone like Petrarch means bridging time, not piercing a veil.[29] But this means reawakening an antique spirit instead of reconstructing original meanings. It was no trouble for Petrarch to imagine himself rendering Cicero's contemporaneity, conversing with him, exchanging letters ("Franciscus sends his greetings to Cicero. I have been hunting for your letters long and persistently. I discovered them where I least expected to, and avidly read them. I could hear your voice, Marcus Tullius").[30] Petrarch reads Cicero in the spirit of Cicero, where "spirit" is not a metaphor (not just a metaphor) but characterizes the condition of intimacy in which understanding takes place. It would not be too much to describe this condition as ethical in the sense in which Emmanuel Levinas uses this term when he speaks of our relation to the other as a condition of proximity and exposure. This condition is not, he says, "a modality of cognition" but one of openness and vulnerability in which one's self-identity is interrupted by the other. The other is no longer external to the subject as an object that reposes in itself and waits to be acted upon. On the contrary, subjectivity itself is structured "as the other in the same," that is, it is no longer a consciousness beholding its objects but a subject disturbed and even invaded by what is alien.[31] In roughly this wise, when Luther speaks of the Spirit inscribing itself in the heart of one who reads, what he is getting at is precisely this sort of condition of openness, intimacy, and vulnerability of the subject to the text. The text in this event is irreducible to its grammatical character; it is no longer intelligible purely in terms of the letter inscribed on the page. It is now a pneumatic text that enters into and inhabits (indicts and identifies) the one who reads.

This is far from the condition of cognitive objectivity in which one reflects oneself out of the hermeneutical situation and regards the text from a historical-critical or analytical distance—as in Spinoza's *Tractatus Theologico-Philosophicus* (1670), in which he proposes to study the Bible purely in the light of natural reason and "to accept nothing as an authoritative Scriptural statement which we do not perceive very clearly when we examine it in the light of its history," that is, in terms of the language and intentions of the original authors.[32] Unfortunately, as Spinoza emphasizes, most of what we need to know in this regard is irrevocably lost to us. Indeed, the "difficulties in this method of interpreting Scripture from its own history, I conceive to be so great that I do not hesitate to say that the true meaning of Scripture is in many places inexplicable, or at best mere subject for guesswork" (p. 112). Spinoza adds, however, that "such difficulties only arise when we endeavour to follow the meaning of a prophet in matters which cannot be perceived, but only imagined, not in things whereof the understanding can give a clear and distinct idea, and which are conceivable through themselves: matters which by their nature are easily perceived and cannot be expressed so obscurely as to be unintelligible; as the proverb says, 'a word is enough to the wise'" (pp. 112–13). This means that, quite apart from what the author might have originally meant, whatever in the text answers to what is rational—what does not impinge against reason—is to be accepted as the meaning of the text. ("We are at work not on the truth of passages," Spinoza says, "but solely on their meaning" [p. 101].) The model, as we might expect, is Euclid's *Elements.* "Euclid, who only wrote of matters very simple and easily understood, can easily be comprehended by anyone in any language; we can follow his intention perfectly, and be certain of his true meaning, without having a thorough knowledge of the language in which he wrote. . . . We need make no researches concerning the life, the pursuits, or the habits of the author; nor need we inquire in what language, nor when he wrote, nor the vicissitudes of his book, nor its various readings, nor how, nor by whose advice it has been received" (p. 113). It follows that the power and authority of interpretation rest with whoever can determine whether a statement answers to the claims of reason; in short, since the power of reason is equally distributed in all human beings, interpretive authority belongs to everyone—so long as he or she approaches the text "in a careful, impartial, and unfettered spirit, making no assumptions concerning it, and attributing to it no doctrines" except those which can be perceived clearly and distinctly in the light of natural reason (p. 9). Call this Cartesian hermeneutics, or the allegory of suspicion, in which the text comes under the control of the reader as disengaged rational subject, unresponsive except to its own self-certitude. Spinoza, in effect, restores the hermeneutical condition of allegory in which one rationalizes the alien text or naturalizes it within a prevailing philosophical outlook. Only now it is hard to speak of an appropriation of the text because the point is to adopt an attitude of detached regard that preserves the distance and strangeness of what is written. The Scriptures are taken out of sacred history and recontextualized within a history of historical documents as fragments from a lost world impinging on the present only as so many museum pieces. The motive of Cartesian hermeneutics is to preserve alienation as a condition of freedom from the text (a motive aroused all the more when, as in the case of the Scriptures, the texts do "not teach philosophy but merely obedience" to religious authority [p. 190]). Not surprisingly, therefore, Spinoza concludes his treatise with an assertion of the freedom and autonomy of the rational subject ("That in a Free State every man may Think what he Likes and Say what he Thinks" [p. 257]).[33]

So in contrast to the idea of a pneumatic text that inscribes itself in the reading subject, Cartesian hermeneutics proposes the idea of a text as dead letter, a purely analytical object. In a sense, such an idea brings the history of interpretation to an end, as that which is always over and done with, *vergangen*—like a history of philosophy conceived as the simple accumulation of local opinions and perspectives. Of a history so conceived, Hegel says, "we are finished with it, and have got beyond it." For if "the peculiarities of other people are external and foreign to me, purely historical and dead material, [then] the history of philosophy is superfluous, wearisome, devoid of interest except to scholars; what I get in it is a trivial mass of details, a trivial subject-matter. It does not belong to me and I am not in it."[34] Further, "the possession of purely historical facts is like the legal possession of things that I do not know what to do with" (p. 133 / p. 99). These things are now mine, I have (so to speak) inherited them, but my relation to them is merely external. Hegel gives the example of "a teacher of the history of philosophy [who] is supposed not to be partisan. This demand for neutrality has generally no other meaning but that such a teacher is to act in expounding the philosophies as if he were dead, that he is to treat them as something cut off from his spirit, as something external to him, and that he is to busy himself with them in a thoughtless way. . . . But if we are to study the history of philosophy in a worthwhile way . . . we must . . . not restrict ourselves to, or content ourselves with, merely knowing the thinking of other people. Truth is only known when we are present in it with our own spirit; mere knowledge of it is no proof that we are really at home in it." (p. 134 / p. 100). It is not enough to reproduce another's thought; it is necessary to think it as one's own. The dead letter must be reinvested with one's own spirit, meaning that one takes it up, resituates it in one's own present, appropriates it, not merely as a preserved artifact but as something internalized, that is, essential to one's self-reflection and self-identity.[35]

Hegel takes the same approach to the history of religion and to the Scriptures in particular. In his lectures of 1824 on the philosophy of religion he says that

> there is a type of theology that wants to adopt only a historical attitude toward religion; it even has an abundance of cognition, though only of a historical kind. This cognition is no concern of ours, for if the cognition of religion were merely historical, we would have to compare such theologians with countinghouse clerks, who keep the ledgers and accounts of other people's wealth, a wealth that passes through their hands without their retaining any of it, clerks who act only for others without acquiring assets of their own. They do of course receive a salary, but their merit lies only in keeping records of the assets of other people. In philosophy and religion, however, the essential thing is that one's own spirit itself should recognize a possession and content [einen Besitz und Inhalt], deem itself worthy of cognition, and not keep itself humbly outside.[36]

So understanding means appropriation, but it is important to notice that Hegelian appropriation is powerfully allegorical in character. For example,

Hegel complains that the so-called rational theology of the Enlightenment seeks merely to reproduce an original doctrine and to interpret the Scriptures in its own terms.

> But where interpretation is not mere explanation of the words but discussion of the content [*Erörterung des Inhalts*] and elucidation of the sense [*Erklärung des Sinnes*], it must introduce its own thoughts into the word that forms the basis [of the faith]. There can only be mere interpretation of words when all that happens is that one word is replaced by another with the same scope. If interpretation is elucidation, then other categories of thought are bound up with it. A development of the word is a progression to further thoughts. One seemingly abides by the sense, but in fact new thoughts are developed. Bible commentaries do not so much acquaint us with content of scripture as with the mode of thought of their age." (p. 39 / p. 123)

For Hegel, interpretation is always radical in the sense that the alien text can be elucidated only within the conceptual order (or, say, the spirit) of the one who interprets. "No one," he says, "can escape the substance of his time any more than he can jump out of his skin."[37] There is no going back in history; rather, one takes history forward into (and so by means of) one's thinking. This is the meaning of *Aufhebung*. As Hegel puts it in his lectures of 1831 on the philosophy of religion, "It is, indeed, the sense contained in the words which is supposed to be given. The giving of the sense means, however, the bringing forward of the sense into consciousness, into the region of ideas; and these ideas, which get determinate character elsewhere, then assert their influence in the exposition of the sense supposed to be contained in the words. It is the case even in the presentation of a philosophical system which is already fully developed, as, for example, that of Plato or of Aristotle, that the presentation takes a different form, according to the definite kind of idea which those who undertake thus to expound it have already formed for themselves."[38] We understand differently, as Gadamer will later say, if we understand at all.

The point is that there is no understanding at a distance. Understanding means having an internal connection with what is understood. But this notion of internal connection is highly ambiguous. In a text from 1819, Friedrich Schleiermacher says: "The task [of hermeneutics] is to be formulated as follows: 'To understand the text at first as well as and then even better than its author.'"[39] This means situating the text in the time and place of its composition, as in the logical reconstruction of meaning based on formal analysis and historical research; but it also means retracing the process of composition so that, as Schleiermacher had once phrased it, "the interpreter can put himself 'inside' the author [*dass man sich dadurch in den Schriftsteller 'hinein' bildet*]" (p. 50 / p. 64). Here, in contrast to Hegel, the point is not simply to appropriate another's idea but to enter into another's subjectivity, as if to understand the other from the inside out. What is it to grasp the self-experience or self-intimacy of another?

Gadamer in *Truth and Method* has emphasized the difference between understanding the subject matter of a text (Hegel) and understanding the subjectivity of the text's author (Schleiermacher). This distinction forms the basis of his critique of Schleiermacher's romantic subjectivism and his argument that we understand a text when we understand things (ourselves, for example, or the world) in its light.[40] But one could emphasize just as well the difference between Hegel's interest in what is universal ("the peculiarities of other people are external and foreign to me") and Schleiermacher's idea that understanding and interpretation are always of what is singular and unique. As Levinas says, "A universal thought dispenses with communication" (*Totality and Infinity*, p. 72). What is universal does not need to be interpreted, whereas what is singular is never anything less than many-sided and opaque. For Hegel, intelligibility means the subsumption of the singular into a higher conceptual order; for Schleiermacher it means, or at least entails, the recovery of the singular from a background in which it is part of a whole or a representative case. Grammatical and historical interpretation, that is, the reconstruction of the linguistic and historical context of an utterance, is only preliminary to an understanding that requires us to work back through the utterance to the person who originally produced it. Understanding is of other people, not simply of meanings or concepts. As Schleiermacher says, "We must not only explain the words and the subject matter [*Wort- und Sacherklären*] but the spirit of the author as well" (p. 155 / p. 212).

Schleiermacher appears to mean this in both a strong and a weak sense, as when he distinguishes between two methods of psychological or, as he sometimes called it, technical or artful interpretation, namely, the divinatory and the comparative: "By leading the interpreter to transform himself, so to speak, into the author, the divinatory method seeks to gain an immediate apprehension of the author as an individual [*das individuelle unmittelbar aufzufassen sucht*]. The comparative method proceeds by subsuming the author under a general type" (p. 105 / p. 150). To be sure, Schleiermacher did not inquire into what happens when the spirit of another is understood in this immediate way. What would it be to transform oneself into someone else?[41] As Heinz Kimmerle notes, for Schleiermacher hermeneutics is more method than experience.[42] Schleiermacher is perhaps more Hegelian than Gadamer makes him out to be, particularly in a late text in which he emphasizes the limitations of the divinatory and comparative methods and the need to subsume them into a higher understanding of the interplay between the spirit of the author and the spirit of the age. But it does not appear that for Schleiermacher the task of hermeneutics is simply to overcome our historical and cultural differences from the texts that we study; rather, it is also to overcome our separateness from one another, our psychological solitude, our condition as solitary subjects for whom misunderstanding or alienation is a condition that has always got to be assumed as the starting point of hermeneutics (p. 110). For the point is not just to think another's thoughts but to encounter, as if in the intimacy of self-experience, another mind.[43] Understanding is of minds rather than of thoughts.

This idea stands out more sharply in Friedrich Dilthey's historicist elaboration of Schleiermacher's concept of *verstehen*.[44] For Dilthey overcoming my own solitude means bringing the dead letter of history to life through the mediation of my own subjectivity. Except that the texts that come down to me from the past are not dead. They are more than simply sources and documents for historical reconstruction conducted from a transcendental viewpoint. Dilthey's theory of the text, like Luther's, is *geistlich,* or pneumatic, and his hermeneutics is likewise one of experience rather than of exegesis. The construction of meaning is more than exegesis, because meaning is not a logical entity but a life-expression (*Lebenaüsserung*), that is, the expression of the lived experience (*Erlebnis*) of other people. Experience is something that cannot be understood from the outside or at a distance but only by living through it, and insofar as history is composed of experience it can only be understood internally, that is, by reliving it, or what Dilthey calls *Nacherleben,* the key word of Dilthey's hermeneutics. It means projecting myself into the expressions that come down to us in order to breathe my life into them and make them live within me as my own. *Nacherleben,* reliving the lived experience of another, is a mode of appropriation in which I overcome the otherness of other people by integrating their experiences of the world into my own self-understanding; and this means an enlargement of self-understanding to include the objective spirit of mankind.[45]

Gadamer complains that in Dilthey's hermeneutics, for all of its emphasis on life and experience, the "I" of interpretation remains an abstraction, a transparent, disembodied subject that merely deciphers history but does not experience it (*Truth and Method,* p. 241). This perhaps misses Dilthey's insistence that understanding is not just something mental but means belonging to a historical and already-understood world.[46] The real issue between Gadamer and Dilthey lies in the difference between two conceptions of hermeneutical experience—*Nacherleben* and *Erfahrung* (Hegel's word for experience). In the one the subject internalizes its object, consumes it, adds it to itself; in the other the subject is divested, exposed, and transformed by what happens to it. One could clarify this difference with the help of Robert Solomon's remark that in Hegel's *Phenomenology* consciousness is "downright cannibalistic"; that is, it is repeatedly characterized as something "voracious, as 'gobbling up' (Hegel's term) everything it confronts."[47] The same can be said, if less colorfully, about Dilthey's notion of *Nacherleben*. By reliving the experiences of others, my own horizon of experience expands in the direction of universality. *Nacherleben* is a species of Hegelian *Aufhebung*.

But what of the text that refuses to be assimilated in this way? Of course, I can always find ways of reading that overcome this refusal. I can always perform various sorts of translation of the text into my own ways of thinking. But Gadamer's idea is that it is not always possible to bring the text under such hermeneutical control. Gadamer restores Luther's idea of being exposed to a text and interpreted by it. This comes out in his attempt to recuperate the notion of the classical. The classical, Gadamer says, "does not refer to a quality that we assign to particular historical phenomena, but to a notable mode of being historical, the historical process of preservation [Bewahrung] that, through the constant proving of itself [Bewährung], allows something true [ein Wahres] to come into being" (*Truth and Method*, p. 271 / p. 287). Granted that the task of historical criticism is to situate the text in the time and place of its composition. But what happens if the text refuses to remain situated in this way? What if the work proves uncontainable and breaks out of the context we have constructed for it? "The classical," Gadamer says, "is something that resists historical criticism" (p. 271 / p. 287). It is something inescapable in the sense that we cannot reflect ourselves out of the situation that it defines. There is no getting around behind its normative power. It bears upon us with exactly the force that Luther reserved for the Scriptures. "The classical," says Gadamer (quoting Hegel, although the language is Luther's),

is "that which is self-significant [selbst bedeutende] and hence also self-interpretive [selber Deutende]." But that ultimately means that the classical preserves itself precisely *because* it is significant in itself and interprets itself; i.e., it speaks in such a way that it is not a statement about what is past—documentary evidence that still needs to be interpreted—rather, it says something to the present as if it were said specifically to it. What we call "classical" does not first require the overcoming of historical distance, for in its own constant mediation it overcomes this distance by itself. The classical, then, is certainly timeless, but this time-lessness is a mode of historical being. (pp. 273–74 / pp. 289–90)

It is easy to misunderstand this idea. One could say that the classical appears self-interpreting because it is the expression of universal genius, and so what it says makes itself plain to every age. What it says is just universally the case. Call this a neoclassical theory of the classical. But for Gadamer the truth of the classical is not of this sort; it is, in a sense, not something that can be reproduced but, paradoxically, something that can occur only once. This is because the truth of the classical—or perhaps of any text—is comparable to the truth of experience, where experience is not Dilthey's *Erlebnis* but Hegel's *Erfahrung*, namely, an event that one undergoes and from which one cannot turn back because one has been turned into some-one else by the experience. Experience as *Erfahrung* is dialectical rather than inductive. For Hegel it is a way of negation in which one recognizes the untruth of what one had thought. Its structure is that of "a reversal [*Umkehrung*] of consciousness itself."[48] This means more than simply an alteration of perspective or change of mind. Hegel thinks of it in terms of a transition from natural to philosophical consciousness, as progress toward the self-certainty of absolute knowledge. But Gadamer emphasizes the ne-gativity of experience in an entirely different way. For him, experience is a process of disillusionment or divestiture that leaves us standing before the world without the protection of familiar concepts. It is not a kind of knowl-edge, he says, but is opposed to knowledge. Experience puts us in touch with reality not by revealing it to us but by exposing us to it.[49] Imagine a text that could situate us in the world in this way, by divesting us of our concepts and removing us from familiar ground. Such a text of course could never be simply a formal object for us. The truth of such a text could never be formulated simply in terms of meanings, much less in universal terms. On the contrary, it could only be formulated as a narrative of what hap-pened to us in our encounter with the text.

We can distinguish between mundane and sublime versions of this idea. The mundane version would be Gadamer's notion of being opened up by a text. This occurs whenever a text resists our efforts to integrate it into our conceptual horizon. For Gadamer, the resistance of the classical or eminent text is always critical rather than merely passive; the text resists our under-standing in such a way as to bring into the foreground the historicality—the limits or finitude—of our hermeneutical situation. Gadamer speaks of historicality in terms of prejudices, but what he has in mind is not just the

subjective attitude of expectation and prejudgment but also the cultural for-
mations, the social, political, and intellectual constructions (call it the
world) within which our encounter with the text occurs and which the text
always unsettles, always puts at risk. The breakdown of prejudices (that is,
of the forestructure of understanding) that occurs in hermeneutical experience amounts to a breakdown of a world that requires a radical reinterpretation. A dramatic, vaguely frightening example of this sort of thing might
be Jorge Luis Borges's story "Tlön, Uqbar, Tertius Orbis," in which the discovery of an encyclopedia for an imaginary planet causes a conceptual revolution that transforms Western culture into a facsimile of the alien world.
A less dramatic textbook example might be the transformation of medieval
culture by the recovery of ancient texts. Gadamer's model, meanwhile, is
the Platonic dialogue. For him every text occupies the position of Socrates
with respect to the one who seeks to interpret it, so that even when we try
to reduce a text formally by means of analysis and exegesis, we are nevertheless (know it or not) always in a position of being interrogated, opened
up and exposed in the manner of one of Socrates' interlocutors. As in
Luther's hermeneutics, interpretation is an event that moves in two directions. It is not possible to interpret a text without being interpreted by it in
turn.

The sublime (one could almost say mystical) version of this idea would
be Heidegger's notion of "undergoing an experience with language [*mit der
Sprache eine Erfahrung zu machen*]." In an essay entitled "The Nature of
Language," Heidegger writes:

> To undergo an experience with something—be it a thing, a person, or
> a god—means that this something befalls us, strikes us, comes over us,
> overwhelms and transforms us. When we talk of "undergoing" an ex-
> perience, we mean specifically that the experience is not of our own
> making; to undergo [*machen*] here means that we endure it, suffer it,
> receive it as it strikes us and submit to it. It is this something itself that
> comes about, comes to pass, happens.
>
> To undergo an experience with language . . . means to let ourselves
> be properly concerned by the claim of language by entering into and
> submitting to it. If it is true that man finds the proper mode of his
> existence in language—whether he is aware of it or not—then an ex-
> perience we undergo with language will touch the innermost nexus of
> our existence. We who speak language may thereupon become trans-
> formed by such experiences, from one day to the next or in the course
> of time. But now it could be that an experience we undergo with lan-
> guage is too much for us moderns.[50]

Experience in this sense is not merely a subjective encounter with an object that reposes quietly in itself. Language at all events is not any such object— is not an object of any sort—whence it is quite beyond our ability to step outside of it and grasp it from a distance. Of course, we imagine that in learning a language, for example, we come to master it, to appropriate it and make it our own. This instrumental view is, so to speak, our natural (or at all events modern) attitude toward language. But an experience with language turns this attitude upside down. Appropriation is no longer an act that we perform but an event in which we are taken up and which brings us out into the open, exposes us to what we cannot control, to words and things exceeding the grasp of our concepts. There is no short way of saying what this means, unless it were to say that from the beginning it is language that appropriates us, catches us up in its play and "transforms us into itself [*es uns zu sich verwandelt*]" (p. 177 / p. 74). Heidegger emphasizes that an experience with language does not occur in our speaking of it; on the con- trary, it is when language withholds itself, when words fail or get away from us, when we are struck dumb or left bewildered by the excessiveness of language, that language overwhelms and transforms us. An experience with language turns us into something other than speaking subjects; it takes us out of the propositional attitude in which we assert our mastery over words and things and resituates us in an attitude of listening.[51]

Listening is the key word of Heidegger's hermeneutics. Our relation to language, and by extension to whatever is put into language and whatever comes down to us in tradition, is not the Hegelian *Aufhebung* but the an- cient contemplative and mystical attitude of listening. One recalls the mo- nastic tradition of reading with one's ears. In an commentary on the Heraclitean Fragment 50—"When you have listened not to me but to the Logos . . ."—Heidegger asks what it is that happens when true listening occurs. In true listening one enters not simply into another's subjectivity but into what is said; or rather it is the other way around, because in listening one is open and vulnerable in a way that one is not when simply looking or probing. It matters to Heidegger that in German the word for listening and hearing is also the word for belonging. "We have heard [*gehört*]," Heidegger says, "when we belong to [*gehören*] what is said."[52] When one listens one steps out of the aggressive mode of grasping and knowing into the mode of belonging. In the mode of listening and belonging, one is in the grasp of what is said, no longer in the attitude of domination and control. It is pre- cisely at this point that Heidegger seems reactionary by comparison with Hegel. Hegel's *Umkehrung* is progressive, that is, a movement toward en- lightenment and the self-certainty of absolute consciousness. In contrast to the voraciousness of Hegel's *Aufhebung,* Heidegger says, his own approach to the history of thinking is not an approach at all but a "step back," a refusal of appropriation and conceptual control in order to listen for what remains unthought and unspoken in all that comes down to us from the past.[53] Thinking, Heidegger says, is not reasoning or questioning but listening; its goal is not conceptual representation but *Gelassenheit,* or a letting go, releasement, and "openness to the mystery."[54]

Heidegger always rejected the idea that his work contains hidden theological motives, but its movement vis-à-vis Hegel and the philosophical tradition duplicates Luther's movement away from the appropriation and mastery of the text toward openness and self-reflection in light of the text. It is Gadamer who makes this Lutheran connection explicit when, following Heidegger's *Umkehrung,* he appeals to the "forgotten history of hermeneutics" in which "understanding always involves something like applying the text to be understood to the interpreter's present situation" (*Truth and Method,* p. 291 / p. 308). Gadamer is, in a way, a secular Luther who has substituted tradition for the Holy Scriptures, where tradition is likewise a discourse, or (better) a history or crush of histories that cannot be brought under the control of interpretation. Like Luther, his concern is not with the production of interpretations but with the question of what it is to inhabit a given hermeneutical situation. And this is as good a way as any of characterizing the regulating question of this book. In the following chapters, I want to continue to give some different senses to this question.

Wordsworth at the Limits of Romantic Hermeneutics

8

> However exalted a notion we would wish to cherish of the
> character of a Poet, it is obvious, that while he describes
> and imitates passions, his employment is in some degree
> mechanical, compared with the freedom and power of real and
> substantial action and suffering. So that it will be the wish of
> the Poet to bring his feelings near to those of the persons
> whose feelings he describes, nay, for short spaces of time,
> perhaps, to let himself slip into an entire delusion, and even
> confound and identify his own feelings with theirs; modifying
> only the language which is thus suggested to him by a
> consideration that he describes for a particular purpose, that
> of giving pleasure.
> —Wordsworth, Preface to *Lyrical Ballads*

In this chapter I want to try to gloss the above passage, with its reference to something that looks very much like the Stanislavsky method of getting into character, where one loses oneself in the construction of someone else. Imagine a theory of poetry as acting, in which the distinction between being and acting loses its ontological force. As it happens, glossing this passage will mean situating Wordsworth within the history of interpretation, by which I mean the history that concerns itself with the question of understanding. What is it that happens when something, or someone, makes sense, or maybe stops making sense, or is just plain inaccessible to sense, as most of us are? What is this word *sense,* and why do we make so much of it? What is it to make sense of other people? The history of interpretation is the history of coping with the irreducible difficulty of these questions.

Wordsworth enters this history at one of its richest and most critical moments. We ourselves are still very much a part of this moment, because we define ourselves as having gotten beyond it. It is the point at which the question of understanding gets formulated for the first time as a problem about other minds, that is, as a project of entering into and experiencing alien subjects—experiencing them from the inside out, as they experience themselves, which is to say as we experience *our* selves: the idea is to enter into the self-experience of another, inhabiting the other as other. This project defines what is romantic about romantic hermeneutics, whose goal is summarized by Schleiermacher in a famous formulation: "To understand the text at first as well as and then even better than its author."[1] Understanding in this historical context goes by the German word *verstehen:* it means getting inside the author's time and place but also, in some sense, getting inside the author's head in order to reproduce, in Schleiermacher's words, "the original psychic process of producing and combining images and ideas" (p. 204). There is a postulate of inner space here that carries interpretation considerably beyond the analytical construction of meaning. For Schleiermacher, objective interpretation has a psychological, divinatory component that "leads the interpreter to transform himself . . . into the author" (p. 150): so the goal of interpretation is to inhabit—inhabit immediately, without mediation, as in moment of psychic identity—the self-understanding, the inner space, of the one who writes. Dilthey, following Schleiermacher, puts the romantic idea this way: "We strain," he says, "to get inside a speaker."[2] This is what motivates hermeneutics, the study of history, and indeed all the human sciences; perhaps it is the motivation of thinking itself, in the sense that what calls for thinking is always the thinking of another and not just a disembodied problem or transcendental question. To think is to enter into the consciousness that thinks, which for Dilthey is ultimately human consciousness as such, the "objective mind" of humankind or human culture; but this objective mind is always mediated by the lived experiences (*Erlebnisse*) of individuals, and to interpret is to enter into this mediation. Lived experience has no reality at the level of general law. Thus Dilthey describes the motivation of thought underlying the human sciences as the "infinite desire to surrender to, and lose oneself in, the existence of others" (p. 215). *Verstehen,* in Dilthey's terms, is *Nachbildung,* the logical (but also imaginative) reproduction of the "mental life of another person" (p. 227), but because one's own consciousness is the medium of this construction, understanding is also *Nacherleben,* or reexperiencing the lived experience of another, that is, experiencing a Thou as an I, understanding the other the way we understand ourselves, or perhaps better. For Dilthey there can be no self-understanding that is not mediated by the hermeneutical experience of the other. As he wrote in his famous essay on "The Development of Hermeneutics," "The inner experience of my own states can never, by itself, make me aware of my own individuality. Only by comparing my-self to others and becoming conscious of how I differ from them can I ex-perience my own individuality" (p. 247).

All of this is close to the kind of thing Plato warned us about in the *Republic* (book 2), where *mimesis* means slipping into the feeling or delu-sion that we are someone else (Achilles, say, or some other heroic or maybe not-so-heroic character). As if understanding other people carried with it the risk of madness, which perhaps it always does, because evidently no one is ever driven mad alone; on the contrary it is philosophical lucidity, rational self-possession, that consists in the mind's uninterrupted, not to say simple or uncomplex, self-identity. One never associates this sort of self-identity with poetic consciousness. "When the mind is like a hall in which thought is like a voice speaking," Wallace Stevens says, "the voice is always that of someone else."[3] Stevens thought this pretty scary, because hearing voices, after all, *is* a bit scary, and as I've tried to show elsewhere a good deal of Stevens's imaginative energy went into the construction of a monological attitude that reduces heterogeneous voices to a single harmonious chorus. The question is whether this amounts to getting rid of the human.[4] Perhaps getting rid of the human is the price the imagination asks us to pay for art—but I don't want to tangle with this monstrous question here: not exactly. All I want to hold onto for the present is the idea that there is always more than one of us inside of us, as Marx, Freud, and Nietzsche thought. The hermeneutics of suspicion is very much in the romantic tradition, where being conscious entails the problem of internalizing whole structures of other people. We can think of *Dr. Jekyll and Mr. Hyde,* for example, as a story about ideology ("There is no document of civilization which is not at the same time a document of barbarism"). It is certainly an allegory of ro-mantic hermeneutics, and so is Schleiermacher's speculation that "each per-son contains a minimum of everyone else," as if we were not sealed-off subjects the way philosophers imagine but so many incarnations of one an-other *(Hermeneutics,* p. 150). *"Je est un autre,"* says Rimbaud in a famous line. "I am Heathcliff," says Cathy. Or think of Yeats's idea that we are all inhabitants of antithetical selves, like mask wearers. From Yeats's stand-point it would be misleading to ask what sort of understanding goes into, or underwrites, the wearing of masks, because for him understanding flows from the direction of the other, from the mask to the self, which is a sort of metaphorical version of Dilthey's idea. Understanding, whether of oneself or another, is just the wearing of masks. What would it be for me to inhabit your persona? This is a thought that probably crosses every actor's mind; Yeats merely thought that it would cross ours as well if there were any substance to us: getting into a role, he thought, is not just the romantic but the heroic or mythic mode of being.

Formerly people thought of understanding as a matter of entering into the mind of God, becoming privy to his secrets or his will or what he knows of the future, mystically entering into his own spirit or life, hearing him speak, seeing him, quite possibly, face-to-face—but of course there was never thought of turning into God, only of being appropriated by him, of being made his own or one of his own, his chosen or betrothed. So understanding might be figured as a form of initiation into a secret relationship, into mystery or a community of the faithful or into a body of sometimes recondite teachings or a mystical body that overrides the distinction between the living and the dead; or it might be a matter of throwing light on what is dark, or of being illuminated as by a divine flash or warmed by God's sweet breath, or of crossing a threshold into another order of existence where understanding is no longer necessary. Most often understanding what is said or written just means understanding how it applies to you, how it fits you, how it was meant for you, a message uttered like a whisper for no ears but your own, so that taking a text in the right spirit means taking it to heart, not trying to evade it, which is the mistake tragic heroes always make, seeking by disguise or flight to empty prophecies of their force. The history of interpretation is, not surprisingly perhaps, preoccupied with the questions of prophecy and law, where there can be no such thing as interpretation at a safe distance.

After Luther, however, these various hermeneutical traditions begin to drift to the margins, to be repressed or reassimilated in various obscure ways by a figure of the reader as a solitary subject alone with a printed text, that is, a demystified or reduced text, the text as decontextualized object whose sense and force are, in a manner of speaking, enclosed in brackets or quotation marks, placed in suspension or suspended animation: distanced. Of course a legal text cannot be bracketed quite so easily as this (certainly not in the way we have learned to bracket literary texts), but even with legal texts the idea is also very strong that one can understand the text only from the outside as someone not addressed by it; which is what our idea of objectivity comes to, namely, that if a text is meant for you, if you're subject to it in some way, bound by it, you're not in a position to make sense of it, as if making sense meant making the text subject to the hypnotic power of your analytical gaze, bringing it under your conceptual control.

There is a complicated story here that remains to be told—about how the printing press produced a culture of reading radically different from anything that had existed before: a culture in which the individual reader can appropriate the act of reading, where reading can now mean (or seem to mean) reading for oneself, say, independently of the sort of institutionalized setting in which one would be read to ceremoniously by a figure of forbidding authority: read to moreover from a text that one was not allowed to touch and rarely even to see—a text that looms invisibly, whose mode of existence is a disembodied or apocalyptic voice out of nowhere, echoing and reechoing in one's ear: a transcendental or mystified text, a text warm and reverberating with pneumatic energy: a dark, closed, reserved, infinitely intended or bottomless text: a text with its face turned away in a gesture of hermeneutic refusal, but a text that nevertheless bears down upon everyone, impressing the whole world or even the cosmos with the force of law: a text no one can stand up to or apart from: a text that brings the world to its knees. To be a text (to be worth reading) is to be an extension or version or semblance of this transcendental scripture.

Dante and Petrarch still knew such a text. It is the one in which letter and spirit are both to be taken literally, a pneumatic text that enables one (literally) to enter into a dialogue with its author. Think of Dante's encounter with Virgil or of Petrarch's letters to his friend and contemporary Cicero. Later we will ask about the difference between entering into a dialogue with an author and entering into the author as a subject endowed with an interior distance. The difference is the difference between ancient and modern hermeneutics. Luther is very much the crucial figure here. In Lutheran hermeneutics the Spirit that inscribes the text does so in the heart of the one who reads. Luther restructured hermeneutics around the individual reader, but he retained the ancient notion of the text as (literally) a spiritual medium, a place or region of inspiration in which the spirit of the author enters into the reader, inhabits the reader, transforms her, graces her, sanctifies or elects her, fills her with enthusiasm. One can think of romantic hermeneutics as a sort of reversal of this idea, call it a secularized theory of inspiration in which the reader enters into a dead author and breathes new life into *her:* call it restoring the dead letter to pneumatic presence, lending it spirit.

Dryden is somewhere between Luther and Wordsworth in this regard. The idea of being inhabited by an author's spirit still makes not just metaphorical sense to him. He has this remark in *Preface to the Fables, Ancient and Modern* (1700): "Spenser more than once insinuates that the soul of Chaucer was transfused into his body."[5] Dryden insinuates no less. When he translated Chaucer he thought he could do a good job of it—indeed, thought he had the right to rewrite Chaucer, improve upon him—because he was, in some not just metaphorical sense, a reincarnation of Chaucer's spirit; Dryden is Dryden, but in the bargain, or because of the way he *is*

Dryden, he is also, in some real sense, Chaucer. To get into the spirit of romantic hermeneutics, however, we would have to imagine Dryden trying to reincarnate himself *as* Chaucer, annihilating himself as Dryden and inhabiting another self, translating himself, as if by a psychic metamorphosis, into someone completely different, someone strange or alien, someone from another world.

The note of self-annihilation seems distinctive. Understanding the other means becoming the other, means (therefore) unbecoming oneself, being objective where being objective means being subjective for someone else's subject. Think of the way Descartes, in *Discourse on Method,* turns himself into someone radically different from himself, someone (something?) no longer Descartes: "I then examined closely what I was, and saw that I could imagine that I had no body, and that there was no world nor any place that I occupied, but that I could not imagine for a moment that I did not exist . . .; therefore I concluded that I was a substance whose whole essence or nature was only to think, and which, to exist, has no need of space nor of any material thing. Thus it follows that this ego, this soul, by which I am what I am, is entirely distinct from the body and is easier to know than the latter, and that even if the body were not, the soul would not cease to be all that it now is."[6] This disembodiment of the spirit, this disincarnation, is laid down as a foundation for philosophy, that is, for knowledge, specifically of the sort that knows itself as such. No disincarnation, no knowledge (no *real* knowledge). We know that Socrates expressed some such idea as this in the *Phaedo,* but he knew that he was thoroughly embodied as Socrates and would not see justice face-to-face until after his death. But with Descartes the idea is that this disembodiment is *methodologically* possible; one can systematically disembody oneself, turn oneself, by methodical acts of suspicion, into a pure spirit, or anyhow purely thinking thing: whence one can travel anywhere, on any strange seas of thought, so long as one holds fast to the principles of algebraic reasoning.

Descartes seems to me to set the stage for the famous romantic idea of the excursive or excursionary imagination, of the mind that can situate itself anywhere, occupy any perspective, understand any point of view, transcend any horizon, the subject turning into the objective. We know this idea in its original form from poems like Coleridge's "This Lime-Tree Bower My Prison," in which the disabled poet is nevertheless able to accompany his friends on a walking tour because the body is not in fact a prison-house so long as imagination has not been stayed or stilled by abstruse research. There is no scene we cannot inhabit, and we do not need a body to take us there. But we also know how this is so from Wordsworth, whose excursionary nature made him, among other things, a connoisseur of epitaphs (he wrote a series of essays on epitaphs—texts that are, in their way, allegories of disembodiment and mental transport).

If you don't mind a pun, you could say that the epitaph is a species of necromantic hermeneutics. Its task, Wordsworth says, is to resurrect the mind of the person whose remains lie a few feet below; and the stress is on *mind,* not life or character or object of beloved memory. Wordsworth complains that Pope's epitaphs are mere character portraits; they do not give us the sense of the living mind of the deceased. In a good epitaph the mind of the dead one is made to appear and felt to be present, not of course as it was before death but in its disembodied or heavenly form: as if the understanding of an epitaph therefore entailed something like the experience of ghosts. So an epitaph is not a pneumatic text—the spirit has departed—but the hereabouts are haunted, and one is in on the haunting in a rather indispensable way. It is not surprising, Wordsworth says, that "epitaphs so often personate the deceased."[7] But Wordsworth prefers that writers of epitaphs speak in their own voices, because in fact understanding an epitaph means getting a feel not just for the mind of the deceased but, more important, for the mind of the mourning epitaph-writer—getting a feel for that mind in just that moment when it experiences the absent or ghostly presence of another, disembodied, departed but living spirit.

Wordsworth's idea, remember, is that epitaphs are windows onto eternity. Through them we have intimations of immortality. What they give us is an experience of the union of the living and the dead, or, say, an experience of the livingness of the dead. But the hermeneutical point is that getting into the spirit of epitaph reading entails something like having an experience of an alien consciousness. Wordsworth suggests as much when he compares the epitaph experience to a sudden rupture in a seaside reverie:

Amid the quiet of a Church-yard thus decorated as it seemed by the hand of Memory, and shining, if I may so say, in the light of love, I have been affected by sensations akin to those which have risen in my mind while I have been standing by the side of a smooth Sea, on a Summer's day. It is such a happiness to have, in an unkind World, one Enclosure where the voice of detraction is not heard; where the traces of evil inclinations are unknown; where contentment prevails, and there is no jarring tone in the peaceful Concert of amity and gratitude. I have been rouzed from this reverie by a consciousness, suddenly flashing upon me, of the anxieties, the perturbations, and, in many instances, the vices and rancorous dispositions, by which the hearts of those who lie under so smooth a surface and so fair an outside must have been agitated. The image of an unruffled Sea has still remained; but my fancy has penetrated into the depths of that Sea—with accompanying thoughts of Shipwreck, of the destruction of the Mariner's hopes, the bones of drowned Men heaped together, monsters of the deep, and all the hideous and confused sights which Clarence saw in his Dream! (pp. 134–35)

We have long since learned to see something quintessentially Wordsworthian in this cemetery scene. Geoffrey Hartman, for example, wonders whether there could be "a more archetypal situation for the self-conscious mind than this figure of the halted traveler confronting an inscription, confronting the knowledge of death and startled by it into feeling 'the burden of the mystery.'"[8] In the epitaph experience the mind is wakened to a heterogeneous consciousness, a consciousness not *of* but *as* someone else, in this case a whole graveyard of others whose "anxieties, perturbations, and . . . rancorous dispositions" are reconstituted in the wandering or excursive subject. Imagine feeling another's feelings; imagine feeling the disembodied feelings of the dead. Feeling disembodied feelings is a condition of transport, which is doubtless why suddenly Wordsworth's mind no longer inhabits his body but all at once has "penetrated into the depths of that Sea," which is either Sex or Death or Mind with a capital *M*—perhaps all three at once: in any case, a Davey Jones's locker filled with "the bones of drowned Men heaped together, monsters of the deep, and all the hideous and confused sights" that Clarence in Shakespeare's *Richard III* recalls from his dream of drowning:

> What dreadful noise of waters in mine ears!
> What ugly sights of death within mine eyes!
> Methought I saw a thousand fearful wrecks;
> Ten thousand men that fishes gnaw'd upon. (1.4.22–25)

Call it, just to call it something familiar, a descent into the unconscious, or into that alien mode of consciousness that our own self-consciousness, our self-possession or self-identity, requires that we repress; elsewhere Wordsworth will call it the "mind's abyss," whence the Imagination rises up "Like an unfathered vapour that enwraps, / At once, some lonely traveller" and disconnects him utterly from himself (*Prelude*, 6.594–96).

We know this Wordsworth well—Poet of the Mind, than which there is nothing lovelier on earth. But I want to take half a step back to "the anxieties, the perturbations, and . . . rancorous dispositions, by which the hearts of those who lie under so smooth a surface and so fair an outside must have been agitated." The grave, like the body, seals us off from the other; its serene surface conceals the reality that we desire to know or to experience from the inside out—experience in the sense of appropriating or possessing as our own (the way we know, or think we know, or possess, or think we possess, ourselves). What we desire is the reality of the other; and this is, of course, just what we cannot know, not to say possess.

Romantic hermeneutics is interesting because in large part it is an attempt to answer the problem of skepticism concerning other minds. We cannot know another's pain. This is not, in Stanley Cavell's words, because of "an intellectual lack."[9] It is like Othello's not knowing that, or whether, Desdemona is faithful. It is an untranscendable doubt produced not so much by the limits of reason as by the limits of the human itself. Doubting the existence of objects we can see and touch is one thing. What Cavell calls the "truth of skepticism," its moral, hits home when it comes to the existence of the other's inner space, filled with I know not what fearful message withheld from me. "A statue, a stone, is something whose existence is open to ocular proof," says Cavell. "A human being is not" (*The Claim of Reason*, p. 496). Romantic hermeneutics is, among other things, made up of compelling fantasies in which I imagine myself exceeding the finitude that withholds the other from me. Romantic hermeneutics belongs to the culture of enlightened skepticism. It is born of the impossible desire to possess the self-possession of the other, knowing the other from the inside out, with the self-certainty of Descartes's self-experience, not doubting the other as one not-doubts oneself. But this desire, like all other desires, has its corresponding horror, which is that if I enter the inner sanctum of the other, no one will ever hear of me again. It will be like sex or death or the descent into the unconscious; or castration or animal metamorphosis or the dispossession of madmen, murderers, and sinful women. What I must give up is precisely my self-possession, my consciousness; I must evacuate my inwardness, leave my body, turn myself into I know not what, become a body for another to inhabit, or a mind for another's will to control. The mystique of mesmerism, or belief in animal or personal magnetism, is relevant here— Maria Tatar's book *Spellbound*, on the prehistory of psychoanalysis, covers valuable ground on this point—but I suppose that vampire stories show best the darker side of romantic hermeneutics.[10]

The lighter, coolheaded, ratiocinative side is represented by stories like Edgar Allan Poe's "The Purloined Letter," in which, to make a point, Dupin tells the anecdote about the schoolboy who guesses correctly in the game of odd and even because he is able to identify so thoroughly with his opponent's consciousness. The boy's explanation of how he does it illustrates well the practical, businesslike side of romantic hermeneutics: " 'When I wish to find out how wise, or how stupid or how good, or how wicked is any one, or what are his thoughts at the moment, I fashion the expression of my face, as accurately as possible, in accordance with the expression of his, and then wait to see what thoughts or sentiments arise in my mind or heart, as if to match or correspond with the expression.' "[11] The idea is that if I can imagine myself as you, turn myself into you as if from the outside in, I can know your secrets (that is, know you from the inside out). It turns out that this power of empathic imagination, the ability to turn oneself into another, is what has made Dupin such a great detective. It is also, on the romantic view, what makes the poet.

In *The Poetry of Experience* Robert Langbaum said that what distinguishes romanticism is "the role-playing or projective attitude of mind."[12] According to Langbaum, "the act of knowing spontaneously and completely is an act of imaginative projection into the external object, an act of identification with the object; so that the living consciousness perceived in the object is our own" (p. 24). This is *Einfühlung,* or "the romantic way of knowing" (p. 79). "To know an object," Langbaum says, "the romanticist must *be* it" (p. 25). This is safe enough if the object is just an object, the table or chair or text whose material appearance holds the skeptic at arm's length, just short of knowing for sure; or say that the object is a natural scene whose genius the poet is able to enliven—

> O Lady! we receive but what we give,
> And in our life alone does Nature live.

—but what if the object is another person? The problem with other people is that our knowledge of them tends to be reciprocal, intersubjective, dialogical. They are not just objects of our possessive gaze but are possessive, sometimes Dracula-like, in their turn. *Einfühlung* as the romantic way of knowing, becoming what you know, sounds like a good idea until you run up against a monster. What if the other *is* a monster, is just corrosively evil? Knowing as becoming what you know has its mortal risks.

I've often wondered if this is why Wordsworth seems to prefer the company of the dead, as if out of disappointment with the living, or a conviction, or fear, that most human beings are, up close, monstrous, devouring, so that one had better keep one's distance, never stepping outside the safe precinct of the spectator's mode where one can regard solitary reapers and highland girls without being seen. As Sartre would later analyze it, being seen, being exposed to another's gaze, is a moment of shameful dispossession, of alienating self-consciousness in which I am no longer a subject of my self-experience but am now an object for another, as is my world, which suffers what Sartre calls an "internal hemorrhage," as if my world had "a kind of drain hole in the middle of its being and [were] perpetually flowing off through this hole."[13] I think Wordsworth would have understood Sartre perfectly. Anyhow a dialogue with hoot owls suits the boy of Winander just fine. Apart from Wordsworth, the most famous character in Wordsworth's poetry is Lucy, dead before her years. Wordsworthian intimacy with nature is not something convertible to social reality. Intimacy with one's sister is mainly an extension, or reproduction, of one's own self-experience, as "Tintern Abbey" makes plain. This problem of antipathy seems to have been part of Keats's insight when he distinguished between Wordsworth's "Egotistical Sublime," his introspective hermeneutics, and his own (Keats's own, every poet's own) lack of character, that is, the "chameleon-poet's" ability to turn into other people. Antipathy toward the other in this case would be the essence of the antiromantic, call it the self-refusal of romanticism, its disavowal of itself as the mode of spiritual life motivated by *Einfühlung* or, in Dilthey's language, by the desire to lose oneself in another's existence. Here we have the workings of something like Browning's distinction between subjective and objective poets. The one follows the idea that poetry is the spontaneous overflow of powerful feelings. The other follows the same idea, except that before one experiences this powerful overflow one must turn oneself into a character who feels these things. Romantic characterization is characterization from the inside out, getting into character, Stanislavsky-style. The dramatic monologue, with its impersonation of pathological states, is the distinctive genre of romantic hermeneutics, with autobiography close behind.

Just so, the distinction between subjective and objective is hard to maintain with respect to Wordsworth because his own self-relation is, as we know, powerfully mediated by memory, by the person (he thinks) he once was, which is why, as a hermeneutical personality, a self-construction, he is more interesting than Descartes, whose *Prelude* was *Discourse on Method*. "I have said that Poetry is the spontaneous overflow of powerful feelings," Wordsworth says in a famous pronouncement: "It takes its origin from emotion recollected in tranquillity: the emotion is contemplated till, by a species of re-action, the tranquillity gradually disappears, and an emotion, kindred to that which was before the subject of contemplation, is gradually produced, and does itself actually exist in the mind. In this mood successful composition generally begins" (*Wordsworth's Literary Criticism*, p. 85). Here again is the psychic transformation that is the keystone of romantic hermeneutics. The difference between turning oneself into another and turning oneself into what one once was is perhaps not a difference in kind: it is "a species of re-action," call it reanimation, where in one case character and emotion are mediated by imagination, in the other by memory. As every student of autobiography knows, the difference between memory and imagination is epistemologically uncertain. From a hermeneutical standpoint, the difference is irrelevant, because in either case the task, or mode, of understanding remains the same: understanding means entering into the other, awakening the other in oneself, experiencing the other *as* oneself or in the medium of one's own self-experience. In Wordsworthian hermeneutics, self-understanding means reexperiencing the consciousness one once possessed (was once possessed by); it is not to know oneself as one now, presently, is; it is not Cartesian self-presence but consciousness of one's former consciousness, a doubling, a fusion of autobiographical horizons:

> The vacancy between me and those days
> Which yet have such self-presence in my mind,
> That, musing on them, often do I seem
> Two consciousnesses, conscious of myself
> And of some other Being. (*Prelude*, 2.29–33)

What about this other? Understanding in romantic hermeneutics means the appropriation of an alien consciousness, making it one's own (one's own consciousness). The Wordsworthian version of this entails the reappropriation, from within one's own memory, of a consciousness that specifically has not yet been alienated from itself by "the heavy weight / Of all this unintelligible world" ("Tintern Abbey," 39–40), a consciousness not yet estranged from itself by human experience or by the experience of the human. In Wordsworth *Nacherleben* means reexperiencing the self-experience of a consciousness still sealed off from other minds, a consciousness pure in the sense of undivided by the encounter with the otherness of other people: one should not hesitate to call this the experience of a *philosophical* consciousness—which is, I imagine, the upshot of Wordsworth's "Intimations" ode, with its memorable line about who the "best philosopher" is.

Let me step back and come round to this from another side by recalling Dilthey's theory of autobiography as the highest form that understanding can take, the perfect instance of what *verstehen* ought to be. "In autobiography," he says, "we encounter the highest and most instructive form of the understanding of life. Here life is an external phenomenon from which understanding penetrates to what produced it within a particular environment. The person who understands it is the same as the one who created it. This results in a particular intimacy of understanding" (*Dilthey: Selected Writings*, pp. 214–15). The hermeneutical genius is the interpreter who achieves this intimacy of understanding with respect to texts created by someone else. Here one has to imagine what it would be to write someone else's autobiography: it would mean living, which is to say reliving (*Nacherleben*) someone else's life: becoming, being, another—but of course this is what every autobiographer goes through, as we know starting at least from Wordsworth's case, where autobiography is not merely a reflexive account of one's past, not mere self-characterization, but, on the contrary, a *Nachbildung* and *Nacherleben* that has the effect of both reanimating an original, plenary consciousness and then restoring a secondary, evacuated consciousness to this original plenitude of feeling: what one was inhabits the hollowed-out inner space that one has become. In the "spots of time" idea, *Nacherleben* means restoring the present by means of the past, bringing back a life of feeling that seems to have dropped out of human experience. Imagine bringing oneself to life by reliving the life one once lived. Wordsworth here gets us close to Dilthey's ideal conception of interpretation as foundational for human culture, I mean foundational for the life, which is to say vitality, of culture, where the goal of the human sciences is to keep culture alive by endlessly reexperiencing, in a kind of Kierkegaardian forward repetition, the once-and-future lived experiences (*Erlebnisse*) on which its monuments are grounded.

But there is this other, darker side that Wordsworth seems to edge away from into autobiographical refuge and that Dilthey's idealism seems unable to acknowledge: namely, the fear that intimacy with another mind carries with it a risk of transformation into the strange, the monstrous, the more-or-less-than- or other-than-human. Possibly it means more: exposure to the uncanny and the horrible, to violence and madness, to a secular damnation far more unbearable than anything the religious imagination could devise. Stanley Cavell, near the end of *The Claim of Reason*, speculates briefly on romanticism's shocking discovery, that it is no problem to prove the existence of God, but proving the existence of the human unfailingly brings us up short. He mentions the wonderful passage in *Essay on the Origin of Language*, in which Rousseau has "a savage man" encountering other people for the first time and experiencing a sort of foundational fear. Cavell's gloss on this passage reads as follows:

> Fright (anyway, the experience of others as fearful) remains the basis of the knowledge of the existence of others; only now we no longer interpret the threat as a function of the other's bulk or body. We seem left with the other's sheer otherness, the fact that he, too, is an I, hence can name and know us. One can regard this moment in Rousseau as an effort to answer the question of others formed in Wittgenstein's *In-*

vestigations—or, removing the surface anachronism, one can regard Wittgenstein's question as a rediscovery of the moment discovered in Rousseau: "What gives us so much as the idea that living beings— things—can feel?" (*Investigations*, §283). (*The Claim of Reason*, p. 466)

Let us say that understanding another means reexperiencing the other's lived experience, call it (romantically) the other's "life of feeling." What we find in Wordsworth is something like a realism concerning the limits of such understanding, but perhaps it is more like what Cavell has in mind when he speaks of encountering the limits of the human, where the idea is that only by encountering these limits, where the human is caught in the moment of slipping into something else, something more-or-less or frightfully other-than-human, are we able to determine, with some approximation of philosophical self-certainty, the existence of the human. What gives us the idea, or assurance, that human beings feel? We cannot settle this question by consulting ourselves, as Wordsworth testifies in *The Prelude*. Indeed, romantic writing can be said to register in many ways the horror of turning into a human being who does not feel, which is to say, does not feel human; it is the horror of turning into an other, crossing the threshold into the not-human—I have mentioned animal metamorphosis, which Irving Massey has talked about in his book *The Gaping Pig*, but more terrifying still is metamorphosis into the nonnaturally human, say into that most loathsome of romantic creatures, the artificial man, one of Hoffmann's automatons, for example, a *mere* creature of artifice, of culture, of knowledge or science, whatever separates the child from the man.[14] What's the difference between a human being and someone made to look human, someone who walks and talks, dances and sings, plays flawlessly at the piano (a perfectly social being)? Cavell has some terrific pages on this question in the last part of *The Claim of Reason* (pp. 403–11). Hoffmann's great story "The Sandman" is in part about what happens when we discover that someone we know turns out not to be human after all but to be a technological product: what happens is that a general suspicion spreads across society like a deep stain— a suspicion that if one of us is not human, perhaps no one is. In any case, no one is above suspicion—we might all, in ways hidden from us, be merely humanoid: androids wrought to perfection, so perfectly human that we are reduced, as only civilization can reduce us, to skepticism concerning our own real existence. (There is a splendid replay of this idea in Ridley Scott's movie *Blade Runner*). Here we get some idea of what skepticism really feels like: what is it not to be able to know (not to be able to be certain, philosophically certain) that someone (oneself, for example) is human? The thrust, or trust, of romantic hermeneutics is that if we could get inside, we could be sure, that is, we could know firsthand, with more than "ocular proof," as by magical autopsy, seeing into the life of things: because admittedly one can't tell from the outside. Which is perhaps the pathos of interiority.

But what if interiority is not what is behind the barrier? What if there is no inside, or anyhow no knowing for sure that human beings have insides, inner spaces inhabited by lives of feeling or recuperable memories of lived experience? This question seems to disclose the limits of romantic hermeneutics (you will recognize it as a sort of basic postmodern question: in our own intellectual milieu we have replaced belief in interiority with belief in ideology). Wordsworth's formulation of this question, his perception of these hermeneutical limits, occurs in these lines from *The Prelude:*

> Awed have I been by strolling Bedlamites;
> From many other uncouth vagrants (passed
> In fear) have walked with quicker step; but why
> Take note of this? When I began to enquire,
> To watch and question those I met, and speak
> Without reserve to them, the lonely roads
> Were open schools in which I daily read
> With most delight the passions of mankind,
> Whether by words, looks, sighs, or tears, revealed;
> There saw into the depths of human souls,
> Souls that appear to have no depth at all
> To careless eyes. (13.157–68)

This passage gives us a sort of parable of romantic hermeneutics, including its dark side: "Awed have I been by strolling Bedlamites," among other borderline cases of human existence: "but why / Take note of this?" Good question. "We strain to get inside," says Dilthey, in the predicate that the mind is an inhabitable place, but was there ever a postulate more delicate, fragile, eager to go to pieces? After all, there are human beings who, to all appearances, just don't have such a place, or don't occupy it, who are elsewhere, or whose "words, looks, sighs, or tears" are opaque, sealing off consciousness in an uninhabitable otherness that we call madness: a place where we are always beside ourselves, never in our right minds, therefore beyond interpretation. Worse yet, we just might be one of these vagrants, because we know from sad experience what it is not to have eyes to see "into the depths of human souls." In the famous mental crisis recorded in *Prelude*, Wordsworth turns into one of these creatures of pure externality:

> I speak in recollection of a time
> When the bodily eye, in every stage of life
> The most despotic of our senses, gained
> Such strength in *me* as often held my mind
> In absolute dominion. (12.127–31)

As if the hermeneutical problem of understanding other people resolved itself into a problem of being, or staying, human, that is, not so much a problem of consciousness as a problem of being in which one's own being as human becomes sufficiently questionable as to require a constant working out and endless, as well as endlessly unsatisfied, interpretation. On a certain way of reading Wordsworth's poetry, the problem of being human, of being certain of one's humanity or of one's real human existence, is not one that one knows how to solve: certainly it is not a problem that goes away when one becomes full-grown; rather, it gets worse, one's humanness grows the more questionable, so that one can no longer see or feel in oneself quite what (one thinks) one once saw and felt: one has to turn elsewhere, to someone else, some simulacrum or reconstruction of oneself—in Wordsworth's case, his sister:

> Nor perchance,
> If I were not thus taught, should I the more
> Suffer my genial spirits to decay:
> For thou art with me here upon the banks
> Of this fair river; thou my dearest Friend,
> My dear, dear Friend! and in thy voice I catch
> The language of my former heart, and read
> My former pleasures in the shooting lights
> Of thy wild eyes. Oh! yet a little while
> May I behold in thee what I was once,
> My dear, dear Sister! ("Tintern Abbey," 111–21)

One can imagine a Hoffmannesque version of this moment: Wordsworth looks into Dorothy's eyes and—but what would it be to look into the eyes of an android that looks back at you with cool recognition and the nod of kinship? The technological irony, the disappointment with the human implicit here, is what Villiers d'Isle-Adam tried to exploit in his novel, *L'Eve future* (1883), in which Thomas Edison creates a beautiful woman who is more human, more high-spirited, more intellectually, psychologically, and morally compelling, more capable of being loved, than a real, or at least naturally born, human being.[15] One recalls Descartes's conception that an embodied human being is simply an automaton that thinks; and at any moment we expect a Nobel-prize-winning word from scientists at Berkeley or Chicago that we have at last broken the barrier that separates artificial from human intelligence. The scary part is our frank inability to say exactly why this will never happen.

Returning to Wordsworth, however, a more sober thought would be to ask with whom, or before whom, is Wordsworth not afraid? I mean, with whom, or in whose eyes, is he himself? Romanticism, Cavell says, "can be thought of as the discovery, or one rediscovery, of the subjective; the subjective as the exceptional; or the discovery of freedom as a state in which each subject claims its right to recognition, or acknowledgment" (*The Claim of Reason*, p. 466). We are not human, our existence is not proven, until we are acknowledged as such by those we take to be human. Here getting into the hermeneutical circle in the right way is all in all: getting into it, and also perhaps staying in it. The problem with "strolling Bedlamites"—why we avert our eyes and hurry on—is that they just might catch our eye and show some sign of recognition, causing an internal hemorrhage that drains us out of ourselves and into the nowhere of their alien space. "In order to make myself recognized by the Other," Sartre says, "I must risk my own life" (*Being and Nothingness*, p. 320). What Cavell calls "the experience of others as fearful," or the experience of their sheer otherness, entails an experience of self-doubt, perhaps a momentary self-alienation—think about those uncanny moments when someone you do not know mistakes you, or perhaps just takes you, for an old friend. My favorite example of this sort of epistemological crisis is the female Yahoo who throws herself passionately upon Gulliver.

Gulliver, whose self-interpretations are repeatedly undermined by his encounter with others, is an important case for study in this connection, but again I cannot help thinking of Kafka's story about poor Gregor Samsa, whose interior distance survives for a while his startling metamorphosis; but slowly he turns inwardly into a bug as well, chiefly because of the brute empirical difficulty that others have in recognizing his humanness. Gradually this recognition is withdrawn by his family, the crucial point occurring when his sister and mother remove his furniture from his room. Little did they know, much less did he, how thoroughly his inwardness, his humanity, was embedded in his furniture. As if being human depended on belonging to a human world, a human (as against, say, a horse or buggy) form of life; at which point we encounter the anthropological problem of getting into, being accepted by, and remaining a part of a human form of life, or maybe of coping with a form of life radically different from the one in which we grew up, or of coping with an alienating trajectory of growth, as if there were any other.

The postmodern critique of the subject thinks of itself as having got "beyond hermeneutics," by which it means romantic hermeneutics—for example, the Husserlian idea of interpretation as the reproduction of an author's intentional experience. Among the casualties of this critique is Georges Poulet, whose famous essay "Criticism and the Experience of Interiority," is a sort of textbook of romantic hermeneutics. Whenever I take up a book, Poulet says, "I realize that what I hold in my hands is no longer just an object, or even simply a living thing. I am aware of a rational being, of a consciousness; the consciousness of another, no different from the one I automatically assume in every human being I encounter, except that in this case the consciousness is open to me, welcomes me, lets me look deep inside itself, and even allows me, with unheard-of license, to think what it thinks and feel what it feels." But it is not, of course, simply that I now inhabit another's consciousness; on the contrary, it is that another's consciousness has displaced my own, and I, Rimbaud-like, am another: "Here I am thinking a thought which manifestly belongs to another mental world, which is being thought in me just as though I did not exist . . . as though reading were the act by which a thought managed to bestow itself within me with a subject not myself. Whenever I read, I mentally pronounce an *I,* and yet the *I* which I pronounce is not myself. . . . Reading is just that: a way of giving way not only to a host of alien words, images, ideas, but also to the very alien principle which utters them and shelters them."[16]

Poulet thinks that all of this is purely methodological, however, as if one could pick books up and put them down as one pleases, without suffering any serious transformation; as if one could read Nietzsche, for example, without turning into a Nietzschean; as if one could experience Nietzschean consciousness for a while, then dispense with it, going on as before. This is a highly aestheticized picture of reading. Call it hermeneutical consumerism. We should think of Wordsworth as buying none of this, as setting limits to Poulet from the anterior side, giving a critique of the subject by dramatizing its vulnerability to otherness, the abysmal risks that hover and loom both inside and out. I read Wordsworth's celebrated and guarded approach to the reading of books as being of a piece with his desire to keep his distance from others, to preserve self-possession against the demonic character of another's discourse. Discourse *is* demonic, possessive, dispossessing. It is perhaps the demonic nature of discourse that gives us the idea that we have consciousness, feelings, imagination, a poet's mind. Who needs to be told that nothing is more possessive than language? We cannot get it out of our

heads, cannot not be linguistical except by way of terrible injury. The sur-
mise now is that it is the possessiveness of language that generates belief in
such things as mind, conscious, spirit, interior distance—the superstition of
"mental experience." At the far end of this belief is Beckett's *The Unnamable,* which is a narrative about the demonic nature of discourse. It gives us
a disembodied subject, a pure "voice," whose self-experience is just the experience of being possessed by discourse ("It issues from me, it fills me, it
clamours against my walls, it is not mine, I can't stop it, I can't prevent it,
from tearing me, racking me, assailing me. It is not mine, I have none, I
have no voice and must speak, that is all I know").[17] As if consciousness
were a conspiracy, a trick of language designed "to make me believe I have
an ego all my own, and can speak of it" (p. 345).

Hartman asks: "Is Wordsworth afraid of his own imagination?" *(Wordsworth's Poetry,* p. 39)

> Imagination—here the Power so called
> Through sad incompetence of human speech,
> That awful Power rose from the mind's abyss
> Like an unfathered vapour that enwraps,
> At once, some lonely traveller. *(Prelude,* 6.592–96)

The dark truth of the imagination is that it is just the demonic, apocalyptic
discourse of the sort that compels the Unnamable to speak: "in such
strength / Of usurpation, when the light of sense / Goes out" (6.599–
601), one is just no longer in one's right mind, or in possession of any mind
at all. This used to be called divine inspiration, or the workings of the Muse,
or the

> workings of one mind, the features
> Of the same face, blossoms upon one tree;
> Characters of the great Apocalypse,
> The types and symbols of Eternity,
> Of first, and last, and midst, and without end. (6.636–40)

But Wordsworth's reiteration of the transcendental view is loomed with uncertainty. One can sense that what Wordsworth is afraid of is turning into
the Unnamable, into a pure threshold through which everything drains
away in the stream of discourse. It's a question of discovering the other
already inside of you, usurping your interiority, turning you into itself with
its impressive talk—I mean impressive as the opposite of expressive. Imagine
getting sucked into "the mind's abyss" (6.594), as if expression were suddenly to reverse itself and words were to flow in the opposite direction,

drawing ego and world into a black hole (recall the image of drowning from the "Essay upon Epitaphs"). In this context it is easy to think of *The Unnamable* as the last gasp of the egotistical sublime, the endgame of romantic hermeneutics. It is the expression of a consciousness discovering that consciousness is something else entirely, belongs elsewhere, is not one's own, is only just talk, does not exist. ("Does Consciousness Exist?" asks William James.) Possibly it is not too much to say that skepticism concerning the existence of Mind is to Wordsworth what skepticism concerning the existence of God was to Pascal.

I began with a quotation from the "Preface to *Lyrical Ballads*" about the poet who lets himself "slip into an entire delusion" that he is someone else. It is probably true that in Western culture this idea will always make sense, always have something to it, always be part of our self-definition: Western culture has from the beginning been a rhetorical culture of impersonation, empathy, consummate acting, getting into and projecting character: a culture in which narcissism is the name of a psychic disorder—a disorder, however, that is also essential to our self-definition. It has never been difficult to imagine ourselves, as sociologists now regularly do, as a culture of narcissists: not just a culture that could no longer interpret itself according to narratives of self-sacrifice and acting in the other's interest or the interests of solidarity but a culture that repressed such narratives in favor of stories about self-sufficient philosophers and brains in a vat. The opposite of this would perhaps be an anthropological culture, a culture absorbed in the question of the other, intoxicated by difference and strangeness; a culture that tells itself endless stories about the encounter with what is alien, where each of these stories is a narrative of a self-interpretation that we can never quite appropriate as our own. Wordsworth helps us to understand the sense in which we *are* these two cultures—a rhetorical, role-playing, Protagorean, Keatsian, Nietzschean, Erving Goffmanesque culture that depends for its self-definition on critiques of the subject, of the egotistical sublime; and a philosophical culture of the self, of *sōphrosunē* and reason and autobiography and cognitive self-identity (*cogito ergo sum*): a culture that depends on Socratic critiques of the unexamined life, not to mention critiques of mimesis, discourse, reason itself—all with a view toward justifying (in its own eyes) its transcendental self-image.[18] It is hardly surprising that, Wordsworth-like, we are demonstrably unsatisfiable with respect to either culture, at home in neither, and think of ourselves as belonging instead to the condition of crisis, as if crisis were not just a condition but a category, possibly the basic category of modernist self-understanding.

On the Tragedy of Hermeneutical Experience

9

Breakdown and failure reveal the true nature of things.
—Karl Jaspers, *Tragedy Is Not Enough*

Hermeneutics is made up of a family of questions about what happens in the understanding of anything, not just of texts but of how things are. This is different from the usual question about how to make understanding happen, how to *produce* it the way you produce a meaning or a statement where one is missing. For hermeneutics, understanding is not (or not just) of meanings; rather, meaning is, metaphorically, the light that a text sheds on the subject (*Sache*) that we seek to understand. Think of *Sache* not as an object of thought or as the product or goal of conceptual determination but as a question that comes up or confronts you—a question not of your own devising and perhaps one you don't know how to put into words, like the questions of horror and death that hover and loom from life's onset. No one thinks up questions like these; rather they encroach and bear down, and we just find ourselves exposed to them. Frequently the *Sache* of thinking makes itself felt as just this sort of question without words; it is that which resists conceptual framing and leaves one dumbstruck with its evasions. Hermeneutics has to do with these evasions. However, it is not a method of preventing or outwitting them. It is not always the case that what happens in understanding is that one understands something in the sense of grasping or solving it. What happens, what happens also or instead, is that one *always* confronts the limits—in Gadamer's language, the finitude or historicality, the situatedness—of understanding itself.

In the essay "Text and Interpretation," which was part of his so-called encounter with Derrida, Gadamer characterized these limits in terms of the "impenetrability of the otherness of the other."[1] For Schleiermacher the task of hermeneutics had been to (explain how to) understand the other, as if from inside the other's own subjective condition. After Gadamer, however, one would say that in understanding one encounters the other in its otherness, not as an object in a different time and place but as that which resists the grasp of my knowledge or which requires me to loosen my hold or open my fist. It is that which will not be objectified before me. Whether I take the other ethically as a person (Levinas) or thoughtfully, thinkingly, as a subject matter like the question of language (Heidegger), what happens in understanding is that I always experience the refusal of the other to be contained in the conceptual apparatus that I have prepared for it or that my own time and place have prepared for it; and of course this alters my own relation to this framework, not to say my own self-relation or my own standing. So one could say that what happens in understanding is not so much the familiarization of the other as self-estrangement. But perhaps it is enough to say that in this event one is left unguarded or exposed to the other as well as to oneself and the world, which is now implicated in the strangeness of the other.

It is not easy to say what sort of experience this is, however, partly because of the limitations of the concept of experience. When Gadamer's *Truth and Method* was first published (1960), the notion of experience, among other cherished ideas, had already begun to disappear from our conceptual horizon. Reasons for this certainly include the development of structuralism, which redesigned Kant's theory of the transcendental subject as a concept of a total system immanent in its results. Henceforward experience would only be a metaphor of surface structure. Moreover, structuralism provided the language for powerful new interpretations of Marx, Nietzsche, and Freud, which Paul Ricoeur summarized with the phrase "hermeneutics of suspicion." Crucially, critique of ideology, deconstruction, and psychoanalysis make complete sense only when defined critically against various German philosophies of the Spirit, where the concept of experience is a fundamental category. In the German idealist tradition experience is the domain of the creative subject. It is where we form the world and ourselves in it. For example, in 1957 Robert Langbaum argued that modern literature is a "poetry of experience," that is, a poetry of worldmaking and the formation of new values to replace an obsolete cultural inheritance.[2] The romantic motto is: there is nothing outside of experience. But now we say that everything is outside of it; it is an empty concept, a category of false consciousness. History, for example, never occurs at the level of experience.

Certainly, the foremost philosopher of experience was Wilhelm Dilthey, for whom *Erlebnis*, usually translated as "lived experience," is the basic unit of time, history, and human culture. Experience here is not of phenomena or of objects like desks and chairs; it is the existence of human subjects within a temporal order that cannot itself be objectified the way empirical data can, because one can never stand outside of temporality and observe it as it goes by (like Quine's "passing show"). Rather, one can enter into it only in reflection, and of course what one encounters then is not experience itself but only the mediating constructions produced by experiencing subjects.

For experience in the romantic sense is essentially expressive. It produces works or narratives of itself that make possible the reexperiencing of all that happens. This reexperiencing—Dilthey's *Nacherleben*—is the task of hermeneutics or, more broadly, of the hermeneutical disciplines that Dilthey called the *Geisteswissenschaften*. In Dilthey's theory what distinguishes hermeneutical understanding from scientific explanation is that understanding can never occur at an analytical distance; it always means living through what is understood. Its goal is the intelligibility of what cannot be conceptualized or reduced, namely, human life in all its singularity. The point is that in the romantic view what calls for understanding is never just a text but another subject. The text is always understood as a mediation between subjects of historical experience. The thought that one can never work through these mediations to relive the experience that produced them—the idea that one mediation simply opens onto another—is what separates us from Dilthey.

Now in *Truth and Method*, in the context of Heidegger's historicizing of the romantic subject, Gadamer has harsh words for Dilthey, whom he sees as clinging to a Cartesian theory that conceives the subject as disengaged from history and sustaining itself entirely from within. This criticism is not entirely just, but it is true that *Nacherleben* implies something like an out-of-body hermeneutics, through which the interpreter is able to escape his or her historicality and enter into the subjectivity of another. "By transposing his own being experimentally, as it were, into a historical setting," Dilthey says, "the interpreter can momentarily . . . reproduce an alien life in himself

[*Nachbildung fremden Lebens in sich herbeizuführen*]."³ This reproduction of the other in oneself is what Gadamer wants to reexamine in the light of Heidegger's historicism. One can never extricate oneself from one's own historical situation. One always reads the other from within one's own time and place. But what happens in this reading? Gadamer's idea is that we always encounter the resistance of the other to the way we make sense of things and that this encounter has important critical consequences. One cannot reproduce an alien life in oneself without risk to one's self-identity.

Indeed, Gadamer's critique of Dilthey does not do away with experience but simply brings it down to earth. Gadamer works along the lines of Heidegger's readings of Hegel, perhaps not so much the early lectures on *Hegel's Phenomenology of the Spirit* (first delivered in 1930–31) as on "Hegel's Concept of Experience" (1942–43), first published in *Holzwege* (1950). The second text is a close reading of the ten pages or so that make up Hegel's introduction to *Phenomenology*, in which experience is characterized as a reversal of consciousness (*Umkehrung des Bewusstseins*).⁴ Experience here is *Erfahrung* rather than *Erlebnis*, but it also means living through an event as against merely responding to it as a spectator. Hegel stresses that his idea "does not seem to agree with what is ordinarily meant by experience" (p. 79 / p. 55), and Heidegger emphasizes that this is because experience has nothing to do with empirical knowledge, nor is it anything like Husserl's phenomenological experience, where experience is still reducible to the self-evidence of objects.⁵ For in Hegel's idea nothing is acquired, nothing is grasped or objectified in its essence; instead, *everything is taken away*.

Hegel thinks of *Erfahrung* as a reversal of consciousness that elevates it to a higher ground called philosophy or science. The model of this reversal has to be something like the Copernican Revolution, but as Heidegger reads him, Hegel is interested mainly in the truth that consciousness discovers about itself in this event. Experience as *Umkehrung* is, to be sure, a movement of enlightenment for Hegel, who calls it "a way of the Soul which journeys through . . . its own configurations as though they were stations appointed for it by its own nature, so that it may purify itself for the life of the Spirit, and achieve, finally, through a completed experience of itself, the awareness of what it really is as such" (p. 72 / p. 49). But the way of purification is (as always) through suffering and destitution. What consciousness discovers about itself is that its knowledge of the world, and so of itself, is not "real knowledge." As Hegel says, the journey that consciousness undergoes, its experience of itself, "has a negative significance for it." "The road can . . . be regarded as the pathway of *doubt*, or more precisely as the way of despair" (p. 72 / p. 49). Experience does not simply lead to hesitation and uncertainty; it is a "thoroughgoing skepticism" (p. 72 / p. 50), a self-alienation in which "consciousness suffers violence at its own hands" (pp. 74–75 / p. 51). Not to put too fine a point on it, experience is essentially satirical, a self-unmasking, as if reason could only discover the truth of things, and so of itself, when it sees that it is a fool.

For Gadamer the understanding of a text always has the structure of a reversal. At the most elementary level there is "the experience of being brought up short by the text" that is essential to philology or to any effort to determine what a text is saying (*Truth and Method,* p. 268). Just when we think we have the meaning of a text pinned down, it confronts us with something that puts our understanding in question. At a higher level, the classical text, as Gadamer says, "is something that resists historical criticism" (p. 287), that is, it refuses to be contained in the contexts that our research arranges for it; it is always breaking free of our constructions and intervening in our own situation. Indeed, a recurrent theme of the history of interpretation is that the understanding of a text always requires, in some sense, a conversion to the text's way of thinking, and what this means is that we always end up having to reinterpret ourselves, and even change ourselves, in the light of the text. To understand a text is not only to grasp its meaning; it is to understand the claim that it has on us. Most often this claim is critical in the strong sense, as when a text exposes us to our prejudices, by which Gadamer means not only our private, subjective dispositions but, more important, the conceptual frameworks we inhabit and to which we appeal when we try to make sense of things. More is at stake in interpretation than interpretation. What would it be for a text to explode the conceptual world of the one who seeks to interpret it?

This is really what is at issue in *Truth and Method* in the chapter on "The Concept of Experience and the Essence of Hermeneutical Experience," a chapter that more than thirty years later remains pretty much unread. Here Gadamer emphasizes the negativity of experience. Paraphrasing Hegel, Gadamer calls *Erfahrung* "skepticism in action" (p. 353) because it throws what one knows, or rather what one *is*, into question, that is, into that open place of exposure where everything is otherwise than usual. In experience one does not acquire anything, unless it is just experience itself, where being experienced is not the same as being in possession of something objective and determinate; rather, experience is always of limits and refusal. This is why it is so hard to communicate experience, as from parents to children. Experience in this sense can only be put into stories; it cannot be contained within propositions or underwritten by the law of contradiction. It has the universality of proverbs rather than of principles. It is never rule-governed.

Experience is inevitably painful, because it entails the defeat of will or desire, the breakdown of design or expectation, of power or projection, but this breakdown is also an opening, even a sort of emancipation or releasement. Gadamer thinks of it in terms of insight, where insight means less a metaphysical grasp of something, however, and less an illumination of transcendence than an "escape from something that had deceived us and held us captive [*ein Zurückkommen von etwas, worin man verblendeterweise befangen war*]" (p. 338 / p. 356), a releasement, say, from some prior certainty or ground, some vocabulary or framework or settled self-understanding; or say that the hermeneutical experience always entails an "epistemological crisis" that calls for the reinterpretation of our situation, or ourselves, a critical dismantling of what had been decided.[6] Thus the negativity of hermeneutical experience is not merely nugatory and ironic or logically absurd; it is a negativity that places us in the open, in the region of the question. Were we to ask what a hermeneutical experience is like, Gadamer would certainly point us to Plato's dialogues, where Socrates is seen reducing the cultural experts of Athens to bewilderment or aporia. We call aporia "undecidability," but it is what Gadamer means by openness. Openness is not the open-mindedness of the liberal enlightenment, which is mostly a condition of disengagement that comes from having reflected ourselves out of the world. For Gadamer openness is a condition of exposure in which one's conceptual resources have been blown away by what one has encountered. In this event one finds oneself radically situated with no place to hide. Now insight and recognition become, as Gadamer likes to say, inescapable.

Hence the relevance of tragedy, as Gadamer himself suggests when he refers to the motto of Aeschylus, *pathei mathos*, learning through suffering (p. 356). Learning what, however? The traditional thought is that tragedy is always about self-knowledge, as when Oedipus learns the terrible truth about himself. But of course, to speak strictly, there never was a time when Oedipus did not know the truth about himself. Self-knowledge was never something that Oedipus lacked. His problem is that self-knowledge was never enough. More accurately, his relation to himself is neither a relation of knowing nor a relation to a self. What Oedipus knows is his name, that is, the name he has made for himself: Oedipus, "wise above all other men to read / Life's riddles and the ways of Heaven" (33–34). (Remember, he is famous for having solved the riddle of the Sphinx.) There is nothing false about this name, as the action of the play confirms, but the paradox is that the action confirms the identity of Oedipus by estranging him from it. This self-estrangement begins when Oedipus is asked to live up to his name, be the same man still, emancipate Thebes (again) from its curse, which he does of course; but this time *he* is the curse—as, in fact, he knows well enough, though he doesn't see it yet, for he has heard more than once, and from no less than the oracle at Delphi, what his fate was to be, that he was to murder his father and marry his mother, else why did he flee from Corinth? Oedipus never misunderstands himself—he will always be the man who solved the riddle of the Sphinx—but this self-understanding cannot contain the other that his fate inscribes. The story of Oedipus is about the implacable reality of this otherness, its inescapability as Fate. Fate is not just the inevitability of events; it is the otherness of identity, or reality, that which we seek to avoid but meet willy-nilly at the crossroads. It is this other that Oedipus must finally acknowledge; this is the meaning of the recognition scene. Exactly what this means, what it comes to, is that the self of Oedipus must now abide with this other, who becomes his sole society and the region of his exile. As if the point about Oedipus were that he is no longer the same as us, being no longer the same as himself. Sameness is just what he is exiled from; he can never be the same again, although nothing about him has changed (except of course his self-interpretation). Recall that the hermeneutical genius of Oedipus was that he was able to solve the riddle of the Sphinx by seeing himself in it, recognizing himself as human (the secret of the riddle); but the action of the play takes us to the limits of this self-recognition. Now Oedipus is required to acknowledge what lies on the other side, beyond self-recognition, of which Oedipus now deprives himself, because by blinding himself he can no longer see himself in the eyes of his children, where recognition means kinship. One could say that Oedipus encounters the limits of self-understanding, or that his self-understanding encounters the limits of the human or the same, which is to say, the limits of the speakable. The double meaning of his blindness is that what he can no longer see is himself as one of us. He understands himself as belonging elsewhere, beyond the reach of language.

> Drive me at once beyond your bounds, where I
> Shall be alone, and no one speak to me. (1375–76)

But Oedipus was always already beyond this threshold. That is the meaning of Fate, which inscribes not our identity (in the sense of kinship) but our difference (in the sense of the mark that singles us out, separates us, like the difference the name "Oedipus" inscribes: "lame-footed," the sign that links him to his fate). Miasma or pollution is the social form of this difference that Thebes cannot abide. Oedipus is uncontainable. In his otherness, he is reality. It is this, if anything, that he understands.

One can clarify some of this by appealing to Stanley Cavell's writings on tragedy, most notably "The Avoidance of Love: An Essay on *King Lear*."[7] Cavell's idea is that in tragedy we discover the moral or truth of skepticism, which is that "the human creature's basis in the world as a whole, its relation to the world as such, is not that of knowing, anyway not what we think of as knowing" (*Claim of Reason*, p. 324). Each of Shakespeare's great plays starts out with a will-to-certainty—a will to be absolutely certain of the world, to have it absolutely present to one's mind and senses, to make it subject to one's knowing, hence to bring it or keep it under control. The lesson of tragic action is the refusal of the world to be subjected in this way. This refusal is summarized by Cordelia's answer to Lear ("Nothing, my Lord" [1.1.89]), but one could just as well refer to Desdemona's inaccessibility to the demands that Othello's doubt places upon her, her inescapable otherness that Othello would either know or destroy. Like the skeptic, Cavell says, the tragic hero finds that the world "vanishes exactly with the effort to *make* it present" (*Disowning Knowledge*, p. 94). What he learns, or needs to learn, is to forgo the knowing that presentness calls for. But how "do we learn that what we need is not more knowledge but the willingness to forgo knowing? For it sounds to us as though we are being asked to abandon reason for irrationality . . . or to trade knowledge for superstition. . . . This is why we think skepticism must mean that we cannot know the world exists, and hence that perhaps there isn't one (a conclusion some profess to admire and others to fear). Whereas what skepticism suggests is that since we cannot know the world exists, its presentness to us cannot be a function of knowing. The world is to be *accepted*; as the presentness of other minds is not to be known, but acknowledged" (p. 95).

Acknowledgment is how we connect up with reality as historicality or limit. It is what happens in hermeneutical experience, where understanding is an achievement not of objective consciousness but of openness and answerability, where openness means exposure. "Experience," Gadamer says, "teaches us to acknowledge the real." What is recognized is reality as other, not as the same: reality as that which is more Fate than Fact. "The genuine result of experience," Gadamer says, "is to know what is. But 'what is,' here, is not this or that thing, but 'what cannot be done away with [*was nicht mehr umzustossen ist*]' (Ranke)" (pp. 339–40 / p. 357). Tragedy is that which does away with everything except "what is." This is, so to speak, the key to its philosophical, or at all events critical, nature as a hermeneutics of the inescapable. If we think of Shakespeare's great plays, we see that tragic learning (*pathei mathos*) is always a radical divestiture in which nothing is left to the tragic figure, everything is taken away, leaving the person radically exposed to reality, as if the whole category or project of presentness were reversed. What is it to be present to reality? It takes a Macbeth or Lear to know. The whole movement of *King Lear* is to expose Lear to his own otherness. His daughters are the first to do this, but from the start he encounters his other in the unmaskings of his Fool:

> LEAR. Doth any here know me? This is not Lear:
>   Doth Lear walk thus? speak thus? Where are his eyes?
>   Either his notion weakens, his discernings
>   Are lethargied—Ha! waking? 'tis not so.
>   Who is it that can tell me who I am? (1.4.246–50)

(To which Lear's Fool darkly replies: "Lear's shadow.") But above all there is the unforgettable image of Lear naked before the storm:

> LEAR. Why, thou wert better in thy grave than to answer with thy un-
>   covered body this extremity of the skies. Is man no more than
>   this? Consider him well. Thou owest the worm no silk, the beast
>   no hide, the sheep no wool, the cat no perfume. Ha! here's three
>   on 's are sophisticated! Thou art the thing itself: unaccommo-
>   dated man is no more but such a poor, bare, forked animal as
>   thou art. Off, off, you lendings! come, unbutton here.
>   [*Tearing off his clothes.*]
>   (3.4.105–13)

One wants to say that hermeneutical experience always entails the event of exposure that belongs to tragedy. Cavell even suggests that exposure is exactly what happens to us in reading the text of a tragic drama. "I have more than once suggested," Cavell says, "that in failing to see what the true position of a character is, in a given moment, we are exactly put in his condition, and thereby implicated in the tragedy." But how? "What is the medium of this drama, how does it do its work upon us?" One could, Cavell says, describe it this way: "The medium is one which keeps all significance continuously before the senses, so that when it comes over us that we have missed it, this discovery will reveal our ignorance to have been willful, complicitous, a refusal to see" (*Disowning Knowledge*, p. 85), that is, a failure not of exegesis but of acknowledgment. Understanding a tragic action, Cavell says, is "different from the experience of comprehending meanings in a complex poem or the experience of finding the sense of a lyric. These are associated with a thrill of recognition, an access of intimacy, not with a particular sense of exposure. The progress from ignorance to exposure, I mean the treatment of an ignorance which is not to be cured by information (because it is not caused by a lack of information) outlines one motive to philosophy; this is a reason for calling Shakespeare's theater one of philosophical drama" (p. 85).

This seems very close to what Gadamer had said in *Truth and Method* about the tragic effect, that is, about the way tragedy (on Aristotle's analysis) appropriates its audience and exposes it to the tragic experience. I mean the idea that the tragic audience is not kept at a distance by tragic representation but is on the contrary overwhelmed and transformed by it. Thus Aristotle speaks of the pity and fear (*eleos* and *phobos*) that tragedy induces in the audience. Gadamer takes these in the sense of misery and apprehension, the anguish and cold horror that come over us when we see someone rushing to his destruction. "Misery and apprehension [*Jammer und Bangigkeit*]," Gadamer says, "are modes of ekstasis, being outside oneself, which testify to the power of what is being played out before us" (p. 124 / pp. 130–31). Yet what can it mean to say that tragedy is *kathartic*, that it "purifies" us of these disturbances? Gadamer says:

> It seems clear to me that Aristotle is thinking of the tragic pensiveness that comes over the spectator in tragedy. But pensiveness is a kind of relief and resolution, in which pain and pleasure are peculiarly mixed. How can Aristotle call this condition a purification? What is the impure element in feeling, and how is this removed in the tragic emotion? It seems to me that the answer is as follows: being overcome by misery and horror involves a painful division [*Entzweiung*]. There is a disjunction [*Uneinigkeit*] with what is happening, a refusal to accept [*Nichtwahrhabenwollen*] that rebels against the agonizing events. But the effect of the tragic catastrophe is precisely to dissolve this disjunction with what is [*diese Entzweiung mit dem, was ist*]. It effects the total liberation of the constrained heart. We are freed not only from the spell in which the misery and horror of the tragic fate had bound us, but at the same time we are free from everything that divides us from what is. (pp. 124–25 / p. 131)

In Cavell's language, we may imagine that the tragic audience is distributed along a moral plane between "acknowledgment and avoidance" (*Claim of Reason*, p. 329) and that the resolution of the tragic action means not just the working out of catastrophe but the overcoming of that "refusal to accept" that Gadamer identifies as our characteristic response to the unfolding of what happens (call it our characteristic response to reality as Other or as Fate: we are always fleeing Corinth). Again the idea is that tragic knowledge is closer to what Cavell calls acknowledgment and what Gadamer calls hermeneutical experience than it is to what we normally think of as knowledge, namely, knowledge as conceptual representation. "Tragic pensiveness," says Gadamer, "does not affirm the tragic course of events as such, or the justice of the fate that overtakes the hero but rather a metaphysical order of being that is true for all. To see that 'this is how it is' is a kind of self-knowledge for the spectator, who emerges with new insight from the illusions in which he, like everyone else, lives. The tragic affirmation is an insight that the spectator has by virtue of the continuity of meaning in which he places himself" (pp. 125–26 / p. 132). The point to understand is that tragic affirmation is not pretty; it means acknowledgment not just of the difficulty but of the horror of life. Tragic knowledge thus entails what elsewhere is called the "critique of the subject." It is emancipation from false consciousness achieved not by methodological application or analysis but by hermeneutical experience, that is, by the encounter with the otherness of reality, or with that which refuses to be contained within—kept at bay by—our conceptual operations and results. The difference between hermeneutical experience and logical forms of critique, however, is just the difference between tragedy and comedy, between the cold shock of recognition and the joyful exuberance of liberation from the constraints of historicality. In hermeneutical experience there is little comfort, unless it is simply that now we know how awful things can get. Tragic serenity consists of being beyond surprise.

In antiquity it was philosophy's claim that it alone could safeguard us against tragedy. The counterclaim is that tragedy cures us of philosophy. This comes out in Martha Nussbaum's *Fragility of Goodness,* which tries to situate Aristotle's account of tragedy within the framework of Plato's attempt in his middle dialogues to imagine a life secured against disaster (beyond hermeneutical experience).[8] For Plato the goal of the good life is to become rationally self-sufficient, impervious to events or circumstances, essentially sealed off from adversity (which is to say, from other people). It is not that terrible things cannot happen to the good or just man; it is that these terrible things cannot deprive him of his self-possession, his sense of being at home with himself; catastrophe cannot deprive him of his well-being and self-sameness. So Socrates is not just not a tragic figure; he is, as Nietzsche figured him, antitragic. I mean that Plato seems to have set out to create a character to whom tragedy could never happen. The Socratic good life is free from pity and fear. Socrates would have never fled from Corinth. He would never have met himself at the crossroads. Otherness never accrues to Socrates. (Recall the unLear-like image from the *Sympo-*

sium: Socrates standing motionless for hours in the snow, impervious to the cold.) His ignorance is never fatal and neither, one is tempted to say, is his death. Whereas for Aristotle (on Nussbaum's reading) the good life is exactly that which risks tragedy by not sealing itself off; on the contrary, risk is essential to the good life precisely because what the good life requires is openness and responsiveness to what cannot be controlled, namely the world of action, events, and other people. As Nussbaum says, for Aristotle there are "central human values"—friendship, for example, and justice—that "cannot be found in a life without shortage, risk, need, and limitation. Their nature *and* their goodness are constituted by the fragile nature of human life" (p. 341). Whether Aristotle would go so far as the chorus in *Antigone*—"Nothing very great comes into the life of mortals without disaster"—is arguable, because his view of life (like Martha Nussbaum's) is comic rather than tragic, but his conception of the good life as exposed to the world rather than sealed off in philosophical asceticism led him to seek in tragic drama the experience of what it is to be fully human, as if this were of greater philosophical importance than the experience of unqualified *eudaimonia.*

Of course Nietzsche thought that on this precise point Aristotle had confounded everything, missing not only the musical foundations of tragedy but the purpose, which is to induce in us an experience of transcendental joy:

Let the reader invoke, truly and purely, the effects upon him of genuine musical tragedy by harkening back to his own experience. . . . He will remember how, watching the myth unfold before him, he felt himself raised to a kind of omniscience, as though his visual power were no longer limited to surfaces but capable of penetrating beyond them; as though he were able to perceive with utter visual clarity the motions of the will, the struggle of motives, the mounting current of passions, all with the aid of music. Yet, though he was conscious of a tremendous intensification of his visual and imaginative instincts, he will nevertheless feel that this long series of Apollonian effects did not result in the blissful dwelling in will-less contemplation which the sculptor and epic poet—those truly Apollonian artists—induce in him by their productions. He will not have felt that justification of the individuated world which is the essence of Apollonian art. He will have beheld the transfigured world of the stage and yet denied it, seen before him the tragic hero in epic clarity and beauty and yet rejoiced in his destruction. He will have responded profoundly to the events presented on the stage and yet fled willingly into that which passes understanding. He will have considered the actions of the hero and yet divined in them a higher, overmastering joy.[9]

Hence W. B. Yeats's notion of tragic gaiety—

> Hector is dead and there's a light in Troy;
> We that look on but laugh in tragic joy.[10]

—which subsumes even the tragic heroes themselves:

> All perform their tragic play.
> There struts Hamlet, there is Lear,
> That's Ophelia, that Cordelia;
> Yet they, should the last scene be there,
> The great stage curtain about to drop,
> If worthy their prominent part in the play,
> Do not break up their lines to weep,
> They know that Hamlet and Lear are gay;
> Gaiety transfiguring all that dread.
> ("Lapus Lazuli," p. 295)

Nietzsche says: "In thus retracing the experience of the truly responsive listener we gain an understanding of the tragic artist, of how, like a prodigal deity of individuation, he creates his characters—a far cry from mere imitation of nature—and how his mighty Dionysiac desire then engulfs this entire world of phenomena, in order to reveal behind it a sublime esthetic joy in the heart of original Oneness" (p. 133). The "spirit of the sublime," Nietzsche says, "subjugates terror by means of art" (p. 52).

Yet what is missing from hermeneutical experience, what this experience fatally lacks, is precisely the sort of distancing factor that informs the Nietzschean-Yeatsian theory of tragedy. Here again Cavell is helpful. In "The Avoidance of Love" he says that our experience of *King Lear* is different from our experience of Racine's *Phèdre* or Ibsen's *Hedda Gabler:*

> In *Phèdre* we are placed unprotected under heaven, examined by an unblinking light. In *Hedda Gabler,* we watch and wait, unable to avert our eyes, as if from an accident or an argument rising at the next table in a restaurant, or a figure standing on the ledge of a skyscraper. In *King Lear* we are differently implicated, placed into a world not obviously unlike ours (as Racine's is, whose terrain we could not occupy), nor obviously like ours (as Ibsen's is, in whose rooms and rhythms we are, or recently were, at home), and somehow participating in the pro-

ceedings—not listening, not watching, not overhearing, almost as if dreaming it, with words and gestures carrying significance of that power and privacy and obscurity; and yet participating, as at a funeral or a marriage or inauguration, confirming something; it could not happen without us. It is not a dispute or a story, but history happening, and we are living through it; later we may discover what it means, when we discover what a life means. (*Disowning Knowledge*, p. 97)

Participating, not watching, not listening, not overhearing—or reading. Cavell says that my relationship to the characters on the tragic stage is not (or not just) literary or aesthetic, much less cognitive, that is, they are not just present to me in the usual theatrical or imaginative or projective fashion: rather, I belong to their present, am present to *them*, meaning that they have a claim on me, not just on my attention but on *me*. What sort of claim is this? And how am I to respond? I am, to be sure, in a theater, in the dark, present at what transpires, but part of the tragic *ekstasis* is that the dark no longer conceals me, I am outside the distance between the stage and my self-possession, facing the characters not so much as if they were real but as if my separateness from them no longer derives from their ontological peculiarity as aesthetic objects or fictional representations. It is now a human separateness, something different from aesthetic distance or the cognition of a disengaged, punctual ego; it is something intimate and harrowing, like a cold sweat. (Cavell writes: "Calling the existence of Lear and others 'fictional' is incoherent [if understandable] when used as an explanation of their existence, or as a denial of their existence. It is, rather, the name of a problem: *What* is the existence of a character on the stage, what kind of [grammatical] entity is this?" [p. 103].)

Cavell wants to say that tragedy, or at all events this tragedy, exposes me to this fact of (my) human separateness; that is, *King Lear* does not simply show or disclose or teach or illustrate this separateness, it is *die Sache Selbst*, the tragic *ekstasis*.

Catharsis, if that is the question, is a matter of purging attachment from everything but the present, from pity for the past and terror of the future. My immobility, my transfixing, rightly attained, is expressed by that sense of awe, always recognized as the response to tragedy. In another word, what is revealed is my separateness from what is happening to them; that I am I, and here. It is only in his perception of them as separate from me that I make them present. That I make them *other*, face them.

And the point of my presence at these events is to join in confirming this separateness. Confirming it as neither a blessing nor a curse but a fact, the fact of having one life—not one rather than two, but this one rather than any other. I cannot confirm it alone. Rather, it is the nature of this tragedy that its actors have to confirm their separateness alone, through isolation, the denial of others. What is purged is my difference from others, in everything but separateness. (p. 109)

I am external to the world, and (radically) to others—not, however, as a transcendental spectator ("We that look on but laugh in tragic joy")—but rather as confined in myself and in my horror as events unfold, belonging to a time in which I do not intervene, which knows nothing of me: "Their fate, up there, out there, is that they must act, they are in the arena in which action is ineluctable. My freedom is that I am not now in the arena. Everything which can be done is being done. The present in which action alone is possible is fully occupied. It is not that my space is different from theirs but that I have no space within which I can move. It is not that my time is different from theirs but that I have no present apart from theirs. The time in which that hint is laid, in which that knowledge is fixed, in which those fingers grip the throat, is all the time I have. There is no time in which to stop it" (pp. 110–11). And then it is too late, in a twinkling it is over, vanished, leaving me divested of the world, staring blankly at the darkness that has me all to itself. Cleansed I certainly am, as of everything but the extremity of my being human. "Because the actors have stopped," Cavell says, "we are freed to act again; but also compelled to. Our hiddenness, our silence, and our placement are now our choices" (pp. 114–15).

In an essay entitled "Politics as Opposed to What?" Cavell speaks of the scene of interpretation as a drama of "reading and being read."[11] His example is from psychoanalysis, where "the situation of reading has typically been turned around, that it is not first of all the text that is subject to interpretation but we in the gaze or hearing of the text" (p. 200). An analogous case would be the reading of a Platonic dialogue, in which our understanding of the text is of the way the text appropriates us, makes us answerable to its interrogations; and for Gadamer this is the model of all eminent texts and of tradition as well (*Truth and Method*, pp. 362–79). Cavell understands this hermeneutical situation as being redemptive or therapeutic, rather (for him) like the reading of Wittgenstein's *Philosophical Investigations*, which like tragedy cures us of philosophy, or (for Wittgenstein) like the reading of the *Tractatus Logico-Philosophicus*, which cures us of itself.[12] One moral at least is that our relation to tragic drama is not one of reading, although of course it is not one of *not* reading; rather, we are taken by the text out of our usual position with respect to it, so that among other things as an expression of our understanding it would no longer be enough to give a reading of it, checking ourselves against the text, as if that were simply to go on as before (as if we hadn't read it correctly). We could put this another way by saying that our understanding of tragedy can be satisfied not by our reading of it but only by our actions in the world. If we go on as before, we are, Cavell would say, evading the text. In this respect tragedy resembles the law and the Scriptures, which we understand only insofar as we understand where they have taken us, and where we go from here. Understanding a text means being resituated not only in relation to the text but with respect to the present and future.

The concept of hermeneutical experience thus sheds some useful light on the idea that we understand differently if we understand at all. This does not mean that we periodically assign new meanings to a text or that the text, as someone might put it, is susceptible to indefinitely many interpretative readings (all at once?). *King Lear* has never meant anything except what it says, except when revised so that Cordelia might be allowed to live. But now it seems far from clear that our understanding of this or any text can be adequately characterized as a grasp of meanings. The concept of meaning has always seemed overpriced for the return we get on it. So much indeed seems to have been conceded over the centuries by grammarians, logicians, and various sorts of philosophers of language who, against the principle of Ockham's Razor, find themselves having to multiply categories of meaning—literal versus figurative, meaning versus significance, deep versus surface structure—just to keep pace with the sorts of things hermeneutical experience exacts from us. Perhaps this only means that, as with everything else, the extension of the concept of meaning cannot be closed by a frontier. If we understand differently when we understand at all, it is because of the way a text like *King Lear* resituates us in the world—exposes us to it despite our best conceptual defenses, for example the idea that poetry makes nothing happen, or maybe deprives us of these defenses, which we sometimes mistake for meanings.

What Is Tradition?

10

It might be as well to ask Gadamer whose and what "tradition" he has in mind. For his theory holds only on the enormous assumption that there is indeed a single "mainstream" tradition; that all "valid" works participate in it; that history forms an unbroken continuum, free of decisive rupture, conflict, and contradiction; and that the prejudices which "we" (who?) have inherited from the "tradition" are to be cherished. It assumes, in other words, that history is a place where "we" can always and everywhere be at home; that the work of the past will always deepen—rather than, say, decimate—our present self-understanding; and that the alien is always secretly familiar. It is, in short, a grossly complacent theory of history, the projection on to the world at large of a viewpoint for which "art" means chiefly the classical monuments of the high German tradition. It has little conception of history and tradition as oppressive as well as liberating forces, areas rent by conflict and domination. History for Gadamer is not a place for struggle, discontinuity and exclusion but a continuing "chain," an ever-flowing river, almost, one might say, a club of the like-minded.
—Terry Eagleton, *Literary Theory*

My purpose in this chapter is not to try to clarify the hermeneutical concept of tradition in the usual analytical style but rather to work through a number of dialectical reversals in which the concept seems to play itself out, as if it were trying to resist conceptualization. Anyhow I cannot promise to produce a clear idea of what tradition is. Possibly it will be enough if I can just make it harder for people to speak of tradition in the usual way, which is to say, without a second thought—much the way Terry Eagleton speaks of it in the epigraph I've chosen.

For several chapters now (in fact from the start) I've been trying to urge the idea that the main question in hermeneutics is reflective and historical rather than formal and exegetical; the question is not how do we analyze and interpret but how do we respond to hermeneutical situations (or to any situation in which we find ourselves)? A critical form of this question is: How do we stand with respect to all that comes down to us from the past? In our own time we have brought this question under the rule of an analytical distinction between the hermeneutics of faith and the hermeneutics of suspicion, that is, between interpretation as recollection or retrieval and interpretation as unmasking or emancipation from mental bondage. The one seeks to overcome the alienation of forgetfulness or of historical or cultural difference; the other seeks to produce this alienation where historical and cultural difference has been repressed in favor of institutionalized systems or doctrines that claim to speak all at once and once for all.

Faith and suspicion are sometimes figured as methodological options that one can pick up as one pleases, but in fact one does not so much choose between them as abide within their opposition and interplay. They are the way we conceptualize the old quarrel of ancients and moderns, which is essentially a quarrel about which way history moves. The Modernist takes it that everything comes down to us from the future and recedes into the past, often taking its own sweet time; in fact much of what is *vergangen*, or over and done with, gets left behind and accumulates so that we never have enough museums or junkyards. For the Modernist the museum or cultural prison is the prototype of the institution. Its function is to objectify or reify the past, maintain possession of it, or hold it in place so that it won't disappear or grow disruptive; which is to say that its function is also exclusionary. The university is a type of museum, and so in an analogous way is the state. Also language and culture and even whole metaphysical epochs. The idea is not to get locked inside these things, lost or employed in them. Our own time has seen a proliferation of prison-house theories of language, culture, and ideology that testify to the anxiety of Modernism—I mean the anxiety of a modernity that has been around for a while, what we now call the Postmodern, which is just the cold recognition, after years of radical aspiration, that there is no breaking free of the systems that contain us. It is an awakening to the universal scope of the museum, whose serene aesthetic surface now dissolves to reveal a vast labyrinthine bureaucracy and dedicated guardians of obsolescence. Imagine Descartes adjusting the mirror of the *cogito* and seeing himself as dean of studies after all. Call this the horror of the Same.

The Classicist, on the other hand, thinks that things come down to us from the past and that unless everything goes to pieces, the future will be a version of what has proven itself over time, something to live up to or shoot for. Such things as come down to us in this way are normative and binding. Here the prototype of the institution is the Temple of the Law, that is, the Church, the State, and the School. This edificial system condenses easily into the figure of the Book. The nightmare of the Classicist is that the Book when opened will turn out to be *Finnegans Wake*. Call this the horror of the Other. It is a repressed fear that time moves, after all, in the other direction, toward strangeness and difference, and that what lies ahead will be full of primitive rage and incoherence, a rocky horror picture show, Chaos and Old Night, which is what the Modernist sees when he looks into the past. Indeed, we can think of Classicism and Modernism as attempts to escape one another's failure to understand historicality or to cope with the contingencies of historical being. The thought naturally occurs that, like most antagonists, they form a Janus face, but the more basic point is that both are products of the same deep anxiety about historicality.

In antiquity the question of how we stand with respect to the past was understood chiefly, or anyhow frequently, as a problem of translation, as in the topos of the *translatio studii,* the transference of the empire of learning across boundaries of regional and linguistic difference. The metaphor of empire is important because what is transferred in the translation of the archive is not just meaning but also authority, which is to say the right to speak and to interpret, that is, the right to rule in matters of discourse, or the right to say how things are, or how they are to be written and understood. The apostolic concept of the Rule of Faith, for example, concerns the question of who can say what the store of revelation comes down to, or rather *who* it comes down to—who owns it or has a right to it, who is to be allowed to dwell in the kingdom of God and who will be the outcast or exile. Tradition here is a category of inheritance. It is a deposit of faith that needs to be preserved against false claimants in behalf of rightful heirs. It is this picture that arouses most people against the idea of tradition. Derrida's postal-service theory of hermeneutics is a sort of parody of this idea.[1]

Mainly, the topos of *translatio studii* traces the *lateral* movement of the imperium from east to west, from Greece to Rome, from Paganism to Christianity. It is not until Petrarch that this translative movement comes to be thought of as historical in the sense of a struggle against the alienation of temporality, or what upscale critics call "distanciation." Here the imperium is no longer something alive and in transport but dead and buried or dispersed into fragments, and there is nothing for it but to walk among the ruins, looking for the scattered remains of a burned or looted archive. Indeed, Petrarch's letters are filled with stories of wandering back and forth in what looks for all the world like a postnuclear or postapocalyptic age: "When I was about twenty-five," he writes, "I made an excursion among the Belgians and the Swiss. When I reached Liège I heard that a good supply of books was available. I called a halt and made my companions wait until I could copy an oration of Cicero with my hand, and have another copied by a friend. Later I circulated these throughout Italy. You will be amused to hear that in that great city of the barbarians we had the greatest difficulty in finding any ink, and what we did find was yellower than saffron."[2] Thomas Greene gives a very compelling account of Petrarch's archaeological and necromantic hermeneutics that disinters the ruined empire of Rome and tries not only to reconstruct it but also to reinstitute its authority.[3] This hermeneutical necromancy produced an uncanny result, namely, a new imperium made of contemporary "buildings and statues and poems" filled with the ghosts who used to haunt the monasteries and ruins, as if translation now meant not simply the transference of an archive to yet another region of the world but, rather, the reincarnation of antique spirits in modern forms. So the humanist text, Greene says, calls for an act of "subreading" that awakens "the latent presence of an ancient author" (p. 95). The idea is to catch the spirit of Cicero (among many others) lurking in the Petrarchan text.

Yet we also find Petrarch trying to reverse this process as if to reincarnate himself in the antique world. The medium of this self-translation, Petrarch says, is the quotation. "Yes, I use a great many quotations," he says. "People say that I could use fewer. Of course I could; I might even omit them entirely. I won't deny that I might even be totally silent; and perhaps that would be the wisest thing." But such people misunderstand the nature of quotation. Quotation is not a mode of adornment that is incidental to writing. Nor is it the reinsertion of antiquity into the discourse of modernism, as if to turn such discourse into a museum or library or some other edifice of memory. On the contrary, a text without quotation is not writing. In fact, it would not be too much to say that one quotes *in order* to write, because quotation mediates one's distance from the ongoing world of writing. It is a threshold or window. Writing is not for one's own age or even for posterity; it is emancipation from modernity. Quotation is a mode of dialogue with antiquity in which one restores oneself to the life (that is, the company) of authorship. Think of canto 4 of the *Inferno*: "I write for myself," Petrarch says, "and while I am writing I eagerly converse with our predecessors in the only way I can; and I gladly dismiss from mind the men with whom I am forced by an unkind fate to live. I exert all my mental powers to flee contemporaries and seek out the men of the past. As the sight of the former offends me, so the remembrance of the latter and their magnificent deeds and glorious names fill me with unthinkable, unspeakable joy. If this were generally known, many would be stunned to learn that I am happier with the dead than with the living" (*Letters from Petrarch*, p. 68). For the dead, of course, are not dead at all. They do not require to be disinterred and reanimated; rather it is the other way around: it is we who require to be unearthed from the interment of the present. The dead live in their texts, which constitute an ongoing discourse in which one's own writing can participate. One does not insert quotations into one's own text; rather, quotation is a mode of inserting one's own text into the discourse of the other, that is, into that distant and alien text that no longer makes sense to us, that is inscribed in a language we no longer understand, that belongs to a world from which we are in endless exile, and that everyone around us regards as a world well lost.

The lesson of Petrarch would be that tradition is not an empire of the dead whose ruins litter the contemporary landscape; not the *bricoleur*'s debris. It is not something that requires to be disinterred and reinstituted in a museum or on a throne. It is not *vergangen*, or gone for good. Petrarch's letter in defense of quotations gives us the model of the hermeneutical concept of tradition as an ongoing conversation from which modernity (by definition) excludes itself. I say "by definition" because modernity is, in Paul de Man's phrase, a "ruthless forgetting"; that is, modernity defines itself in terms of an "epistemological break" with the merely ongoing as that which has ceased to make sense, that which speaks in tongues gone strange, or which no longer fits the conceptual schemes in which we want to take things in hand and make them intelligible to ourselves, bring them under our control, answerable to our programs and justified by our projects. For the Modernist, history is always in a state of ending or, say, a repetition of crisis and exhaustion. ("'Well now that's done: and I'm glad it's over.'") We are always in the post position, primed and impatient to start history over again in an endless recuperation of the Cartesian moment of self-fathering.[4]

The interesting thing about Petrarch, however, is that he is just as much a Modernist as Descartes, that is, he sees himself in history as a solitary subject, an alien. But whereas Descartes turns his back on what comes down in tradition in order to secure the subject against subtexts or false consciousness (elevating alienation into a method), Petrarch enters into tradition in a mutual appropriation that he describes vividly in the famous letter to Boccaccio:

> I have read Vergil, Horace, Livy, Cicero, not once but a thousand times, not hastily but in repose, and I have pondered them with all the powers of my mind. I ate in the morning what I would digest in the evening; I swallowed as a boy what I would ruminate upon as a man. These writings I have so thoroughly absorbed and fixed, not only in my memory but in my very marrow, these have never become so much a part of myself, that even though I should never read them again they would cling in my spirit, deep-rooted in its inmost recesses. But meanwhile I may well forget the author, since by long usage and possession I may adopt them and regard them as my own, and, bewildered by their mass,

I may forget whose they are and even that they are others' work. This is what I was saying, that sometimes the most familiar things deceive us the most. They recur perhaps to memory, in their wonted way, when the mind is busied and concentrated on something else, and they seem to be not merely one's own thoughts but, remarkably indeed, actually new and original. (*Letters from Petrarch*, p. 183)

We can call Petrarch's appropriation of tradition dialogical; it is an event of mutual belonging from which it is no longer possible to extract and objectify either the monumental text or the pure thinking subject, much less a message passing between the two. Appropriation in this sense is what keeps tradition from turning into a museum. Tradition is not mere repetition but is the modern subject's mode of being historical. Here it is natural to think of Gadamer's "effective-historical consciousness" and the "fusion of horizons," where the subject is no longer a logical spectator at a passing show but belongs to a heterogeneous play of voices that calls it away from itself. "Our historical consciousness," Gadamer says, "is always filled with a variety of voices in which the echo of the past is heard. It is present only in the multifariousness of such voices: this constitutes the nature of tradition in which we want to share and have a part" (*Truth and Method*, p. 268 / p. 284). This is quite different from the monumental idea of tradition that we get from T. S. Eliot, with his pantheon or five-foot shelf whose order is periodically adjusted to make room for new members. Eliot's is still your basic museum-piece theory of tradition, which helps to explain why in *The Waste Land* each quotation or subtext is separated out into a footnote. Eliot is still the Modernist driven by Descartes's jealousy of the subject—I mean, the subject's desire to seal itself off or to keep its thinking pure or uncontaminated by the horizon of the other—whereas Petrarch is open and porous and heterogeneous. His relation to tradition is not that of a link in a chain of transmission or authorship; rather, tradition is the medium of his formation as Petrarch, as a historically singular individual who is never fully present in any of his incarnations or inscriptions, never properly identifiable, unlike Descartes's purely logical subject, the transcendental and monumentally self-possessed "thinking thing," or Eliot's serene or possibly anxious aesthetic monad, the pure perceptual consciousness isolated in its epiphanies, escaping memory and desire at "the intersection of the timeless moment" ("Little Gidding").

Of course, it is possible to see in Petrarch's conception the humanist idea of tradition as a refuge, as if tradition were not historical but transcendental, adjacent to history as an alternative to the discontinuous and fragile construction of modernities. The first circle of Dante's hell is Petrarch's heaven. Greene speaks of Petrarch's "lifelong anxiety of temporality," of the alienation that does not belong to our relationship with the past but is instead the condition of our belongingness to a present that always withholds itself, absents itself by withdrawing into a future that never arrives but is always deferred or displaced by the unexpected. Greene remarks how for Petrarch the "ancient texts . . . were exempt from this unstable play of displacements" (*Light in Troy,* p. 126). What compels Petrarch into the discourse of tradition is the inability to achieve the self-presence of modernity, call it the failure to become Descartes, that is, the failure to achieve philosophy, where philosophy is to be understood in its antique sense as the desire to seal oneself off from facticity or the contingencies of historical being, that is, the desire to possess the present by framing it within a purely logical space.

But we must not imagine Petrarch in the posture of withdrawing from history into tradition; rather, one should say that tradition is his mode of entering into history, of belonging to his time. Petrarch fashions himself out of the conversation with tradition, even as tradition fashions itself out of Petrarch, but this mutual appropriation entails a critical event. Greene puts it succinctly when he says that Petrarch was "the first to notice that classical antiquity was very different from his own medieval world, and the first to consider antiquity more admirable." But this is not just a moment of nostalgia. "Petrarch," Greene says, "took more or less alone the step an archaic society must take to reach maturity: he recognized *the possibility of a cultural alternative.* With that step he established the basis of a radical critique of his culture: not the critique that points to a subversion of declared ideals, but rather the kind that calls ideals themselves into question" (p. 90). It tells us something about Thomas Greene's modernism, or his allegiance to a progressive theory of history, that he should see this as "the step an archaic society must take to reach maturity." It's not by any means clear that one grows more philosophical as time goes by. But what Petrarch's recognition of cultural alterity entails is a statement about the otherness of tradition—the idea that what comes down to us in tradition, what tradition preserves or rather entails, is not a deposit of familiar meanings but something strange and refractory to interpretation, resistant to the present, uncontainable in the given world in which we find ourselves at home, the world that makes sense to us and promises us a future that has a place for us. In a critical theory of tradition, tradition is not the persistence of the same; on the contrary, it is the disruption of the same by that which cannot be repressed or subsumed into a familiar category. The encounter with tradition, to borrow

Gadamer's language, is always subversive of totalization or containment. For Gadamer, this means the openness of tradition to the future, its irreducibility to the library or museum or to institutions of interpretation, its refusal of closure or of finite constructions. Tradition in this respect is infinite in Levinas's ethical sense of the Infinity of the Other that discloses itself in conversation (*Totality and Infinity*, pp. 48–52). In the discourse of the other, says Levinas, there is always "the experience of something absolutely foreign . . . *a traumatism of astonishment*" (p. 73). One must not conflate and confuse tradition with the forms of cultural transmission that try to fix and control it. Tradition must always be distinguished from institutions of interpretation.

One way to summarize this point would be to say that in Petrarch we see a critical turn from allegory to satire as a mode of coping with the historicality of being. Instead of rewriting the discourse of the other in order to remove its strangeness or to fit it into the conceptual framework of the present, Petrarch enters into this discourse to shake the present (or his own self) loose from the dogmatism of its self-possession. This comes out in his letter on quotations, in which he says that he studies the texts of antiquity in order "to find if my mind has been lying to me about itself" (*Letters from Petrarch*, p. 68). This critical moment is radically different from the methodological critique that we find in Descartes, who imagines himself able to be deceived only from the outside in, not from the inside out. Descartes repudiates all that is not intelligible in terms of his self-certainty, but Petrarch's self-certainty is always open to question by the mediation of tradition, that is, by the discourse of the other or of what has otherwise been said. The discourse of Descartes is one of worldmaking predicated on the exclusion of the uncontainable; the discourse of Petrarch is uncontainable from the start: "I won't deny," he says, "that I might [remain] totally silent; perhaps that would be the wisest thing. But in view of the world's ills and shames it is hard to keep silent. I think I have been patient long enough in not yet trying my hand at satire, since, long before our present horrors, I find it written: 'it is very hard not to write satires'" (p. 68). So far from integrating the writer into a cozy refuge, tradition sets him apart from his age, places him in the classical position of the satirist, namely, that of the wanderer, the solitary, the alien or exile, the wild man raging against his own image.

It might be worth expanding on this opposition of allegory and satire, which is a sort of premodern way of facing off the hermeneutical postures of faith and suspicion, which Modernism has got backwards. All interpretation is certainly allegorical in the sense of being a conversion of the strange into the familiar, or of the different into the same. Allegory is a mode of translation that rewrites an alien discourse in order to make it come out right—according to prevailing norms of what is right. On its face allegory appears benevolent and accommodating. It exhibits generously what logicians call the doctrine of charity, which just means, as Donald Davidson says, that "if we cannot find a way to interpret the utterances and behavior of a creature as revealing a set of beliefs largely consistent and true by our own standards, we have no reason to count that creature as rational, as having beliefs, or as saying anything at all."[5] Almost always this means reading a text like the Homeric poems or Ovid or the Scriptures in such a way as to remove their scandal with respect to reason or philosophy. In fact it would not be too much to say that allegory is essentially philosophy's (or any dominant culture's) way of overcoming its suspicion of whatever is not itself. Allegory is philosophy's way of keeping itself pure. So Philo reads the Book of Genesis as being largely consistent with Hellenistic moral philosophy; he assigns to the Mosaic text truth conditions that will make the text right according to the standards of what is right as first put in place in Plato's academy. The Cain and Abel story meets these conditions when the conflict between the two brothers is understood as a conflict between two fundamental principles of the human soul: self-love and love of God. In any soul, human or otherwise, you can count on the one principle resenting, despising, and finally destroying the other. Call this mode of reading Saving the Text, which otherwise would get used for wrapping fish. It is the mode of interpretation of the institution whose task is to identify everything in terms of itself, not just (of course) academically, but to lay claim to it or keep it under control. Allegory is appropriative discourse with implicit claims to universality in the sense that there is, theoretically, nothing that it is required to reject as alien or just plain false. It enlarges its empire of learning by taking the strangeness at its borders as a difference of letter and spirit, the way Christianity takes Judaism, where Judaism is no longer the other but is an intelligible component of Christianity and even foundational for the theological narrative of promise and fulfillment by which Christianity understands itself. So there is nothing that is not a component of faith. The same goes for fabulous narratives vis-à-vis the philosophical spirit that redescribes whatever is offensive to reason so as to make it rational after all.

The standard idea is to identify tradition with allegory, that is, with that which converts everything into itself and fixes every alien or random particle so as to rescue it from its randomness or preserve it against its own contingency or otherness. So tradition comes to be thought of as a structure of subsumptive thinking. But this misses Petrarch's lesson about the way the encounter with tradition exposes one's self-image to alternative descriptions, producing an irrepressible satirical desire. Satire is the discourse of the Other against the Same: counterallegory. Satire explodes the conceptual schemes or mechanical operations of the spirit by which we try to objectify and control things, including all that comes down to us from the past. Satire is unconvertible, uncontainable, uncontrollable; it rages at the gates for all the world like the voice of a madwoman. The complication here is that most of us, creatures of the seminar room, know satire chiefly in its allegorized form as a *Dunciad,* where Reason savages the children of Chaos and Old Night, but we also know (from Swift, for example) that satire always precedes and surpasses the norms that try to justify it—or, to put it bluntly, the satirist is always a little out of control, more subversive than corrective, as if Reason were the agent of the Scurrilous Body rather than the other way around. Satire resists the institution of allegory and frequently, or say in its very nature, breaks out against it. The model for satire in this case would be prophetic outrage against the Temple of the Law and the scribes inside who say that prophecy is dead. If you ask where satire comes from, the answer is that it is a return of the forgotten, the pagan, the forbidden or repressed, the voice out of the past whose task is not to reveal and redeem but to torment and scourge and even to bring the house down.

On this line of thinking a good example of the encounter with tradition would be the story of Oedipus and his discovery of the truth of what has been said about him by seers, drunks, and oracles, not to mention what his own awakened memory can tell him. I mean that from a hermeneutical standpoint the encounter with tradition is more likely to resemble satire than allegory, unmasking of the present rather than translation of the past. Or, as I've tried to suggest, the hermeneutical experience of what comes down to us from the past is structurally tragic rather than comic. It is an event that exposes us to our own blindness or the limits of our historicality and extracts from us an acknowledgment of our belongingness to something different, reversing what we had thought. It's just the sort of event that might drive us to put out our eyes.

This thought requires a conception of tradition very different from the gentleman's-club theory proposed by Terry Eagleton (among many others), which confuses tradition with the institutions that try to allegorize it or read it as a homogeneous master narrative in which everything is joined together in a vast program of conceptual integration. From a hermeneutic standpoint, tradition is more accurately not a structure of any sort but just the historicality of open-ended, intersecting, competing narratives that cannot be mastered by any Great Code. My claim would be that a careful reading of Gadamer produces an antitotalist conception of tradition that bears no resemblance to the sort of thing Eagleton and others claim to see in him. We miss the heteroglossia in Gadamer's notion of tradition.[6] Gadamer's idea is that the encounter with tradition always brings our desire for totality up short. This is why (as I argue in chapter 9) the hermeneutical question of how we stand with respect to what comes down to us from the past receives its most powerful answer in stories of epistemological crises, as when Oedipus discovers that he can no longer contain himself in his official self-interpretation as the man who solved the riddle of the Sphinx. Not that he didn't solve such a riddle. It's just that there is also that otherness about him that cannot be confined within a finite interpretation. So the idea is to see tradition not as the repository of official interpretations but as that which resists the institutionalizing of interpretation and forces radical unmaskings of the kind Oedipus suffers. Tradition is seamed in just this way, as a conflict of interpretations that cannot be resolved or harmonized by allegory but instead must be suffered or lived through.

The suffering of such conflicts is basic to what Gadamer calls hermeneutical experience, where experience is always an experience of negation or reversal, as in "the reversal of direction that consciousness undergoes when it recognises itself in what is alien and different."[7] Nowhere does Gadamer suggest that these conflicts are to be overcome by final (much less official) interpretations. Rather, his concern is with the openness that these conflicts produce. Only in this condition of openness can the understanding of anything occur. So Oedipus understands himself only through the negativity of hermeneutical or tragic experience; he understands himself, one might say, *as* that which is disclosed in such experience. As if one could say that the understanding of anything is not the product of interpretation, rather it is the product of the failure of interpretation to hold its ground. This is what Gadamer means when he says, in a notorious line, that we understand differently if we understand at all (*Truth and Method*, p. 280 / p. 297). It is certainly what is meant by the historicality of hermeneutical experience. No method could produce the moment in which Oedipus recognizes the truth about himself. So let us think of tradition as inscribing, in its irrepressibility and irreducibility, what cannot be done away with or that which must be faced.

In his book *Radical Hermeneutics*, John Caputo complains that Gadamer "describes the continuity of tradition, but leaves unasked the question of whether the tradition is all that unified to begin with. He never asks to what extent the play of the tradition is a power play and its unity something that has been enforced by the powers that be. His 'tradition' is innocent of Nietzsche's suspicious eye, of Foucauldian genealogy. He does not face the question of the ruptures within tradition, its vulnerability to difference, its capacity to oppress."[8] Yet this is again to think of tradition spatially and hierarchically as edifice and institution or as the accumulation and weight of custom, whereas Gadamer's line of thinking stresses tradition as event, as a dialectical encounter that puts what we think in question and calls for the revision rather than the institution of interpretation. As such, the so-called unity of tradition cannot be thought of organically or geometrically—in fact it is very difficult to conceptualize. Indeed, a fruitful way to understand the nature of tradition would be to study such things as the relation of Judaism and Christianity. This is not the same as studying typology or salvation history or even the history of religions; it means entering into this relation as into a breach or wound that can never be healed. Theologians of a hermeneutical rather than dogmatic cast would call this entering into a mystery, which is very much like entering into the conflict of interpretations. As a way into this mystery or conflict, I have found it helpful to borrow Martin Heidegger's notion of the "rift" as that dif-ference (*Unter-Schied*) that holds apart what it calls together. The virtue of this idea is that it is flatly antifoundational without, however, being just anarchic.[9] It is antifoundational because there is nothing there on which to ground the operations of an exclusionary logic. But it is not just anarchic, because it is a figure of commonality or mutual belonging, where what is common, what is shared, is not an identity but a difference—and, moreover, not a dialectical or systematic difference within a totality but a radical difference that is not to be overcome or subsumed in a higher order, one that calls for acknowledgment and acceptance, much the way a limit or one's own mortality calls not so much for knowledge as acknowledgment. What is it to share a difference or hold a difference in common? It is perhaps like sharing a history or a mode of being historical. But it is a sharing in which neither side gives up its singularity, its freedom, its otherness or self-refusal, its capacity for satire.

Martin Heidegger introduces the "rift" (*Riss*) in his crucial essay "The Origin of the Work of Art" (1935), where he speaks for the first time of the mysterious opposition of earth and world. "Upon the earth and in it," he says, "historical man grounds his dwelling in the world."[10] The world is the human world that comes into the open or into its own in the work of the work of art, which is a clearing in which we can enter into time and being. The earth, by contrast, is that which withholds itself from this opening of the world. The earth is characterized by reserve, concealment, and refusal.

It resists every effort that we make to break into it and bring it under control. The earth is undisclosable. As Heidegger says, "It shrinks from every disclosure and constantly keeps itself closed up [*sich verschlossen hält*]" (p. 36 / p. 47).

One could just as well say that the world is allegorical in its movement; in its worlding, the world tries to find a place or a home for all that is. But all that is nevertheless resists this movement that calls it forward. The earth is the region or power of this resistance. In the language of Levinas, it is the uncontainable, the other, the infinite. It would not be too much to say that the earth is satirical with respect to the world precisely because its resistance is world's limit and finitude, its situatedness or belongingness to history, its exposure to contingency. "Upon the earth and in it, historical man grounds his dwelling in the world." But the earth is not therefore foundational in the sense of *Letztbegrundung;* one could think of it instead as subversive—not Ultimate Ground but Underground, although Heidegger himself seems to prefer the figure of moving or shifting ground, the ground that alters or withholds itself every time we try to lay claim to it as the bedrock that justifies us.

Heidegger thinks of earth and world in terms of the intimacy of antagonists rather than in terms of foundational metaphors. "The opposition of earth and world," he says, "is a striving [*Streit*]. But we would surely all too easily falsify its nature if we were to confound striving with discord and dispute, and thus see it only as disorder and destruction. In essential striving, rather, the opponents raise each other into the self-assertion of their natures. . . . In the struggle, each opponent carries the other beyond itself. . . . The more the struggle overdoes itself on its own part, the more inflexibly do the opponents let themselves go into the intimacy of simple belonging to one another" (p. 35 / p. 49). Earth and world, Heidegger says, "are always intrinsically and essentially in conflict, belligerent by nature" (p. 44 / p. 55). But this conflict, this rift, is not "a mere cleft ripped open; rather it is the intimacy with which opponents belong to each other. . . . It is a basic design, an outline sketch [*Auf-Riss*], that draws the basic features of the lighting of beings. This rift does not let opponents break apart; it brings the opposition of measure and boundary into their common outline [*Umriss*]" (p. 51 / p. 63). Moreover, there is no harmony, no pleasure, no plenitude in this intimacy. In his essay on "Language" (1950), Heidegger characterizes the rift as *pain*. "Pain rends," he says. "It is the rift. But it does not tear apart into disparate fragments. Pain indeed tears asunder, it separates, yet at the same time it draws everything together, gathers it to itself. Its rending, as a separating that gathers, is at the same time that drawing

[*Ziehen*] which, like the pen-drawing of a plan or a sketch [*wie der Vorriss und Aufriss*], draws and joins together what is held apart in separation. Pain is the rending that divides and gathers. Pain is the joining of the rift. The joining is the threshold. It settles the between, the middle of the two that are separated in it. Pain joins the rift of the difference. Pain is the dif-ference [*Unter-Schied*] itself."[11]

What if we were to think of tradition as designed or sketched—structured—in this way, as rift rather than ground? Here it would not be enough to think of tradition as an allegorical process that integrates the other into an edifice of the same, say, a vast typological master narrative; it would also have to be thought of as a satirical process in which the other is encountered in its otherness as a radical difference, a singularity, a refusal of typology, a questioning of self-identity, a resistance to interpretation, an unsilenceable questioning. Speaking from the side of Christianity, the other in this event (namely, Judaism) is not just the indifferent alien; it is one's own other, the difference of one's belonging, that which one's self-identity can neither exclude nor contain, the conflict of interpretation in which one lives and which one cannot transcend. Do not think of it as a diacritical difference that determines one's identity systematically, that is, as belonging to a totality; it is a historical difference (call it, if you like, a deconstructive difference) that makes possible one's self-interpretation only in the bargain of calling it into question and requiring its constant modification. If one maps this Heideggerian design onto the relation of Christianity and Judaism, one does not get a typology of testaments but a mutual and painful antagonism that cannot be resolved, not even by the monumental deception of doing away with history itself, say, by writing dissertations on the nonoccurrence of the Holocaust. Christianity interprets itself as a Modernism by dividing time into New and Old, where the one appropriates the other, dispensing with it as part of its self-dispensation as history's new beginning, as if Judaism were mere prehistory. But in fact time is split lengthwise as a rift among adjacent histories, not hierarchically as a progression of epochs. So Judaism is not *vergangen* but confronts Christianity all along its way or all the way down as an irrepressible prophetic voice, not the voice of the precursor awaiting final interpretation but the voice of the outsider still awaiting acknowledgment. From the standpoint of interpretation, this means acknowledgment of a double reading of the Scriptures as well as of history, a reading that calls each side into its own self-assertion but also places each side at risk, always exposing its self-image to alternative descriptions, threatening allegory with satire. This means taking the hyphen in "Judeo-Christian tradition" as a figure of dissemination, that is, as a seam, where, as Heidegger says, "the seam that binds their being toward one another is pain" (p. 205). This pain is far from at an end. The seam itself is plural, because Islam, for example, is also that which can be neither excluded nor contained. As we now painfully know, the Islamic world belongs dramatically to the conflict of interpretations; it cannot be interpreted away, that is, there is no coping with it allegorically. It confronts us like a satirist; it must be acknowledged.[12]

Thinking this way forces us to look twice at Gadamer's celebrated notion of the fusion of horizons.[13] Caputo, for example, says that

> Gadamer understood everything that was healing and restorative about Heidegger's notion of retrieval but . . . he lacked the heart for Heidegger's more radical side. He produced an impressive philosophy of the "tradition" and of the dynamics of its transmission. His concern was always with the horizons, with their mutual nourishment and interaction, with a certain wedding or joining of the horizons such that each draws strength from the other and all in the service of the present. He understood what Heidegger had to say about the truth of Being and the experience of the work of art, but he had no interest in the more deeply critical side of Heidegger which had inspired Heidegger's talk of destruction and overcoming. (*Radical Hermeneutics,* p. 96)

This certainly summarizes the general view, which sees hermeneutics as a program of cultural unification or the totalization of horizons. But Gadamer had directed his thinking against the Kantian idea of the subject that reflects itself out of its own historicality (compare Kant, "What Is Enlightenment?"). "Historical consciousness," Gadamer says, "is aware of its own otherness and hence distinguishes the horizon of tradition from its own horizon."[14] This self-identity, however, can only be preserved by sealing the subject off from the horizon of tradition, and this means the repression of what cannot be contained within its self-definition. Self-possession cannot survive the encounter with what comes down to us from the past. In this encounter the subject discovers itself as "only something laid over a continuing tradition"; it is not just itself but also that which it finds strange and unintelligible in its own terms. Gadamer formulates this in the language of Hegel—the subject "immediately recombines what it has distinguished in order, in the unity of the historical horizon that it thus acquires, to become again one with itself" (*Truth and Method,* p. 290 / p. 306)—but what this means is that one is always in a fundamental dilemma with respect to tradition, that is, one is always in a condition of crisis in which either one must try the harder to enclose oneself in one's own self-certainty (the way of philosophy), or one must revise oneself and maintain oneself in revision because one can never exclude the other from one's self-understanding (the way of hermeneutics). From a hermeneutic standpoint, the idea of the fusion of horizons is very different from a totalist scheme of integration in which all differences and singularities are to be effaced. For why else, Gadamer asks, would "we speak of the fusion of horizons and not simply of the formation of the one horizon, whose bounds are set in the depths of tradition?" The fact is there is never any possibility of "one horizon" grounded in an synthesis of the many. We must not be misled by the perspectival metaphor of horizon. The fusion of horizons is not a unification of perspectives. On the contrary. "Every encounter with tradition that takes place within historical consciousness involves the experience of the tension between the [traditional] text and the present. The hermeneutic task consists in not covering up this tension by attempting a naive assimilation but consciously bringing it out" (p. 290 / p. 306). The fusion of horizons is not an allegorical process; its structure is intrinsically satirical. In the fusion of horizons I am always exposed to what refuses me—always, in short, the naked emperor.

This is what Gadamer means when he says that the end of hermeneutical experience is not meaning or knowledge but openness, where openness, however, means not simply open-mindedness, tolerance for another's views, or the mutual indulgence of liberal pluralists but acknowledgment of what is alien and refractory to one's categories. It means acknowledging the being of what refuses to fit or refuses to be known, that which says no to me. What is it to face what refuses my language and my allegories? How do we stand with respect to such refusal? According to Levinas, the uncontainability, that is, the transcendence or infinity of the other, is the beginning of the ethical.

> The Other who can sovereignly say *no* to me is exposed to the point of the sword or the revolver's bullet, and the whole unshakeable firmness of his "for itself" with that intransigent *no* he opposes is obliterated because the sword or the bullet has touched the ventricles or auricles of his heart. In the contexture of the world he is a quasi-nothing. But he can oppose to me a struggle, that is, oppose to the force that strikes him not a force of resistance, but the very *unforeseeableness* of his reaction. He thus opposes to me not a greater force, an energy assessable and consequently presenting itself as though it were part of a whole, but the very transcendence of his being by relation to that whole; not some superlative of power, but precisely the infinity of his transcendence. This infinity, stronger than murder, already resists us in his face,

is his face, is the primordial expression, is the first word: "you shall not commit murder." The infinite paralyses power by its infinite resistance to murder, which, firm and insurmountable, gleams in the face of the Other, in the total nudity of his defenceless eyes, in the nudity of the absolute openness of the Transcendent. There is here a relation not with a very great resistance but with something absolutely *other:* the resistance of what has no resistance—the ethical resistance.[15]

I could break off my reflections with this quotation, even though I am far from having reduced my subject to clarity and self-consistency. I began with a fundamental hermeneutical question: How do we stand with respect to all that comes down to us from the past? It appears now that we cannot address this question purely in terms of cognition, as if tradition were simply an object calling for attention and asking not to be abandoned. Now we have this thought to chew on, that what comes down to us from the past says no to us, is not obsolete but refractory and resistant, excessive with respect to interpretation, satirical with respect to our allegories, and so it will not serve as foundation and testimony, background or thesis; indeed it will not serve at all except to draw us out of ourselves, leaving us, Oedipus-like, exposed and possibly horrified at our own image.

I want to conclude, however, with another thought, some parts of which I will try to clarify in the final chapters of this book. Any reflection on the nature of tradition entails a corresponding need to work through the nature of authority. If we take the line of thinking I have tried to follow—turning the imperial or museum-piece theory of tradition on its head—how are we to understand the nature of authority? Gadamer speaks of rehabilitating authority as well as tradition on the idea that what comes down to us from the past is binding on us in some way. In what way? The quotation from Levinas helps us distinguish between two sorts of authority. There is most obviously the authority of rule in which we are coerced along a certain path. In our own time we have dreamed of a nonideological place or region of discourse and action that is free from coercion, and this means freedom from authority, where authority means essentially the (mostly unjustified) exercise of power or force. Tradition, Caputo says in the passage cited earlier, is a "power play and its unity something that has been enforced by the powers that be." But this seems too simple. For there is, after all, a difference between being under a rule or under someone's power or control and being under a claim. The authority of the claim is not imperialist. It cannot be institutionalized, that is, it is not a claim whose power lies in its self-justification—the only claim that philosophy recognizes. Hermeneutics acknowledges another sort of claim, however, which does not need to be backed up by force or domination, whether by argument or superior numbers. This claim demands not obedience but openness, acknowledgment, and acceptance of what is singular and otherwise. I take it that it is a claim of this sort that Cavell and Levinas, in their different ways, are trying to understand. I think of satire as the social medium of such a claim and of tradition as the place where it is registered.

On the Radical Turn
in Hermeneutics

11

Nach
dem Unwiederholbaren, nach
ihm, nach
allem.
—Paul Celan, "A la pointe acérée"

Hermeneutics belongs to multiple histories and so cannot be made into any one thing that begins and ends and suffers conceptual revolutions along the way, although in our effort to make sense of hermeneutics this is very much the sort of story we are apt to be looking for and inevitably come to rely on. Thus in the second part of *Truth and Method* Gadamer sketches out a history of hermeneutics that begins with the romantic idealism of Hegel, Schleiermacher, and Dilthey, where hermeneutics is defined in terms of a consciousness whose objects are the products of an expressive spirit and whose task is to reconstruct this originating spirit in order to clarify and participate in, or to appropriate and go beyond, its self-understanding. But with Heidegger, as the story goes, this history splits in two. There are those who continue Dilthey's Kant-like concern with how knowledge of historical and cultural products is possible. Husserl's phenomenology, with its transcendentalist conceptions of meaning and consciousness, is regarded by many as a way of determining the logical conditions of *verstehen*. But those who follow Heidegger understand that consciousness is never alone with its objects but is always situated, always historical and

213

contingent, so that it is no longer enough to think of understanding as an activity of consciousness at all. Here the other always constitutes the limit of understanding as such. The other can never be objectified; it can never be appropriated once and for all in any finite interpretation. For Gadamer, it is this excessiveness of the other, this finitude or situatedness of understanding, that calls for reflection. Historicality, not history or historical transmission, is the true object, the *Sache,* of hermeneutics.

One problem with Gadamer's history of hermeneutics is that it leads up to and stops with *Truth and Method* (1960), in which he explicates the notion of historicality initially in terms of authority and tradition; and taken in their customary senses, authority and tradition seem notoriously to blame whenever historicality is denied or repressed. If we imagine that this is all Gadamer is saying, that historicality is simply the uncritical perpetuation of authority and tradition, then more radical accounts of historicality are certainly both possible and desirable. A radical account is what John Caputo is after in *Radical Hermeneutics.* For Caputo the true *Sache* of hermeneutics begins to emerge only in the later Heidegger (who is roughly contemporaneous with the writing of *Truth and Method*) and in Jacques Derrida's critical readings of Heidegger. Caputo sketches out a history of hermeneutics that bypasses Gadamer and the romantics almost completely. His history is an end-of-philosophy story about the way deconstruction shakes us loose from our categories and exposes us to the "original difficulty of life."[1] What is hermeneutical about deconstruction is precisely its concern with concrete situations in which meaning is constituted; and what is radical about it is that it is not just a critical reflection on these situations but an intervention in them. "Deconstruction," Caputo says, "is an exercise in disruption which displaces whatever tends to settle in place" (p. 193).

For Caputo, the starting point of radical hermeneutics is the problem of repetition. Taken schematically, romantic hermeneutics is, let us say, a hermeneutics of retrieval. The idea of understanding the other as well as it understands itself looks back to a moment of self-presence that it is the task of hermeneutics to re-present. In certain regions of discourse—geometry, say, or the region of the assertion—this task seems easy. Univocal meanings seem to make possible what Derrida calls "pure traditionality," in contrast to expressions of genius, which are frequently not translatable.[2] In either case, however, the task is the same: to recover the original moment of expression, live through it once more, restore its animating spirit to the life of immediate experience. This was Dilthey's idea of *Nacherleben.* Reexperiencing the lived experience of another is the romantic theory of hermeneutical experience.

Caputo, borrowing from Derrida, calls this the postal-service theory of hermeneutics, the theory of pure traditionality in which something original or originary gets transmitted or reproduced:

> The postal principle is the principle of message bearing and hence the principle of all hermeneutics. Hermes, as the message bearer from the gods, is the first of all postmen, and it is to Hermes that the later Heidegger attaches the only possible sense that hermeneutics can have. "Only a god can save us now," he said, that is, only a dispatch carried by Hermes. Now it is just such an epistolary service that Derrida wants to show is always already confounded and thrown into disarray: letters are lost, messages garbled, and neither the proper senders nor the proper addressee can be identified. If the history of the West is the collected and collective (*Ge-*) history of Being's sendings (*Schickungen, Ge-schicke,* from the verb *schicken,* to send or mail), the confounding of the postal principle is likewise a confounding of Being's own delivery service. (*Radical Hermeneutics,* p. 160)

The reference here (both Derrida's and Caputo's) is to "Dialogue on Language" in *Unterwegs zur Sprache,* in which Heidegger, as a way of getting "beyond hermeneutics," gives an allegorical interpretation of Hermes the faithful message bearer. Hermeneutics is message bearing, but message bearing is always a referring-back-to the sender, just as Dilthey's notion of experience, Heidegger says, "always means to refer back—to refer life and lived experience [*Erlebnis*] back to the 'I.' Experience is the name for the referral of the objective back to the subject. The celebrated I / Thou experience, too, belongs within the metaphysical sphere of subjectivity" (*On the Way to Language,* pp. 35–36). But we know, or by now ought to know, that Hermes was never simply our friendly postman but the granddaddy of tricksters, a figure of anarchy or misrule, of thievery, treachery, and deceit, someone always a little out of control, the bringer of truth who doubles as the thief of reason and who therefore leaves you in perpetual hesitation as to what you have just heard or said, written or read; in short, a polytropic figure, someone mischievous and untrustworthy, like the language we speak when we try to make sense of anything. This is not Hermes the friendly postman but Hermes the many-sided, uncontainable, nocturnal transgressor who, among other things, fathered Pan upon a faithless Penelope and then taught the goat boy how to masturbate.

There is, of course, an obvious or trivial sense in which repetition is foundational for understanding (and so for hermeneutics), namely, that without repetition we would never be familiar with anything; there would only be unrelenting strangeness or aphasia. Problems start when philosophers begin worrying the distinction between identity and difference, sameness and otherness, and then imagine a world divided between those who come down on the side of sameness, who desire familiarity and cultivate nostalgia, and those who seek emancipation from this state of affairs, who want to get us beyond the pleasure principle and to face reality, horrible as it may be. In a world structured in this way into radicals and reactionaries, hermeneutics is just a philosophy of repetition. Instead of dumping hermeneutics in the usual postmodern style, however, Caputo wants to save it, or to save repetition by thinking of it as an open-ended project. And this makes some obvious sense. Think of exegesis. Exegesis is a term of retrieval—you take out what was put in. When the meaning of a word has been forgotten, it is the task of exegesis to recover it. What is lost must be looked for. But what is it to look for something? This project also has the structure of repetition, but rather the way a quest or question does. Remembering has the structure of repetition, but so does expectation: remembering is a repetition backward, but expectation, or, say, hope, is a repetition forward. Things lost in the past are found in the future. What is it to follow advice, or a hunch, or a hint? And what is it for something to be possible? Possibility is a repetition that moves forward. What is it to make a promise and then keep it (or not)? These are the Kierkegaardian waters in which Caputo wants to redeem hermeneutics.

Still, it is too much to say that the postal-service theory gives us "the only possible sense that hermeneutics can have," and it is certainly false to say (as Caputo does) that with this theory one has got to the heart of Gadamer's philosophical hermeneutics. But no matter. It is enough (for a start) to see that both philosophical and radical or deconstructive hermeneutics are antiromantic. Instead of regarding the hermeneutical scene in terms of plenitude, say the replenishment of meaning or experience (*Erlebnis*), they regard it as a scene of conflict and disruption, where experience means *Erfahrung*, that is, something that one undergoes, something overwhelming and uncanny that exacts a radical transformation that leaves everything otherwise, no longer recognizable in the sense of familiar or the same. For convenience we can borrow from our earlier discussion of tradition and describe this sort of hermeneutical scene in terms of a basic opposition between two categories or genres of discourse, allegory and satire. Possibly one could study the history of hermeneutics extending back into antiquity as an endless movement back and forth, indeed an endless and sometimes violent struggle, between these two modes of discourse.

The idea that all interpretation is fundamentally allegorical is as old as writing itself, possibly older, but it received a new and powerful reformu-

lation in section 32 of Heidegger's *Being and Time,* with the idea that interpretation is in every case grounded in what we already have in place (in the
situation at hand). Allegory is a form of understanding that doesn't try to
conceal the forestructure or scene of its interpretations but, rather, asserts
this structure by translating everything into it. It is not a technique of exegesis in the philological sense but a mode of appropriation or a way of
assimilating another's discourse into one's own conceptual scheme or forestructure of understanding; it is a way of reinscribing the alien text within
one's own hermeneutical circle.

Basic to hermeneutical experience, however, is the way texts (among
other things) refuse to be appropriated, the way they are refractory to the
categories that we use to make sense of them (the way they end up meaning
something different from what we intend, whether as writers or interpreters). What interests Gadamer, for example, is the experience of being
"pulled up short by the text" (*Truth and Method*, p. 268). In our encounter
with a text that comes down to us from the past (or from another culture,
or perhaps from our very midst), we always find that what the text says is
not what we thought (or what we would say) but something else, something
other that brings us up hard against the presuppositions or forestructures
that we inhabit and that underwrite and make possible our efforts of understanding. The satirical effect of this encounter is to disrupt and fragment
our self-possession. It is an event that alters our relation to the conceptual
frameworks within which things are otherwise familiar and intelligible to
us. So we are always in the position of having to revise these frameworks—
an obligation that allegory helps us avoid. Sometimes this hermeneutical
event is emancipatory in the sense that, as Gadamer says, we are released
"from something that had deceived us and held us captive" (*Truth and
Method,* p. 356), and we can think of comedy as the form of discourse that
celebrates these moments of freedom from mental bondage. But sometimes
these revisions take a negative form, and one can understand tragedy as the
genre of discourse that tries to give an account of such events, as when
Lear's construction of how things are, including above all his own self-understanding, comes completely apart, leaving him naked and alone before
the world, freezing in the storm, exposed to the limits of understanding itself
(there is nothing left for Lear to revise himself into; he is unaccommodated
man teaching us how cold hermeneutics can get). The hermeneutic point is
that the relation of the alien text to the conceptual framework that tries to
appropriate it is always satirical, always resistant and explosive in virtue of
being uncontainable within the interpretation that tries to hold itself together and maintain its authority. It is easy to think of Cordelia's "Nothing,

my Lord" as such an alien text; the loony unmaskings of Lear's Fool are another example; the play is full of such examples. The alien text (every text) is always excessive, and this excessiveness is always satirical in the sense that it exposes the "beforehand" in which interpretation is grounded and can cause the whole forestructure (possibly a whole cultural system) to go crashingly to pieces.

The satirical, potentially tragic structure of the hermeneutical scene holds even in the case of what Gadamer calls classical texts, those that belong to our canons and that form the background and medium of our self-understanding. Yet the classical text always remains external to these mediations, uncontainable as mere background or as a component of a conceptual scheme. As Gadamer says, the classical text is "self-interpreting," resistant to the allegories in which we appropriate it. When Gadamer speaks of allowing the text to address us, he is speaking Luther's language; nor is it any accident that Luther was the greatest antagonist of allegorical interpretation. He understood that in allegory we (tacitly) revise the text in order to protect ourselves from it, that is, to avoid seeing ourselves in its light and having to revise ourselves under the pressure of its claim on us. The motto of Reform hermeneutics, *Scriptura sui ipsius interpres,* means that we haven't control of this text; it means the disappropriation of our schemes and concepts, which can no longer mediate the strangeness of what is said. Heideggerian listening, which catches us up in an experience (*Erfahrung*) we may not be able to withstand—that may transform or destroy us—is very much in the Lutheran tradition.

Caputo's *Radical Hermeneutics* is about one way in which this classic hermeneutical scene has been played in the history of philosophy since Hegel and Kierkegaard, the one being (on a certain traditional view) the great allegorizer of philosophy, the genius of subsumptive thinking, and the other the great satirist who celebrates "the foundering of all human categories" (p. 34). Caputo sees Derrida, quite rightly, as repeating Kierkegaardian satire, subjecting Husserl's allegorical edifice, his "metaphysics of re-presentation" (p. 121), to an earthly shaking, not from the outside in, as if Derrida were from another planet, but from the inside out, by reading Husserl with himself against himself, that is, reading one side of Husserl (say, his geometric side) in terms of his other, alien, repressed, pun-filled side—the side open or exposed to historicality or to the "contingency and alterability" of the life-world (which Caputo summarizes throughout with the word *flux* [p. 121]). Speaking hermeneutically, deconstruction is counterallegorical; it is satirical with respect to allegory as such (satirical, one might say, with respect to philosophy as a discourse or institution that has, among other things, authorized itself to make judgments about the legitimacy of other discourses). At the same time, however, as Caputo makes clear (and Derrida himself insists on this), deconstruction is comic rather than tragic. It aims at emancipation, not tragic divestiture (not destruction); so it is not as cold as cold can be. Its mode of existence, or of liberation, takes the form of parody, or, say, of poetry or literature, or (to speak strictly) the pun, that most alien and philosophically trivial of discourses (the other of the concept).

In a fine exposition, Caputo shows (that Derrida shows) that James Joyce is the natural companion—the logical supplement, the other—of Husserl; that is, geometry is always underwritten by the pun, or the idea of speaking several words or texts or several languages at once, as against translating one into another according to the principle of the ideality of meaning (an essentially allegorical concept); and one can read Derrida's texts as mediating or at least traversing the enormous gap between these two contemporaries and their discourses or institutions, giving us thereby the plain sense in which *Finnegans Wake* is a monumental satire upon, among other texts, *Logical Investigations* (this is the point, I take it, of Derrida's essay "Two Words for Joyce," which is itself a supplement to two crucial pages in Caputo's favorite and least punful of all Derrida's texts, namely, the introduction to his translation of Husserl's *Origin of Geometry*).[3] Whence it would follow, on the construction I am trying to hold together, that *Logical Investigations* can be taken as an allegorical reinscription of *Finnegans Wake*, that is, as an interpretation that proposes to lay bare the deep structure of what, on the surface, is an uncontrollable, uninterpretable simultaneity of heterogeneous languages ("once current puns, quashed quotatoes, messes of mottage" [*Finnegans Wake*, p. 183]). Strictly speaking, the reduction is an allegorical move that philosophy has always made against literature understood as a canonical deposit of the "madness of words." On a charitable view the reduction is philosophy's attempt to salvage something from this madness; on Derrida's view it is a sort of police action, a movement of repression against what is alien and uncontainable, a movement of aggression against Hermes the outlaw, thief, and playful decentered phallus.

The pun deserves a moment's attention, the more so because (on an argument I have made elsewhere) it is the basic unit of Heidegger's discourse in his later writings on language and poetry and has done more than anything to arouse the institution of philosophy against him. So Jürgen Habermas: "Heidegger flees . . . to the luminous heights of an esoteric, special discourse generally and is immunized by vagueness against any specific objections."[4] But of course the opposite is the case; Heidegger does not ascend to the Empyrean but falls to the lowly pun (*a-lētheia, Er-eignis*), which is (strictly speaking) not so much unspeakable as untranslatable, refractory to our allegories, satirical with respect to the propositional style that for Habermas is canonical for philosophy. This seems the upshot of Derrida's contra-Husserlian remark, apropos a translation of *Glas* into English, that

> the analytic experience of the pun, in its very possibility, remains foreign to the pun, as *strictly* foreign to its facility or to its temptation as possible. But by definition a *pun* must not be absolutely controllable and subject to the censorship of rational consciousness and its representatives. On the other hand, everything is played out in this economy of "the more or less strictly," of forces in play, of the interest there is in evaluating the power of a condensation or a displacement, of interests there can be in prohibiting every pun in certain places, in the name of this or that socio-institutional norm—perhaps it is necessary to recall here that the law of this *strict-ure* constitutes the very focus of reflection for a book [namely, *Glas:* "a book on theft," which is to say a book about Hermes (18)] that interrogates itself on right, the right of property, theft, notably the theft of the name and all the police forces of language. In the name of what does one condemn these deviations [*écarts*] that are *Witz*, wordplay, spirit, *pun?* Why does one do it most often in the name of knowledge, in the academic institutions that feel themselves responsible for the seriousness of science and philosophy, by supposing one has nothing to learn, nothing to know from a pun? Better still, or worse, by supposing that the pun must be morally condemned and as such proscribed, for the pun signals some malice [*malignité*], a perverse tendency to transgress the laws of society? The critics are also guardians of these laws, whether they declare it or not. As such, and in their traditional function, they must denounce those that take to the pun. Let us recall the *Dunciade* [the French translation of what is arguably the greatest satire in English]: "A great Critic formerly . . . declared He that would pun would pick a pocket." Signed Pope (pun / pick / po).[5]

The pun is a piece of Hermes-talk, outlaw discourse or discourse that is out of control. In Poststructuralist thinking it is what is called Text, or textuality, which is not just the material written or printed text but a traversal (*l'écriture*) that occurs whenever we speak or write and that is always foregrounded when someone takes what we say differently from the sense intended, forcing us to say: "No pun intended." It is a species of *Gelassenheit* or the letting go of language, stepping back from the rule of representational-calculative thinking where *s* is either *p* or nothing. When Joyce writes, "Psing a psalm of psexpeans, apocryphul of rhyme" (*Finnegans Wake*, p. 242), he is not in any sense the author of this line (which he recites, as one does, from a nursery rhyme); rather, he lets it happen, lets it slip, allows the slippage of the signifier that always occurs whenever we traverse the gap between one text and another (which is what is called speaking or writing). Plato in *Seventh Letter* calls this slippage "the weakness of the logos" (342e); it is the wandering of words that ought to be tethered like slaves. Philosophy, on a certain psychoanalytic view of philosophy as the Law of the Father, was invented to keep this sort of thing from happening; so we drove the poets out, into exile, like the words they write, into endless wandering (thinking without why), which is the fate of Hermes and Cain.

A pun is also a repetition in Derrida's and Caputo's sense of repetition as that which disseminates as well as duplicates; it is, in Aristotle's or Caputo's word, a kinesis of language that does not, however, move forward in Caputo's still-constructive or edificial sense of repetition but *explodes* uncontrollably in every direction without foreseeable consequences, perhaps without any consequences, unless it is just to explode some prior edifice of discourse. As in the Joycean "Lard, have mustard on them" (*Finnegans Wake,* p. 409), the pun is a repetition of a petition that profanes or demystifies it, robs it of its force, keeps it from working or getting the results intended or prayed for; it is playful in the satirical sense of fragmenting the allegorical construction, showing it to be of no consequence or without the why (or the answer to Why write?)

I began this book by asking what hermeneutics is *about*. One could say that it is about the moment when philosophy confronts poetry or whatever is not itself—whatever is resistant to itself: that which refuses to be philosophized. This encounter, this resistance of language to philosophy, is, so to speak, the primal hermeneutical scene. What is deconstructive about deconstruction is simply its attempt to return philosophy to this primal scene, perhaps to cure it of its logophobia. In the introduction I quoted the following from Foucault's "The Order of Discourse":

> What civilization, in appearance, has shown more respect toward discourse than our own? Where has it been more and better honoured? Where have men depended more radically, apparently, on its constraints and its universal character? But, it seems to me, a certain fear lies behind this apparent supremacy accorded, this apparent logophilia. It is as though these taboos, these barriers, thresholds and limits were deliberately disposed in order, at least partly, to master and control the great proliferation of discourse, in such a way as to relieve its richness

of its most dangerous elements; to organise its disorder so as to skate round its most uncontrollable aspects. It is as though people had wanted to efface all trace of its irruption into the activity of our thought and language. (*Archeology of Knowledge,* p. 228)

I have always thought that one could detect Heidegger's hand in this passage—I mean the punning Heidegger who became increasingly preoccupied with the relationship between poetry and thinking. It was Heidegger's idea that by exposing thinking (*Denken*) to the refusal of language, its resistance to conceptual control, poetry (*Dichten*) turns it away from philosophy, that is, sets it free—teaches it, one might say, the meaning of *Gelassenheit,* or the tricks of Hermes.[6]

But if not Foucault, then certainly Derrida draws his inspiration from this region of Heidegger's thought. In "The Time of a Thesis" Derrida asked: "What is literature? And first of all what is it 'to write'? How is it that the fact of writing can disturb the very question 'what is?' and even 'what does it mean?' To say this in other words—and here is the *saying otherwise* that was of importance to me—when and how does an inscription become literature and what takes place when it does? To what and to whom is this due? What takes place between philosophy and literature, science and literature, politics and literature, theology and literature, psychoanalysis and literature? It was here, in all the abstractness of its title, that lay the most pressing question." Nothing less than philosophy itself is at stake in this question. How is it, Derrida wants to know, "that philosophy finds itself inscribed, rather than inscribing itself, within a space which it seeks but is unable to control, a space which opens out to another which is no longer even *its* other. . . . How is one to name the structure of this space?"[7] But the task of thinking is not to "name the structure of this space," as if it were above and beyond it in the manner of the transcendental, analytic spectator; it is to enter into it, turn itself loose in it, risk itself in this space of exposure to whatever is not itself.

Here, one wants to say, in this space, in this place of exposure, is where hermeneutics is to be found. But in what form, exactly?

Caputo divides Heidegger and Derrida into country mouse and city mouse, the *Schwarzwalder* as against the Parisian intellectual, the solitary walker along country paths versus the restless, Cain-like, streetwise wanderer, the meditative versus the disruptive thinker. True to the fable, Caputo gives the country mouse the last word even though the city mouse has all the good lines. He separates cleanly the textual moment of slippage, of free-fall into the *abîme,* from the mystical moment in which we are "open to the mystery" in the sense of exposed to the *Abgrund* that fills us with awe.

What about this mysticism? At a decisive point in his reading of the Hei-degger-Derrida connection, when deconstruction, on Caputo's analysis, ap-pears to have settled everybody's hash, including Heidegger's, Caputo has Heidegger whisper something in Derrida's ear (p. 190). We aren't able to overhear anything, of course, but whatever Heidegger said so secretly, it is no secret how Derrida would react. Derrida's response—given, in effect, in an essay called "Comment ne pas parler" (1985)—would be not to answer Heidegger, as if to whisper something back or to fix him with a horrified look, but to call attention to the whispering itself as an instance of the dis-course of "negative theology," in which, by saying nothing, by speaking and (to all appearances) saying nothing, say by punning, one starts to speak of God, that is, of a hyperessentiality beyond Being. Derrida wants to say that, the punning opacity of its language aside, deconstruction is not a negative theology, even though the ontotheological reappropriation of deconstruc-tion is always a possibility.[8] Perhaps more than a possibility. After all, with the later Heidegger, who wants to avoid speaking about language, for ex-ample, not to mention Being, we are squarely in the extradiscursive realm of Meister Eckhart, so it is not clear who is appropriating whom. The claim of negative theology—its claim upon hermeneutics, radical or otherwise—is perhaps as inescapable as it is untheorizable, because negative theology defines more sharply than anything else the point at which language, in the bargain of going to pieces, transgresses the unnameable. But what interests hermeneutics in negative theology is not so much the mysteries it holds open as its satirical power with respect to the discursive cultures of religion, with their complex forms of legal and conceptual organization and restraint. The point about negative theology is that it causes the languages of religion to ring hollow. Undoubtedly mystical in character, negative theology possesses a demystifying power that would fill a Nietzschean with envy. It is no won-der that Heidegger could not keep his hands off of it.

In an earlier study Caputo had worked out some of the internal connec-tions between Meister Eckhart and Heidegger.[9] And he says that Meister Eckhart is "one of the background heroes" of *Radical Hermeneutics,* "one of the great masters of disruption, of thinking through and thinking against the grain of everyday conceptions. He is adept at throwing the guardians of Being and presence (and of their version of 'the true faith') into confusion and consternation. . . . Eventually the Curia made him pay for this sort of thing, but not before he was able to cut into the garment of medieval onto-theo-logic, disrupt the mail of the medieval *Seinsgeschick* and set it spin-ning" (p. 268). But it is not easy to say how far Caputo is willing to act on this in his own thinking. He seems more allegorist than satirist. After a chapter on "Cold Hermeneutics" that leaves both Heidegger and Derrida exposed to each other, or to their worst fears, with philosophy seemingly in bits and pieces everywhere, there is a Back-to-Kant movement, a repetition; it is, to be sure, not just a recitation but a kinesis, whose story line reads: Beyond Radical Hermeneutics; Or, What to Do After the Storm Has Passed?—

> What are we to do now, after the "end" of metaphysics? How does one go about one's business after giving Heidegger and Derrida so much? How are the sciences possible if one talks in terms of a child-king and the foundering of principles? And what guidelines can there be for action if the *archai* are so many sendings, if there are no "metaphysical foundations"? If there is no master name, if there are too many truths, what has become of science and ethics, thought and action, theory and practice (provided we can make such distinctions)? If the flux is all, and linguistic, historical structures are nothing more than writings in the sand which we manage to inscribe in between tides, what then? What can we know? What ought we to do? What can we hope for? Who are we, we who cannot say "we," we who are divided from ourselves, our (non)selves? (p. 209)

Unlike Lear, Caputo weathers the storm of hermeneutics and comes out with his (philosophical) faculties staggering but intact. Part 3 of *Radical Hermeneutics* reads like a comedy (or, say, a tragicomedy) in which the institution of philosophy, purged and sobered, to be sure, after its night on the stormy heath or dark night of the soul, is otherwise untransfigured and so resumes a reasonable facsimile of its former life: "How are the sciences possible?" asks the Postmodern Kant. "What can we know? What ought we to do?" Caputo may now be in a better position than before to face the difficulty of life—to give different answers to Kant's questions—but certainly he has no difficulty facing philosophy, I mean the institution of philosophy, with its lore of Kantian questions that give the theory of what it is to think (or to "do" philosophy): I mean the institution which is, if I understand, the major concrete difficulty that people like Heidegger and Derrida struggle against in order to alter radically the limits of philosophy, say, the boundary that it shares with poetry.

Caputo speaks not of the end (or limits) of philosophy but of its renewal. What this renewal will look like is sketched out in part 3 of *Radical Hermeneutics*, with its account of a Post-Enlightenment conception of rationality, a rationality that Caputo tries to characterize as a kind of "play" as against methodical progress, the rigorous construction and clarification of concepts, problem solving, argumentation, and propositional control. Here we must imagine reason not as founding, ordering, and containing but as subversive, disruptive, and liberating; reason as crazy rather than serene, on the move rather than sitting in repose; reason, as Heidegger might put it, emancipated from logic. Interestingly, Caputo elucidates his notion of playful rationality by opposing it to Gadamer's notion of *phronēsis*. Caputo says:

> *Phronēsis* functions only within an existing framework, an established paradigm. It is a fundamentally conservative notion in the best sense of the word, that is, it knows how to keep something alive, to renew it in changing circumstances but always within the compass of an established order. It requires a stable paradigm, a more or less fixed order. Aristotle conceived of the functioning of *phronēsis* within a fundamentally stable *polis*, not within a period of revolutionary conflict. *Phronēsis* is the virtue which enables us to apply courage, e.g., to a new situation. It is acquired slowly, by practice, by imitating the moves of the prudent man. But suppose the *polis* is divided among itself, torn into competing factions, each of which has its own ideas about the prudent man. Suppose the *polis* is decentered, ruptured, in conflict? Suppose it is a mixed *polis*, populated with Athenian democrats and Spartan warriors (and Chinese wise men), each of whom speaks of loving the gods and the city and of doing one's civic duty but each of whom has entirely different ideas and practices, so that one does not know whether it is courage which is called for? *Phronēsis* cannot function if there is a conflict about who the prudent man is. (p. 217)

This is forcefully expressed, and as philosophers like to say, it surely captures something, because Gadamer's idea is that there is no such thing as rationality as such; rather, norms of rationality are internal to specific cultures and traditions, such that moral and practical reasoning has the character and coherence of cultural practices rather than the logical coherence of rule-governed behavior. Hence Gadamer speaks of the rationality of dialogue, where the idea is not to reduce the cultural world to a harmonious system but to allow for the interplay of rival and perhaps even incompatible social arguments.[10]

Which is all very well, but what Caputo wants to know is what happens if a culture or tradition goes to pieces. What if the background against which *phronēsis* is possible, not to say intelligible, breaks down into fragments of competing moral schemes and norms of rationality? What if our social practices multiply incoherently into various competing and mutually incompatible forms of life?[11] The problem is that Caputo tries to elucidate these questions with the help of Thomas Kuhn's theory of revolutionary science, with its notion of paradigms shaken by the introduction of alien concepts. Caputo states:

> *Phronēsis* is the virtue of older men, and young men have only the be-
> ginnings of it. *Phronēsis* is a process of deliberation and not the product of
> a midnight visitation, of a breakthrough to a new way of seeing things
> which is most likely to occur in the young and inexperienced. *Phronēsis*
> does not come in a flash but is slowly nurtured through years of train-
> ing. Times of scientific crisis are times of a certain freeplay, when the reg-
> ular business of science is in jeopardy, when the best minds are loose, in
> play with the play of the issues before them, on their own. Incommen-
> surability occurs at the interstices between scientific epochs, in moments
> of epochal play (Heidegger), points of Foucaultian rupture. (p. 220)

But my thought, as I have said, is that a richer and certainly colder example of what Caputo is getting at (or drawing back from) can be found in
tragedy, where an epistemological crisis is not something that goes on in the
head or in theory or in a clean, well-lighted place like the history of science.
Indeed, it can hardly be any trouble to find room for playful rationality
within the world of science, which, after all, brackets human life as a thing
of little consequence, a mere superficial contingency; whereas it is far from
clear whether such a thing as playful rationality can even be conceptualized
in the context of tragic divestiture, where one is *in extremis,* on the verge
(maybe no longer on the verge) of madness, all hope of renewal gone. Whatever else might be wrong with Gadamer's notion of *phronēsis,* it is nevertheless a conception of rationality that depends for its intelligibility on
situations of tragic consequence where one is caught, for example, between
equally compelling claims as to what is just or good. As Gadamer says,
phronēsis presupposes not age but experience. The lesson of tragedy—of
Hamlet, for example—is that the young are not prepared for tragic conflict,
and so events must wait for them. Or, as the concluding lines of *King Lear*
have it:

> The weight of this sad time we must obey,
> Speak what we feel, not what we ought to say.
> The oldest hath borne most: we that are young
> Shall never see so much, nor live so long. (5.3.323–26)

But as for tragedy, Caputo will have none of it:

The tragic does not allow suffering its play, which is to cut into and
waste life. The tragic view, against its own rhetoric, is in fact not hard

enough: it accepts, embraces, and makes light of just what it should resist. It is tolerant of that against which it should raise its voice in protest. It accepts just what it should defy. It lets violence off too easily. Its notion of the justice of strife is that of a weak-willed judge. It has no nerve for a real fight, which means to resist the wasteful effects of suffering. (p. 285)

From the point of view of a religious *memoria passionis,* the tragic view has a short memory and is a pawn in the hands of those who know how to play the game of power. It is the religious view which is radical and liberating, while the tragic view is the laughing gas of the suffering. It asks them to love their exploitation and affirm it in a Dionysian dance. (p. 286)

Whereas I take tragedy to be asking a truly radical hermeneutical question—not What is it to understand *King Lear?* but What is it to *be* King Lear? What is it to live through not just the *ébranlement* of one's concepts but the complete destruction of one's world? Tragic drama is the concrete working out of this question. In so doing, it acknowledges the horror of life, is responsive and open to it, does not refuse to mourn. What philosophy (including philosophy of religion)—what Caputo—objects to is tragedy's refusal to propose solutions to the problem of this horror. But one could just as well take it that tragedy is making a claim *against* philosophy: namely, that living through the destruction of the world discloses (Gadamer would say: exposes us to) what cannot be done away with by means of philosophy, much less philosophy of religion. In his *Aesthetic Theory* Theodor Adorno says at one point: "rational cognition has one critical limit which is its inability to cope with human suffering" (p. 27). It is not so much that cognition finds such reality too horrible to contemplate as that it cannot cope with this reality's refusal to function as a problem it might solve or as a condition it might transcend. Tragedy is, among other things, the disclosure of this "critical limit," this refusal of philosophy, and so it seems to throw in with the horror of life. As Martha Nussbaum says, "We have not fully understood the 'tragic view' if we have not understood why it has been found intolerably painful by certain ambitious rational human beings" (*The Fragility of Goodness,* p. 50).

Think of tragedy as a sort of originary crisis of modernity or Enlightenment. As Charles Segal puts it, "Tragedy . . . deals with situations where the division between civilization and savagery no longer seems to apply. Where this division is disturbed, so is the very nature of man and humanity. Tragedy no longer locates the boundary between the civilized and the savage on the frontiers of society, at the limits of the inhabited world, but brings it within the polis itself, within the very hearts of its rulers and citizens."[12] Or, much to the same point, in a famous study Jean-Pierre Vernant, referring specifically to Greek tragedy in the context of the crisis of law within the ancient city-state, says that "what tragedy depicts is one *dike* in conflict with another, a law that is not fixed, [but] shifting and changing into its opposite. To be sure, tragedy is something quite different from legal debate. It takes as its subject the man actually living out this debate, forced to make a decisive choice, to orient his activity in a universe of ambiguous values where nothing is ever stable or unequivocal."[13]

By contrast we can think of Caputo's radical hermeneutics (like Derrida's deconstruction) as an attempt to work through our present-day crisis of rationality or Enlightenment from within philosophy itself, or in philosophy's own terms, and this means working to resolve this crisis before it is too late—before the end of philosophy, as if the end of philosophy would mean the return of tragedy, where the crisis can no longer be conceptually contained but threatens a regression to that originary struggle with poetry, that is, the struggle of reason with darkness, madness, anarchy, or with the horror of human life as such. The idea of radical hermeneutics, one might say, is to sustain the comedy of life in which the hope of the renewal (of philosophy, science, the disciplines of reason) is never lost.

Against Poetry

12

HEIDEGGER, RICOEUR, AND THE

ORIGINARY SCENE OF HERMENEUTICS

> But there is another side to literature. Literature is a concern
> for the reality of things, for their unknown, free and silent
> existence; literature is their innocence and forbidden presence,
> it is the being which protests against revelation, it is the
> defiance of what does not want to take place outside. In this
> way, it sympathizes with darkness, with aimless passion, with
> lawless violence, with everything in the world that seems to
> perpetuate the refusal to come into the world. In this way, too,
> it allies itself with the reality of language, it makes language
> into matter without contour, content without form, a force
> that is capricious and impersonal and says nothing, reveals
> nothing, simply announces—through its refusal to say
> anything—that it comes from night and will return to night.
> —Maurice Blanchot, *La part du feu (1949)*

The title is meant to take us back to the quarrel between philosophy and poetry that Socrates already regarded as ancient. My sense is that every hermeneutical situation has the structure of this quarrel, which is governed by a logic that is by turns exclusionary and allegorical. Plato's idea seems to have been that poetry embodies something (we're not sure what) that interferes with the sort of discourse Socrates is trying to set up and that he seems to be practicing in texts like the *Republic,* where one statement follows another more or less justifiably or according to some principle of internal necessity. Call this saying what has to be said. Poetry is somehow not this sort of saying. Whatever it is, poetry seems subversive of justice and necessity. It seems to be on the loose in our talk, or in our world, causing things to go out of control. It is of course in the nature of words to run around loose—we are never really able to pin them down—but poetry seems to institute this ambiguity or misrule, as if poetry were some sort of antiprinciple principle, or as if there were some internal or even metaphysical link between poetry and anarchy, say, of the sort Antonin Ar-

229

taud imagined when he said that whenever "the poetic spirit is exercised, it always moves toward a kind of seething anarchy, a total breakdown of reality by poetry."[1] Philosophy at all events is principled; it stakes itself on saving us from precisely such things as the "breakdown of reality by poetry." It seeks, among other things, a world in which things are just so and not otherwise. Moreover, it is the sort of discourse that helps to produce such a world by keeping things straight and getting them down exactly. Philosophy is that discourse that makes a point of keeping itself under control and works to make the world behave likewise, teaching every discourse to be ever watchful, as if to bring the world under its claim. In a world presided over by philosophy's kind of self-control—in a world instituted by the propositional style of philosophical discourse—it's hard to see how poetry, on Plato's (or Artaud's) description of it, could be tolerated.

The *Republic* is, of course, a principal chapter in Plato's story about the self-sufficiency of philosophy. It is in the nature of philosophy, or of reason, to seal itself off from whatever is not itself, or, much to the same point, to convert whatever is not itself into some simulacrum or facsimile answerable to its norms. The logic of appropriation is simply a working out, in another form, of the logic of exclusion, rather in the sense that Aristotle's *Poetics* is not so much a reversal of book 10 of the *Republic* as an extension of it. Aristotle understood that a less draconian method of getting rid of poetry would be to redescribe it so as to make it a systematic part of philosophy. Martha Nussbaum has shown that in the *Phaedrus* Plato had already worked out the possibility of a philosophical poetry more or less as a lesson in how to take up the challenge Socrates lays down in the *Republic*, namely, that having heard the case against her, all lovers of poetry should now come to her defense (*The Fragility of Goodness*, pp. 200–33). But it was Aristotle who actually made a place for poetry in the organon or general theory of the logos, which we might think of as a sort of Republic of Discourse. The idea is, first, to read poetry so as to count it, in some sense, as knowledge, that is, as connecting us up, in some hypothetical fashion, with reality; and second, it is to lay bare poetry's deep structure so as to say that it has a kind of necessary consecutiveness about it and therefore can be made to work as kind of reasoning, say a logic of discovery. So it is no trouble to get poetry to meet the claims of justice and necessity. The concepts of mimesis and plot, one might say, have no other justification.

In thinking this way about poetry, giving it a logic and a power of cognition, Aristotle was following the ancient and abiding rule of allegory, which is that if a poetic text is scandalous with respect to reason, we must rewrite it or, much to the same point, find a way of reading it that removes

the scandal. Western culture has always been deeply allegorical in its operations and results; it has a special genius for constructing ways of reading
poetry, or any alien discourse, so as to make it consistent with its own prevailing cultural norms. It was nothing to convert Homer and the Hebrew
Bible into foundational texts. Aristotle's achievement was to make tragic
poetry a branch of moral philosophy, and doubtless he did much the same
for comedy, although maybe not, since comedy, being so completely at home
with anarchy and misrule, is probably unphilosophizable.

Historically there are two faces of allegory, one formal, the other transcendental. On the one side there is the tradition of poetics, whose task has
always been the demystification of divine madness, the restraint of genius
by rules. Poetics turns poetry to rational account by seeming to make it
teachable, even though it is still theoretically mad. This is the classical or
sober Latin view that reigned from Roman antiquity to Milton. Poetry is
poiēsis, a craft of language, a branch of rhetoric concerned with versifica-
tion and the use of figures: in short, a school subject. Poetry has no matter
intrinsic to itself but draws its meaning from philosophy, theology, and history. The modern version of this idea comes down to us from Kant in the
form of a theory of aesthetic differentiation and, more recently, in the history of literary criticism, in which poetry is set apart as an object of various
competing forms of analytic, strategic, instrumental, or calculative reasoning. In structuralist poetics this instrumental approach is expanded to a
global interest in the rules by which texts as such are constituted. Whatever
it is on the surface, poetry has a lawlike deep structure or textual logic
continuous with the logic of culture itself, whence it is but a short step to
convert poetics into a general cultural analytic in which all discursive and
non-discursive modes of production can be examined from within the conceptual frame of a single methodological outlook. Richard Rorty summarizes a general view when he says that we would be better off dropping the
distinction between poetry and philosophy altogether and speaking instead
of a "general undifferentiated text."[2] One could describe this idea as a sort
of Postmodern Aristotelianism, in which the quarrel between philosophy
and poetry is not so much resolved as absorbed into a total organon of
discourse or the theory of vast networks of weaving and reweaving
vocabularies.

On the other hand there is the idea, sometimes underwritten by appeals
to Plato's *Phaedrus*, that poetry is more vision than craft and that at a certain level philosophy and poetry are identical—they are expressions of the
same transcendental spirit. Marx turned this romantic idea more or less on
its head and so recovered something of the original radicalism of Platonic

hermeneutics. Louis Althusser, for example, sees Marx as antiallegorical, dissipating the "religious myth of reading" that has always tried to save texts by integrating them into an "expressive totality" organized around a transcendental Logos (*Reading Capital*, p. 24). Henceforth the constitution of a culture free from mental bondage requires the exclusion of the text that, however beautiful in itself, is nevertheless an ideological instrument; and perhaps the more beautiful it is, the more sinister. Like the Platonist, the historical materialist cannot contemplate poetry without horror or, at least, without "cautious detachment."[3] Like Aristotle, the historical materialist will allow only a poetry of realism, plenty of Balzac but no *Finnegans Wake*, narrative logic but no lyrical density. But naturally there is some question (which Althusser readily acknowledges) as to whether such a constitution of an ideology-free culture is possible. The idea of a true consciousness or a consciousness purified of whatever is not itself is just what Nietzsche ridiculed with his idea that Western culture is poetic all the way down. Nietzsche reminds us of what embarrassed Socrates, namely, that the Republic has to be founded, if founded at all, on the repressed or forgotten lie. Nietzsche parodies the visionary politics of romanticism, where poetry is transcendental and foundational, no longer the art of making verses but a theory of worldmaking in which, as Friedrich Schlegel says, "the human spirit impresses its law on all things and ... the world is its work of art" (Atheneum Frag. 168). Nietzsche just gives this idea a Nietzschean interpretation.

Schlegel and Nietzsche come together in Heidegger's theory of poetry as a sort of primordial discourse that is foundational for the world and at the same time a constant danger to it. In his Hölderlin lectures from the 1930s Heidegger says that, contrary to the metaphysical tradition, language is not to be understood as any sort of linguistic or conceptual system; rather, it is an event in which all that is is summoned for the first time into openness of being; and this event is what Heidegger calls poetry (*Dichtung*, not *Poesie*). "The poet," Heidegger says (in "Hölderlin and the Essence of Poetry" [1936]), "names the gods and names all things in that which they are. This naming does not consist merely in something already known being supplied with a name; it is rather that when the poet speaks the essential word, the existent is by this naming nominated as what it is. Poetry is the establishing of being by means of the word." "The speech of the poet," Heidegger says, "is establishment ... in the sense of the firm basing of human existence on its foundation."[4] Rather than being the logical foundation of the philosophers, however, this foundation is entirely historical and contingent, an opening into time and the future instead of onto some absolute antecedent ground. The world opened up in poetry is not (or not yet) a Kantian world answerable to the laws of reason. The poet's naming is not conceptual determination but a calling of what is singular and ungraspable as such. In the history of the West philosophy originates as that which tries to rationalize this naming, that is, to interpret or make sense of it; but poetry can never be part of this interpretation. Philosophy tries to stabilize the world conceptually by means of the logical determination of what poetry brings into the open, but poetry refuses to be stabilized in this way. Philosophy's task is to preside over the open, taking the measure of what is, fixing things in place, but poetry is a turning loose. Or, in short, poetry is foundational but not philosophical: it does not try to bring things under control; rather, it lets them go, lets them turn this way and that, luxuriates in ambiguity. But philosophically this is madness. Which is just to say once more that there is a primordial opposition between philosophy and poetry that cannot be done away with. Heidegger is foursquare with Plato on this point. But for Heidegger it is not so much that philosophy must therefore summarily banish the poet according to the old story. Poetry, although an event of worldmaking, is not itself a worldly sort of speaking, that is, it is not a speaking that the world can contain. Poetry cannot be brought into the light of being; there is no place for it in the clearing that it opens up. As Heidegger puts it, "The excessive brightness [of the world] drives the poet into the dark." As if exile, or blindness, or madness, were the poet's natural condition. For Heidegger, in any case, the poet is always set apart, a Cain-like wanderer, both founder and exile.

It is possible to see in the Hölderlin lectures something like Heidegger's version of Plato's *Republic*. One can see this even more clearly in "The Origin of the Work of Art," with its strange, almost gnostic opposition of world and earth.[5] Heidegger says that the *work* of the work of art, its truth, is to set up a world, but this event does not occur within an absolute or transcendental space. On the contrary, the world is finite, surrounded everywhere by what is not itself. Its disclosure occurs within the horizon of that which refuses disclosure, refuses the open: and this refusal is what Heidegger calls earth. If the work of art makes manifest the world, it also makes manifest the refusal of the earth. Indeed, the conflict of world and earth, what Heidegger calls the *rift* (*Riss*), is inscribed in the very structure, or *Gestalt*, of the work. This rift shows itself in the withdrawal (*retrait*) of the work, its self-refusal with respect to the world. The work is uncontainable within the world, resistant to its reasons, excessive with respect to the boundary that separates world from earth. The paradox of the work of art is that there is no place for it in the world it works to establish. Its sort of speaking, its words, cannot be made sense of in worldly terms. With respect to the light, it is all materiality and density (*Dichte*). For indeed the work of art is not an object that we can possess and visit on pilgrimages to caves or museums or antique ruins. To be sure, the world can seem to appropriate the work, find places and uses for it. This is just the basic allegorical task of criticism, aesthetics, and the philosophy of art (to name only these three). The work of art can be made part of the world's equipment, reduced equipmentally. But in every appropriation of the work we will find that the work has withdrawn, that it no longer works its work. For the word *work* means both being and event. It has a double inflection as both the thingly work and the *working* of the work, that is, its work as art. For the mode of existence of the work of art, its work, the happening of its truth, is a movement (Heidegger does not hesitate to call it a struggle or strife) of disclosure and concealment, of self-showing and self-exile, of the lighting or clearing of beings and the self-refusal or withdrawal of all that is into ambiguity and darkness. As if the work of the work of art were not just a worldmaking but also a limit of the world and an encroachment upon it; as if the work not only opened up the world but also exposed it to what is not itself or to what refuses it, namely, the self-secluding earth. "The world," Heidegger says, "in resting upon the earth, strives to surmount it. As self-opening it cannot endure anything closed. The earth, however, as sheltering and concealing, tends always to draw the world into itself and keep it there" (*Poetry, Language, Thought,* p. 49). The work of the work of art opens a world, but the work as a work is self-closing; it remains of the earth, belongs to it, as Heidegger would say, primordially. Which is why the world, as self-opening, can finally not endure the work of art.

The work, indeed, is nothing but trouble to the world. In "The Origin of the Work of Art" Heidegger speaks of the "createdness" of the work, which is not so much a formal condition as a condition of its singularity and refractoriness within the world. In the world, the work is solitary, enigmatic, unapproachable, not for us, inhuman. The work of art opens a world, and it remains within the world as a breach, a rupture, a shaking that allows nothing to settle into place. "All art," he says, "as the letting happen of the advent of the truth of what is, is, as such, essentially poetry. . . . It is due to art's poetic nature that, in the midst of what is, art breaks open an open place, in whose openness everything is other than usual." In this breach, nothing seems to remain: "everything ordinary and hitherto becomes an unbeing" (*Poetry, Language, Thought,* p. 72). The task philosophy sets for itself is to interrupt this event, to close the breach, to preserve the identity and self-sameness of the world, that is, to set logical limits to the opening of the Open, to establish the measure and boundary of the world, to settle the world and civilize it, bringing it under control. If the work of the work of art is to set up a world, the task of philosophy is to stabilize this event, perhaps to cut it off as if to prevent the endless dissemination of worlds. This is, in effect, the work of the logos, namely, to intervene in the work of the work of art, to master its effects, to render it accessible to the comportments of reason, thereby instituting the world as a Republic. If there is a quarrel between philosophy and poetry, it begins here.

And here, one might say, is where Paul Ricoeur is to be found vis-à-vis Heidegger. We can think of Ricoeur's hermeneutics of the text or his hermeneutics of narrative as philosophy's attempt to get on top of the event of art that Heidegger describes; it is to overcome the struggle of world and earth and to establish the world, not to say the work of art, on properly philosophical foundations, freeing it, one might say, from the earth. Aristotle-like, Ricoeur's approach is not so much to banish poetry as to appropriate it, or anyhow to take over in the name of philosophy the worldly project of the poetic work.

The starting point of Ricoeur's hermeneutics of appropriation is the well-known distinction between system and history, structure and event. This distinction derives from an encounter between existentialism and structuralism—between a tradition that concerns itself with the ontological condition of belonging to a concrete historical situation and a tradition that is concerned, Kant-like, with the formal or logical conditions that make things intelligible. The structure-event distinction, Ricoeur says, gives us two ways of thinking about language—the way of linguistics and the way of what he calls hermeneutics, where the one is concerned with *langue,* or with how language works as a system of signifiers, and the other is concerned with what is said, or *parole.*[6] Thus we can think of language in terms of signs or in terms of saying; that is, we can think of what words mean in relation to other words in any linguistic or semiotic system or of what they mean when they are used in actual speech, say, in sentences. Somewhat loosely, Ricoeur maps onto this difference Frege's distinction between *Sinn und Bedeutung,* or between ideal meaning, which has no internal connection with how things are in the world, and actual meaning, which is always the product of assertion, of something said about something. Sometimes Ricoeur refers to the connection between these two orders of meaning in terms of a dialectic of semiotics and semantics, where semiotics has to do with the differential character of signifying systems, and semantics with the referential meaning of sentences. For Ricoeur, the importance of the semiotic approach to language is that it disconnects meaning from the speaking subject.[7]

Meaning is entirely internal to the linguistic system; it is not the product of consciousness or intentionality or any activity of the spirit. It is no longer anything occult; it is not anything that needs to be reconstructed or reproduced. On the other hand, for Ricoeur semiotics has this weakness: it also disconnects meaning from the world, because if meaning is internal to the system, that is, simply a function of a chain of signifiers, then it becomes impossible to speak of anything outside the system. This is why Ricoeur wants to go beyond the semiotics of signifying systems to what he calls a "semantics of the sentence," because it is in the *use* of language—in the making of predications in the world of everyday discourse—that language is reconnected to reality. Speaking does not occur inside a system; it is a practice that belongs to the environing world of circumstances in which human life runs its course, and it cannot help being about this world. In speaking, the meaning of signs is predicated of the world in which we find ourselves.

What happens, however, when we shift discourse from the level of the sentence to the level of the text? In the first place, the situation of discourse is obliterated. A text is never the cry of its occasion. It is not anything one engages in a conversation. It does not have an inside and an outside like a speaking subject; it does not express itself like a "thou." A text is a structural object with its own intrinsic intelligibility; it is never an utterance. It can be addressed only by means of formal analysis. Moreover, the obliteration of the situation in which speakers discourse about the world also means that the referential movement of discourse is suspended by the text. There ceases to be a world referred to by the text. The text is not only self-contained but autotelic, closed off to its author and to the world of its composition, existing only for itself. This "leaves the text 'in the air,'" says Ricouer, "outside or without a world. In virtue of this obliteration of the relation to the world, each text is free to enter into relations with all other texts which come to take the place of the circumstantial reality referred to by living speech. This relation of text to text, within the effacement of the world about which we speak, engendered the quasi-world of texts or *literature*."[8] Literature is external to the world, and not only external. As Ricoeur says, "The role of most of our literature is . . . to destroy the world" (p. 141).

I want to come back to this last line. But for now it is enough to say simply that texts are always alienating in the nature of the case; their autonomy means that they are always estranged from whatever is not a text—so that formally speaking, only by translating ourselves into texts could we enter into the region where intelligibility, not to say self-understanding, is possible—a thought that Ricoeur pursues in "The Question of Proof in Freud's Psychoanalytic Writings," in which he claims that the "truth" of psychoanalysis is the product of "constructing or reconstructing a coherent story or account from the tattered remains of our experience" (*Hermeneutics and the Human Sciences*, p. 267). More important, however, the text's power of estrangement makes possible the reintroduction into hermeneutics of the historical, aesthetic, and critical distance that the ontological condition of belonging calls into question. We are always outside the texts that come down to us from the past or from alien cultures; these texts always project before us a difference from the situation in which we find ourselves. For Ricoeur, this difference, or distanciation, restores the possibility of something like a critique of ideology. Ricoeur rejects the possibility of critique as someone like Althusser understands it, namely, a critical analysis conducted from "a non-ideological place called science."[9] The "critique of ideology," Ricoeur says, "never breaks its link to the basis of belonging," that is, it can never emancipate itself from its own historicality (p. 245). But this does not rule out the possibility of a "critical hermeneutics" that would be able to situate itself analytically outside of what it nevertheless belongs to ontologically. Tradition, after all, is always textual; it is not a "thou." In this respect the encounter with tradition would never be simply an act of recognition and acceptance (what Gadamer calls naïve assimilation); it would always require a critical appropriation of otherness, which is what Gadamer has in mind when he speaks of horizons that are fused but never unified or identical or subsumed into a higher or wider perspective. Horizon for Gadamer is not a perspectival concept.

For Gadamer, of course, this appropriation of the other is radically unstable; one is always in danger of going to pieces in the encounter with alterity. This is not Ricoeur's view at all. For Ricoeur the critical appropriation of otherness is methodological, more logical than ontological, in any event, without any dark side. To understand what Ricoeur means by appropriation, one has to go back to the inaugural distinction between the semiotics of signifying systems and the semantics of referential discourse. Ricoeur elevates this distinction into what he calls a second-order dialectic of structural explanation and hermeneutical understanding, where understanding fulfills itself in action in the world rather than in intellectual agreement with intentions, truth claims, concepts, or states of affairs. For Ricoeur the text that comes down to us, say, in tradition or from another culture, is before everything else a structural object that possesses its own intrinsic sense, its own laws of formal intelligibility. Its meaning is not anything that lies behind it in the form of an original intention or even an original reference to the time and place of its composition. Its meaning *is* its textuality. Textuality obliterates intentionality and referentiality in the process of objectifying itself. This is so particularly with literary texts in which, Ricoeur says, "language seems to glorify itself at the expense of the referential function of ordinary discourse" (*Hermeneutics and the Human Sciences*, p. 141).

What Ricoeur wants to argue is that the power of estrangement that texts exhibit nevertheless allows for the reconnection of discourse and a world outside of the text. "My thesis," Ricoeur says, "is that the abolition of first order reference, an abolition effected [for example] by fiction and poetry, is the condition of possibility for the freeing of a second-order reference, which reaches the world not only at the level of manipulable objects but at the level that Husserl has designated by the expression *Lebenswelt* and Heidegger by the expression 'being-in-the-world'" (p. 141). For Ricoeur, the meaning of a text does not lie behind it in the region of intention and ostensive reference but *in front of it* in the space of interpretation. He writes as follows: "If we can no longer define hermeneutics in terms of the search for the psychological intentions of another person which are concealed *behind* the text, and if we do not want to reduce interpretation to the dismantling of structures, then what remains to be interpreted? I shall say: to interpret is to explicate the type of being-in-the-world unfolded *in front of the text*" (p. 141). This explication is not something to be worked out on paper. It is not an analytical project. Following the early Heidegger and Gadamer, Ricoeur emphasizes that understanding is a mode of being rather than simply an act of consciousness. "The moment of 'understanding,'" he says, "corresponds dialectically to being in a situation: it is 'the projection of our ownmost possibilities,' applying it to the theory of the text. For what must be interpreted in a text is a *proposed world* which I could inhabit and wherein I could project one of my ownmost possibilities. This is what I call the world of the text, the world proper to this unique text" (p. 142).

Ricoeur proposes something like a magical looking-glass theory of textual meaning. The discourse of texts is phenomenological rather than logical or semiotic, in the sense that reference means disclosure, bringing-to-appearance, rather than designation and representation. Texts *mean* not by corresponding to states of affairs, not by satisfying truth conditions, but by manifesting or opening up a region of existence whose reality is not simply matter for analysis but is, on the contrary, matter for appropriation, for intervention and action. The task of discourse in this sense would be not merely to picture reality but to throw light on the situation in which we find ourselves historically and to open up a path for us to follow in the way of action and conduct. The looking-glass theory of meaning presupposes an ontological turn away from epistemology toward a hermeneutics of praxis and action. It presupposes that our relationship with the world is not simply one of knowing but of being-with-others in states of affairs that require our intervention. "World" here is to be understood in its Heideggerian sense of ontological horizon rather than in the Kantian sense of objective representation. Thus the world that is disclosed in the text is not to be thought of as discontinuous from our world but as an enlargement of it, a movement of our world into the future; but it is a movement that can be actualized only to the extent that we act on what the text proposes, bring the text about by entering into our actual world in light of the world proposed by the text.

So we should think of ourselves as standing *before* the text and not only outside of it in some purely analytical space. The space of interpretation is always historical, always political and ethical as well as analytical—as it is, for example, in the case of legal interpretation, where we are always within the jurisdiction of what we seek to understand, whence our understanding is necessarily more than just the construction and analysis of legal propositions or more than the logical application of rules; it is a way of construing situations with respect to the action we are called upon to take in them. This interpretive action is always an intervention in reality; it alters reality for better or for worse—but always in the positive or negative light of the law. The law is a text that always projects consequences for those who find themselves before it or within its jurisdiction; its meaning lies therefore in its fulfillment in the future, not in the logical analysis of its internal structure or in the reconstruction of its originating intention. The law is always utopian. It projects a world, that is, a mode of being that bears upon our present existence in a historical time and place. Our relationship to the text, therefore, like our relationship with the world, is not merely theoretical; it is not just a relationship of knowing, or what we think of as knowing. The understanding of a text—any text, whether literary or legal, political or scientific—begins to show itself only in action.

It seems to me that what we have here is a basic Aristotelian theory of the text, and what is Aristotelian about it is the way the text is saved or justified by being systematized and then reconnected to reality according to an up-to-date conception of mimesis—a looking-glass theory of mimesis that is, so to speak, beyond representation. As Ricoeur says in *Time and Narrative*, mimesis "takes on its full scope when the work deploys a world that the reader appropriates."[10] Were this the place to do so, I would go on to mention a number of interesting versions of this theory developed by people like Arthur Danto, Alasdair MacIntyre, Martha Nussbaum, Richard Rorty, and Fredric Jameson (good, cloth-coat Aristotelians one and all).[11]

But in fact one could trace the idea back through Luther and Augustine to the earliest beginnings of scriptural hermeneutics, where the idea is to interpret a text by understanding oneself and one's historical situation in its light. The intelligibility of a text lies in its potential for fulfillment in the oncoming world of conduct and action, not in the reconstitution of an original message or state of affairs. In its heart of hearts hermeneutics is prophetic rather than nostalgic. So for Ricoeur even mythic narratives cannot simply be framed as imaginary or aesthetic; they are not simply traces of a vanished world but texts that expose our actual world to alternative possibilities, and as such they cannot help bearing upon our world in critical ways, not just by exposing us to the world's limits but by exposing these limits as historical and contingent. The idea that poetry makes nothing happen could only be true in a nonhistorical world. The world that recovers an ancient or alien text is always altered by it: in Western culture this is an enduring fact of historical experience.[12]

Obviously, this is a satisfying way of thinking about texts and interpretation, and I think one will never understand hermeneutics either philosophically or historically unless one works out an idea roughly along these Aristotelian lines. However, I also think that one will always fall short of grasping the hard reality of hermeneutics if one simply stops where Ricoeur and others seem to stop, without asking whether this way of thinking does not entail a reduction of the literary work of art to what one might call the bare narrative function of projecting a possible world onto the space of interpretation. Ricoeur himself acknowledges, always impatiently and on occasion derisively, that the literary work of art, and particularly the modern avant-garde text, is always excessive with respect to this narrative or mimetic function. For Ricoeur, whatever is written, or considered materially as a text, remains in suspension, in the air, outside the world, mere literature, until it is appropriated in a certain way, the way one appropriates a legal or sacred text, a philosophical argument, a political constitution, a scientific model, or an ethical narrative. The literary text, by contrast, is that which resists appropriation or withholds itself from our hermeneutical tasks. The literary text is one whose looking glass remains opaque. Ricoeur does not hesitate to say that the task of the reader in such an event is to clean and polish the glass in order to render it transparent. The literary work of art, after all, is only an incomplete sketch, a fragment of what needs to be translated into a complete world by the appropriative act of reading. As Ricoeur puts it in *Time and Narrative*, the literary work, considered as a text, "consists of holes, lacunae, zones of indetermination, which, as in Joyce's *Ulysses*, challenge the reader's capacity to configure what the author seems to take malign delight in disfiguring. In such an extreme case, it is the

reader, almost abandoned by the work, who carries the burden of emplot-
ment," that is, the burden of allegory or of reconstructing from the textuality of the text the narrative that projects a world (p. 75). The point is always
to rewrite the literary text as if it were, in its deep structure, a philosophical,
legal, sacred, or political text. This recomposition of the dark or recalcitrant
text is all that allegory has ever meant.

But what would it be for the reader to engage the text at the level of its
resistance to philosophy, that is, prior to reduction, in its refusal of allegory?
What would it be to engage the text in its excess and in its density—or as
Ricoeur says, in its disfigurement and Joycean malignancy? This is the unasked question, the unthought thought, of Ricoeur's philosophy, and of philosophy generally, and for that matter of the university study of literature,
which remains basically an Aristotelian scholasticism in spite of its recent
theoretical adventures.

The question here is one that Heidegger tried to formulate in his later
writings on language, poetry, and thinking, in which language is no longer
conceivable as a logical or linguistic system but is an irreducible, untheorizable place or region or event that Heidegger calls Saying (*Sage*). Poetry and
thinking (*Dichten und Denken*) belong together in this place; that is, prior
to their formal reduction as Literature and Philosophy, prior to their logical
construction as modes or institutions of discourse, poetry and thinking already confront each other, are exposed to each other, within the event of
Saying. What sort of happening is this? What is the site or event of poetry
and thinking? What does this mutual exposure entail? What are its philosophical consequences?[13]

These are the basic questions of a Platonic hermeneutics. To get a sense
of these questions (for it is not clear that we know how to ask them), we
need to take a step back from Aristotle and Ricoeur and imagine something
like the following. Suppose you grant all that Plato says about poetry, suppose that what Plato says is true, namely, that poetry belongs with darkness
and ambiguity, outside the philosophy of light, therefore outside the domain
of justice and necessity, not just radically unstable but linked metaphysically
to anarchy and the derangement of the senses and of reason, not only external to the world, uncontainable within it, but set against it a danger to it
("The role of most of our literature . . . is to destroy the world")—suppose
you grant all of this, but instead of banishing the poet or making her write
philosophical novels, you just linger in her company. What then? What happens to philosophy (or the world) in this event?

A paragraph from Emmanuel Levinas's *Otherwise than Being* might clarify these questions, or at least make them less rhetorical.

Philosophy is disclosure of being, and being's *essence* is truth and philosophy. Being's essence is the temporalization of time, the diastasis of the identical and its recapture or reminiscence, the unity of apperception. *Essence* does not first designate the edges of solids or the moving line of acts in which a light glimmers; it designates this "modification" without alteration or transition, independent of all qualitative determination, more formal than the silent using up of things which reveals their becoming, already weighted down with matter, the creaking of a piece of furniture of the night. This modification by which the same comes unstuck or parts with itself, undoes itself into this and that, no longer covers over itself and thus is disclosed (like in Dufy's paintings, where the colors spread out from their contours and do not rub up against them), becomes a phenomenon—is the *esse* of every being. Being's essence designates nothing that could be a nameable content, a thing, event, or action; it names this mobility of the immobile, this multiplication of the identical, this diastasis of the punctual, this lapse. This modification without alteration or displacement, being's essence or time, does not await, in addition, an illumination that would allow for an "act of consciousness." This modification is precisely the visibility of the same to the same, which is sometimes called openness. The work of being, essence, time, the lapse of time, is exposition, truth, philosophy. *Being's essence is a dissipating of opacity,* not only because this "drawing out" of being would have to have been first understood so that the truth could be told about things, events and acts that *are;* but because this drawing out is the *original dissipation* of opaqueness. In it forms are illuminated where knowledge is awakened; in it being leaves the night, or, at least, quits sleep, that night of night, for an unextinguishable insomnia of consciousness. Thus every particular knowledge, every factual exercise of understanding—ideology, faith, or science—every perception, every disclosing behavior whatever it be, would owe their light to essence, the first light, and to philosophy which is dawn or its twilight. Temporality, in the divergence of the identical from itself, is *essence* and original light, that which Plato distinguished from the visibility of the visible and the clairvoyance of the eye. The time of the essence unites three moments of knowing. Is the light of essence which makes things seen itself seen? It can to be sure become a theme; essence can show itself, be spoken of and described. But then light presents itself in light, which latter is not thematic, but resounds for the "eye that listens," with a resonance unique in its kind, a resonance of silence. Expressions such as the eye that listens to the resonance of silence are not monstrosities, for they speak of the way one approaches the temporality of the true, and in temporality being deploys its essence.[14]

Here Levinas tells, or retells, ambiguously, the story of philosophy's genesis in "an original dissipation of opaqueness," that is, being's departure from Chaos and Old Night. Philosophy *discloses* this event—but what does this mean, exactly? Levinas has it that philosophy preserves being from the non-identical not so much by grasping being as such, since being is unnameable, as (oddly) by determining its essence as so many oxymorons—modification without alteration, mobility of the immobile, multiplication of the identical, the self-estrangement of the punctual, and (more strangely still): *lapse,* as of time, when "the same comes unstuck or parts with itself, undoes itself into this or that, no longer covers over itself and thus is disclosed . . ., becomes a phenomenon." This phenomenon is like a phenomenon "in Dufy's paintings, where colors spread out from their contours and do not rub up against them." This reference to Dufy is worth a moment's study, because in his writings Levinas rarely gives examples. Raoul Dufy (1877–1953) was a French painter usually counted among the Fauvists, who championed the motto "color for color's sake." He is perhaps most famous for a splendid and massive mural—some two hundred feet by thirty-five feet—called "The History of Electricity," which was commissioned by the Paris Electrical Supply Company and exhibited in the firm's pavilion at the 1937 World's Fair in Paris. But given the context in which he appears in Levinas's reflections, it seems most important to know that Dufy followed closely, and made use of, the experiments of Jacques Maroger, a chemist who attempted to rid pigments of opacity, thus producing radiant colors or colors through which light seems to shine.[15] So perhaps "The History of Electricity" is allegorical of the history of philosophy.

By ridding things of their opacity philosophy enables them to appear not as things but as beings, that is, not in the materiality of their existence (furniture creaking in the night) but in their translucent essence, as if dematerialized or spiritualized, all thickness dissipated, so that nothing about them is hidden. Whereas (following Heidegger's analysis) poetry discloses or, more accurately, summons things not as beings but precisely as things— earthly, singular or nonidentical, opaque, refractory to the light, impenetrable to analysis, always withdrawing from view. Likewise, as if executing a classical decorum, poetry itself is thinglike discourse: material, dense (*dicht*), as in the dark saying in which nothing is ever itself or capturable but is always interpretable otherwise, forever running loose, anarchic and dangerous.

Hence the idea, basic to a Platonic hermeneutics, that poetry's natural or, rather, originary condition is one of exile. On this condition one can learn most from Maurice Blanchot:

> The poem is exile, and the poet who belongs to it belongs to the dis-satisfaction of exile. He is always lost to himself, outside, far from home; he belongs to the foreign, to the outside which knows no inti-macy or limit, and to the separation which Hölderlin names when in his madness he sees rhythm's infinite space.
>
> Exile, the poem then, makes the poet a wanderer, the one always astray, he to whom the stability of presence is not granted and who is deprived of a true abode. And this must be understood in the gravest sense: the artist does not belong to truth because the work is itself what escapes the movement of the true, eludes signification, designating that region where nothing subsists, where what takes place has nevertheless never taken place, where what begins over has never begun. It points to the realm of the most dangerous indecision, toward the confusion from which nothing emerges. This eternal outside is quite well evoked by the image of the *exterior* darkness where man understands that which the true must negate in order to become possible and to progress.[16]

Thoughts of this character tend to turn people into Aristotelians—or, in more up-to-date fashion, into either Kantians or Hegelians. Literary critics on the whole interpret the idea that poetry "escapes the movement of the true" by following Kant in resolving the question of truth procedurally, so that the truth of the poem (its point, say) becomes a function of the strategy used to approach it. Philosophers, meanwhile, mostly follow Hegel's "death of art" idea, namely that poetry may once have determined "the movement of the true" but has since been superseded by philosophy: "Art, considered in its highest vocation, is and remains for us a thing of the past."[17]

On closer look there may be little to choose between Kant and Hegel, who says that "what is now aroused in us by works of art is not just im-mediate enjoyment but our judgement also, since we subject to our intellec-tual consideration (i) the content of the art, and (ii) the work of art's means of presentation, and the appropriateness of one to another. The *philosophy* of art is therefore a greater need in our day than it was in days when art by itself as art yielded full satisfaction. Art invites us to intellectual consider-ation, and that not for the purpose of creating art again, but for knowing philosophically what art is" (p. 11). The point is that we have distanced ourselves from art; it can no longer do us any harm—this being, from a certain point of view, as Danto suggests, the whole definition of philosophy, or at least "the reason philosophy was invented," as if "philosophical systems [were] finally penitentiary systems [or] labyrinths for keeping monsters in and so protecting us against some deep metaphysical danger." Naturally, as Danto says, one cannot help asking "what power finally is that philosophy is afraid of" (*Philosophical Disenfranchisement of Art*, p. 12).

Perhaps the answer is: whatever turns people into poets, that is, wanderers, people incapable of philosophy, that is, people suffering, as Blanchot says, "the inability to abide and stay. For where the wanderer is, the conditions of the definite here are lacking. . . . The wanderer's country is not truth, but exile; he lives outside, on the other side which is by no means a beyond, rather the contrary. He remains separated, where the deep of dissimulation reigns, that elemental obscurity through which no way can be made and which because of that makes its awful way through him" (*The Space of Literature*, p. 238). One has only to recall the status of wandering in Plato's texts to understand what is at stake here for the philosopher who goes astray, into the wanderer's country.

In this context it seems right to think of Derrida, who says that the central task of his philosophical work has been to find a nonphilosophical place in which "philosophy as such can appear to itself as other than itself, so that it can interrogate and reflect upon itself in an original manner."[18] Derrida is of two minds as to whether literature can provide such a nonphilosophical place. It doesn't seem that it can, because literature is from the beginning saturated with philosophy; it has already, under the rule of poetics, transformed itself into a discourse of lucidity, a self-allegorizing or self-interpreting, self-justifying text. It has made itself over from something earthly into a worldly and even heavenly good. It is at all events something stable, something recognizable, and not apt to unravel us. Anyway, insofar as this is true there would be no getting around behind Aristotle and Ricoeur, or Kant and Hegel, to recover that originary hermeneutical situation that Heidegger characterizes as a "rift of poetry and thinking," before Literature and Philosophy are stabilized or established as discursive institutions or systems of discursive constraint. Poetry, as such—as *Dichten*, Heidegger's strange word for poetry—does not exist. There is, one might say, no such thing; in any case we are hardly in a position to recognize such a thing. There are only philosophical constructions of poetrylike objects—epics and tragedies, novels and lyrics, whose transparency avant-garde writers like Mallarmé and Artaud and Joyce and John Cage interfere with by means of their bizarre disfigurations of art and language. But whereas for Ricoeur these disfigurations are indeed aberrations, interferences with philosophical reading and its projects of worldmaking, for Derrida they are exactly what must be appropriated, taken up and put into play, precisely because they are external to the philosophy of light. In other words they are what the philosopher must throw in with—as a philosopher. For what interests Derrida is resistance to philosophy as such. It is this resistance that he wants to act out within the institution of philosophy itself in order (this is my guess) to unseal it, to expose it to what is not itself, exposing its limits as historical and contingent, showing it how to become different things—showing, as Wittgenstein might say, that the extension of the concept of philosophy cannot be closed by a frontier. As if wandering were not just poetic madness but something else—for example, a side of philosophy concerned not with the movement of the true but with another sort of movement that one could call freedom.

But how far this movement can be made intelligible by further reflection remains open to question.

Conclusion

TOWARD A HERMENEUTICS

OF FREEDOM

> We may conclude this history of hermeneutics with the
> following remark. The initial purpose of hermeneutics was to
> explain the word of God. This purpose was eventually
> expanded into the attempt to regulate the process of explaining
> the word of man. In the nineteenth century we learned, first
> from Hegel and then more effectively from Nietzsche, that God
> is dead. In the twentieth century, Kojève and his students, like
> Foucault, have informed us that man is dead, thereby as it
> were opening the gates into the abyss of postanthropological
> deconstruction. As the scope of hermeneutics has expanded,
> then, the two original sources of hermeneutical meaning, God
> and man, have vanished, taking with them the cosmos or
> world and leaving us with nothing but our own garrulity,
> which we choose to call the philosophy of language, linguistic
> philosophy, or one of their synonyms. If nothing is real, the
> real is nothing; there is no difference between the written lines
> of a text and the blank spaces between them.
> —Stanley Rosen, *Hermeneutics as Politics*

I've said in this book that our relationship with texts, or
with the world (or with other people), seems inadequately served by the
concept of meaning. I expect now that someone will take me to be saying
that texts, etcetera, are meaningless and that hermeneutics is one more thief
in the postmodern night. It is true that hermeneutics is not always reputable
and that one should always double one's locks. But a serious hermeneutical
lesson that one might draw from this book is that nothing, unfortunately,
is meaningless; rather there are more meanings than we know what to do
with, and not even texts that resist our efforts of interpretation will save us.
We are like Odysseus, accumulating more stories than we could possibly
want, but not too many to tell. Or maybe we are like Oedipus, who finds
to his horror that everything he hears is the truth. Like Oedipus, we spend
our lives trying to get on top, or to the bottom, of what is said. But someone
always comes along, one more old retainer with impractical news. Some
believe, Jocasta-like, that if we could cut down on our stories we could
avoid the desperate conclusion Oedipus arrives at.

For example, in an essay called "Relativism, Power, and Philosophy," Alasdair MacIntyre makes an interesting distinction between modern and premodern languages. A premodern language is one used in a culture with a coherent system of concepts and beliefs and a regularly consulted canon of narratives or texts that show how to use such concepts and what the upshot is of holding such beliefs, and also why one would be justified (or not) in saying that something is true, and how one would go about developing arguments to that effect, and further how to go about settling disputes rationally or without recourse to force or manipulation or mechanical operations of the spirit. A modern language is one used in a culture in which none of this is any longer possible because that culture is now overdetermined by too many narratives. MacIntyre describes as follows "the historical process which made the language of modernity what it is":

> A central feature of that process had to be . . . the detachment of the language-in-use from any particular set of canonical texts; and an early stage in that history was the gradual accumulation in the culture of so many different, heterogeneous, and conflicting bodies of canonical texts from so many diverse parts of the cultural past that every one of them had to forego any exclusive claim to canonical status at all. So the accumulation of Greek, Hebrew, and Latin texts at the Renaissance proved only a prologue not only to the annexation of Chinese, Sanskrit, Mayan, and Old Irish texts, and to the bestowal of equal status upon texts in European vernacular languages from the thirteenth to the nineteenth centuries, but also to the discovery of a wide range of preliterate cultures, the whole finally to be assembled in that modern liberal arts college museum of academic culture, whose introductory tour is provided by those Great Books courses which run from Gilgamesh to Saul Bellow via Confucius, Dante, Newton, *Tristram Shandy*, and Margaret Mead.[1]

The modern world (on this view) is one in which we have lost the use of our concepts because there is no longer any coherent background of texts that show what such use looks like.[2] Instead there is a plurality of rival and competing backgrounds—so many that we cannot even sort them out any more in order to get a fix on where we come from or where we stand. Anything we might coherently say or believe about the world is beyond our competence, not because skepticism has it right, but because our language is a "conceptual *mélange*" (*After Virtue*, p. 210). Our world is a contest of narratives, a whirl of theories and practices. It is not one thing but an accumulation of forms of life both ancient and modern, near and remote, advanced and backward, alien and familiar, all arriving in California and spreading outward in bits and pieces in every direction. I am modern, a creature of modernity, just insofar as I don't know where I belong in any of this; or rather, I float free among all the fragments of discourse and action that swirl through time and space like radio waves and electronic images. No one can pin me down.

Is this altogether bad? This is perhaps another way of putting the question of how we stand with respect to all that comes down to us from the past, or (same question, really) of how we stand with respect to the world and others with whom we find ourselves. And in addition it is a way of putting the old question of individual freedom (or is it individual fate?). Sometimes hermeneutics gets taken as, and in a certain sense it is, a theory of confinement, because it is preoccupied with our belongingness, or, roughly, with the idea that none of us ever comes floating freely into the world; rather, we are from the start initiated into ongoing forms of life or contexts of practice and action that make themselves felt internally not only as claims upon our ownmost existence but as indispensable features of our self-recognition. We are social before we are individual, and so we are always to some extent "individual" in quotation marks, and perhaps one ought to come out and confess the point that hermeneutics, like most European theory, is frankly anti-individualist, a beneficiary (at least) of the many-sided critique of the subject that characterizes so much of twentieth-century intellectual culture; and it is also true, as a further twist, that hermeneutics is drawn historically toward a Levinasian ethics of vulnerability that turns the self or ego inside out, defines it as responsibility for another.[3] Hermeneutics takes no interest in Cartesian, Lockean, Kantian, Husserlian, Sartrean, and other sorts of famous subjects; its concern is for what Cornelius Castoriadis calls "the actual subject traversed through and through by the world and by others."[4] But for all of that it remains an open question, at least for hermeneutics, of how confined we finally are to our constitutive forms of life and cultural practice, which after all, with due respect to long-running prison-house theories of language, culture, and ideology, may themselves be heterogeneous, porous, and open-ended—not, finally, structured like a language or a system of rules or even as a conceptual scheme, but rather structured like the weather owing to their historicality; in which case we might think of hermeneutics as a kind of chaos theory interested in the historical turbulence of systems. The question MacIntyre is asking, if I understand, is whether *this* sort of loose multifariousness, call it a cultural lack of schematic coherence, doesn't come down finally to a kind of moral and intellectual anarchy; in which case isn't hermeneutics, with its love of the surface and the singular and its distrust of deep-structure logic, a symptom or accomplice of deterioration into Chaos and Old Night (the very thing, for example, that Stanley Rosen warns us against)?[5]

The sense of this question is not easy to clarify. I want to conclude this book by struggling with some of its difficulties—without being sure where I will end up. What I call a hermeneutics of freedom is not a theory of anything but, rather, an effort to enter into a subject that (like hermeneutics itself, perhaps) does not seem to have a coherent place or ongoing life in our present intellectual culture.

In an essay entitled "Losing Your Concepts," Cora Diamond reformulates MacIntyre's criticism of modernity as a problem not of too many texts but of too few, that is, as a problem of inarticulateness or the inability of some people to give accounts of their experience owing to a lack of vocabulary.[6] She mentions as an example *Habits of the Heart,* by Robert Bellah and others, which argues that the ideology of radical individualism in American culture has produced a society of empty, disengaged, drifting selves incapable of memorable experience or coherent expression.[7] And she quotes John Berger's statement, in *The Fortunate Man,* that "there are large sections of the English working and middle class who are inarticulate as a result of wholesale cultural deprivation. They are deprived of the means of translating what they know into thoughts which they can think. They have no examples to follow in which words clarify experience. Their spoken proverbial traditions have long been destroyed: and, although they are literate in the strictly technical sense, they have not had the opportunity for discovering the existence of a written cultural heritage. . . . A great deal of their experience—especially emotional and introspective experience—has to remain *unnamed* for them."[8] Cora Diamond sees these cases as part of the more general problem first sketched out by Iris Murdoch in a famous essay, "Against Dryness," in which Murdoch said that we moderns have "suffered a general loss of concepts, the loss of a moral and political vocabulary. We no longer use a spread-out substantial picture of the manifold virtues of man and society. We no longer see man against a background of values, of realities, which transcend him. We picture man as a brave naked will surrounded by an easily comprehended empirical world."[9] This problem (says Diamond) tends to be lost on modern Anglo-American philosophers, who think that concepts are simply categories under which things fall, whereas Diamond argues that our capacity to use a word "is a capacity to participate in the life from which that word comes" (p. 267). "Part of the difficulty here" she says, "is that we think of learning to use a term as learning to follow the rules for that use; we think of language in terms of rules fixing what can and cannot be done. But the most essential thing about language is that it is *not* fixed in that way. Learning to use a term is coming into life with that term, whose possibilities are to a great extent to be made" (p. 268). As Stanley Cavell once put it: "In 'learning a language' you learn not merely what the names of things are, but what a name is; not merely what the form of expression is for expressing a wish, but what a wish is; not merely the word for 'father,' but what a father is; not merely what the word for 'love' is, but what love is. In learning a language, you do not merely learn the pronunciation of sounds, and their grammatical orders, but the 'forms of life' which make those sounds what they are, what they do—e.g., name, call, point, express a wish or affection, indicate a choice or an aversion, etc."[10] So inarticulateness suggests a problem not just in one's vocabulary but in one's relation to the form of life in which that vocabulary has application. If, as Diamond says, "learning to use a term is coming into life with that term," losing one's concepts means falling out of life with them.

But Diamond wants to know whether this is always or necessarily a bad thing. Her essay is mainly about how difficult it is to get a clear shot at this question, but finally she asks: "What if we have lost concepts? Might we not have gained more than enough to counterbalance that loss, in the general shift of modes of thought and action, and forms of social life, of which the supposed conceptual loss was part? If Progress brings with it the loss of some concepts, may its other blessings not outweigh the loss? Is it not perhaps possible to suffer from conceptual nostalgia, in which the good of the good, old, now vanished concepts is detached from the evils—the tyranny and oppression and grinding poverty—of the life to which those concepts belonged?" (pp. 266–67). She has in mind particularly the

debate about whether we should be better off without our present concept of sexual difference. Suppose we gave up the idea that a person is essentially characterized as a man *or* a woman, that this belongs to who he is, who she is, and that one's sex is not like the color of one's hair. Suppose all that were given up, and the old concepts of man and woman were to be found, two hundred years from now, only in the literature of bygone days that people could hardly any longer understand, would people have gained? Any adequate discussion of that question depends on some understanding of what it is for us to live with our present concept of the difference: how it enters into the ordering and articulating of our experience, how it contributes both to the ways we make sense of what we do and what happens to us, and to how we see the shape of our lives. (p. 268)

The difficulty is that people live with the concept of sexual difference un-equally, or anyhow differently, depending on an extraordinary variety of social, regional, economic, educational, cultural, and sexual circumstances. Feminists argue that getting rid of the concept would loosen things up for the better. The point being that the loss of a concept is, depending on the situation, either a deprivation or a freedom.[11] Whether it is one or the other looks like a political question.

That is, the question is not so much whether our culture has too many texts as how we live with them, which is why MacIntyre does not think it enough, whatever its pedagogical convenience, to fix a canon and lay it out on a five-foot shelf. His idea is that we have to change completely the con-ditions under which texts are studied, and this means, for him, transforming universities into cultures of argument in which, as in a medieval university, one's beliefs are really at stake, where "really" means that what is really at stake in a dispute is one's existence in the world.[12] Such a transformation would mean, for MacIntyre, getting rid of healthy portions of hermeneutics (for example, the part that looks for all the world like a branch of Nietz-schean genealogy that historicizes everything and answers to nothing), meanwhile retaining from it the concepts of authority and tradition refor-mulated as a theory of a culture's ability to legitimate itself, or parts of itself, as something like "the best theory so far."[13] But basic to hermeneutics both ancient and modern is the idea that there is no making sense at a distance; one must always work out some internal connection with what one seeks to understand. It would help to distinguish here, as maybe MacIntyre does not, between Gadamer's old-fashioned historicism and Richard Rorty's ironic or mildly Nietzschean version of it, because Gadamer after all follows pretty straightforwardly the Socratic idea that it's an empty dispute when one can exempt oneself from the consequences of its outcome, whereas for Rorty disputed questions need to be cushioned or kept at bay by a strong distinction between private beliefs and public needs, meaning particularly that our texts, whatever they are and however many, ought not to be taken so seriously as to be given application in the public realm. Which is perhaps how the liberal ironist squares it with Plato.[14]

Rorty's notion of irony, to characterize it very roughly, starts with the belief, or recognition, that there is no getting outside of our conceptual schemes, that is, no such thing as a transcendental standpoint from which to judge how well our versions of things (our "vocabularies") stand up against how things are. Everything, from whatever point of view, is "inter-pretable otherwise"; everything, as Rorty likes to say, can be made to look good or bad by being redescribed, which is what Rorty means by "contingency." But there is a distancing factor in this recognition, which is what Rorty means by freedom, or the "recognition of contingency" (p. 26), namely, that if everything is schematic, nothing is deserving of our countenance, nothing has a claim on us; rather, everything is under our command, and up to the limits of our private chambers we can redesign ourselves at will. As Rorty says, "[Nietzsche] thinks a human life triumphant just insofar as it escapes from inherited descriptions of the contingencies of its existence and finds new descriptions. This is the difference between the will to truth and the will to self-overcoming" (p. 29). Irony is (as it was, in a sense, for Socrates, although not for Nietzsche's Socrates) a nonmetaphysical way of getting outside of one's metaphysics, as if putting it in quotation marks. Thompson Clarke once said that "we philosophers apart from 'creating concepts' and providing their mental upkeep, are outsiders, standing back detached from concepts and items alike (even when items are aspects of ourselves), purely ascertaining observers who, usually by means of our senses, ascertain, when possible, whether items fulfill the conditions legislated by concepts."[15] Rorty's irony means giving up the monitoring of the life world while remaining an outsider. Or in other words we give up God's point of view but not his option of withdrawing from his handiwork. In effect, Rorty stares down Kierkegaard, who complained that "because the ironist poetically produces himself as well as his environment with the greatest possible poetic license, because he lives completely hypothetically and subjunctively, his life finally loses all continuity."[16] But if continuity is another word for getting trapped in outdated schemes or descriptions, then for Rorty continuity is what needs losing; or, to put it plainly, for Rorty losing one's concepts becomes a style of philosophy. Either lose your concepts or grow obsolete.

It looks from this crude summary as if there's wide disagreement between MacIntyre and Rorty. MacIntyre's complaint against the Great Books course is, after all, that it both presupposes and encourages the enlightened liberal's self-image as a free-floating agent of self-creation who is able to construct a private moral outlook from among the ingredients of various and possibly rival and incompatible schemes of human values.[17] Against liberalism MacIntyre holds, as if he had studied hermeneutics, that one could not make sense of any given value, say, justice or mercy, nor could one even recognize a value as such, except as a believer in it, or at all events as one who belongs to or has some internal sense of the specific, historically contingent moral scheme in which that value has a practical meaning—and this means expressly in terms of the (presumably canonical) library of narratives and texts that show what it would be for such a value to have application in this or that particular ongoing form of life. Or, in short, values are not detachable from forms of life and neither are words or concepts or texts; or when they do become detached, they are no longer values, and quite possibly we do not have a name for what they have become because their intelligibility has just drained away. So on MacIntyre's reasoning the idea that in the intimacy of my rooms I could pick and choose among the best that various moral schemes have to offer, and so re-create myself anew, which seems to be what Rorty is proposing—this idea is so much transcendental buffoonery, because what irony detaches me from is simply my ability to make any coherent sense of myself or anything at all. What it gets me into, MacIntyre would say, is "a state of intellectual and moral destitution" in which self-creation could never get under way (*Whose Justice? Which Rationality?* p. 367; compare *After Virtue,* pp. 103–13, 238–45).

One can imagine Rorty shrugging this off as overserious, but he wouldn't have to. For if Rorty sides with Nietzsche, he still, unNietzsche-like, or at all events unironically, can see the enlightened liberal ironist spending "her time worrying about the possibility that she has been initiated into the wrong tribe, taught to play the wrong language game. She worries that the process of socialization which turned her into a human being by giving her a language may have given her the wrong language, and so turned her into the wrong kind of human being." To be sure, as a Nietzschean rider Rorty adds that "she cannot give a criterion of wrongness" (*Contingency, Irony, and Solidarity,* p. 75), that is, she cannot produce, bad as she feels, a moral argument to the effect that the whole phallocentric system in which she finds herself is botched all the way down—botched as if in the nature of the case. But on MacIntyre's theory she *could* give a criterion of wrongness just insofar as she could derive an argument from within an alternative moral scheme, for what makes us rational moral agents is not our ability to ground our judgments on universal principles but simply our ability to criticize and correct ourselves by comparing our own moral scheme with alternative and possibly, from our point of view, better moral traditions ("Relativism, Power, and Philosophy," pp. 201–02). I don't find Rorty saying anything that disagrees with MacIntyre on this point; in fact, he says, sounding for all the world like MacIntyre, that "for us ironists nothing can serve as a criticism of a final vocabulary save another such vocabulary. . . . Nothing can serve as a criticism of a person save another person or of a culture save an alternative culture—for persons and cultures are, for us, incarnated vocabularies" (*Contingency, Irony, and Solidarity,* p. 80).[18]

Thus the most interesting difference between MacIntyre and Rorty might come down to a problem of how to evaluate the categories of public and private, and even here seemingly large differences may narrow once one gets down to the fine print. Thus for MacIntyre no one is a self except in the context of a shared tradition (*After Virtue*, pp. 204–05), whereas for Rorty no one is a self except in the context of a shared tradition from which one has freed oneself and created oneself anew, as if the task of liberalism were to win an atomistic freedom from a holistic embrace. To which MacIntyre might be imagined to reply: How can one create oneself anew if all one is is an incarnated vocabulary, unless it is by converting, Augustine-like, to an alternative vocabulary, assuming one to be available? That is, there is no escape into the privacy of unencumbered selfhood, only into alternative communities, and the devil is to find one that is being maintained in good working order.[19] Or, to put it another way: "The perspectivist," MacIntyre says, "fails to recognize how integral the concept of truth is to tradition-constituted forms of inquiry. It is this which leads perspectivists to suppose that one could temporarily adopt the standpoint of a tradition and then exchange it for another, as one might wear first one costume and then another, or as one might act one part in one play and then a quite different part in a quite different play" (*Whose Justice? Which Rationality*, p. 367).[20] To which Rorty might reply: so much the worse for the concept of truth. For the point about irony is precisely that it is a strategy of disencumbrance, or of self-mastery, in a holistic world of tradition-constituted identities. Whence Rorty appeals to Hegel, who, as Rorty reads him, "dropped the idea of getting at the truth in favor of the idea of making things new. His criticism of his predecessors was not that their propositions were false but that their languages were obsolete" (*Contingency, Irony, Solidarity*, p. 78).

As if the sense of our question about too many narratives came down to a choice between truth and freedom, with Rorty and MacIntyre differing chiefly about what they are prepared to give up, given that one can't have everything. There is something initially attractive in this way of framing the problem, which is roughly what John MacCumber does in *Poetic Interaction*, where the question of too many narratives turns on whether you take narrative to be a mode of truth telling, or whether it is something else:

> Any narrative is . . . only one of many possible stories, and as more of these possibilities are actualized the better off, narratively speaking, we are. There is reason to believe that our store of philosophical narratives is presently rather low. Why, for example, has no one advanced the idea that our concept of the state, the centerpiece of European political theory (if not of European politics itself), grows from Aristotle's abstruse critique of the Platonic theory of self-motion? Why has it not been suggested that Kant's philosophy not merely takes up Platonic themes,

but is largely a rewriting of Plato in which the modern rational mind (one from which eros has been eliminated) replaces the ancient cosmos? Why have modernists and postmodernists, in the lulls between their recurrent skirmishes, failed to see that their respective viewpoints co-exist as sweetly as twin embryos in a womb, in Kant's doctrine of reflective judgment? Again, I suspect, the reason for this is not want of intelligence and industry, but rather the conviction that narrative is a form of truth telling, that there can be only one true story, and that the proliferation of narratives would (as indeed it does) undermine the truth claim of any one of them. But narrative connecting is like a rope rather than a chain; there is no more need for different narratives to harmonize fully with one another than there is for all the strands of a rope to twist in the same direction at the same point.[21]

There is an interesting point here, which MacCumber does not quite make, about the systematic inarticulateness of philosophy. MacCumber aims rather at the thought that "language is oriented to freedom as inherently as it is to truth. More so, indeed, because some language games are intrinsically emancipatory while—in spite of what we think philosophers have told us—none is intrinsically true." The argument, in fact, is that "freedom and truth are not only separate values served by speech, but that they are complementary; that language becomes, in certain senses, intrinsically emancipatory when truth claims are not made, and vice versa" (p. 1).[22] So on the one side, or in the interests of truth, it is necessary to regiment language in order to tighten up what we say, and this is the task of philosophical analysis, which seeks to restrict the stories we tell to the one that, if not absolutely the right one, we are nevertheless justified in telling, at least for now. Whereas on the other side, in the interests of freedom, one allows language to gyre and gimble in the wabe, to multiply itself, Babel-like, into a confusion of tongues, which is not, however, a condition of meaninglessness but, on the contrary, one in which "there are no predetermined criteria by which an utterance is to be excluded as senseless" (p. 413). If you try to imagine a culture in which "there are no predetermined criteria by which an utterance is to be excluded as senseless," you get a sense of what terrified Plato, and enchanted Nietzsche, and why it is prudent even for liberal ironists to put their trust in Aristotle.

How would we stand with respect to texts oriented toward freedom rather than truth? A nice hermeneutical question, one that we don't really know how to formulate, and so we make do as follows: if you think of a culture as a conceptual scheme organized according to the principle of non-contradiction, that is, as a fabric of interwoven sentences or sentences hanging together according to rules of argument or inferential reasoning, then chances are the multiplication of random utterances or sentences that don't fit in is going to be disruptive, producing maybe even a crisis, possibly a crisis of rationality that seems a chronic feature of modernity, or of the Enlightenment (or, on the long view, of Western culture since Plato). But, imagining yourself as Laurence Sterne, you might want this. So Rorty, up to a point. Or if you think of a culture as a form of life with a coherent background of narratives that show what it is to participate in that form of life, then the introduction of narratives from alien cultures, or from else-where in history, or from unconstrained and possibly deranged imagina-tions, is going to produce some sort of crisis in that form of life, maybe a serious epistemological crisis or maybe a comic one, depending on whether these narratives can be rewritten or allegorized in such a way as to integrate them into the canon, or if not then set aside, as on Habermas's model, in a special region of discourse where they will not interfere with the everyday intercourse—the communicative praxis—that holds the form of life to-gether.[23] But is interfering with this praxis altogether a bad thing? Not if it needs critical redirection. So MacIntyre, up to a point.

So the question is: How tight or loose do you want your conceptual scheme? MacIntyre wants one that functions rationally, although perhaps not quite as rigorously as physics, this being perhaps too tight; but physics (or, more accurately, the history of physics) is a good model for what it would be, for MacIntyre, for a culture or tradition to persist in good work-ing order, namely, as a self-critical system that is able to resolve or at least work through its internal contradictions by periodically restructuring itself, so far as it can, depending on what comes in contact with it.[24] By contrast, Rorty, in the tradition of William James and John Dewey, slightly updated by a reading of Nietzsche, is happy to keep things loose. For him, as for MacIntyre and most analytical philosophers after Quine, human cultures (or human minds) can be thought of "as webs of beliefs and desires, of sentential attitudes—webs which continually reweave themselves so as to accommodate new sentential attitudes."[25]

It is no trouble to think of this reweaving or recontextualizing as problem solving, self-correction, or maintaining the equilibrium or coherence of the system—this is the task of allegory, or of philosophy, or for MacIntyre just. the task of rational inquiry—but Rorty thinks it might be a good idea "to recontextualize for the hell of it" (p. 110), not simply to keep things in good working order but to keep things loose, multifarious, open-ended, on the principle that "good working order" means a system that accommodates as many random particles as possible rather than one that is self-identical or self-consistent from center to periphery. Rorty is agreeable to the idea that keeping things loose is the task of literature, on a good, nonthreatening Aristotelian theory of literature (that is, narrative descriptions of possible worlds). Imagine, however, a conceptual scheme designed according to other principles than the rules of reason, for example the principles of composition that guided the weaving and reweaving, or unweaving, of *Tristram Shandy*. Thus MacCumber thinks that Rorty's pragmatism will require him to stop short of promoting runaway recontextualizing or the "unchecked proliferation of vocabularies. . . . Vocabularies are, pragmatically speaking, different ways to conceptualize a problem or situation. A person who had an infinite number of them would be unable to settle on any finite number as 'best' for the situation at hand and hence would be unable to act. The more vocabularies we have at our disposal the closer we come to this situation."[26] Tristram Shandy is perhaps something like a person with too many vocabularies. But one wonders whether in practice there aren't historical constraints that hold the number down, much the way that in art history not everything is possible in every place at every moment.

Or is it that one ought not to think of vocabularies or narratives or traditions as systems of rules to be applied beforehand to cases as a way of getting a logical grip on them? This seems to be what Cora Diamond was trying to get at. Thus *phronēsis*, for example, implies not the having of vocabularies, however few or many, but the ability to act in situations that can't be described or conceptualized in advance. Living through situations, after all, is much harder than describing them or grasping them conceptually. One could say about modernity that it has lost, among other things, the concept of practical reasoning—this is the form that Gadamer's critique of modernity takes, namely, that what modernity recognizes as practical rationality mostly reduces to a theory of instrumental control, or the idea that we can't let the situations in which we find ourselves (or the texts that we read, or the people with whom we exist, or the forms of life in which we live, or the natural world) get out of hand.[27] The sense that we have too many narratives expresses among other things the conviction that modernity is the same as anarchy, whence our increasing dependence on the elaboration of administrative and managerial systems (*After Virtue*, pp. 103–04). Anthony Giddens's characterization of modernity as a juggernaut seems to catch this spirit. He likens it to

> a runaway engine of enormous power which, collectively as human beings, we can drive to some extent but which also threatens to rush out of our control and which could rend itself asunder. The juggernaut crushes those who resist it, and while it sometimes seems to have a steady path, there are times when it veers away erratically in directions

we cannot foresee. The ride is by no means wholly unpleasant or unre-warding; it can often be exhilarating and charged with hopeful antici-pation. But, so long as the institutions of modernity endure, we shall never be able to control completely either the path or the pace of the journey. In turn, we shall never be able to feel entirely secure, because the terrain across which it runs is fraught with risks of high conse-quence. Feelings of ontological security and existential anxiety will co-exist in ambivalence.[28]

Gadamer meanwhile interprets *phronēsis* as responsiveness rather than con-trol. This means being responsive to what situations call for in the way of action, but because situations are always made of other people, *phronēsis* in particular means responsiveness to others, granting an open space in which others can come forward, not foreclosing events by strategic inter-vention and taking command like Robinson Crusoe. The logical weakness of *phronēsis* is what comes across in modern theory, faced as it is with a juggernaut to ride.[29] *Phronēsis* is different from a rationality of problem solving, which is why for someone like Gadamer experience is always more important than principles, vocabularies, concepts, procedures, and rules. As we have seen, experience does not consist in positive knowledge; rather (useless as it sounds) being experienced consists in openness to experience, tragic as it often is, which is perhaps another way of characterizing the recognition of contingency (*Truth and Method,* pp. 355–57). As the saying goes, a tragic sense of life helps one to achieve the flexibility and resilience of the comic hero. In the case of *phronēsis* one can never have too many narratives. Having too many narratives would be like having too many ex-periences: one can't imagine what it would mean to reach such a point, unless it were just the weariness or garrulous serenity of old age. Although we often approach them in the spirit of deep-structure logic, narratives are not forms of mediation like conceptual schemes. They do not inculcate prin-ciples and views; rather, they remind us of what we leave out of account and so tend to expose us to what cannot be done away with or brought under control (history, for example, not to say tragedy).

In an essay on "Freedom and Contingency" William Connolly suggests that a good deal of our thinking about human freedom is confused because of the way we associate freedom with being in control, not under the sway of outmoded concepts, in tune with the right communal order or system of virtues.[30] All of our ideas of freedom, Connolly says, are informed by the belief that "the order of things [is] susceptible to human mastery or to a harmonization that approaches the highest human essence. The world, at least in the final instance, must be *for us* in one way or the other. It—

including external nature and the human material from which unified selves are constructed—must be either formed for us or plastic enough to be mastered by us" (p. 181). Connolly calls this belief "ontological narcissism." But what if one does not share this belief? What if one loses the concept of a world as an orderly system, say, a conceptual framework maintained in equilibrium by regular internal adjustments by appropriate experts. What if the world is not structured as a language but as a juggernaut? Connolly says:

> Suppose internal and external nature contains, because it was neither designed by a god nor neatly susceptible to organization by human design, elements of stubborn opacity to human knowledge, recalcitrance to human projects, resistance to every model of normal individuality and harmonious community. Suppose these elements of strife and dissonance enter into life, creating disturbances in the designs we inevitably impose upon it: each worthy design of the normal self, the common good, and justice, while realizing something good, encounters resistances that inhibit its transparency, coherence, and responsiveness and impede its harmonization with the other elements of social life to which it is bound by ties of interdependence. (p. 183)

Here is a conception of contingency somewhat darker, less (or differently) comic than Rorty's—but the internal link between freedom and contingency may still hold. What if freedom itself has to do with this opacity, recalcitrance, or resistance of both human beings and things in the world to the designs of reason? What if it is linked with the tendency of things to careen out of control? Bernhard Waldenfels reminds us that there is, of course, no "realm" of freedom outside of all design and constraint.[31] Rather freedom is internal to constraint as resistance of the constrained. "Something unruly is to be found within what is ruled," Waldenfels says, "just as the invisible or unsayable is not beyond what is seen or said, but within. This unruly may be called *sens sauvage*, a sense that cannot be completely domesticated. Searle's distinction between 'brute facts' and 'institutional facts' has to be modified. In every work of culture, there remains some brutishness, which is not to be devalued as simply awaiting rationalization or fleeing from it. Rather we should take it in the sense Dubuffet intends when he speaks of *art brut*. If we should one day succeed in taming all that resists, in ruling out the unruly and in filling in all the blanks, the game would be up" (p. 192). This is also the moral of *Tristram Shandy*.

This brings us around again to the problem that has turned up repeatedly in this book, namely, the problem of the singular, of what doesn't fit in, of what goes its own way. For hermeneutics this problem of the singular is, so to speak, one to be cherished and preserved rather than resolved or overcome. One wants to say, for example, that freedom is something like the claim of the singular upon our constructions or our sense of the order of things, our principles and rules, as if freedom were just the fact of being singular, unsubsumable, excessive with respect to the way things make sense to us. If this is so, freedom as the refractory and unsubsumable need not be thought of as (just) a subjective possession—for example, a right (*my* right). The concept of freedom as an individual right is simply one way of interpreting the primacy of the singular. Freedom concerns the world and not only human beings. Think of freedom as a space (sometimes, alas, quite small) in which the singular is just what it is and not something answerable to or legislated by concepts and principles. Heidegger discovered in this space a way of turning the concept of truth inside out. Truth is no longer what fits but what goes free.[32]

Not that this idea is so easy to translate into the language of social theory—but then freedom may not be something that can be brought under theoretical management. A useful guide here is Albrecht Wellmer, whose "Models of Freedom in the Modern World" lays out the differences between communalist and individualist theories of freedom, that is, "rational freedom as it is connected with the concern for the common good, the virtues of citizens, communal action, public debate, and the political control of the economy" (p. 231), as against a natural-rights theory that begins by situating the individual outside all constraints, and which comes down, as Wellmer sees it, to a theory of negative freedom, or "the right *not* to be rational."[33] Wellmer sides with Habermas and other communalists or communitarians in thinking that before everything else human culture must be rational and just, and he thinks that Habermas's procedural theory of communicative action comes close to giving us the picture of just such a culture. But what gets left out? "Every communalist," Wellmer says, "as long as he unmistakably wants to side with the Enlightenment tradition, has to come to terms with the fact that modern bourgeois society is the paradigmatic society of the Enlightenment in the modern world: the only society in which human rights, the rule of law, public freedom, and democratic institutions have to some extent become safely institutionalized." This means (as Hegel saw) coming to terms with civil society—"a society of property owners who, notwithstanding their religious, racial, political, and other differences, are equal before the law, and who, in accordance with general laws, are permitted to pursue their personal interest and their idiosyncratic ideas of happiness, and who, finally, are free to choose careers, professions, employments, or places for living and working" (p. 230). The question is whether the bourgeois theory of freedom implied in civil society can be made compatible with the rational theory of freedom favored by communitarians. Or, in short, is a just and rational state compatible with a strong theory of negative freedom?

Wellmer's example of such a strong theory is Robert Nozick's famous idea of a society in which "visionaries and crackpots, maniacs and saints, monks and libertines, capitalists and communists and participatory democrats, proponents of phalanxes (Fourier), palaces of labor (Flora Tristan), villages of unity and cooperation (Owen), mutualist communities (Proudhon), time stores (Josiah Warren), Bruderhof, kibbutzim, kundalini yoga ashrams, and so forth, may all have their try at building their vision and setting an alluring example"?[34] I am not sure whether Nozick really gives us a theory of freedom, in that he seems mainly interested in property rights. Wellmer thinks of Nozick's idea as a nightmare, but actually it looks this way only if one imagines that each of these groups is out to destroy the other and to possess the whole country for themselves. It all depends on how freedom is contextualized historically. There may be in the abstract, or against a background of ethnic rivalry or long-standing cultural hatreds, good Hobbesian reasons to imagine this, but a hermeneutical utopia of the sort that Georgia Warnke, for example, has imagined would have these groups confronting one another dialectically and undergoing internal transformations (for better or worse) as a consequence.[35] A stronger, although perhaps less negative, account of the "negativity" of freedom might be found in some of George Kateb's writings on Emersonian individualism. To be sure, the standard theory of rights includes "the right to life, the right to a full range of expression, the right to be let alone, the right to ownership, and the right to equal citizenship in a constitutional representative democracy."[36] But only a purely analytic philosopher lets it go at that. Writers like Emerson, Thoreau, and Whitman, Kateb says, wanted to understand and develop the "sense of life" that is lodged in this theory.

> A sense of life certainly inheres in the theory and practice of rights. The individualism of personal and political rights *is* a sense of life. It is best described in negatives, just as its morality is largely negative. There is no good life, only lives that are not bad. The mere absence of oppression and degradation are sweet. A person's equal acceptance by the rest removes the heavy weight of inferiority, contempt, invisibility. That too is sweet. The weakening of traditional enclosure in status, group, class, locality, ethnicity, race—the whole suffocating network of ascribed artificial, or biological but culturally exaggerated, identity opens life up, at least a bit. The culture of individual rights has lightness of being;

free being is light. It seems insubstantial and lacking in positivity. Yet all its negativity, all its avoidances and absences and abstentions, are a life, and a life that it takes patient eyes to see, and a new sense of beauty to admire. The life that is not the good life is good in itself. (pp. 188–89)

The point of Emersonian individualism, Kateb says, is that this negativity is not the *end* of life but only its starting point: "living a life should mean more: a life should gain in definition; it should be more *assertive* or *expressive*. The regime of habit or custom or convention should be 'thrown off'" (p. 189). The Emersonian acts on "the wish to be different; the wish to be unique; the wish to go off in one's own direction; the wish to experiment, to wander, to float" (p. 191). It is a mistake, however, to map onto this a theory of the disencumbered ego. "The stark dualism of ego and other that we associate with the teaching of Fichte and Stirner, and with the antagonism posited by Hegel between lord and bondsman, is not part of the mentality of democratic individuality" (p. 190). On the contrary, the Emersonians, according to Kateb, "are saying that the readiness to assert a claim in behalf of others who are denied some crucial right should convert itself into the readiness to *resist* political power when it oppresses others, even when oneself and many others like oneself are safe and free. The sense of indirect responsibility is as important as the sense of direct responsibility. And the real grievances of others must be felt as real, must be felt as if they were one's own." Add to this the idea that what this life calls for is "a *receptivity* or *responsiveness* that aims to take in on its own terms what presents itself" (p. 189)—in other words, openness to what is nonidentical—and it becomes clear that in Emersonian individualism the distinction between negative and positive freedom becomes hard to maintain. Indeed (but of course without a thought of doing such a thing), Kateb speaks the language of hermeneutics when he explicates Whitman's "ethics of the open road" as an openness to experience and "a readiness to convert tolerance into recognition; to admire and appreciate, especially that which may be overlooked or despised; to acknowledge that one is not the only real thing in the world, and that others are just as real to themselves. . . . The effort to live outside oneself, to lend oneself to the acknowledgment of other persons, to creatures, and things, exists and is underwritten by the sense that one is multiple, various, full of contradictions, full of moods that 'do not believe in each other'" (pp. 203–04).[37]

Nozick's analytical conception of negative freedom does not have these ethical complications but has, for Wellmer, a different sort of turbulence. What bothers Wellmer about Nozick's idea is that there is frankly something to it—call it a concept that, incoherent and perhaps even frightening as it may be to communitarians, one would not want to lose. As Wellmer understands it,

> Negative freedom—in the sense of a universalist institutionalization of abstract right—is the precondition of communal freedom in the modern world to the same degree as it is also the condition under which individuals have a right *not* to be fully rational. . . . Negative freedom as a human right of self-determination, includes the right to be—within certain limits—selfish, crazy, eccentric, irresponsible, deviant, obsessive, self-destructive, monomaniac, etc.; what needs to be added is only that what at some point *appears* to others as crazy, eccentric, deviant, etc.—and even as selfish—may at some other point appear, even from the point of view of communal rationality, as reasonable and justified. (pp. 241–42)

This was, in so many words, Hegel's insight.

> For Hegel [says Wellmer] civil society—the sphere of institutionalized negative freedom—was ethical life lost in its extremes. It represented for him that aspect of *disunity* (*Entzweiung*) in modern life which, being the big scandal of modernity in the eyes of Rousseau, the early romantics, and, later on, Marx, he considered to be the price to be paid for the restoration of communal freedom under conditions of modernity: i.e., under conditions of a fully emancipated human individuality, of universal human rights, and of an emancipation of science, art, and professional life from the political and religious constraints of premodern society. As a price to be paid it was, at the same time, the *precondition* for that modern form of communal freedom which, in contrast to the classical Greek form of ethical life, would not tolerate any limitations of rational discourse and rational investigation. For civil society as the sphere of disunification was for Hegel, at the same time, a sphere of learning, of the education (*Bildung*) of individuals in a practical, cognitive, moral, and aesthetic sense; consequently, it had also a *positive* role with regard to the formation of individuals who would have the intellectual and moral qualifications as citizens of a modern state. (p. 242)

Wellmer wants to retain this insight, but can one do so without compromising the idea of a society that is rational and just?

Not easily, according to Wellmer. After all,

> how could a principle of rationality, even if it is a [Habermasian] principle of "communicative" and / or "discursive" rationality, say any-

thing about a *right not* to be rational? The point of a principle of rationality is to delimit the sphere of rational communication and rational discourse, as it were, *from within:* it reminds us that we have *no* "right" *not* to be rational and it spells out *what* it is that we have no right to be (what the norms are which we have no right to violate). Now if this principle is an a priori principle [as Habermas argues], it must be valid for any possible speaker at any time; it cannot possibly allow for exceptions. Consequently, if there is anything like a right *not* to be rational, it must be a different *sort* of right. (p. 245)

That is, not a right that can be derived, for example, from a theory of communicative action or indeed from any theory of a just and rational society, but from a theory of natural rights that seems to do little but expose us to chaos and old night. As Wellmer says, whereas communicative rationality as understood by Habermas aims at the "reduction of complexity" in human culture, "from the point of view of a principle of negative freedom not the *reduction,* but the *creation* of complexity is the redeeming feature of that aspect of 'disunification' which is built into modern civil society." Whence Wellmer concludes: "It is in this sense that freedom and reason do *not* coincide in the modern world—even if the demand for freedom is a rational demand and if the telos of negative freedom is a rational, communal freedom" (p. 247).[38]

The moral of Wellmer's story, in plain English, might be this: freedom is a many-sided background assumption in our modern bourgeois societies, part of our self-interpretation, and therefore something we couldn't do without (certainly in the United States) without undergoing first a considerable transformation, perhaps something on the order of a science-fiction mutation. At the same time, however, every effort to clarify this background assumption, this untheorized self-interpretation, seems to turn reason against it precisely because clarification leans so heavily in the direction of fragmentation and anarchy as the "price to be paid" for freedom.[39] No freedom without the scandal of modernity (the juggernaut!). Hence, perhaps the prudence of so much of modern social theory, which in general, as Robert Flathman says, allows questions of freedom to remain "well into the background of much thought and action."[40] Freedom, Flathman says, "is elemental in that it is elementary—assumed, not explicitly attended to or controverted, below the surface of self-conscious acting and interacting (pp. 316–17). This is different from saying that freedom is (or ought to be made) foundational in the sense of justifiable in terms of principles and rules (Rawls); rather, freedom, says Flathman, depends exactly on *not* being foundational in this way—on *not* being rationally defensible, that is (if I understand), not fully compatible with the sort of theory of the just and rational state that one gets, for example, from Habermas. As if, as Rainer Schürmann says, freedom were "without why"—anarchic, not so much in the sense that worries Wellmer (refusing to be rational, claiming that anything goes) as in the sense of being without principle, as in Meister Eckhart's saying, "Only that which is without a principle properly lives."[41]

A hermeneutics of freedom might take this saying to heart as it shuttles between communitarians and liberals, or more accurately, as it tries to negotiate between the Scylla and Charybdis of MacIntyre and Rorty, who when taken together are certainly more treacherous and interesting than the communitarian-liberal debate, which seems at times to hang in the air.[42] On the one side, freedom confronts squarely the ancient claims of rationality, with its inescapable exclusionary logic—for example, the idea that "membership in a particular type of moral community, one from which fundamental dissent has to be excluded, is a condition for genuinely rational inquiry" (Three Rival Versions of Moral Inquiry, p. 60). This idea cannot be wrong, which oddly may be why the ethical and reflective interests of hermeneutics, committed as they are to things like openness to the non-identical, are at the receiving end of this logic. Hermeneutics, like freedom itself, may not be compatible with ontological security. On the other side, freedom confronts ironic modernity, or the idea that once we understand that history is the history of obsolescence, that we are only so many webs of belief and that the point is, Penelope-like, to unweave and reweave these so as not to get caught by them, there is really nothing left to call freedom, unless it is just being mistress in one's own house, full of undesirable hangers-on as it is likely to be. This can't be wrong, either, but it makes an interest in the question of freedom seem, well, quaint, which must be ironic liberalism's ironic point. If this book shows anything at all, it is that a point of this sort is bound to be lost on hermeneutics.

Given its history, or histories, hermeneutics is rather more bound to be haunted by Hannah Arendt's old line, apropos of promises, that "man's inability to rely upon himself or to have complete faith in himself (which is the same thing) is the price human beings pay for freedom; and the impossibility of remaining unique masters of what they do, of knowing its consequences and relying upon the future, is the price they pay for plurality and reality, for the joy of inhabiting together with others a world whose reality is guaranteed for each by the presence of all."[43] A thought like this, which may of course not be anything one can take up within current theories of freedom, will keep hermeneutics, like old Odysseus, on the way.

Notes

Preface

1. Hans Kimmerle, "Hermeneutical Theory or Ontological Hermeneutics," in *Hermeneutics and History*, ed. Robert W. Funk, trans. Freidrich Seifert (New York: Harper & Row), pp. 106–21.

2. One is "The Problem of Figuration in Antiquity," which I presented at a conference on hermeneutics at the University of Kansas in 1981. The paper, which inspired a good deal of low humor among the conferees, who thought that I was proposing a method of nostalgia or the reconstitution of metaphysics, was published in *Hermeneutics: Questions and Prospects*, ed. Gary Shapiro and Alan Sica (Amherst: University of Massachusetts Press, 1984), pp. 147–64. The other is "The Weakness of Language in the Human Sciences," which I first presented under the title "Structure and Hermeneutics" at an annual meeting of the Metaphysical Society at Northwestern University in 1984. The society had heard the word *hermeneutics* before and didn't like it a bit, associating it with the belief, which naturally they couldn't help attributing to me, that *Hamlet* is meaningless. I regret that I was unable to persuade the society that on this and many related points it is mistaken. A later version of this paper was presented at a conference

at the University of Iowa and subsequently published in *The Rhetoric of the Human Sciences: Language and Argument in Scholarship and Public Affairs,* ed. John S. Nelson, Allan Megill, and Donald N. McCloskey (Madison: University of Wisconsin Press, 1987), pp. 239–62.

3. The poem, which appears in *Northern Summer: New and Selected Poems* (Athens, Ohio: Swallow Press, 1984), pp. 127–34, is a dedication to Matthias's friend and collaborator Vladeta Vuckovic.

Introduction

1. A sense of the cross-disciplinary range of hermeneutics can be gained from some of the excellent anthologies of critical essays on hermeneutics that have appeared in recent years, particularly in the social sciences. A short checklist: *Understanding and Social Inquiry,* ed. Fred R. Dallmayr and Thomas A. McCarthy (Notre Dame: Notre Dame University Press, 1977); *Hermeneutics: Questions and Prospects,* ed. Gary Shapiro and Alan Sica (Amherst: University of Massachusetts Press, 1984); *Hermeneutics and Praxis,* ed. Robert Hollinger (Notre Dame: University of Notre Dame Press, 1985); *Hermeneutics and Modern Philosophy,* ed. Brice Wachterhauser (Albany: SUNY Press, 1986); *Interpretive Social Science: A Second Look,* ed. Paul Rabinow and William M. Sullivan (Berkeley: University of California Press, 1987); *Antifoundationalism and Practical Reasoning: Conversations Among Hermeneutics and Analysis,* ed. Evan Simpson (Edmonton, Canada: Academic Publishing, 1987); *Hermeneutics and Psychological Theory,* ed. Stanley B. Messer, Louis A. Sass, and Robert L. Woolfolk (New Brunswick: Rutgers University Press, 1988); *Interpreting Law and Literature: A Hermeneutic Reader,* ed. Sanford Levinson and Steven Mailloux. (Evanston: Northwestern University Press, 1988); *Hermeneutics and Medieval Culture,* ed. Patrick J. Gallacher and Helen Damico. (Albany: SUNY Press, 1989); *Hermeneutics and Critical Theory in Ethics and Politics,* ed. Michael Kelly (Cambridge: MIT Press, 1990).

2. *Hermeneutics* (Evanston: Northwestern University Press, 1969). Useful textbooks containing primary material include: *The Hermeneutic Reader,* ed. Kurt Mueller-Vollmer (New York: Continuum, 1985); *The Hermeneutic Tradition: From Ast to Ricoeur,* ed. Gayle L. Ormiston and Alan D. Schrift (Albany: SUNY Press, 1990); and *Transforming the Hermeneutic Context: From Nietzsche to Nancy,* ed. Gayle Ormiston and Alan D. Schrift (Albany: SUNY Press, 1990). A two-volume anthology with excellent introductory material is *Hermeneutical Inquiry,* ed. David Klemm (Atlanta: Scholars Press, 1986), which emphasizes the theological dimensions of hermeneutics. Each of these anthologies contains valuable bibliographies. Also valuable is Josef Bleicher, *Contemporary Hermeneutics: Hermeneutics as Method, Philosophy, and Critique* (London: Routledge & Kegan Paul, 1980).

3. *The Monist,* 64, no. 2 (April 1981), 175–94. For the story of hermeneutics from ancient Alexandria to the nineteenth century, see Georges Gusdorf, *Les origines*

de l'herméneutique (Paris: Payot, 1988). Very valuable is Hans Frei's *The Eclipse of Biblical Narrative: A Study in Eighteenth and Nineteenth Century Hermeneutics* (New Haven: Yale University Press, 1974). See also *About Interpretation: From Plato to Dilthey—A Hermeneutic Anthology,* ed. Barrie A. Wilson (New York: Peter Lang, 1989).

4. "The Development of Hermeneutics," in *Dilthey: Selected Writings,* ed. and trans. H. P. Rickman (Cambridge: Cambridge University Press, 1976), p. 249.

5. See Husserl, *Logical Investigations,* trans. John Findlay (New York: Humanities Press, 1970), vol 1, pp. 321–29. See Ronald McIntyre and David Woodruff Smith, "Husserl's Identification of Meaning and Noema," *The Monist,* 59, no. 1 (January 1975), 115–32. See especially Rüdiger Bubner, "Is Transcendental Hermeneutics Possible?" in *Essays on Explanation and Understanding: Studies in the Foundations of the Humanities and Social Sciences,* ed. Juha Manninen and Raimo Tuomela (Dordrecht: D. Reidel, 1976), pp. 59–77.

6. Perhaps not exactly absolutely translatable. See Jacques Derrida, *Edmund Husserl's Origin of Geometry: An Introduction,* trans. John P. Leavy (Stony Brook, N.Y.: Nicholas Hays, 1978), pp. 87–107.

7. See Levinas, *Totality and Infinity,* trans. Alfonso Lingis (Philadelphia: Duquesne University Press, 1961), p. 72.

8. See *The Will to Power,* trans. Walter Kaufmann and R. J. Hollingdale (New York: Vintage, 1968), p. 267.

9. See *Being and Time,* trans. John Macquarrie and Edward Robinson (New York: Harper & Row, 1962), esp. pp. 182–203 (sects. 31–34).

10. See Hubert L. Dreyfus, "Holism and Hermeneutics," in *Hermeneutics and Praxis,* ed. Robert Hollinger (Notre Dame: University of Notre Dame Press, 1985), pp. 227–47.

11. In fact it was already Dilthey's idea that understanding is rooted in the everyday and does not require a special mental act like inferential reasoning until one encounters something that doesn't make sense. Here's Dilthey's version of the hermeneutics of the everyday: "The great outer reality of mind always surrounds us. It is a manifestation of the mind in the world of the senses—from a fleeting expression to the century-long rule of a constitution or code of law. *Every single expression represents a common feature* in the realm of objective mind. Every word, every sentence, every gesture or polite formula, every work of art and every political deed is intelligible because the people who expressed themselves through them and those who understood them have something in common; the individual always experiences, thinks and acts in a common sphere and only there does he understand. Everything that is understood carries, as it were, the hallmark of familiarity derived from such common features. We live in this atmosphere, it surrounds us constantly. We are immersed in it. We are at home everywhere in this historical and understood world; we understand the sense and meaning of it all; we ourselves are woven into this common sphere" (*Dilthey: Selected Writings,* p. 191).

12. I discuss this problem at greater length in "On the Weakness of Language in the

Human Sciences," in *The Rhetoric of the Human Sciences: Language and Argument in Scholarship and Public Affairs*, ed. John S. Nelson, Allan Megill, and Donald N. McCloskey (Madison: University of Wisconsin Press, 1987), pp. 239–62.

13. See *Being and Time*, pp. 190, 200–01.

14. "Understanding a Primitive Society," *American Philosophical Quarterly*, 1, no. 4 (October 1964), 307–24.

15. *The Idea of Social Science and Its Relation to Reality* (London: Routledge & Kegan Paul, 1958), p. 100.

16. "Is Understanding Religion Compatible with Believing?" in *Rationality*, ed. Bryan R. Wilson (New York: Harper & Row, 1970), p. 67. The essay was first published in *Faith and the Philosophers*, ed. John Hick (London: Macmillan, 1964).

17. The question of how we know what to look for might, of course, be taken as a methodological problem of sorts. Winch writes: "I wish to point out that the very conception of human life involves certain very fundamental notions— which I shall call 'limiting notions'—which have an obvious ethical dimension, and which indeed in a sense determine the 'ethical space,' within which the possibilities of good and evil in human life can be exercised. The notions which I shall discuss very briefly here correspond closely to those which Vico made the foundation of his idea of natural law, on which he thought the possibility of understanding human history rested: birth, death, sexual relations. Their significance here is that they are inescapably involved in the life of all known human societies in a way which gives us a clue where to look, if we are puzzled about the point of an alien system of institutions. The specific forms which these concepts take, the particular institutions in which they are expressed, vary very considerably from one society to another; but their central position within a society's institutions must be a constant factor. In trying to understand the life of an alien society, then, it will be of the utmost importance to be clear about the way in which these notions enter into it. The actual practice of social anthropologists bears this out, although I do not know how many of them would attach the same kind of importance to them as I do" (p. 322). In other words, the question of what to look for in an alien society is only a problem for those whose approach is defined exclusively in terms of methodological procedures, and it is hard to imagine that anyone really enters into the study of alien cultures (or anything at all) in this way. Winch seems here very close to Rudolf Bultmann's formulation of a basic hermeneutical principle: "The presupposition of any understanding interpretation is a prior life relation to the subject matter that is directly or indirectly expressed in the text and that provides the objective in questioning it. Without such a life relation in which text and interpreter are bound together, questioning the text and understanding it are impossible, and questioning it is not even motivated. This is also to say that any interpretation is necessarily sustained by a certain preunderstanding of the subject matter that is expressed or asked about." See "The Problem of Hermeneutics" (1950), in

New Testament Theology and Other Basic Writings, ed. and trans. Schubert M. Ogden (Philadelphia: Fortress Press, 1984), p. 82. What can we learn from what we study about what matters to us? Of course if nothing matters to us . . . .

18. *Whose Justice? Which Rationality?* (Notre Dame: University of Notre Dame Press, 1988), esp. pp. 361–66. See also MacIntyre, "Rationality, Power, and Philosophy," in *Relativism: Interpretation and Confrontation,* ed. Michael Krausz (Notre Dame: University of Notre Dame Press, 1989), pp. 199–202. In "Is Understanding Religion Compatible with Believing It" MacIntyre had acknowledged that anthropology is inescapably in a dialogical relation with what it studies. We may not be able to help seeing the incoherence of an alien practice, and insofar as "we cannot avoid doing this it is better to do it self-consciously. Otherwise we shall project on to our studies, as Frazer notoriously did, an image of our own social life. Moreover, if we are sufficiently sensitive we make it possible for us to escape our own cultural limitations. For we shall have to ask not just how we see the Trobrianders and the Nuer, but how they do or would see us. And perhaps what hitherto looked intelligible and obviously so will then appear opaque and question-begging" (pp. 71–72). But after his debate with Winch, MacIntyre seemed ready to examine more critically what escaping our own cultural limitations might involve. See especially his "Epistemological Crises, Dramatic Narrative, and the Philosophy of Science," *The Monist,* 60, no. 4 (October 1977), 453–72. See "Conclusion: Toward a Hermeneutics of Freedom," this vol.

19. "Understanding and Ethnocentricity," in *Philosophy and the Human Sciences: Philosophical Papers,* 2 (Cambridge: Cambridge University Press, 1985), p. 129. For a provocative and comprehensive series of discussions of these issues and the many philosophical quarrels that inform them, see Joseph Margolis, *Pragmatism Without Foundations: Reconciling Realism and Relativism* (London: Basil Blackwell, 1986).

20. *Anthropology as Cultural Critique: An Experimental Moment in the Human Sciences* (Chicago: University of Chicago Press, 1986), pp. 137–38. See p. 140: "An argument could be made that to date the most effective form of cultural criticism offered by anthropology has been essentially satirical." Marcus and Fischer describe here a fundamental scene in hermeneutics. See chaps. 9–12, this vol.

21. Marcus and Fischer remark that "the study of the mass-culture industry, popular culture, and the formation of public consciousness has emerged as one of the most vigorous of the new research directions" (p. 153), and they single out the famous Culture Studies Group of Birmingham, England, as a model of what they call "strong epistemological critique." The problem is the deracination that occurs when the practice of cultural critique is converted into a scholastic method or the newest New Criticism adopted by the advanced seminar. There is a good discussion of this problem by Joel Pfister in "The Americanization of Cultural Studies," *Yale Journal of Criticism,* 4, no. 2 (1991), 199–229.

22. Marcus and Fischer seem to me to conceptualize ethnography explicitly as a

hermeneutical discipline when they speak of "the Janus-faced nature of ethnography as cultural criticism," whose task is "to provide a convincing access to diversity in the world at a time when the perception, if not the reality, of this diversity is threatened by modern consciousness. This is what makes ethnography, long seen as merely description, at present a potentially controversial and unsettling mode of representation. Difference in the world is no longer discovered, as in the age of exploration, or salvaged, as in the age of colonialism and high capitalism, but rather must be redeemed, or recovered as valid and significant, in an age of apparent homogenization and suspicion of authenticity, which, while recognizing cultural diversity, ignores its practical implications" (p. 166). Cultural studies sometimes seems to take diversity as its endpoint, something to affirm for its own sake, rather than as a starting point for a genuine politics. What can we learn from what we study about what practically matters to us, that is, matters to us in the way of conduct and action in the world at hand? Anthony Giddens, in *The Consequences of Modernity* (Stanford: Stanford University Press, 1990), seems right when he says that *"emancipatory politics* needs to be linked with *life politics,* or a *politics of self-actualization.* By emancipatory politics, I mean radical engagements concerned with the liberation from inequality or servitude. If we see once and for all that history does not obey a master-slave dialectic, or that it only does so in some contexts and circumstances, we can recognize that emancipatory politics cannot be the only side of the story. Life politics refers to radical engagements which seek to further the possibilities of a fulfilling and satisfying life for all, and in respect of which there are no 'others' " (p. 156).

23. See Anthony Giddens, "Hermeneutics and Social Theory," in *Hermeneutics: Questions and Prospects* (Amherst: University of Massachusetts Press, 1984), pp. 215–30. This is a valuable account of what a "hermeneutically informed social theory" might look like. See also Giddens, "The Prospects of Social Theory Today," in *Central Problems in Social Theory: Action, Structure, and Contradiction in Social Analysis* (Berkeley: University of California Press, 1979), esp. pp. 245–57. Giddens is critical of Winch's conception of social theory as stopping short of the problem of human action that, for Giddens, is the main problem of a hermeneutic social theory, but I take Winch's essay on "Understanding a Primitive Society" to be going further in this regard than his earlier *Idea of a Social Science* and to foreshadow Giddens's own point about modernity's need for a "life politics." See Giddens, *The Consequences of Modernity,* pp. 154–58.

24. Tübingen: Mohr, 1960; 2d ed., trans. Joel Weinsheimer and Donald G. Marshall (New York: Continuum, 1989).

25. See Hirsch, *Validity in Interpretation* (New Haven: Yale University Press, 1967), pp. 245–64; and Caputo, *Radical Interpretation: Repetition, Deconstruction, and the Hermeneutic Project* (Bloomington: Indiana University Press, 1987).

26. See MacIntyre, *After Virtue* (Notre Dame: University of Notre Dame Press, 1981).

27. Reference here is to *Truth and Method*, sect. 2 of pt. 2, "Elements of a Theory of Hermeneutical Experience," pp. 265–379. See Joel Weinsheimer's commentary in *Gadamer's Hermeneutics* (New Haven: Yale University Press, 1985), pp. 164–212. History is not of course objective in the sense that we can stand outside of it and see it whole; rather it is, as Gadamer would say, what cannot be done away with—it is what always intervenes in our constructions of meaning or in our efforts to reduce things to conceptual arrangement. It has always seemed to me that the argument that anti-relativists have with Gadamer is actually not with Gadamer but rather with the historicality of existence.

28. See Habermas, *On the Logic of the Social Sciences,* trans. Shierry Weber Nicholson and Jerry A. Stark (Cambridge: MIT Press, 1988), esp. pp. 168–70. The term "depth hermeneutics" comes from Habermas's essay "The Hermeneutic Claim to Universality" (1973), trans. Joseph Bleicher, in Bleicher, *Contemporary Hermeneutics: Hermeneutics as Method, Philosophy, and Critique,* pp. 200–02. My reading of Gadamer on this point derives from his account of the negativity of hermeneutical experience and its consequences (see chaps. 9–12, this vol.) and differs perhaps from the views developed by other of Gadamer's readers whom I greatly admire. See, for example, Georgia Warnke, *Hermeneutics, Tradition, and Reason* (Stanford: Stanford University Press, 1987), esp. pp. 134–38; and Joel Weinsheimer, *Gadamer's Hermeneutics,* esp. pp. 199–212.

29. "On the Very Idea of a Conceptual Scheme," in *Inquiries into Truth and Interpretation* (Oxford: Oxford University Press, 1984), p. 185.

30. *The Birth of the Clinic: An Archeology of Medical Perception,* trans. A. M. Sheridan Smith (New York: Vintage, 1975), pp. xvi–xvii.

31. See Michael Shapiro's account of Foucault's "antihermeneutics" in "Literary Production as a Politicizing Practice," *Political Theory,* 12, no. 3 (August 1984), esp. 392–93.

32. Louis Althusser and Etienne Balibar, *Reading Capital,* trans. Ben Brewster (London: New Left Books, 1970), p. 17.

33. *Illuminations,* trans. Harry Zohn (New York: Schocken, 1969), p. 79.

34. *L'ordre du discours* (Paris: Gallimard, 1971). Translated as "The Discourse on Language" by Rupert Swyer, *Social Science Information,* 10, no. 2 (April 1971), 7–30; reprinted in *The Archeology of Knowledge,* trans. A. W. Sheridan Smith (New York: Harper & Row, 1972), pp. 215–37. Reference below is to this last text.

35. How to characterize these systems remains an open question. I have always found Anthony Giddens helpful for the way he can loosen up concepts of structure and system. A valuable piece of work in this regard is his "Agency, Structure," in *Central Problems in Social Theory,* pp. 49–95. See "Conclusion: Toward a Hermeneutics of Freedom" (this vol.), where this question is taken up in somewhat more detail.

36. See *The Archeology of Knowledge,* p. 203: "[The] essential task [is] to free the history of thought from its subjection to transcendence. For me, the problem was certainly not how to structuralize it, by applying to the development of

knowledge or to the genesis of the sciences categories that had proved themselves in the domain of language [*langue*]. My aim was to analyse this history, in the discontinuity that no teleology would reduce in advance; to map it in a dispersion that no pre-established horizon would embrace; to allow it to be deployed in an anonymity on which no transcendental constitution would impose the form of the subject; to open it up to a temporality that would not promise the return of any dawn. My aim was to cleanse it of all transcendental narcissism." One might compare this what Joseph Margolis has to say about eliminationists and reductionists in *Texts Without Referents: Reconciling Science and Narrative* (London: Basil Blackwell, 1989), pp. xiii-xv.

37. See *Heidegger on Being and Acting: From Principles to Anarchy*, trans. Christine Marie-Gros (Bloomington: Indiana University Press, 1987).

Chapter 1. Truth and Power in the Discourse of Socrates

1. Unless otherwise indicated, translations of the Presocratics are from G. S. Kirk, J. E. Raven, M. Schofield, *The Presocratic Philosophers: A Critical History with a Selection of Texts*, 2d ed. (Cambridge: Cambridge University Press, 1983).
2. "Gorgias and the Socratic Principle: nemo sua sponte peccat," in *Sophistik*, ed. Carl Joachim Classen (Darmstadt: Wissenschaftliche Buchgesellschaft, 1976), pp. 408–21.
3. *The Route of Parmenides: A Study of Word, Image, and Argument in the Fragments* (New Haven: Yale University Press, 1970), p. 139. See also R. G. A. Buxton, *Persuasion in Greek Tragedy: A Study in Peitho* (Cambridge: Cambridge University Press, 1982), pp. 29–66.
4. See Eric A. Havelock, "The Socratic Self as It Is Parodied in Aristophanes' *Clouds*," *Yale Classical Studies*, 22 (1972), 1–18.
5. *Dialogue and Dialectic: Eight Hermeneutical Studies on Plato*, trans. P. Christopher Smith (New Haven: Yale University Press, 1980), p. 153.
6. *The Composition of Plato's* Apology (Cambridge: Cambridge University Press, 1933), pp. 101–02.
7. See Martha Nussbaum, "The Speech of Alcibiades: A Reading of Plato's *Symposium*," *Philosophy and Literature*, 3, no. 2 (Fall 1979), esp. 167–68; reprinted in *The Fragility of Goodness: Luck and Ethics in Greek Tragedy and Philosophy* (Cambridge: Cambridge University Press, 1986), pp. 165–99.

Chapter 2. Thucydides, Plato, and the Historicality of Truth

1. See Kathy Eden, "Hermeneutics and the Ancient Rhetorical Tradition," *Rhetorica*, 5, no. 1 (Winter 1987), 59–86.
2. This is the Loeb translation, which I have emended in one crucial place, 22.2. I have translated *tōn alēthōs lechthentōn* as "the truth of what was said" instead of "the general sense of what was said."

3. "I have adopted the scholastic method and preferred it to the free play of mind and wit, although I indeed found, since I wanted every thoughtful mind to share in this investigation, that the aridity of this method would frighten off readers of the kind who seek a direct connection with the practical. Even if I had the utmost command of wit and literary charm, I would want to exclude them from this, for it is very important to me not to leave the slightest suspicion that I wanted to beguile the reader and gain his assent that way, but rather I had to anticipate no concurrence whatsover from him except from the sheer force of my insight. The method actually was the result of deliberation on my part." Quoted by Ernst Cassirer, *Kant's Life and Thought* (New Haven: Yale University Press, 1981), p. 140. Cf. Heidegger, *Being and Time,* trans. John Macquarrie and Edward Robinson (New York: Harper, 1953), p. 63: "With regard to the awkwardness and 'inelegance' of expression in the analyses to come, we may remark that it is one thing to give a report in which we tell about *beings,* but another to grasp beings in their *Being.* For the latter task we lack not only most of the words but, above all, the 'grammar.' If we may allude to earlier researches on the analysis of Being, incomparable to their own level, we may compare the ontological sections of Plato's *Parmenides* or the fourth chapter of the seventh book of Aristotle's *Metaphysics* with a narrative section from Thucydides; we can then see the altogether unprecedented character of those formulations which were imposed upon the Greeks by their philosophers."

4. See "The Consequences of Literacy," in *Literacy in Traditional Societies,* ed. Jack Goody and Ian Watt (Cambridge: Cambridge University Press, 1968), pp. 27–68. See also Goody, *The Domestication of the Savage Mind* (Cambridge: Cambridge University Press, 1977), esp. pp. 36–51.

5. *The Literate Revolution in Greece and Its Cultural Consequences* (Princeton: Princeton University Press, 1982), p. 24.

6. *Preface to Plato* (Cambridge: Harvard University Press, 1965), pp. 36–86.

7. *Analytical Philosophy of History* (Cambridge: Cambridge University Press, 1965), p. 127.

8. Voegelin, *Order and History: The World of the Polis* (Baton Rouge: Louisiana University Press, 1957), vol. 2, pp. 353–58.

9. See Friedrich Solmsen, *Intellectual Experiments of the Greek Enlightenment* (Princeton: Princeton University Press, 1975), p. 174; and Virginia Hunter, *Past and Process in Herodotus and Thucydides* (Princeton: Princeton University Press, 1982), pp. 93–118.

10. See Adam Milman Perry, *Logos and Ergon in Thucydides* (New York: Arno, [1957] 1981).

11. See Hornblower, *Thucydides* (Baltimore: Johns Hopkins University Press, 1987), esp. pp. 34–44. Hornblower sees Thucydides as divided between producing a historical record of events (an objective program) and giving an interpretation of events (a subjective program). There is no squaring these programs. See also Virginia Hunter, *Thucydides: The Artful Reporter* (Toronto: Hakkert, 1973), pp. 177–84.

12. See, for example, N. G. L. Hammond, "The Particular and the Universal in the Speeches of Thucydides, with Special Reference to That of Hermocrates at Gela," in *The Speeches of Thucydides: A Collection of Original Studies with a Bibliography* (Chapel Hill: University of North Carolina Press, 1973), pp. 49–59.

13. *Phoenix*, 36, no. 2 (Summer 1982), 95–103. On the difficult last line of this passage, Wilson suggests: "keeping as closely as possible to the main points of what was actually said."

14. See Gerhardsson, *Memory and Manuscript: Oral Tradition and Written Transmission in Rabbinic Judaism and Early Christianity*, trans. Eric J. Sharpe (Uppsala: Acta Seminarii Neotestamentiei Uppsaliensis, 1961).

15. "History-Writing as Answerable Style," in *The Fate of Reading and Other Essays* (Chicago: University of Chicago Press, 1975), pp. 101–13.

16. *Greek Political Theory: The Image of Man in Thucydides and Plato* (Chicago: University of Chicago Press, [1950] 1965), p. 122.

17. See Gadamer, *Truth and Method*, pp. 291–300, on the primacy of *die Sache* in the understanding of an utterance or text—that is, "understanding means, primarily, to understand *die Sache*, and only secondarily to isolate and understand another's meaning as such" (p. 291).

18. *The Post Card: From Socrates to Freud and Beyond*, trans. Alan Bass (Chicago: University of Chicago Press, 1987).

19. A thought like this has crossed Donald Davidson's mind. See "A Nice Derangement of Epitaphs," in *Philosophical Grounds of Rationality: Intentions, Categories, Ends*, ed. Richard E. Grandy and Richard Warner (Oxford: Clarendon, 1986), esp. p. 173.

Chapter 3. Canon and Power in the Hebrew Bible

1. P. R. Ackroyd, "The Old Testament in the Making," in *The Cambridge History of the Bible*, 3 vols. (Cambridge: Cambridge University Press, 1963–70), vol. 1, *From the Beginning to Jerome*, ed. P. R. Ackroyd and C. F. Evans (1970), p. 112.

2. Brevard S. Childs, *Introduction to the Old Testament as Scripture* (Philadelphia: Westminster Press, 1979), p. 78.

3. On early rabbinic textual scholarship see J. Weingreen, *From Bible to Mishna: The Continuity of Tradition* (Manchester: Manchester University Press, 1976), pp. 1–33.

4. See J. R. Roberts, "The Textual Transmission of the Old Testament," in *Tradition and Interpretation: Essays by Members of the Society for Old Testament Study*, ed. G. W. Anderson (Oxford: Clarendon Press, 1979), pp. 1–30.

5. See M. H. Segal, "The Promulgation of the Authoritative Text of the Hebrew Bible," *Journal of Biblical Literature*, 72 (1953), 35–47; reprinted in *The Canon and Masorah of the Hebrew Bible*, ed. Sid Z. Leiman (New York: KTAV, 1974),

pp. 285–97. See esp. p. 289: "We have conclusive evidence, both internal and external, that for a long time in the age of the sopherim the text was in a fluid condition, and that scribes were not tied to a standard model text."

6. See Albert C. Sundberg, Jr., *The Old Testament of the Early Church*, Harvard Theological Studies, no. 20 (Cambridge: Harvard University Press, 1964), and Childs, *Introduction to the Old Testament as Scripture*, pp. 57–62.

7. See Barnabas Lindars, s.s.f., "Torah in Deuteronomy," in *Words and Meanings: Essays Presented to David Winton Thomas*, ed. Peter Ackroyd and Barnabas Lindars (Cambridge: Cambridge University Press, 1968), pp. 117–36.

8. I have used the Jewish Publication Society of America translation of the Hebrew Bible (Philadelphia, 1917). Unless otherwise indicated, further references will be to this edition.

9. Nineteenth-century biblical scholars (Christian Friedrich Illgen, Hermann Hupfield, Karl Heinrich Graf, Julius Wellhausen) arrived at the view that the Pentateuch was a composite of various sources: J and E, after the two versions of the Genesis story, one of which identifies God as Yahweh (or Jahweh), the other as Elohim. Deuteronomy (D) is a third source, and the Priestly Code (P) is the fourth. The theory of the J, E, D, and P composite is known as the Graf-Wellhausen thesis. Almost no one agrees with this thesis today, because the evidence for it is so thin and confused, but no one has come up with a compelling alternative. Thus the thesis continues to reign, in spite of itself.

10. See Ackroyd, "The Open Canon," *Colloquium: The Australian and New Zealand Theological Review*, 3 (Autumn 1970), 279–91.

11. (Oxford: Clarendon Press, 1972), p. 168 and n. 3.

12. "Torah in the Book of Jeremiah," *Journal of Biblical Literature*, 60 (1941), 384.

13. *Economy and Society: An Outline of Interpretive Sociology*, ed. Guenther Roth and Claus Wittich, trans. Ephraim Fischoff et al., 2 vols. (Berkeley: University of California Press, 1978), vol. 1, p. 244.

14. Weber's sociological analysis of prophecy appears to have little authority among biblical scholars—the major exception of Joseph Blenkinsopp is cited below—but it is indispensable for an understanding of the relationship between prophecy and Scripture from the hermeneutical standpoint of the theme of power. See *Economy and Society*, vol. 1, pp. 439–51; see also pp. 457–63 for Weber's discussion of canonization. For example, Weber says: "Most, though not all, canonical sacred collections became officially closed against secular or religiously undesirable additions as a consequence of a struggle between various competing groups and prophecies for the control of the community" (pp. 458–59). Canon is not a literary concept but a category of power.

15. Julius Wellhausen, *Prolegomena to the History of Israel* (1878), trans. J. Sutherland Black and Allan Menzies (Edinburgh: Edinburgh University Press, n.d.), p. 398.

16. See particularly "The Prophet Jeremiah and the Book of Deuteronomy," in *From Moses to Qumran: Studies in the Old Testament* (New York: Association Press, 1963), pp. 187–208; and "The Early Prophecies of Jeremiah in Their Setting,"

in *Men of God: Studies in Old Testament History and Prophecy* (London: Nelson, 1963), pp. 133–68.

17. "Jeremiah and Deuteronomy," *Journal of Near Eastern Studies*, 1 (1942), 158.

18. See James Muilenburg, "Baruch the Scribe," in *Proclamation and Presence: Old Testament Essays in Honour of Gwynne Henton Davies*, ed. John I. Durham and R. Porter (Richmond, Va.: John Knox Press, 1970), pp. 215–38. See esp. p. 237: "It has been our contention that the so-called 'Deuteronomic additions' by no means represent a separate source, but conform to conventional scribal composition and are therefore to be assigned to Baruch."

19. *Preaching to the Exiles: A Study of the Prose Tradition in the Book of Jeremiah* (Oxford: Clarendon Press, 1970), esp. p. 92. See also Robert P. Carroll, *From Chaos to Covenant: Prophecy in the Book of Jeremiah* (New York: Crossroad, 1981), esp. pp. 158–97.

20. A very valuable book in this connection is Robert P. Carroll's *When Prophecy Failed: Cognitive Dissonance in the Prophetic Traditions of the Old Testament* (New York: Seabury Press, 1979), esp. 111–28.

21. *Prophecy and Canon: A Contribution to the Study of Jewish Origins* (Notre Dame: University of Notre Dame Press, 1977), p. 38.

22. *The Shaping of Jewish History: A Radical New Interpretation* (New York: Scribner's, 1971), p. 30.

23. *The Complete Bible: An American Translation*; the Old Testament, trans. J. M. Powis Smith and scholars; the Apocrypha and the New Testament, trans. Edgar J. Goodspeed (Chicago: University of Chicago Press, 1939).

Chapter 4. Allegory as Radical Interpretation

1. See Quine, *Word and Object* (New York: Oxford University Press, 1960), pp. 26–30, and Davidson, *Inquiries into Truth and Interpretation* (Oxford: Oxford University Press, 1984), pp. 125–39.

2. Edmund Husserl, *Logical Investigations*, trans. J. N. Findlay (New York: Humanities Press, 1970), vol. 1, §30, p. 327. For an account of Husserl's theory, see Ronald MacIntyre and David Woodruff Smith, "Husserl's Identification of Meaning and Noema," *The Monist*, 59, no. 1 (January, 1975), 115–32.

3. *From a Logical Point of View: Nine Logico-Philosophical Essays*, 2d ed. rev. (Cambridge: Harvard University Press, 1980), pp. 42–43.

4. W. Haas has given the best account yet of this whole line of thinking. See "The Theory of Translation," *Philosophy*, 37 (1962), 208–28; reprinted in *The Theory of Meaning*, ed. G. H. R. Parkinson (Oxford: Oxford University Press, 1968), pp. 86–108, esp. p. 101: "But human lives and interests are so varied, and linguistic instruments so subtle, that, again and again, what appears as one and the same fact in one language, corresponds to a number of different facts in another. The range of permissible choices, *which we have no way of surveying*, must *be* tremendously wide. By switching to different languages, or to different

times in the history of the same language, we constantly alter the fact of 'what there is.'"

5. "The Coherence Theory of Truth and Knowledge," in *Truth and Interpretation: Perspectives on the Philosophy of Donald Davidson,* ed. Ernest LePore (London: Basil Blackwell, 1986), p. 316. In this same volume, John Wallace complains that Davidson's principle of charity ignores the principal danger in interpretation, namely, "the danger of projecting onto others our own patterns of thought and action, our own wishes, interests, and plans, our own standards, criteria, ideals, categories, concepts, and forms of life" (p. 212). Davidson's response to this would be that "the point of the principle is to make the [alien] speaker intelligible, since too great deviations from consistency and correctness leave no common ground on which to judge conformity and difference" (p. 316). Davidson's theory would seem to violate the basic principle of historical criticism, which is that you must situate a text in its own time and place before you begin to interpret it. But Davidson's theory point is that you would not know how to do this unless you had already understood the text according to the logic of radical interpretation, which requires you to have already found a great deal of truth and reason in the text in question. Radical interpretation is a precondition of historical criticism.

6. "The law is an ass" is, taken by itself, incoherent and silly, but we know of a sense, that is, a context or set of conditions, in which it is true to say that "the law is an ass." This is the logic of allegory as radical interpretation. See Paul Ricoeur, *Interpretation Theory: Discourse and the Surplus of Meaning* (Fort Worth: Texas Christian University Press, 1976), p. 50: "What we have . . . called the tension in a metaphorical utterance is really not something that occurs between two terms in the utterance, but rather between two opposed interpretations of the utterance. It is the conflict between these two interpretations that sustains the metaphor. In this regard, we can even say, in a general fashion, that the strategy of discourse by means of which the metaphorical utterance obtains its result is absurdity. This absurdity is only revealed through the attempt to interpret the utterance literally. . . . Thus a metaphor does not exist in itself, but in and through an interpretation. The metaphorical interpretation presupposes a literal interpretation which self-destructs in a significant contradiction. It is this process of self-destruction or transformation which imposes a sort of twist on the words, an extension of meaning thanks to which we can make sense where a literal interpretation would be literally nonsensical." The opposite of radical interpretation might be something like a radical self-transformation or conversion to another's way of taking things, that is, to another's language or conceptual scheme, but it is arguable that such a thing is not entirely possible. See Davidson, "On the Very Idea of a Conceptual Scheme," p. 126.

7. Among a handful of fugitive studies, see Edmund Stein, *Die Allegorische Exegese des Philo aus Alexandria* (Naumburg: Alfred Töpelmann in Giessen, 1929); Jean Pépin, "Remarques sur la théorie de l'exégèse allégorique chez Philon," in *Philon d'Alexandrie,* ed. Arnaldez, Pouilloux, and Mondesert (Paris:

Centre National de la Recherche Scientifique, 1967), pp. 131–67; and Irmgard Christiansen, *Der Technik allegorischer Auslegungswissenschaft bei Philon von Alexandrien* (Tübingen: Mohr, 1969).

8. See James Coulter, *The Literary Microcosm: Theories of Interpretation of the Later Neoplatonists* (Leiden: Brill, 1976), in which Philo hardly rates a mention as an antecedent of Neoplatonic allegory; and Richard Lamberton (Berkeley: University of California Press, 1986). See Bruns, "The Hermeneutics of Allegory and the History of Interpretation," *Comparative Literature*, 40, no. 4 (Fall 1988), 385–96.

9. See R. P. C. Hanson, *Allegory and Event: A Study of the Sources and Significance of Origen's Interpretation of Scripture* (Richmond, Va.: John Knox Press, 1959), pp. 44–55, esp. p. 49. See also Jean Daniélou, *Origen*, trans. Walter Mitchell (New York: Sheed and Ward, 1955), pp. 178–91.

10. *Philo*, vol. 1, pp. xv–xvi. See also Maureen Quilligan, *The Language of Allegory: Defining the Genre* (Ithaca: Cornell University Press, 1979), and "Allegory, Allegoresis, and the Deallegorization of Language," in *Allegory, Myth, and Symbol*, ed. Morton W. Bloomfield (Cambridge: Harvard University Press, 1981), pp. 163–86, for an argument (roughly along lines implied by Colson and Whitaker) that allegory proper be sharply distinguished from allegorical interpretation or allegoresis.

11. "The Structure of Allegorical Desire," in *Allegory and Representation*, ed. Stephen Greenblatt (Baltimore: Johns Hopkins University Press, 1981), p. 29.

12. Harry Austryn Wolfson, *Philo* (Cambridge: Harvard University Press, 1947), vol. 1, pp. 115–37, esp. pp. 121–24.

13. "Allegory as Interpretation," *New Literary History*, 3 (1972), 317.

14. However, in his commentary "The Worse Attacks the Better," Philo is able to turn things around in Abel's favor: "So the words that follow 'Cain rose up against Abel his brother and slew him' (Gen. iv.8) suggest, so far as superficial appearance goes [*kata men ten procheiron phantasian hupoballein*], that Abel has been done away with, but when examined more carefully, that Cain has been done away with by himself. It must be read in this way, 'Cain rose up and slew himself,' not someone else. And this is just what we should expect to befall him. For the soul that has extirpated from itself the principle of the love of virtue and the love of God, has died to the life of virtue. Abel, therefore, strange as it seems, has both been put to death and lives: he is destroyed or abolished out of the mind of the fool, but he is alive with the happy life in God. To this the declaration of Scripture shall be our witness, where Abel is found quite manifestly using his 'voice' and 'crying out' (Gen. iv.10) the wrongs which he has suffered at the hands of a wicked brother. For how could one no longer living speak?" (47.1–48.10)

15. Hence Hugh of St. Victor's idea that history is foundational for exegesis. See *The Didascalicon of Hugh of St. Victor: A Medieval Guide to the Arts*, trans. Jerome Taylor (New York: Columbia University Press, 1961), p. 141.

16. *Alien Wisdom: The Limits of Hellenization* (Cambridge: Cambridge University Press, 1975).

17. *Naming and Necessity* (Cambridge: Harvard University Press, 1980), p. 96.

18. See G. E. Dimock, Jr., "The Name of Odysseus," *Hudson Review,* 9, no. 1 (Spring 1956), 52–70.

19. Thomas Wheaton Bestor gives a brief but helpful account of a complicated subject in "Plato's Semantics and Plato's *Cratylus,*" *Phronesis,* 25, no. 3 (1980), 306–30.

20. Philo acknowledges the arbitrariness of names but claims that the scriptural names were not conferred willy-nilly. In the commentary "On the Cherubim," for example, he says: "Elsewhere the universal practice of men as a body is to give to things names which differ from the things [*onomata tithetai pragmasi diapheronta tōn pragmatōn*], so that the objects are not the same as what we call them. But with Moses the names assigned are manifest images of the things [*tōn onomatōn theseis enargeiai pragmatōn eisin emphantikōtatai*], so that name and thing are inevitably [*ex anagkēs*] the same from the first and the name and that to which the name is given differ not a whit" (56.1–8).

21. See R. P. C. Hanson, "Interpretations of Hebrew Names in Origen," *Vigiliae Christianae,* 10, no. 2 (July 1956), 103–23.

22. In an earlier study, "The Problem of Figuration in Antiquity," I think I overemphasized the scandalous nature of the biblical texts and made it sound as if interpretation in antiquity was mainly concerned with the repair and rehabilitation of texts. In that essay I only mentioned in passing what I think should be emphasized now, namely, that the concept of *huponoia,* for example, "seems to presuppose a Platonistic theory of knowledge as the recognition of what is already known to you. An allegorical reading of the Law is in this respect not the introduction of something alien into the Law but rather the recognition in it of what you know to be true. *Huponoia* presupposes a memory-based epistemology, not an epistemology of subjects and objects and methods for certifying their correspondence." See *Hermeneutics: Questions and Prospects,* ed. Gary Shapiro and Alan Sica (Amherst: University of Massachusetts Press, 1984), p. 151.

23. *Porphyry on the Cave of the Nymphs,* trans. Richard Lamberton (Barrytown, N.Y.: Station Hill Press, 1983), p. 38

24. Philo's texts on Abraham, Joseph, and Moses are examples of what Geza Vermes calls "the rewritten bible," after the *Sefer ha-Yashar,* an eleventh-century life of Moses that represents the culmination of centuries of haggadic development that extends all the way back to the biblical period. See Vermes, *Scripture and Tradition in Judaism: Haggadic Studies* (Leiden: Brill, 1973), esp. pp. 67–126.

25. See Wolfson, *Philo,* vol. 2, pp. 7–11. "Philo," Wolfson says, "identifies his third and highest kind of knowledge, the knowledge of ideas, with prophecy, thus substituting the term prophecy for the Platonic term recollection" (p. 10). Understanding as a species of recognition, that is, of an event of illumination in which the text sheds its light on the mind of the interpreter, is a prophetic experience.

26. See Gadamer, *Truth and Method,* p. 293: "The [hermeneutical] circle, then, is not formal in nature. It is neither subjective nor objective, but describes understanding as the interplay of the movement of tradition and the movement of the

interpreter. The anticipation of meaning that governs our understanding of a text is not an act of subjectivity, but proceeds from the commonality that binds us to the tradition. But this commonality is constantly being formed in our relation to tradition. Tradition is not simply a permanent precondition; rather, we produce it ourselves inasmuch as we understand, participate in the evolution of tradition, and hence further determine it ourselves. Thus the circle of understanding is not a 'methodological' circle, but describes an element of the ontological structure of understanding."

Chapter 5. The Hermeneutics of Midrash

1. Until recently commentators on midrash have set it aside as an essentially aesthetic discourse that can be admired for its literariness but not for any light that it sheds on the scriptural texts. As interpretation it is a free-wheeling, unconstrained eisegesis. A long-standing scholarly tradition does try to defend midrash against the charge of irrationality by arguing that it is, despite its chaotic or nonlinear surface structure, basically a rule-governed activity, and therefore rational after all. This view sometimes emphasizes the importance of the *middoth* of Hillel, Ishmael, and Eleazer b. Jose Ha-gelili. See Hermann L. Strack, *Introduction to the Talmud and Midrash* (1931, rpt. New York: Atheneum, 1983), pp. 93–98. However, it is not clear that *middoth* are rules in our sense, nor are we really clear about the context in which the *middoth* that come down to us are to be understood. (They don't seem to have been formulated systematically or intended to hang together as a manual for exegesis.) For many scholars, many of the *middoth* themselves are offensive to reason. See Saul Lieberman, "Rabbinic Interpretation of Scripture," in *Hellenism in Jewish Palestine* (New York: Jewish Theological Seminary, 1950), pp. 47–82. J. Weingreen, in *From Bible to Mishna: The Continuity of Tradition* (Manchester: Manchester University Press, and New York: Holmes and Meier, 1976), esp. pp. 1–33, remarks on the strange incongruity between the analytical rigor of the rabbis as textual critics and their bizarre extravagance as exegetes. Jacob Neusner tries to penetrate this extravagance to lay bare the deep structure or "syllogism" of a midrashic compilation in *Judaism and Scripture: The Evidence of Leviticus Rabbah* (Chicago: University of Chicago Press, 1986). But this is not to defend midrash as interpretation. Neusner's view is that midrash is a perfect example of "the ubiquitous datum of Western Biblical interpretation: it is that people make of Scripture anything they wish." So there is nothing for it but to take midrash as a form of literature, not as hermeneutics. See Neusner, *Midrash as Literature: The Primacy of Documentary Discourse* (Lanham, N.Y.: University Press of America, 1987), p. 20. My view is that, on any hermeneutically informed study of the evidence, midrash is not just eisigesis but a hermeneutical practice that tells us a good deal about what it is to understand a text. A valuable study in this regard is Daniel Boyarin's *Intertextuality and the Reading of Midrash* (Bloomington: Indiana University Press, 1990). See also an excellent study by David Stern, "Midrash and Indeterminacy," *Critical Inquiry*, 15, no. 3 (Autumn 1988), 132–61.

2. The Nature of Aggadah," in *Midrash and Literature*, ed. Geoffrey Hartman and Sanford Budick, trans. Marc Bergman (New Haven: Yale University Press, 1986), pp. 48–49.

3. References to midrashic texts in this chapter are to *Pĕsiḳta dĕ-Rab Kahăna: R. Kahana's Compilation of Discourses for Sabbaths and Feast Days*, trans. William G. (Gershon Zev) Braude and Israel J. Epstein (Philadelphia: Jewish Publication Society, 1975); *Pesikta Rabbati: Discourses for Feasts, Fasts, and Special Sabbaths*, trans. William Braude (New Haven: Yale University Press, 1968), 2 vols.; *Midrash Rabbah*, trans. Harry Freedman and Maurice Simon (London: Soncino Press, 1938), 10 vols.; and *Sifre: A Tannaitic Commentary on the Book of Deuteronomy*, trans. Reuven Hammer (New Haven: Yale University Press, 1986). The quotation above is from the *Pĕsiḳta de-Rab Kahăna*, 12.12.

4. 'Erubin, 21b. *The Babylonian Talmud*, trans. Rabbi Dr. I. Epstein (London: Soncino Press, 1938), hereafter referred to simply as Talmud.

5. The Talmud continues: "R. Jose b Hanina said: What is the meaning of the text, *A sword is upon the boasters* [baddim] *and they shall become fools?* [Jer. 50:36]. A sword is upon the enemies of the disciples of the wise who sit separately [*bad bedad*] and study the Torah. What is more, they become stupid."

6. *Midrash Rabbah*, Naso (numbers) 14.4. See also *The Talmud*, Hagiga, 3a–b. A slightly different version of this midrash appears in the *Pesikta Rabati*, Piska 3.2. I discuss this version in "Allegory and Midrash: The Beginnings of Scriptural Interpretation," in *The Literary Guide to the Bible*, ed. Robert Alter and Frank Kermode (Cambridge: Harvard University Press, 1987), pp. 630–34.

7. See Richard S. Sarason, "Toward a New Agendum for the Study of Rabbinic Midrashic Literature," in *Studies in Aggadah, Targum, and Jewish Liturgy in Memory of Joseph Heinemann*, ed. Jakob J. Petuchowski and Ezra Fleischer (Jerusalem: Magnes Press, 1981), pp. 55–71. Sarason warns, quite rightly, against conflating and confusing two separate questions with respect to midrash: "The first deals with the nature, social setting, and function of the various midrashic compilations as they have come down to us and of the constituent materials in their current literary contexts. The second asks about the nature, social setting, and function of the midrashic activity in general and about the form and nature of the midrashic materials before literary encapsulation in their present contexts" (p. 62). He calls for an approach that gets us "back *onto* the page" of the midrashic text as this comes down to us in the compilations that we have. What picture of midrash as a hermeneutical practice emerges from *these* pages?

8. There is an account of the deposition and restoration of Gamaliel in the Talmud, Berakoth, 27b-28a, reproduced in the appendix to this chapter.

9. A good account of this state of affairs is given by Ephraim E. Urbach in *The Sages: Their Concepts and Beliefs*, 2d ed. (Jerusalem: Magnes Press, 1979), vol. 1, pp. 593–603 ("The Regime of the Sages after the Destruction of the Temple"), and esp. pp. 620–30 ("The Internal Relations in the Academies of the Sages"). Despite the fierce competition among the rabbis, however, Urbach explains that the Sages remained a fairly well-integrated class with a sharp sense of privileges

with respect to the community as a whole (pp. 625–28). We shall see below that we can read this midrash as an appeal to maintain this social and political integrity despite the internal conflicts that threaten to disrupt it. See also Gedalia Alon, *Jews, Judaism, and The Classical World: Studies in Jewish History in the Times of the Second Temple and Talmud* (Jerusalem: Magnes Press, 1977), pp. 314–33, for an account of the political antagonism between the Patriarch and the Sages during the early history of rabbinic Judaism.

10. See James L. Kugel, "Two Introductions to Midrash," in *Midrash and Literature*, pp. 77–104; reprinted in *Prooftexts*, 3 (1983), 141–55. Jacob Neusner aims to dispute a verse-centered view of midrash in the studies cited above (n. 6), which seek to recover the unifying logic underlying such "documents" as the *Leviticus Rabbah*, a midrashic compilation; but Neusner's argument is not very clear, and as developed in his *Midrash as Literature* it seems misdirected, or at least at cross-purposes with Kugel's account, which seems to me far from controversial. Kugel is surely correct in suggesting that the verse-centered character of midrashic interpretation reflects the economy of a culture whose mnemonics are (however graphic) still oral rather than textual. The text in a scribal culture is still housed in the oral-aural library of memory. See "Two Introductions," p. 94. David Stern seems to me to penetrate to the heart of the matter when he locates midrash in the extraordinary intimacy that exists between God and exegete. The language of exegesis, he says, is a "language of havivut," of intimacy and familiarity; it is not the language of the prophetic sublime or of voices thundering from a great distance. So playful attention to detail is not pedantry or low seriousness but represents a new form of religious language. See Stern, "Midrash and the Language of Exegesis," *Midrash and Literature*, pp. 105–24.

11. The Talmud speaks of "the warfare of the Torah," which only means that fierce, free-wheeling argument is the medium of Torah study. See *Hagigah*, 14a.

12. Hence the threat of "two Torahs." See Urbach, *The Sages*, vol. 1, p. 618. But in practice Torah is plural, as for example between Babylonian and Palestinian traditions, but also throughout the Diaspora, where halakhic decisions must be able to address diverse cultural conditions.

13. See Urbach, *The Sages*, pp. 618–20, on the rule of *lo'titgodedu*.

14. *Tanna de Be Eliyyahu*, ed. M. Friedmann (Vienna, 1902), p. 148; quoted in *The Rabbinic Anthology*, ed. C. G. Montefiore and H. Loewe (New York: Schocken, 1974), p. 132.

15. See Stanley Cavell, *The Claim of Reason: Wittgenstein, Skepticism, Morality, and Tragedy* (New York: Oxford University Press, 1971), pp. 3–36.

16. See "The Concept of a Person," in *Philosophical Papers, I: Human Agency and Language* (Cambridge: Cambridge University Press, 1985), pp. 97–114.

Chapter 6: Ṣūfīyya

1. *The Jewels of the Qurʾān: Al-Ghazālī's Theory*, trans. Muhammad Abul Quasem (London: Kegan Paul, 1977), p. 46. This is a translation of al-Ghazālī's *Kitāb Jawāhir al-Qurʾān*.

2. See Sūra 43.1–4:

> By the Clear Book,
> behold, We have made it an Arabic Koran;
> haply you will understand;
> and behold, it is in the *umm al-kitāb*, with Us;
> sublime indeed, wise.

The Koran Interpreted, trans. Arthur J. Arberry (London: George Allen & Unwin, New York: Macmillan, 1955), vol. 2, p. 199. There seems to have been a clear effort to distinguish the Qur'ān from the Torah and the Gospels precisely on the basis of its special character as recitation. Sūra 6.7 says:

> Had We sent down on thee a Book on parchment
> and so they [could touch] it with their hands, yet
> the unbelievers would have said, "This is naught
> but manifest sorcery."

As if a written text handed down from heaven (think of Ezekial eating the scroll given to him by God) were inherently implausible.

3. Zaid's account of the early history of the Qur'ānic text is preserved, among other places, in al-Ṭabarī's *Commentary on the Qur'ān,* trans. J. Cooper (Oxford: Oxford University Press, 1987), pp. 24–27. Evidence for or against Zaid's account is thin. John Wansborough thinks the Qur'ānic text developed into its present form over a period of at least two centuries. See *Qur'ānic Studies: Sources and Methods of Scriptural Interpretation* (Oxford: Oxford University Press, 1977), esp. pp. 43–52. John Burton meanwhile thinks that a text was already pretty much in place in Muhammad's time. See *The Collection of the Qur'ān* (Cambridge: Cambridge University Press, 1977), pp. 117–89.

4. Labīb al-Saīd identifies ten traditions of recitation, divided into two main categories: *mutawātir* and *mashhūr*, that is, those that have been transmitted "by independent 'chains' (*asānīd*) of authorities on a scale sufficiently wide as to rule out the possibility of error," and those in which "the possibility of error is extremely remote," even though they are "not so widely transmitted." See *The Recited Koran: A History of the First Recorded Version,* trans. Bernard Weiss, M. A. Rauf, and Morroe Berger (Princeton, N.J.: Darwin Press, 1975), pp. 53–54. On the relation of text and recitation, see esp. Frederick M. Denny, "Exegesis and Recitation: Their Development as Classical Forms of Qur'ānic Piety," in *Transitions and Transformations in the History of Religions: Essays in Honor of Joseph M. Kitagawa,* ed. Frank E. Reynolds and Theodore M. Ludwig (Leiden: Brill, 1980), pp. 91–123; and also Denny's more recent "Qur'ān Recitation: A Tradition of Oral Performance and Transmission," *Oral Tradition,* 4, nos. 1–2 (1989), 5–26. See also William A. Graham, *Beyond the Written Word: Oral Aspects of Scripture in the History of Religion* (Cambridge: Cambridge University Press, 1987), pp. 79–115.

5. See Kristina Nelson, *The Art of Reciting the Qur'ān* (Austin: University of Texas Press, 1985), pp. 14–31.

6. Cairo: Lajnat Nashr al-Thaqafah al-Islamiyyah, 1357–58 (Islamic calendar), 1937–38.

7. Trans. Sabih Ahmad Kamali (Lahore: Pakistan Philosophical Congress, 1958).

8. Ed. Jamil Saliba and Kamil ʿAyyad, 5th ed. (Damascus, 1956). *The Faith and Practice of al-Ghazālī*, trans. W. Montgomery Watt (London: George Allen & Unwin, 1953). See Abū Bakr al-Kalābādhi (d. 385 / 995), *The Doctrine of the Ṣūfīs* [*Kitāb al-Taʿarruf li-madhhab ahl al-tasawwuf*], trans. A. J. Arberry (Cambridge: Cambridge University Press, 1935), pp. 135–37 (on *tawhīd*); and R. S. Bhatnagar, *Dimensions of Classical Sufi Thought* (London: East West Publications, 1984), pp. 142–43.

9. See *The Faith and Practice of al-Ghazālī*, pp. 74–75: "I believed that it was permissible for me in the sight of God to continue in retirement on the ground of my inability to demonstrate the truth by argument. But God most high determined Himself to stir up the impulse of the sovereign of the time, though not by any external means; the latter gave me strict orders to hasten to Naysabur (Nishapur) to tackle the problem of this lukewarmness in religious matters. So strict was the injunction that, had I persisted in disobeying it, I should at length have been cut off. I came to realize, too, that the grounds which had made retirement permissible had lost their force. 'It is not right that your motive to clinging to retirement should be laziness and love of ease, the quest for spiritual power and preservation from worldly contamination. It was not because of the difficulty of restoring men to health that you gave yourself this permission.'"

10. But God is never an object of knowledge, that is, there is no such thing as seeing him face-to-face. See Fadlou Shehadi, *Ghazālī's Unique Unknowable God* (Leiden: Brill, 1964), pp. 23–36, 68–72.

11. Indeed, from a hermeneutical standpoint the Qur'ān is a remarkably sophisticated text. Sūra 3.5–7, for example, distinguishes between two sorts of verses, the plain (*muhkam*) and the obscure or ambiguous (*mutashābih*). Those *that* are plain are of the essence of the *umm al-kitāb*, whereas only God knows the interpretation of what is ambiguous or mysterious (like the letters that begin certain sūras or chapters). The point that the Qur'ān urges is simply the hermeneutical commonplace that what is obscure should always be interpreted in light of what is plain. What one knows to be the case should always be used to illuminate what is doubtful. Those who do not follow this principle are always to be held in suspicion as innovators or dissenters.

12. In the third century (A.H.) al-Ṭabarī produced a vast commentary on the Qur'ān, the *Jāmiʿ al-bayān ʿan ta'wīl āy al-Qur'ān*, that assembles this great store of traditional exegetical material. See Jane Dammen McAuliffe, "Qurānic Hermeneutics: The Views of al-Ṭabarī and Ibn Kathīr," and R. Marston Speight, "The Function of *hadith* as Commentary on the Qur'ān, as Seen in the Six Authoritative Collections," in *Approaches to the History of the Interpretation of the Qur'ān*, ed. Andrew Rippin (Oxford: Clarendon Press, 1988), pp. 46–62, 63–81, respectively.

13. See *The Jewels of the Qurʾān*, pp. 33–44.

14. See Paul Nwyia, "L'expérience comme principe herméneutique," in *Exégèse coranique et langage mystique: Nouvel essai sur le lexique technique des mystiques musulmanes* (Beyrouth: Dar El-Machreq, 1970), pp. 109–207. See also Gerhard Böwering, *The Mystical Vision of Existence in Classical Islam: The Qurʾanic Hermeneutics of the Sufi Sahl At-Tustari (d. 283 / 896)* (Berlin: Walter de Gruyter, 1979), pp. 135–36.

15. The eighth book has been translated by Muhammad Abul Quasem as *The Recitation and Interpretation of the Qurʾan: Al-Ghazali's Theory* (London: Kegan Paul International, 1982). References below are to this translation.

16. See *The Jewels of the Qurʾān*, pp. 26–27: "The truth is that the seeker and the Sought are comparable to a picture present in a mirror: The picture is not revealed in it because of rust on its surface; when, however, you polish the mirror the picture is revealed in it, neither by the movement of the picture towards it nor by its movement towards the picture, but by the removal of the veil. God (may He be exalted!) is revealed by His essence and is not concealed, for concealment of light is impossible, and by light everything which is concealed becomes obvious, and God is the light of the heavens and the earth. The concealment of light from the pupil of the eye is only caused by one of two matters—either by turbidness in the pupil of the eye, or by weakness in it since it is unable to tolerate the great dazzling light just as the eyes of bats are unable to tolerate the light of the sun. Nothing, then, is incumbent upon you except to cleanse turbidness from the eye of the soul and to strengthen the pupil. In that case God will be in the soul as the picture is in the mirror, so that when He suddenly reveals Himself in the mirror of the Soul, you hasten to say that He is inside the soul and that the human nature [*nāsūt*] has put on the divine nature [*lāhūt*], until God strengthens you with the firm word so that you realize that the picture is not [really] inside the mirror, but [only] reflected in it."

17. *Jewels of the Qurʾān*, p. 81.

18. See Gershom Scholem, *Kabbalah* (New York: Schocken, 1974), pp. 168–72, 180–82, and Perle Epstein, *Kabbalah: The Way of the Jewish Mystic* (New York: Doubleday, 1978), pp. 73–103 (on *tzeruf*, or "The Path of Letters").

19. *Kabbalah: New Perspectives* (New Haven: Yale University Press, 1988), pp. 235–36.

20. *Kabbalah: New Perspectives*, p. 229. Idel gives a detailed account of Abulafia's "path of letters" in *The Mystical Experience in Abraham Abulafia*, trans. Jonathan Chapman (Albany: SUNY Press, 1988), pp. 13–52. See pp. 24–25, on breathing the letters: "One must take each one of the letters [of the Tetragrammaton] and wave it with the movements of his long breath so that one does not breathe between two letters, but rather one long breath, for however long he can stand it, and afterwards rest for the length of one breath. He shall do the same with each and every letter, until there will be two breaths in each letter: one for pausing when he enunciates the vowel of each letter, and one for resting between each letter. It is known to all that every single breath of one's nostrils is composed of taking in of air from the outside, that is, *mi-baʾʾr le-gaʾʾw* [from

outside to inside], whose secrets allude to the attribute of *Gevurah* and its nature, by which a man is known as *gibbor* [mighty]—that is, the word *ga"w ba"r* [a rearrangement of the consonants of the word *gibbor*]—for his strength by which he conquers his Urge. As the secret of *abg yt zqr' stn* with *ygl pzq šqw zyt*, composed of the emission of breath from within to outside, and this second composition is from *g"w* to *b"r*.

Chapter 7.   Scriptura sui ipsius interpres

1. See Beryl Smalley, *The Study of the Bible in the Middle Ages* (London: Basil Blackwell, 1952), pp. 46–66; and Smalley, "The Study of the Bible in the Medieval Schools," in *The Cambridge History of the Bible: The West from the Fathers to the Reformation,* ed. G. W. H. Lampe (Cambridge: Cambridge University Press, 1969), vol. 2, p. 205.
2. See Jean Leclerc, *The Love of Learning and the Desire for God,* trans. Catharine Misrahi (New York: Fordham University Press, 1961), pp. 23–26. Brian Stock gives a good account of the primacy of experience in Bernard's commentaries in *The Implications of Literacy: Written Language and Models of Interpretation in the Eleventh and Twelfth Centuries* (Princeton: Princeton University Press, 1983), pp. 403–54.
3. See Edward L. Greenstein, "Medieval Bible Commentaries," in *Back to the Sources: Reading the Classic Jewish Texts,* ed. Barry W. Holtz (New York: Summit, 1984), pp. 213–59.
4. Quoted by M. F. Miles, "Theodore of Mopsuestia as Representative of the Antichene School," in *The Cambridge History of the Bible,* ed. P. R. Ackroyd and C. F. Evans (Cambridge: Cambridge University Press, 1970), vol. 1, p. 507. See Dimitri Z. Zaharopoulos, *Theodore of Mopsuestia on the Bible: A Study of His Old Testament Exegesis* (New York: Paulist Press, 1989), esp. pp. 110–16.
5. See Smalley, *The Study of the Bible in the Middle Ages,* esp. pp. 281–308; and Preus, *From Shadow to Promise: Old Testament Interpretation from Augustine to Luther* (Cambridge: Harvard University Press, 1969), esp. pp. 61–148. On the difference between scholastic and monastic commentary, see Leclerc, *The Love of Learning and the Desire for God,* p. 91.
6. "New Hermeneutics and the Early Luther," *Theology Today,* 21 (1964), 38–39.
7. *Summa Theologica,* 1a.1.10. *Basic Writings of St. Thomas Aquinas,* ed. Anton Pegis (New York: Random House, 1945), vol. 1, p. 17.
8. For a more detailed account of Augustine's hermeneutics, see Bruns, "The Problem of Figuration in Antiquity," in *Hermeneutics: Questions and Prospects,* pp. 156–62.
9. *On Christian Doctrine,* trans. D. W. Robertson, Jr. (Indianapolis: Bobbs-Merrill, 1958), p. 38. Hereafter cited in the text as CD.
10. The sense in which this is so is spelled out in Augustine's essay on "The Spirit and the Letter," in which St. Paul's famous lines ("The letter killeth," etc.) are taken to refer to the nature of our standing with respect to the text rather than

as a distinction between two sorts of meaning. See *Augustine's Later Works*, trans. John Burnaby (Philadelphia: Westminster Press, 1965), pp. 198–99. Another way to put this would be to say that for Augustine the notion of meaning is not context free. In this he is consistent with some main lines of analytic philosophy of language. See John Searle, "Literal Meaning," in *Expression and Meaning: Studies in the Theory of Speech Acts* (Cambridge: Cambridge University Press, 1979), pp. 117–36. For Searle, as—in obviously different terms—for Augustine, "the notion of the literal meaning of a sentence only has application relative to a set of background assumptions, and furthermore these background assumptions are not all and could not all be realized in the semantic structure of the sentence in the way that presuppositions and indexically dependent elements of the sentence's truth conditions are realized in the semantic structure of the sentence" (p. 120). So what counts as the literal sense of the text is always relative to a set of background assumptions. The hermeneutically relevant question is: What happens to the literal sense when a text is transferred from one background to another so that different assumptions apply?

11. *Luther's Works*, ed. Helmut T. Lehman, trans. Eric W. Gritsch and Ruth C. Gritsch (Philadelphia: Fortress Press, 1970), vol. 39, pp. 178–79. For the German text see the *D. Martin Luthers Werke: Kritische Gesamtausgabe*, called the *Weimarer Ausgabe* (Weimar: Hermann Böhlau, 1892), vol. 7, p. 650: "Der heilig geist ist der aller einfeltigst schreiber und rether, der inn himell und erden ist, drumb auch sehne wortt nit mehr denn einen einfeltigsten sinn haben kunden, wilchen wir den schrifftlichen odder buchstabischen tzungen sinn nennen. Das aber die ding, durch sehne einfeltig wort einfeltiglich bedeuttet, ettwas weitter und ander ding und also ein ding das ander bedeuttet, da sehn die wort auss und hören die zungen auff. Thun doch das auch alle andere ding, die nit inn der schrifft genennet werden, Seintemal alle gottis werck und creaturn eitel lebendig zeichen und wort gottis sein, wie Augustinus saft und alle lerer. Aber darumb soll man nit sagen, das die schrifft odder gottis wort mehr denn einen sinn haben."

12. *Luther's Works*, vol. 39, p. 178: "Man muss Aaron lassenn schlecht Aaron blehbenn um einfeltigen sinn, es sei denn das der geist selb auffs new anderss ausslege, wilchs als denn einn new schrifftlich sinn ist, wie S. Paulus zu den Hebreern auss Aaron Christum macht." *Weimarer Ausgabe*, vol. 7, p. 650.

13. *Luther's Works*, vol. 39, p. 181: "Darumb ists nit wol genennet schrifftlich sinn, weil Paulus den buchstaben gar viel anders deuttet denn sie. Besser thun die, die ihn nennen grammaticum, historicum sensum, unnd were sein, das man ihn nennet der zungen oder sprachen sinn." *Weimarer Ausgabe*, vol. 7, p. 652.

14. See Gerhard Forde, "Law and Gospel in Luther's Hermeneutic," *Interpretation: A Journal of Bible and Theology*, 37, no. 3 (July 1983), 240–52.

15. See Gerhard Ebeling, "Die Anfänge von Luthers Hermeneutik," in *Lutherstudien* (1951; reprint, Tübingen: Mohr, 1971), vol. 1, pp. 32–38.

16. *Luther's Works*, vol. 39, p. 171: "Es leidett die schrifft nit solch spalten des buchstabenss und geistes." *Weimarer Ausgabe*, vol. 7, p. 651.

17. *Luther's Works,* vol. 39, pp. 182–83: "Diessen geist kan man nu in keine buchs-taben fassen, lessit sich nit schreiben mit tindten inn stein noch bucher, wie das gesetz sich fassen lessit, sondern wirt nur inn das hertz geschrieben, und ist ein lebendige schrifft des heiligen geists on alle mittell." *Weimarer Ausgabe,* vol. 7, p. 654.

18. See Heidegger, *Being and Time,* where interpretation is characterized as a "proj-ect" of understanding: "Such interpretation is grounded existentially in under-standing; the latter does not arise from the former. Nor is interpretation the acquiring of information about what is understood; it is rather the working-out of possibilities projected in understanding" (pp. 188–89).

19. On the relation between understanding and experience (*Erfahrung:* experience as something that one undergoes), see Gerhard Ebeling, *Evangelische Evange-lienauslegung: Eine Untersuchung zu Luthers Hermeneutik* (1942; rev. ed., Darmstadt: Wissenschaftliche Buchgesellschaft, 1969) pp. 391–402.

20. See *Luther's Works,* vol. 39, p. 166.

21. *Weimarer Ausgabe,* vol. 7, pp. 97–98: "Scripturas non nisi eo spiritu intelligen-das esse, quo scriptae sunt, qui spiritus nusquam praesentius et vivacius quam in ipsis sacris suis, quas scripsit, literis inveniri potest. Danda ergo fuit opera, non ut, sepositis sacris literis, solum humanis patrum scriptis intenderemus, immo contra, Primum, sepositis omnium hominum scriptis, tanto magis et per-tinacius insudandum erat solis sacris. . . . Aut dic, si potes, quo iudice finietur questio, si patrum dicta sibi pugnaverint. Oportet enim scriptura iudice hic sen-tentiam ferre, quod fieri non potest, nisi scripturae dederimus principem locum in omnibus quae tribuunter patribus, hoc est, ut sit ipsa per sese certissima, facillima, apertissima, sui ipsius interpres, omnium omnia probans, iudicans et illuminans. . . . Sint ergo Christianorum prima principia non nisi verba divina, omnium autem hominum verba conclusiones hinc eductae et rursus illuc redu-cendae et probandae. . . . Nolo omnium doctior iactari, sed solam scripturam regnare, nec eam meo spiritu aut ullorum hominum interpretari, sed per seipsam et suo spiritu intelligi volo."

22. See Forde, "Law and Gospel in Luther's Hermeneutic," pp. 245–56, and esp. p. 249: "The sacred text is at work to change us, incorporate us into its story: the story with a future, not 'the soul's death.' The 'killing' function of the law cuts off every 'metaphysical' escape, every defense mechanism against the text, every self-justification, in order to save, to put us back in the time before the God of time, to make us historical beings, to wait and hope."

23. This point is ably stressed by Scott Hendrix, "Luther Against the Background of the History of Biblical Interpretation," *Interpretation: A Journal of Bible and Theology,* 37, no. 3 (July 1983), 235–38. "One could," Hendrix says, "identify an objective content of the text through analysis, but there was for Luther a sense in which Scripture was not fully interpreted until it encountered and illu-mined the life of the addressee" (p. 236). See also Gerhard Ebeling, "'Sola Scrip-tura' and Tradition," in *Word of God and Tradition,* trans. S. H. Hooke (Philadelphia: Fortress Press, 1968), esp. pp. 129–33.

24. In *The Bondage of the Will* (1526), Luther writes: "To put it briefly, there are two kinds of clarity in Scripture, just as there are two kinds of obscurity: one external and pertaining to the ministry of the Word, the other located in the understanding of the heart. If you speak of the internal clarity, no man perceives one iota of what is in the Scriptures unless he has the Spirit of God. All men have a darkened heart, so that even if they can recite everything in Scripture, and know how to quote it, yet they apprehend and truly understanding nothing of it. They neither believe in God, nor that they themselves are creatures of God, nor anything else, as Psalm 14 says: 'The fool has said in his heart, "There is no God."'" For the Spirit is required for the understanding of Scripture, both as a whole and in any part of it. If, on the other hand, you speak of the external clarity, nothing at all is left obscure or ambiguous, but everything there is in the Scriptures has been brought out by the word into the most definite light, and published to the world" (*Luther's Works*, vol. 33, p. 28).

25. *Luther and Erasmus: Free Will and Salvation,* ed. and trans. E. Gordon Rupp (Philadelphia: Westminster Press, 1969), p. 46.

26. *Dr. Martin Luthers Tischreden (1531–46)* (Weimar: Hermann Böhlaus, 1914), vol. 3, p. 170: "Die schrifft versteht keiner, sie kome den einem zu haus, id est, experiatur."

27. "'Sola Scriptura' and Tradition," p. 131.

28. See Hendrix, "Luther Against the Background of Bible Interpretation," p. 236: "The power of Scripture was such that it was not changed into the one who studied it but instead transformed the admirer into itself and into its own powers."

29. *The Light in Troy,* p. 94.

30. *Letters from Petrarch,* trans. Morris Bishop (Bloomington: Indiana University Press, 1966), p. 206. Of Cicero and Seneca Petrarch writes: "Their sharp, burning words penetrate the heart, rousing the torpid, warming the cold, awakening sleepers, encouraging the timid, lifting up the fallen, raising to lofty thoughts and noble desires minds attached to earthly things; so that vice is shown in all its hatefulness, and the form of virtue, appearing to the inward eye . . . , begets a marvellous love of wisdom and of virtue itself." Quoted by Kenelm Foster, *Petrarch: Poet and Humanist* (Edinburgh: Edinburgh University Press, 1984), p. 151.

31. See *Otherwise than Being,* p. 25: "Subjectivity is the other in the same, in a way that also differs from that of the presence of interlocutors to one another in a dialogue, in which they are at peace and agreement with one another. The other in the same determinative of subjectivity is the restlessness of the same disturbed by the other."

32. Trans. R. H. M. Lewes (New York: Dover, 1951), p. 101.

33. In a valuable essay, Beryl Lang stresses the political character of Spinoza's hermeneutics in "The Politics of Interpretation: Spinoza's Modernist Turn," *The Review of Metaphysics,* 48, no. 2 (December 1989), 327–56. Lang also makes it plain that Spinoza is a sort of secular Luther—or perhaps that Luther's deter-

mination to interpret the Bible from within itself is where the modernist turn
that Spinoza makes explicit begins.

34. *Einleitung in die Geschichte der Philosophie,* ed. Johannes Hoffmeister (Hamburg: Felix Meiner, 1959), p. 89. *Introduction to the Lectures on the History of
Philosophy,* trans. T. M. Knox and A. V. Miller (Oxford: Clarendon Press,
1985), p. 60. In subsequent citations, reference to the German text is given first.

35. In a famous passage in the *Phenomenology of the Spirit,* Hegel writes: "Trust in
the eternal laws of the gods has vanished, and the Oracles, which pronounced
on particular questions, are dumb. The statues are now only stones from which
the living soul has flown, just as the hymns are words from which belief has
gone. The tables of the gods provide no spiritual food and drink, and in his
games and festivals man no longer recovers the joyful consciousness of his unity
with the divine. The works of the Muse now lack the power of the Spirit, for
the Spirit has gained its certainty of itself from the crushing of gods and men.
They have become what they are for us now—beautiful fruit already picked
from the tree, which a friendly Fate has offered us, as a girl might set the fruit
before us. It cannot give us the actual life in which they existed, not the tree that
bore them, not the earth and the elements which constituted their substance, not
the climate which gave them their peculiar character, nor the cycle of the changing seasons that governed the process of their growth. So Fate does not restore
their world to us along with the works of antique Art, it gives not the spring
and summer of the ethical life in which they blossomed and ripened, but only
the veiled recollection of that actual world. Our active enjoyment of them is
therefore not an act of divine worship through which our consciousness might
come to its perfect truth and fulfillment; it is an external activity—the wiping-
off of some drops of rain or specks of dust from these fruits, so to speak—one
which erects an intricate scaffolding of the dead elements of their outward existence—the language, the historical circumstances, etc. in place of the inner
elements of the ethical life which environed, created, and inspired them. And all
this we do, not in order to enter into their very life, but only to possess an idea
of them in our imagination. But, just as the girl who offers us the plucked fruits
is more than the Nature which directly provides them—the Nature diversified
into their conditions and elements, the tree, air, light, and so on—because she
sums all this up in a higher mode, in the gleam of her self-conscious eye and in
the gesture with which she offers them, so, too, the Spirit of the Fate that presents us with those works of art is more than the ethical life and the actual world
of that nation, for it is the inwardizing [*Er-innerung*] in us of the Spirit which
in them was still [only] outwardly manifested [*veräusserten*]; it is the Spirit of
the tragic Fate which gathers all those individual gods and attributes of the [di-
vine] substance into one pantheon, into the spirit that is itself conscious of itself
as Spirit." *Gesammelte Werke* (Hamburg: Felix Meiner), vol. 9, p. 402. Trans.
A. V. Miller (Oxford: Oxford University Press, 1977), pp. 455–56.

36. *Vorlesungen über die Philosophie der Religion,* ed. Walter Jaeschke (Hamburg:
Felix Meiner, 1983), vol. 1, p. 44. *Lectures on the Philosophy of Religion,* trans.

R. F. Brown (Berkeley: University of California Press, 1984), vol. 1, p. 128. There is an excellent and valuable study of Hegel's hermeneutics by Theodore Kisiel, "Hegel and Hermeneutics," in *Beyond Epistemology: New Studies in the Philosophy of Hegel,* ed. Frederick G. Weiss (The Hague: Martinus Nijhoff, 1974), pp. 197–220.

37. *Introduction to the Lectures on the History of Philosophy,* p. 112.

38. *Lectures on the Philosophy of Religion,* trans. E. B. Speirs and J. Burdon Sanderson (1895; reprint, London: Routledge & Kegan Paul, 1962), vol. 1, pp. 28–29. Obviously this critique of the historical attitude does not mean that one should exclude this attitude from one's study of texts that come down to us in history. Concerning "the manner of treating ancient philosophers," for example, Hegel says: "It is easy enough for us to find a philosophical argument and transform it according to our own level of reflection. But the most important thing in the history of philosophy is precisely to know whether such a proposition was already developed or not, because it is in this development that the progress of philosophy consists. In order to grasp this progress in its necessity we must treat each stage in and by itself, i.e. keep solely to the standpoint of the philosopher whom we are studying. In every proposition, every idea, there are of course other further specific propositions inherent, following from it logically, but it is a totally different matter whether they have already been made explicit or not. The entire difference in the various philosophies in the history of philosophy is the difference between thought implicit and thought being made explicit. Everything depends on setting forth explicitly what has been contained implicitly. Therefore we cannot keep too strictly to the actual words of the philosophers themselves. Otherwise we easily introduce further categories which were foreign to their minds" (*Introduction to the Lectures on the History of Philosophy,* pp. 104–05).

39. *Hermeneutik,* ed. Heinz Kimmerle (Heidelberg: Carl Winter, 1974), p. 84. *Hermeneutics: The Handwritten Manuscripts,* trans. James Duke and Jack Forstman (Missoula, Mont.: Scholars Press, 1977), p. 112.

40. "Schleiermacher's particular contribution [to hermeneutics]," Gadamer says, "is psychological interpretation. It is ultimately a divinatory process, a placing of oneself within the whole framework of the author, an apprehension of the 'inner origin' of the composition of a work, a re-creation of an original production." To which Gadamer adds: "Isolating understanding in this way, however, means that the structure of thought we are trying to understand as an utterance or as a text is not to be understood in terms of its subject matter [*nicht auf seinen sachlichen inhalt hin*] but as an aesthetic construct, as a work of art or 'artistic thought.' If we keep this in mind, we will understand why what is at issue is not a relation to the subject matter" (*Wahrheit und Methode,* p. 175; *Truth and Method,* p. 187). A counterstatement to Gadamer's account of Schleiermacher is given by Hans Frei in *The Eclipse of Biblical Narrative: A Study in Eighteenth and Nineteenth Century Hermeneutics* (New Haven: Yale University Press, 1974), pp. 290–300.

41. See chap. 8, this vol.

42. "Hermeneutical Theory or Ontological Hermeneutics," in *History and Herme-neutics*, ed. Robert W. Funk and Gerhard Ebeling (New York: Harper & Row, 1967), pp. 107–121.

43. "The divinatory [method]," Schleiermacher says, "is based on the assumption that each person is not only a unique individual in his own right, but that he has a receptivity [*Empfänglichkeit*] to the uniqueness of every other person. This assumption in turn seems to presuppose that each person contains a minimum of everyone else, and so divination is aroused by comparison with oneself" (p. 150).

44. See especially "The Understanding of Other Persons and Their Life-Expres-sions," which is a section from the unfinished *Construction of the Historical World in the Human Sciences, Gesammelte Schriften* (Leipzig: Teubner, 1942), vol. 7, esp. pp. 205–27. Dilthey distinguishes between elementary and higher forms of understanding, where the one is a species of practical awareness and the other a species of objective consciousness. In elementary forms of under-standing, say in the encounter between people in everyday life, there is no alien-ation, no sense of distance or isolation from the other, because there is no sense of the other at all. But when our interest in the other as an individual is aroused, then we find ourselves in a distinctively hermeneutical situation. "Quite inde-pendently of the practical interest which constantly forces us to reckon with other people, this concern, be it noble or wicked, foolish or vulgar, occupies a considerable place in our lives. The secret of the person [*Das Geheimnis der Person*] lures us on to new attempts at deeper understanding for its own sake. In such understanding, the realm of individuals, embracing men and their crea-tion, opens up. The unique contribution of understanding in the human sciences [*Geisteswissenschaften*] lies in this; the objective spirit and power of the individ-ual together determine the mind-constructed world. History rests on the under-standing of these two." *Dilthey: Selected Writings*, trans. H. P. Rickman (Cambridge: Cambridge University Press, 1976), pp. 224–25. I have amended the translation slightly.

45. *Gesammelte Schriften*, vol. 7, pp. 215–16. That is, understanding in its highest form is an internalizing of history and therefore an extension of individual sub-jectivity beyond its historical and cultural—and, indeed, psychological—limita-tions: "Life progressively limits a man's inherent potentialities. The shaping of each man's nature determines his further development. In short, he always dis-covers, whether he considers what determines his situation or the acquired char-acteristics of his personality, that the range of new perspectives on life and inner turns of personal experience [*innerer Wendungen des persönlichen Daseins*] is limited. But understanding opens for him a wide realm of possibilities which do not exist within the limitations of his real life. The possibility of experiencing religious states in one's own life is narrowly limited for me as for most of my contemporaries. But, when I read through the letters and writings of Luther, the reports of his contemporaries, the records of religious disputes and councils, and

those of his dealings with officials, I experience a religious process [*erlebe ich einen religiösen Vorgang*], in which life and death are at issue, of such eruptive power and energy as is beyond the possibility of direct experience for a man of our time. But I can re-live it [*Aber nacherleben kann ich ihn*]. I transpose myself [*Ich versetze mich*] into the circumstances; everything in them makes for an extraordinary development of religious feelings. . . . Thus the inner-directed man [*innen determinierte Mensch*] can experience many other existences in his imagination. Limited by circumstances he can yet glimpse alien beauty in the world and areas of life beyond his reach. Put generally: man, tied and limited by the reality of life is liberated not only by art . . . but also by historical understanding" (*Dilthey: Selected Writings*, pp. 227–28).

46. Gadamer says that understanding is more being than consciousness. Dilthey's version goes like this: "The totality of understanding reveals—in contrast with the subjectivity of experience—the objectifications of life. . . . The individual, the communities and the works into which life and mind have entered, form the outer reality of mind. These manifestations of life, as they present themselves to understanding in the external world are, as it were embedded in the context of nature. The great outer reality of mind always surrounds us. It is a manifestation of the mind in the world of the senses—from a fleeting expression to the century-long rule of a constitution or a code of law. *Every single expression represents a common feature* in the realm of this objective mind. Every word, every sentence, every gesture or polite formula, every work of art and every political deed is intelligible because the people who expressed themselves through them and those who understood them have something in common; the individual always experiences, thinks, and acts in a common sphere and only there does he understand. Everything that is understood carries, as it were, the hallmark of familiarity derived from such common features. We live in this atmosphere, it surrounds us constantly. We are immersed in it. We are at home everywhere in this historical and understood world; we understand the sense and meaning of it all; we ourselves are woven into this common sphere" (*Gesammelte Schriften*, vol. 7, pp. 146–47; *Dilthey: Selected Writings*, p. 191).

47. *In the Spirit of Hegel* (Oxford: Oxford University Press, 1983), p. 22.

48. *Sämtliche Werke*, vol. 2, p. 79. J. B. Baillie translates *Umkehrung* as "conversion and transformation," in *Phenomenology of the Spirit*, (New York: Harper & Row, 1967), p. 153. One could also translate it as "inversion," as if turning consciousness upside down.

49. See *Truth and Method*, pp. 346–62, and chap. 9, this vol.

50. *Unterwegs zur Sprache* (Pfullingen: Günther Neske, 1959; 7th ed., 1982), p. 159; *On the Way to Language*, trans. Peter Hertz (New York: Harper, 1971), pp. 57–58.

51. For a more detailed account of this, see Gerald L. Bruns, *Heidegger's Estrangements: Language, Truth, and Writing in the Later Writings* (New Haven: Yale University Press, 1989), esp. pp. 99–122.

52. *Vorträge und Aufsätze* (Pfullingen: Günther Neske, 1954), p. 207; *Early Greek*

Thinking, trans. David Farrell Krell and Frank A. Capuzzi (New York: Harper & Row, 1975), p. 66.

53. *Identität und Differenz* (Pfullingen: Günther Neske, 1957), p. 39. *Identity and Difference,* trans. Joan Stambaugh (New York: Harper & Row, 1966), p. 55.
54. *Gelassenheit* (Pfullingen: Günther Neske, 1959), p. 24. Trans. John Anderson and E. Hans Freund (New York: Harper & Row, 1966), p. 55.

Chapter 8. Wordsworth at the Limits of Romantic Hermeneutics

1. *Hermeneutics: The Handwritten Manuscripts,* ed. Heinz Kimmerle, trans. James Duke and Jack Forstman (Missoula, Mont.: Scholars Press, 1977), p. 112.
2. *Dilthey: Selected Writings,* ed. H. P. Rickman (Cambridge: Cambridge University Press, 1976), p. 248.
3. *Opus Posthumous,* ed. Samuel French Morse (New York: Knopf, 1957), p. 168.
4. See Gerald L. Bruns, "Stevens without Epistemology," in *Wallace Stevens: The Poetics of Modernism,* ed. Albert Gelpi (Cambridge: Cambridge University Press, 1985), pp. 24–40.
5. *An Essay of Dramatic Poesy and Other Critical Writings,* ed. John L. Mahoney (Indianapolis: Bobbs-Merrill, 1965), p. 95. See Gerald L. Bruns, *Inventions: Writing, Textuality, and Understanding in Literary History* (New Haven: Yale University Press, 1982), p. 49.
6. Trans. Laurence J. Lafleur (New York: Liberal Arts Press, 1956), p. 21.
7. *Wordsworth's Literary Criticism,* ed. W. J. B. Owen (London: Routledge & Kegan Paul, 1974), p. 132.
8. *Wordsworth's Poetry, 1787–1814* (New Haven: Yale University Press, 1971), p. 13.
9. *The Claim of Reason: Wittgenstein, Skepticism, Morality, and Tragedy* (New York: Oxford University Press, 1979), p. 493.
10. *Spellbound: Studies on Mesmerism and Literature* (Princeton: Princeton Univ. Press, 1978).
11. *The Fall of the House of Usher and Other Tales* (New York: New American Library, 1980), p. 94.
12. *The Poetry of Experience: The Dramatic Monologue in Modern Literary Tradition* (New York: Norton, 1957), p. 25.
13. *Being and Nothingness,* trans. Hazel Barnes (New York: Washington Square Press, 1956), p. 343.
14. Irving Massey, *The Gaping Pig: Literature and Metamorphosis* (Berkeley: University of California Press, 1976).
15. *Tomorrow's Eve,* trans. Robert Martin Adams (Champaign: University of Illinois Press, 1982).
16. "Criticism and the Experience of Interiority," in *The Languages of Criticism and the Sciences of Man: The Structuralist Controversy,* ed. Richard Macksey and Eugenio Donato (Baltimore: Johns Hopkins University Press, 1970), pp. 57, 60.

17. *Molloy, Malone Dies, The Unnamable: Three Novels* (New York: Grove Press, 1958), p. 307.

18. See Richard Lanham's account of "The Rhetorical Ideal of Life," in *The Motives of Eloquence* (New Haven: Yale University Press, 1976), pp. 1–35; and Robert Langbaum on the "romantic self," its breakdown and reconstitutions, in *Mysteries of Identity: A Theme in Modern Literature* (New York: Oxford University Press, 1977).

Chapter 9. On the Tragedy of Hermeneutical Experience

1. *Hermeneutics and Modern Philosophy*, ed. Brice Wachterhauser, trans. Dennis J. Schmidt (Albany: SUNY Press, 1986), p. 385.

2. *The Poetry of Experience: The Dramatic Monologue in Modern Literary Tradition* (New York: Norton, 1963).

3. "The Development of Hermeneutics" (1900), *Gesammelte Schriften*, vol. 5, p. 330; *Dilthey: Selected Writings*, p. 258.

4. *Werke in zwanzig Bänden* (Frankfurt: Suhrkamp, 1970), vol. 3, p. 79; *Hegel's Phenomenology of the Spirit*, trans. A. V. Miller (Oxford: Oxford University Press, 1977), p. 55.

5. *Hegel's Concept of Experience*, trans. Kenley Royce Dove (New York: Harper & Row, 1970), pp. 124–29. See Husserl, *Experience and Judgment: Investigations in a Genealogy of Logic*, trans. James S. Churchill and Karl Ameriks (Evanston: Northwestern University Press, 1973), pp. 27–63.

6. See Alasdair MacIntyre, "Epistemological Crises, Dramatic Narrative, and the Philosophy of Science," *The Monist*, 60, no. 4 (October 1977), 453–72. For a more linear, less apocalyptic view of experience, see Günther Buck, *Lernen und Erfahrung* (Stuttgart, 1969), which follows Husserl's conception of "perceptual experience," where the negativity of experience simply produces an alteration or expansion of horizons without any critical transformation. See also Buck, "The Structure of Hermeneutic Experience and the Problem of Tradition," trans. Peter Heath, *New Literary History*, 10, no. 2 (Autumn 1978), 31–47. Horizonal change, Buck says, "presents itself . . . as a movement from narrower and more specific to wider and more general horizons. A nullified anticipation, in being discredited, frees our view for a more embracing anticipation that arises, as it were, behind it. This process seems repeatable at will. We can think of no final horizon that experience could ever go beyond. The unsteadiness induced by negative experience is always contained within the higher-order steadiness of wider horizons" (p. 38). But the idea of an "epistemological crisis" means that the way one inhabits these horizons undergoes a break and calls for a reinterpretation of oneself and one's history.

7. Cavell's essays on Shakespeare have been gathered together in *Disowning Knowledge in Six Plays of Shakespeare* (Cambridge: Cambridge University

Press, 1987). See Gerald L. Bruns, "Stanley Cavell's Shakespeare," *Critical Inquiry*, 16, no. 1 (Spring 1990), 612–32.

8. Martha Nussbaum, *The Fragility of Goodness: Luck and Ethics in Greek Tragedy and Philosophy* (Cambridge: Cambridge University Press, 1986), esp. the superb reading of *Antigone*, pp. 51–82. See p. 70 on the chorus in *Antigone*: "For these people experience the complexities of tragedy while and by being a certain sort of community, not by having each soul go off in isolation from its fellows; by attending to what is common or shared and forming themselves into a common responding group, not by reaching for a lonely height of contemplation from which it is a wrenching descent to return to political life." See my discussion of Nussbaum's book, "Tragic Thoughts at the End of Philosophy," *Soundings*, 72, no. 4 (Winter 1989), 694–724.

9. *The Birth of Tragedy and the Genealogy of Morals*, trans. Francis Golffing (Garden City, N.Y.: Doubleday Anchor, 1956), pp. 131–34.

10. "The Gyres," in *The Collected Poems of W. B. Yeats* (New York: Macmillan, 1983), p. 293.

11. "Politics as Opposed to What?" *The Politics of Interpretation*, ed. W. T. J. Mitchell (Chicago: University of Chicago Press, 1983), p. 199.

12. Cavell appropriately cites here Stanley Fish's "Aesthetic of the Good Physician," in *Self-Consuming Artifacts: The Experience of Seventeenth-Century Literature* (Berkeley: University of California Press, 1972), esp. p. 13: "To read the *Phaedrus*, then, is to use it up; for the value of any point in it is that it gets *you* (not any sustained argument), to the next point, which is not so much a point (in logical-demonstrative terms) as a level of insight. It is thus a *self-consuming artifact*, a mimetic enactment in the reader's experience of the Platonic ladder in which each rung, as it is negotiated, is kicked away. The final rung, the level of insight that stands (or, more properly, on which the reader stands) because it is the last, is, of course, the rejection of written artifacts, a rejection that, far from contradicting what has preceded, corresponds exactly to what the reader, in his repeated abandoning of successive states in the argument, has been doing." Reading carries us to the limits of reading, as philosophy to the limits of philosophy.

Chapter 10. What Is Tradition?

1. See Jacques Derrida, "Sending: On Representation," trans. Peter Caws and Mary Ann Caws, *Social Research*, 49 (Summer 1982), 295–326; and *The Post Card: From Socrates to Freud and Beyond*, trans. Alan Bass (Chicago: University of Chicago Press, 1987). Derrida's idea, if I understand, would be that tradition is a sort of institutionalizing of representation, where representation is all "repetition and return" ("Sending," p. 308). So tradition is a mode of transmission, say of messages, and hermeneutics is simply the deciphering of these messages, that is, part of the system of repetition and return. Tradition in this sense would be the theoretical opposite of dissemination. But from the standpoint of philosoph-

ical hermeneutics tradition is probably closer to dissemination than Derrida imagines. Anyhow that's part of the upshot of the present essay.

2. *Letters from Petrarch*, trans. Morris Bishop (Bloomington: Indiana University Press, 1966), pp. 295–96.

3. "Petrarch and the Humanist Hermeneutic," in *The Light in Troy: Imitation and Discovery in Renaissance Poetry* (New Haven: Yale University Press, 1982), p. 92.

4. See Paul de Man, "Literary History and Literary Modernity," in *Blindness and Insight: Essays in the Rhetoric of Contemporary Criticism,* 2d ed. (Minneapolis: University of Minnesota Press, 1983), pp. 142–65. Modernity in the sense used here is far from being a period concept or a concept of style; it is not an aesthetic category (as when people speak of "High Modernism") but has to do with the conception of rationality inaugurated by Descartes and characterized by notions of conceptualization and control. The questionableness of this conception is one of the things that comes out in hermeneutics. See Martin Heidegger, "The End of Philosophy and the Task of Thinking," in *Time and Being,* trans. Joan Stambaugh (New York: Harper & Row, 1972), pp. 55–73. Jürgen Habermas speaks of "aesthetic modernity" as a product of romanticism and the development of an avant-garde outlook that self-consciously breaks with whatever has gone before it; but this view strikes me as unhistorical in the extreme. I cannot see how the concept of modernity can be clarified without reference to Descartes and the exercise of methodical suspicion toward tradition. See Habermas, "Modernity—An Incomplete Project?" in *Interpretive Social Science: A Second Look,* ed. Paul Rabinow and William M. Sullivan, trans. Seyla Ben Habib (Berkeley: University of California Press, 1987), pp. 141–56.

5. *Inquiries into Truth and Interpretation*, p. 137.

6. Something closer to Gadamer's view is given by Alasdair MacIntyre in "Epistemological Crises, Dramatic Narrative, and the Philosophy of Science," *The Monist*, 60, no. 4 (October 1977), 453–72. MacIntyre writes: "[The] connection between narrative and tradition has hitherto gone almost unnoticed, perhaps because tradition has usually been taken seriously only by conservative social theorists. Yet those features of tradition which emerge as important when the connection between tradition and narrative is understood are ones which conservative theorists are unlikely to attend to. For what constitutes a tradition is a conflict of interpretations of that tradition, a conflict which itself has a history susceptible of rival interpretations. If I am a Jew, I have to recognize that the tradition of Judaism is partly constituted by a continuous argument over what it means to be a Jew. Suppose I am an American: the tradition is one partly constituted by continuous argument over what it means to be an American and partly by a continuous argument over what it means to have rejected tradition. If I am an historian, I must acknowledge that the tradition of historiography is partly, but centrally, constituted by arguments about what history is and ought to be, from Hume and Gibbon to Namier and Edward Thompson. . . . A tradition then not only embodies the narrative of an argument, but is only to be

recovered by an argumentative retelling of what narrative which will itself be in conflict with other argumentative retellings. Every tradition therefore is always in danger of lapsing into incoherence and when a tradition does so lapse it sometimes can only be recovered by a revolutionary reconstitution" (pp. 460–61). See also MacIntyre on the "rationality of traditions" in *Whose Justice? Which Rationality?* (Notre Dame: University of Notre Dame Press, 1989), pp. 349–69.

7. *Truth and Method*, p. 355. This recognition ought not to be construed as the satisfaction of an expectation or the confirmation of a hypothesis or an agreement between self and image; it is, as we saw in chapter 9, a recognition of the sort that Oedipus suffers.

8. *Radical Hermeneutics: Repetition, Deconstruction, and the Hermeneutic Project* (Bloomington: Indiana University Press, 1987), p. 112.

9. The "between" between the deconstructive and the anarchic is explored ingeniously by Rainer Schürmann, *Heidegger on Being and Acting: From Principals to Anarchy*, trans. Christine-Marie Gros (1982; reprint, Bloomington: Indiana University Press, 1987).

10. *Gesamtausgabe* (Frankfurt: Vittorio Klosterman, 1977), vol. 5, p. 32; *Poetry, Language, Thought*, trans. Albert Hofstadter (New York: Harper & Row, 1971), p. 46.

11. *Unterwegs zur Sprache*, p. 27; *Poetry, Language, Thought*, p. 204.

12. Theologically this acknowledgment might take the form of a Christology that addressed in an unblinking way the Jewishness of Christ, which is, one might say, the irrepressibly satirical dimension of the Incarnation. See Geza Vermes, *Jesus the Jew: A Historian's Reading of the Gospels* (New York: Macmillan, 1974), and *The Gospel of Jesus the Jew* (Newcastle Upon Tyne: University of Newcastle Upon Tyne Press, 1981). See Rosemary Reuther, *Faith and Fratricide* (New York: Seabury Press, 1978), and *Anti-Semitism in Early Christianity*, vol. 1, *Paul and the Gospels*, ed. Peter Richardson and David Granskou; vol 2, *Separation and Polemic*, ed. Stephen Wilson (Waterloo, Ontario, Canada: Wilfrid Lauer University Press, 1986).

13. "Vielmehr ist Verstehen immer der Vorgang der Verschmelzung solcher vermeintlich für sich seiender Horizonte" (p. 289 / p. 306).

14. "Das historische Bewusstsein ist sich seiner eigenen Andersheit bewusst und hebt daher den Horizont der Überlieferung von dem eigenen Horizont ab" (p. 290 / p. 306). Weinsheimer and Marshall translate *hebt daher* as "foregrounds"; the first English edition read: "distinguishes from"—less literal perhaps but a bit clearer.

15. See *Totality and Infinity*, pp. 198–99.

Chapter 11. On the Radical Turn in Hermeneutics

1. *Radical Hermeneutics: Repetition, Deconstruction, and the Hermeneutic Project* (Bloomington: Indiana University Press, 1987), p. 1.

2. *Edmund Husserl's "Origin of Geometry": An Introduction,* trans. John P. Leavey (Stony Brook, N.Y.: Nicolas Hays, 1978), pp. 100–05.

3. "Two Words for Joyce," in *Post-Structuralist Joyce: Essays from the French,* ed. Derek Attridge and Daniel Ferrer (Cambridge: Cambridge University Press, 1984), pp. 145–69.

4. *The Philosophical Discourse of Modernity,* trans. Frederick Lawrence (Cambridge: MIT Press, 1987), p. 185. See also Richard Rorty, "Deconstruction and Circumvention," *Critical Inquiry,* 11 (1984), 1–23.

5. "Proverb: 'He that would pun . . . ,'" in John P. Leavey, GLASsary (Lincoln: University of Nebraska Press, 1986), p. 18.

6. This is the subject of my book *Heidegger's Estrangements: Language, Truth, and Poetry in the Later Writings* (New Haven: Yale University Press, 1989).

7. *Philosophy in France Today,* ed. Alan Montefiore, trans. Kathleen McLaughlin (Cambridge: Cambridge University Press, 1983), p. 45.

8. *Psyché: Inventions de l'autre* (Paris: Galilée, 1987), p. 542.

9. *The Mystical Element in Heidegger's Thought* (Athens: Ohio University Press, 1978).

10. Georgia Warnke has given a good account of Gadamer's conception of cultural coherence in "The Hermeneutical Turn in Political Philosophy," *Yale Journal of Criticism,* 4, no. 1 (1990), esp. 222–26.

11. Caputo borrows his criticism of Gadamer's interpretation of *phronēsis* from Richard Bernstein, *Beyond Objectivism and Relativism* (Philadelphia: University of Pennsylvania Press, 1983), in which Bernstein says that Gadamer "stops short of facing the issues of what is to be done when the *polis* or community itself is 'corrupt'—when there is a breakdown of its *nomoi* and of a rational discourse about the norms that ought to govern our practical lives" (p. 158).

12. Charles Segal, *Tragedy and Civilization: An Interpretation of Sophocles* (Cambridge: Harvard University Press, 1981), p. 30. See also Segal's *Interpreting Greek Tragedy: Myth, Poetry, Text* (Ithaca: Cornell University Press, 1985), p. 25; and Jean-Pierre Vernant and Pierre Vidal-Naquet, *Mythe et tragédie en Grèce ancienne* (Paris: Maspero, 1973), pp. 11–19.

13. Jean-Pierre Vernant, "The Historical Moment of Tragedy in Greece: Some of the Social and Psychological Conditions," in Vernant and Vidal-Naquet, *Myth and Tragedy in Ancient Greece,* trans. Janet Lloyd (New York: Zone, 1988), p. 26.

Chapter 12. Against Poetry

1. From *The Theater and Its Double* (1931–36), in *Antonin Artaud: Selected Writings,* ed. Susan Sontag, trans. Helen Weaver (Berkeley: University of California Press, 1976), p. 241.

2. Richard Rorty, "Deconstruction and Circumvention," *Critical Inquiry,* 11, no. 1 (September 1984), 1–23.

3. Walter Benjamin, "Theses on the Philosophy of History," in *Illuminations,* trans. Harry Zohn (New York: Schocken, 1969), pp. 256–57.

4. *Existence and Being,* trans. Douglas Scott (Chicago: Henry Regnery, 1949), p. 281–82.

5. *Poetry, Language, Thought,* trans. Albert Hofstadter (New York: Harper & Row, 1971), p. 49. I give a detailed reading of "The Origin of the Work of Art" in *Heidegger's Estrangements: Language, Truth, and Poetry in the Later Writings* (New Haven: Yale University Press, 1989), pp. 27–53.

6. See "Structure, Word, Event," in *The Conflict of Interpretations: Essays in Hermeneutics,* ed. Don Idhe, trans. Robert Sweeney (Evanston: Northwestern University Press, 1974), pp. 79–96.

7. "The Hermeneutical Function of Distanciation," in *Hermeneutics and the Human Sciences: Essays on Language, Action, and Interpretation,* ed. and trans. John B. Thompson (Cambridge: Cambridge University Press, 1981), pp. 132–36.

8. "What Is a Text? Explanation and Understanding," *Hermeneutics and the Human Sciences,* pp. 148–49.

9. "Science and Ideology," *Hermeneutics and the Human Sciences,* p. 232.

10. *Time and Narrative,* trans. Kathleen MacLaughlin and David Pellauer (Chicago: University of Chicago Press, 1984), vol 1., p. 50.

11. See Danto, "Philosophy as / and / of Literature," in *The Philosophical Disenfranchisement of Art* (New York: Columbia University Press, 1986), esp. 154–59; MacIntyre, *After Virtue* (Notre Dame: University of Notre Dame Press, 1981), pp. 190–209; Nussbaum, "Flawed Crystals: James's *The Golden Bowl* and Literature as Moral Philosophy," in *Love's Knowledge: Essays on Philosophy and Literature* (New York: Oxford University Press, 1990), pp. 125–47; Rorty, "Private Irony and Liberal Hope," in *Contingency, Irony, and Solidarity* (Cambridge: Cambridge University Press, 1989), pp. 73–95; Jameson, *The Political Unconscious: Narrative as a Socially Symbolic Act* (Ithaca: Cornell University Press, 1982).

12. Michael Shapiro, who thinks of himself as "antihermeneutical," nevertheless brings out this "Aristotelian" character of hermeneutics in a very fine study, "Literary Production as a Politicizing Practice," *Political Theory,* 12, no. 3 (August 1984), 387–422. "Literary discourse," Shapiro says, "particularly in its modern guise, is hyperpoliticizing. By producing alternative forms of thought *in* language, it makes a political point" (p. 410). But there is no reason to think that modern literature is more powerful in this respect than texts that come down from remote times and places; on the contrary, what such texts give us are alternative forms of *life,* that is, not just different ways of conceiving and expressing what is familiar, but forms of social and cultural practice that may require some alteration in our own self-understanding before we can even begin to understand them.

13. I go into these questions in more detail in *Heidegger's Estrangements,* and I mean to address them still further in *Poetry and the Philosophers: A Study in Darkness, or Freedom* (forthcoming).

14. *Otherwise than Being, or Beyond Essence,* trans. Alphonso Lingis (The Hague: Martinus Nijhoff, 1984), pp. 29–30, italics mine.

15. A print of "The History of Electricity" appears in Dora Perez-Tibi, *Dufy* (New York: Abrams, 1989), p. 149.

16. Maurice Blanchot, "Literature and the Original Experience," in *The Space of Literature,* trans. Ann Smock (Lincoln: University of Nebraska Press, 1982), pp. 237–38. See Donald G. Marshall, "The Necessity of Writing: Death and Imagination in Maurice Blanchot's *L'Espace littérature,*" *Boundary 2,* 14, nos. 1–2 (Fall 1985 / Winter 1986), 225–36. Marshall gives a useful characterization of the sort of "space" the space of writing is, "namely the anonymous, impersonal space of creation. This is not simply an 'other' world, but other than any world"—a sort of pure externality or pure exile. "No one can dwell in this literary space, this realm of *l'oeuvre,* of the work of writing; anyone who tried to do so would be lost in the ecstasy of madness or religious transcendence" (p. 230). At the end of this valuable essay Marshall remarks that "as an imaginative writer, Blanchot commits himself to the risk of critical impersonality, surrendering his autonomy as a writer in order to let emerge within him a necessity of writing that comes from outside. This movement gives to Blanchot's criticism the pressure of a truth quite different from that of accurate and verifiable interpretation. His criticism has the flavor not of theory, but—if I may venture the word—ethical writing. And it is from this perspective that I wish to close, despite my admiration for it, with a reservation. Blanchot's style, a masterful vertigo of repetition and reversal, is recognizably the rhetoric of sublimity" (p. 234). Marshall cautions against the sublime style, much as Aristotle would have, because what such a style entails is a repression of what is unheroic, ordinary, everyday, social, comic—and irrepressibly human. This is very sound advice and raises a crucial question, which I can't take up here, as to why Platonic hermeneutics should require the rhetoric of sublimity as part of its essential decorum. Heidegger's later style is nothing if not the recrudescence of the German romantic sublime. The point is perhaps that such a style is precisely the hyperbole of the solitary wanderer unconstrained by the practical exigencies of the everyday social and political world. From an Aristotelian standpoint it is discourse that is completely mad.

17. *Hegel's Aesthetics: Lectures on Fine Art,* trans. T. M. Knox (Oxford: Clarendon Press, 1975), vol. 1, p. 11.

18. *Dialogues with Contemporary Thinkers* (Manchester: University of Manchester Press, 1984), p. 108.

Conclusion

1. *Relativism: Interpretation and Confrontation,* ed. Michael Krausz (Notre Dame: University of Notre Dame Press, 1989), p. 196.

2. This critique of modernity is laid out with great force in MacIntyre's *After Virtue: A Study in Moral Theory* (Notre Dame: University of Notre Dame Press, 1981), esp. pp. 49–59. Compare Cornelius Castoriadis, *The Imaginary Institution of Society,* trans. Kathleen Blamey (Cambridge: MIT Press, 1987), esp. 146–164. Every human culture is constituted, Castoriadis says, by "social imaginary

significations." What is the condition of these significations in the modern world? Something is wrong with them, but it is not easy to say what. Castoriadis has some wonderful pages on "the imaginary significations that constitute the bureaucratic universe" (p. 158).

3. See *Otherwise than Being, or Beyond Essence*, pp. 8–20, and esp. p. 25, where subjectivity is said to be "structured as the other in the same."

4. *The Imaginary Institution of Society*, p. 106. As Castoriadis says, "There is another determination [of the subject], one that does not concern the orientation of the intentional fibres of the subject, but their very material, which carries the world into the subject and introduces the street into what the subject may take to be its own den" (p. 105).

5. See Roberto Ungar's critique of deep-structure theory in *Social Theory: Its Situation and Its Task* (Cambridge: Cambridge University Press, 1987), pp. 87–95. For an application of the hermeneutical distrust of deep-structure logic, see Gerald L. Bruns, "Law and Language: A Hermeneutics of the Legal Text," in *Legal Hermeneutics*, ed. Gregory Leyh (Berkeley: University of California Press, 1991), pp. 23–40.

6. Cora Diamond, "Losing Your Concepts," *Ethics*, 98, no. 2 (January 1988), 255–77.

7. *Habits of the Heart: Individualism and Commitment in American Life* (Berkeley: University of California Press, 1985), esp. pp. 78–81.

8. *The Fortunate Man* (New York: Pantheon, 1982), pp. 98–99.

9. *Revisions: Changing Perspectives in Moral Philosophy*, ed. Alasdair MacIntyre and Stanley Hauerwas (Notre Dame: University of Notre Dame Press, 1983), p. 46. The essay first appeared in *Encounter*, 16, no. 1 (January 1961), 16–20.

10. Stanley Cavell, *The Claim of Reason: Wittgenstein, Morality, Skepticism, Tragedy* (New York: Oxford University Press, 1979), pp. 177–78.

11. Compare Charles Taylor on the breakdown of common meanings during the 1960s, "Hermeneutics and the Sciences of Man," in *Philosophy and the Human Sciences: Philosophical Papers*, 2 (Cambridge: Cambridge University Press, 1985), pp. 48–52.

12. See *Three Rival Versions of Moral Inquiry: Encyclopaedia, Genealogy, and Tradition* (Notre Dame: University of Notre Dame Press, 1990), esp. 230–34. See also pp. 133–38 for what one might call MacIntyre's hermeneutics, which is rooted in the Augustinian-Lutheran question of what sort of person one has to become "in order to read a book aright."

13. *Whose Justice? Which Rationality?* (Notre Dame: University of Notre Dame Press, 1989), p. 355: "Those who have reached a certain stage in that development [that is, the early history of the development of traditions] are then able to look back and to identify their own previous intellectual inadequacy or the intellectual inadequacy of their predecessors by comparing what they now judge the world, or at least a part of it, to be with what it was then judged to be. To claim truth for one's present state of mindset and the judgments which are its expressions, is to claim that this kind of inadequacy, this kind of discrepancy,

will never appear in any possible future situation, no matter how searching the enquiry, no matter how much evidence is provided, no matter what developments in rational enquiry may occur. The test for truth in the present, therefore, is always to summon up as many questions and as many objections of the greatest strength possible; what can be justifiably claimed as true is what has sufficiently withstood such dialectical questioning and framing of objections. In what does such sufficiency consist? That too is a question to which answers have to be produced and to which rival and competing answers may well appear. And those answers will compete rationally, just insofar as they are tested dialectically, in order to discover which is the best answer to be proposed so far." So the legitimacy of a culture is determined not by its correspondence to something outside of itself, some transcendental foundation, but rather in relation to its history. For an example of how this works, see *Three Rival Versions of Moral Inquiry*, pp. 127–48 ("Aquinas and the Rationality of Tradition"), and also p. 150, on the history of physics as a model of tradition as rational inquiry.

14. See *Contingency, Irony, and Solidarity* (Cambridge: Cambridge University Press, 1989), esp. p. 83.

15. "The Legacy of Skepticism," *Journal of Philosophy*, 69 (1972), 761.

16. See Kierkegaard, *The Concept of Irony, with Constant Reference to Socrates*, trans. Lee M. Capel (New York: Harper & Row, 1965), pp. 300–01.

17. See *After Virtue*, pp. 6–34, and esp. p. 30: "The specifically modern self, the self that I have called emotivist [emotivism being the idea that 'all evaluative judgments and more specifically all moral judgments are *nothing but* expressions of preference, expressions of attitude or feeling' (p. 11)], finds no limits set to that on which it may pass judgment for such limits could only derive from rational criteria for evaluation and, as we have seen, the emotivist self lacks any such criteria. Everything may be criticized from whatever standpoint the self has adopted, including the self's choice of standpoint to adopt. It is in this capacity of the self to evade any necessary identification with any particular contingent state of affairs that some modern philosophers, both analytical and existentialist, have seen the essence of moral agency. To be a moral agent is, on this view, precisely to be able to stand back from any and every situation in which one is involved, from any and every characteristic that one may possess, and to pass judgment on it from a purely universal and abstract point of view that is totally detached from all social particularity. . . . This democratised self which has no necessary social content and no necessary social identity can then be anything, can assume any role or take any point of view, because it *is* in and for itself nothing." This pretty much states Rorty's argument, or rather position, with the exception that irony replaces "a purely universal and abstract point of view."

18. At most Rorty wouldn't follow MacIntyre in trying to raise a cross-cultural theory of rationality on its basis. But why not? And if not, how to account for the footnote at the bottom of p. 83 of *Contingency, Irony, and Solidarity*: "Where . . . webs of belief and desire are pretty much the same for large numbers of people [that is, no longer simply private but also social], it does become useful

to speak of 'an appeal to reason' or to 'logic,' for this simply means an appeal to widely shared common ground by reminding people of propositions which form part of this ground. More generally, all the traditional metaphysical distinctions can be given a respectable ironist sense by sociologizing them—treating them as distinctions between contingently existing sets of practices, or strategies employed within such practices, rather than between natural kinds." Rorty has drawn even closer to MacIntyre in an essay, "Cosmopolitanism Without Emancipation: A Response to Lyotard," in *Modernity and Identity*, ed. Scott Lash and Jonathan Friedman (Oxford: Basil Blackwell, 1992), esp. p. 61: "'Rationally' here means being able to give a retrospective account of why one changed— what old beliefs or desires one invoked in justification of new ones—rather than having to say, helplessly, 'it just happened; somehow I got converted.'" Cf. MacIntyre, *After Virtue*, pp. 194–96; *Whose Justice: Which Rationality?* pp. 357–58, and "The Intelligibility of Action," in *Rationality, Relativism, and the Human Sciences*, ed. J. Margolis, M. Krausz, and R. M. Burian (Dordrecht: Martinus Nijhoff, 1986), pp. 63–80.

19. "What matters at this stage," MacIntyre says at the end of *After Virtue*, "is the construction of local forms of community within which civility and the intellectual and moral life can be sustained through the new dark ages upon us" (p. 245). One could say that the difference between MacIntyre and Rorty comes down to a difference between what sort of community each wants, with MacIntyre wanting to retain the idea of a philosophically justifiable form of life and Rorty saying that the good thing about liberal democracy is that it gives us a chance to be whatever we want. See Rorty, "The Priority of Democracy to Philosophy," in *Objectivity, Relativism, and Truth* (Cambridge: Cambridge University Press, 1991), esp. pp. 189–96.

20. Compare Michael Sandel, "The Procedural Republic and the Unencumbered Self," *Political Theory*, 12, no. 1 (February 1984), esp. 90–91.

21. *Poetic Interaction: Language, Freedom, Reason* (Chicago: University of Chicago Press, 1989), p. 12.

22. In the interests of clarity here one should say that "truth" is used in a sense that belongs mainly to analytic philosophy rather than to the Heideggerian and Gadamerian idea of truth as something that cannot be done away with and which breaks in on one's thinking and possibly stops it in its tracks. Truth for MacCumber, or as MacCumber uses it in this context, is a property of sentences, and the idea is to constrain our use of sentences so rigorously as to make them accessible to this property. But language has other orientations—other uses— than to serve as a bearer of this property. The question of what language has to do with freedom is what remains open and, as MacCumber rightly says, mostly unthought within philosophical circles, perhaps because language is conceived mainly as a mechanism of description—even Rorty thinks of language this way. But freedom requires a rather different conception of language and may in fact require that we "lose" the concept of language altogether.

23. In *The Philosophical Discourse of Modernity* (Cambridge: MIT Press, 1987),

Jürgen Habermas warns against "leveling the genre distinction between philosophy and literature" (p. 185). In Habermas's theory, poetry, in which the rhetorical elements of discourse are radically foregrounded and refer only to themselves—as per the structuralist analyses of Roman Jakobson and others—is external to the communicative praxis of everyday discourse. Taken by itself, poetry is not a problem. The problem lies with the experts who are culturally responsible for it. The task of literary criticism, for example, and, at a higher level, of philosophy, is to study poetry in such a way as to integrate it into the culture from which, owing to its language, it excludes itself. This means rewriting, if only tacitly, poetry's wayward language so as to make it consistent with the ideal norms of communicative action (that is, forms of argumentation aimed at problem solving). Or at all events it means keeping poetry under control, confined to the genre of literature and the realm of art. Things begin to break down, however, when philosophy and criticism start to borrow their language from poetry. See esp. pp. 206–20.

24. See *Three Rival Versions of Moral Inquiry*, pp. 149–50, 157–58.

25. "Inquiry as Recontextualization: An Anti-Dualist Account of Interpretation," in *Objectivity, Relativism, and Truth* (Cambridge: Cambridge University Press, 1990), p. 93.

26. "Reconnecting Rorty: The Situation of Discourse in Richard Rorty's *Contingency, Irony, and Solidarity*," *Diacritics*, 21 (Summer 1990), 11. Rorty seems to acknowledge a problem like this, which is perhaps why, at a moment of matchless implausibility in *Contingency, Irony, and Solidarity*, he imagines for the literary critic the cultural task of weaving together the great books so that they will hang together in "a beautiful mosaic" or a "reflective equilibrium" (p. 81). So Rorty splits the difference between Quine and Sterne by calling in Harold Bloom, who shares with Rorty the idea that history is a prison-house and that the worst thing, cruelty aside, is obsolescence. Another way to put this would be to say that MacIntyre and Rorty are working different sides of Thomas Kuhn's street, with the one stressing that in a tradition in good working order conceptual change proceeds rationally, the other that in a tradition in good working order it is enough for conceptual change to proceed at a good pace and without interruption.

27. See "What Is Practice? The Conditions of Social Reason," in *Reason in the Age of Science*, trans. Frederick G. Lawrence (Cambridge: MIT Press, 1981), pp. 69–87, and esp. pp. 82–85. See MacIntyre, "Aristotle on Practical Reasoning," in *Whose Justice? Which Rationality?*, pp. 124–45. On pp. 140–41, MacIntyre illustrates Aristotle's idea with a modern example: "A hockey player in the closing seconds of a crucial game has an opportunity to pass to another member of his or her team better placed to score a needed goal. Necessarily, we may say, if he or she has perceived and judged the situation, he or she must immediately pass. What is the force of this 'necessarily' and this 'must'? It exhibits the connection between the good of that person *qua* hockey player and member of that particular team and the action of passing, a connection such that were such a

player not to pass, he or she must *either* have falsely denied that passing was for
their good *qua* hockey player *or* have been guilty of inconsistency *or* have acted
as one not caring for his or her good *qua* hockey player and member of that
particular team. That is to say, we recognize the necessity and the immediacy of
rational action by someone inhabiting a structured role in a context in which
the goods of some systematic form of practice are unambiguously ordered. And
in so doing we apply to one part of our social life a conception which Aristotle
applies to rational social life as such." A reader of Gadamer might ask why this
isn't an illustration of strategic rather than moral reasoning. See also Martha
Nussbaum, "The Discernment of Perception: An Aristotelian Conception of Private and Public Rationality," in *Love's Knowledge: Essays on Philosophy and
Literature* (Oxford: Oxford University Press, 1991), pp. 54–105; and Gerald L.
Bruns, "Tragic Thoughts at the End of Philosophy," *Soundings,* 72, no. 4 (Winter
1989), esp. 721–22.

28. *The Consequences of Modernity* (Stanford: Stanford University Press, 1990), p.
139.
29. See my discussion of *phronēsis* in chapter 11. Cf. Richard Bernstein's critique of
phronēsis in *Beyond Objectivism and Relativism: Science, Hermeneutics, and
Praxis* (Philadelphia: University of Pennsylvania Press, 1983), esp. 156–65.
30. See "Freedom and Contingency," in *Life-World and Politics: Between Modernity
and Postmodernity,* ed. Stephen K. White (Notre Dame: University of Notre
Dame Press, 1989), 166–90, esp. pp. 180–81; reprinted as, interestingly, "Freedom and Resentment," in *Identity / Difference: Democratic Negotiations of Political Paradox* (Ithaca: Cornell University Press, 1991), pp. 16–35.
31. "The Ruled and the Unruly: Functions and Limits of Institutional Regulations,"
in *The Public Realm: Essays on Discursive Types in Political Philosophy,* ed.
Reiner Schürmann (Albany, N.Y.: SUNY Press, 1989), pp. 191–92. Schürmann
in his introduction recalls Hannah Arendt's appreciation for those rare moments
in history when everything goes to pieces, as if freedom were breaking free (p.
18). Not a happy idea among social theorists. See Gerald L. Bruns, "Cain: Or,
the Metaphorical Construction of Cities," *Salmagundi,* nos. 74–75 (Spring–
Summer 1987), 70–85.
32. See Heidegger, "The Essence of Truth," in *Basic Writings,* ed. David Farrell Krell,
trans. John Sallis (New York: Harper & Row, 1977), esp. pp. 126–35. The best
account of Heidegger's understanding of freedom is Fred Dallmayr, "Heidegger's
Ontology of Freedom," in *Polis and Praxis* (Cambridge: MIT Press, 1984), esp.
pp. 115–21.
33. *The Philosophical Forum,* 21, nos. 1–2 (Fall–Winter 1989–90), 245. The distinction between negative and positive freedom amounts to an effort to purify
freedom of its negative (merely anarchic) elements. Thus negative freedom is not
true freedom and true freedom is something else—for example, belonging to a
certain kind of culture or society and embodying its norms. See Charles Taylor,
"What's Wrong with Negative Liberty?" in *Human Agency and Language: Philosophical Papers, 1* (Cambridge: Cambridge University Press), pp. 211–29.

34. Quoted by Wellmer, "Models of Freedom in the Modern World," p. 239. See Robert Nozick, *Anarchy, State, and Utopia* (New York: Basic, 1974), p. 316.

35. See Warnke, "The Hermeneutical Turn in Political Philosophy," *Yale Journal of Criticism*, 4, no. 1 (1990), 223. John Rawls invented his famous "original position" in order to "nullify the effects of specific contingencies which put men at odds and tempt them to exploit social and natural circumstances to their own advantage. Now in order to do this I assume that the parties are situated behind a veil of ignorance. They do not know how the various alternatives will affect their own particular case and they are obliged to evaluate principles on the basis of general considerations." See Rawls, *A Theory of Justice* (Cambridge: Harvard University Press, 1971), pp. 136–37.

36. "Democratic Individuality and the Meaning of Rights," in *Liberalism and the Moral Life,* ed. Nancy L. Rosenblum (Cambridge: Harvard University Press, 1989), pp. 187–88.

37. See also Kateb, "Democratic Individuality and the Claims of Politics," *Political Theory*, 12, no. 3 (August 1984), 351–52: "The theory of democratic individuality found in the Emersonian tradition is not committed to a *monadic* conception of the 'subject.'"

38. This last point is subtle. Wellmer argues that "the demands of communal rationality in any specific context and at any given point in historical time will have some kind of public definition in terms of institutions, moral beliefs, public opinion, etc., a kind of public definition which must be open for critique and possible revision and which must leave a space for dissent. Negative freedom seen from this angle would be at least the freedom to dissent and to act as a dissenter" (p. 244).

39. As Wellmer says, "While negative freedom is a precondition of communal freedom in the modern world, it is also a potential cause of disintegration, a source of conflicts, a potential threat of the bonds of solidarity between the individuals. Negative freedom represents, as Hegel saw it, the element of disunification which is constitutive for any modern form of communal freedom" ("Models of Freedom in the Modern World," p. 250). Or, in other words, there's no shaking loose from Plato's insight that democracy is a happy form of anarchy (*Republic* 558c).

40. See *The Philosophy and Politics of Freedom* (Chicago: University of Chicago Press, 1987), p. 318.

41. See Schürmann, *Heidegger on Being and Acting: From Principles to Anarchy,* trans. Christine-Marie Gros (Bloomington: Indiana University Press, 1987), p. v. For a counterstatement to Schürmann, see Kenneth Schmitz, "Neither with nor without Foundations," *Review of Metaphysics*, 42 (September 1988), 3–25. Whereas Schürmann thinks of principle as coercive, gathering all things into its embrace and excluding what does not fit, Schmitz thinks of principle as generosity, that is, as having to do with the "communality" of things that does not destroy their singularity but which rather releases the intelligibility of the singular and brings it home. Communality at all events is not a totality in which

things are justified by the way they are derived and hang together. George Kateb captures some of the force of both ideas when he says that it's a mistake to think that respect for rights needs rational justification. The call for justification of rights is already, he says, a move toward "some other kind of society than one in which rights are respected. To keep on demanding an answer to this question [of why rights should be respected]—even to ask it as if it were just another question that could be reasonably argued about—is already to be on the way to abandoning a respect for rights. It is exemplary that the Bill of Rights contains no rationale." See "Democratic Individuality and the Claims of Politics," *Political Theory*, 12, no. 3 (August 1984), 336.

42. See Charles Taylor, "Cross-Purposes: The Liberal-Communitarian Debate," in *Liberalism and the Moral Life*, pp. 159–82, 279–81.

43. Hannah Arendt, *The Human Condition* (Princeton: Princeton University Press, 1957), p. 244.

Index

Aaronides, 79–80
Abel and Cain story. *See* Cain and Abel
  story
Abraham, 99–100
Abulafia, Abraham, 135–36, 288n20
Acknowledgment, 177, 190–91
Ackroyd, Peter R., 64
Adoleschia, of Socrates, 37–38
Adorno, Theodor, 227
Aesthetics, and historicism, 9
Aggadah, versus *halakhah*, 105
Alētheia, etymology of, 22
Allegory, 85–87, 102, 150–51, 230–31;
  versus satire, 202–04, 216–18. *See also*
  Philo Judaeus as allegorist
Althusser, Louis, 14, 232
Answer to the Hyperchristian,
  Hyperspiritual, and Hyperlearned Book
  by Goat Emser in Leipzig (Luther), 143–
  44

Anthropology, 5–8
Apology (Plato), 24–25, 40–41
Appearance, versus truth, 27–28
Appropriation, 76–77, 199–200, 235,
  237
Aquinas, Thomas, 141
Arendt, Hannah, 266
Aristotelian hermeneutics, 239–40
Aristotle, 10, 49, 188, 190, 308n27;
  Poetics, 230–31; *Rhetoric*, 87
Artaud, Antonin, 229–30
Athenian versus Eleatic talk, 36–37
Audience, 48, 49, 50–51, 188–89
Augustine, 11, 140–43, 289n10; *On*
  Christian Doctrine, 142–43;
  Confessions, 143
Authority, 71–72, 113, 119–20, 146, 211–
  12
Autobiography, 170–71
Azande tribe, magical rites of, 5–7